Adult Literacy and New Technologies

Tools for a Lifetime

Office of Technology Assessment
U.S. Congress

CanGraph.pb — /me

State Recycling Campaign
Material Contribution

20.9%

19.3

60.3%

64.7%

5.7

10.2

Seacoast

Pioneer Valley

Delete   Update

Pages
From   To

Cancel   Fax

Frame

Lotus

Word Perfect

ABCD

Preview Edit

Recommended Citation:

U.S. Congress, Office of Technology Assessment, *Adult Literacy and New Technologies: Tools for a Lifetime*, OTA-SET-550 (Washington, DC: U.S. Government Printing Office, July 1993).

For sale by the U.S. Government Printing Office
Superintendent of Documents, Mail Stop: SSOP, Washington, DC 20402-9328
ISBN 0-16-041858-5

Foreword

America's commitment to the importance of the individual has translated into a belief that education is essential for realizing the American dream. Historically, this Nation has moved to increase educational opportunity, because education was considered crucial to personal growth and achievement and because educated individuals were considered essential for an effective democracy.

Adult education needs are difficult to define and difficult to meet; what constitutes adequate literacy changes continually as the demands facing individuals grow more complex. Rapidly changing demographic patterns and rapidly changing technology mean that the United States today faces a massive problem in equipping citizens with the skills needed to participate fully in the workplace and to contribute as members of family and community. OTA's examination of this problem, initiated at the request of the House Committee on Education and Labor and the Senate Committee on Labor and Human Resources, suggests that technology offers particular capabilities for dealing with this issue. This report is an attempt to identify those capabilities, along with limitations, and outline how new information technologies can be marshalled to meet the goal of a fully literate citizenry.

Throughout this study, the Advisory Panel, workshop participants, and many others played key roles in defining major issues, providing information, and championing a broad range of perspectives. OTA thanks them for their substantial commitment of time and energy. Their participation does not necessarily represent an endorsement of the contents of the report, for which OTA bears sole responsibility.

Roger C. Herdman, Director

Advisory Panel

Richard Venezky, *Chairperson*
Unidel Professor of Educational
    Studies and
Professor of Computer and
    Information Sciences
University of Delaware

Christine Cope
President
South Dakota Literacy Council
Yankton, SD

Sharon Darling
President
National Center for Family
    Literacy
Louisville, KY

Allen De Bevoise
President
AND Communications, Inc.
Los Angeles, CA

Ronald Gillum
Director, Adult Extended
    Learning Services
Michigan Department of Education
Lansing, MI

Shirley Brice Heath
Department of English
Stanford University

Jim Kadamus
Assistant Commissioner
Higher and Continuing Education
New York State Department
    of Education
Albany, NY

Irwin Kirsch
Director, Division of Cognitive and
    Assessment Research
Educational Testing Service
Princeton, NJ

William Kolberg
President and CEO
National Alliance of Business
Washington, DC

Ray Marshall
Professor of Economics
    and Public Affairs
University of Texas at Austin
Austin, TX

Earline McNary
Jamaica Plain, MA

Job Moraido
Law Offices of Public Defender
Child Advocacy Division
San Diego, CA

Richard Murnane
Professor of Economics
Harvard Graduate School
    of Education

Reg Murphy[1]
Executive Vice President
National Geographic Society
Washington, DC

Dale Rezabek
GAIN Coordinator
California Community Colleges
Sacramento, CA

Antonia Stone
Executive Director
Playing to Win
New York, NY

Richard Varn
Senator
Iowa State Legislature
Des Moines, IA

George Walker
President
Delta Wire Co.
Clarksdale, MS

---

[1] Formerly Publisher, *Baltimore Sun*

NOTE: OTA appreciates and is grateful for the valuable assistance and thoughtful critiques provided by the advisory panel members. The panel does not, however, necessarily approve, disapprove, or endorse this report. OTA assumes full responsibility for the report and the accuracy of its contents.

Project Staff

John Andelin
Assistant Director
Science, Information, and Natural
  Resources Division

Nancy Carson
Program Manager
Science, Education, and
  Transportation

PRINCIPAL STAFF

LINDA ROBERTS
Project Director

Kathleen Fulton
Senior Analyst

Patricia Morison
Analyst

Carol Edwards
Congressional Fellow

Chris Spelius
Research Analyst

Hunter Heyck
Research Assistant

Kristan Mayer
Research Assistant

OTHER CONTRIBUTING STAFF

Timothy Rogers
Intern

Lynellen Long
In-House Contractor

ADMINISTRATIVE STAFF

Marsha Fenn
Technical Editor

Gay Jackson
PC Specialist

Tamara C. Wand
Administrative Secretary

CONTRACTORS

Nancy Kober
Charlottesville, VA

SL Productions
New York, NY

Center for Literacy Studies
The University of Tennessee,
  Knoxville
Juliet Merrifield, principal investigator

Education TURNKEY Systems, Inc.
  and
Wujcik and Associates
Falls Church, VA

Interactive Educational Systems
  Design, Inc.
New York, NY

Claremont Graduate School
Claremont, CA
J.D. Eveland, principal investigator

Joyce Hakansson
Berkeley Learning Technologies

Stephen Reder
Northwest Regional Educational
  Laboratory

Saul Rockman
San Francisco, CA

Contents

8 Looking Ahead to a Future With Technology, 223

APPENDIXES

Summary and Policy Options | 1

After working all day in a chicken processing plant and cleaning offices until 10:30 pm, Eraclia Benitez has little time to help her children with their homework. Even in those few hours on weekends, when she's finished the cooking, cleaning, and shopping, and has gone to the laundromat, Eraclia cannot read to them or answer their questions about school work. She's caught in a double bind—she is unable to read or write in either Spanish or English.[1]

When the steel mill closed, 48-year-old Howard LeHuquet was laid off after 18 years as a blast furnace worker. He decided to train for a new career in computer repair or air conditioning and heating. When he took the entrance test (almost 30 years after finishing high school), he failed on the math and was told to try something else. "Now why do you need so much math . . . to fix an air conditioner or a refrigerator? I was working all these years, paying the bills, paying off this house, making car payments. You don't realize time goes by and then, *bang*. It's gone. Everything is math," laments LeHuquet. Now he hits the job market every week, looking for any kind of full-time job with health insurance; currently he is working as a security guard 2 nights a week.[2]

Siman Skinner is an independent contractor who tried numerous methods of learning to read before coming to the Columbus, Mississippi, Learning Center. "When I come in here, I couldn't read a lick. I couldn't." As he talks about why he quit school, Siman relates: "I had a lot of problems with my eyes. Plus I was a slow learner, too. And after a while they just move you on up and I got disgusted with it." He's always worked. "I'd run crews for

---

[1] David Fritzse, "De Nada a Literacy—In One Generation," *Listening to Mothers' Voices: A Reporter's Guide to Family Literacy*, Education Writers Association (ed.) (Washington, DC: 1992), pp. 25-29.

[2] Dale Russakoff, "Lives Once Solid as Steel Shatter in Changed World," *The Washington Post*, Apr. 13, 1992, p. A14.

Coors Brewing Co.

For Sonya Davis (left), receiving her GED has opened the door to college, while for Janet Espinal (right), learning how to read has led to a job as a secretary.

companies, and they never knew I couldn't read. There's always somethin' you can do to get by. Loopholes and the like. But it's pretty hard.'' He motions toward the computer as he recalls past efforts: "I tried teaching myself, ordering tapes and such from the TV and all, and that's helped some but not like this." When he came to the Learning Center, they put him on the computers. "Yeah, I got a lot of 100s. I'm going pretty fast. But I've skipped some stuff. Sometimes it's hard to see the pictures, it's not completely clear on the screen." This time he's determined to make it through, changing jobs so he won't be on the road all the time and can stick with the classes. "It takes time, sure. Just a little stump in the road, that's all."[3]

People who seek literacy services come from many different backgrounds and have many different motives for wanting to learn. "The target population [for literacy services] encompasses Americans who are employed, underemployed, and unemployed."[4] They can include:

- women who need to reenter the workforce after a divorce;
- teenage mothers who dropped out of school when they became pregnant;
- immigrants with master's degrees who speak no English;
- children of Hispanic migrant workers whose itinerant way of life limits their time in school;
- recent high school graduates who are having trouble finding a job;
- middle-aged auto workers whose plants recently closed;
- full-time homemakers who want to help their children with their homework;
- people who need to improve their mathematics skills to be promoted at work;
- truck drivers who need to pass a federally mandated written test to keep their jobs; or
- prison inmates who want to be employable when released.

An array of public, community-based, and private adult literacy programs exist to help people like Eraclia, Howard, and Siman. Yet the national approach to adult literacy education falls short in several critical respects. The vast majority of adults with low literacy skills—perhaps 90 percent—do not receive any literacy services. A high proportion of those who do enroll in literacy programs do not stay long. Most of the instruction is provided by part-time teachers and volunteers, and the agencies and organizations that provide literacy services must deal with a host of persistent challenges, including insufficient and unstable funding, complex administrative requirements, multiple funding sources, and inadequate mechanisms for identifying and sharing effective practices.

What can be done to improve this situation? One answer lies in technology. Computer-based instruction, for example, can draw people like

---

[3] SL Productions, video interview at the Columbus Learning Center, Columbus, MS, Nov. 11, 1991.

[4] Larry Mikulecky, "Second Chance Basic Skills Education," *Investing in People*, background papers, vol. 1, Commission on Workforce Quality and Labor Market Efficiency (ed.) (Washington, DC: U.S. Department of Labor, September 1989), p. 218.

Siman into programs and keep them engaged. Interactive video can bring education into the home for busy mothers like Eraclia and link them with other learners with similar concerns. Multimedia technology can provide a rich palette of resources for people like Howard. Sound, intriguing graphics, and live action video can bring new color to the black and white print-based world of learning. But creative uses of technology are the exception rather than the rule in most adult literacy programs today, the dream rather than the reality.

This study, requested by the House Committee on Education and Labor and the Senate Committee on Labor and Human Resources, seeks to answer this and other questions. In this report, the Office of Technology Assessment (OTA) considers why technology could make a difference in adult literacy, how it is used now, and what should be done to seize its potential for the future.

WHAT IS THIS STUDY ABOUT?

To assess the current and potential impact of technologies for literacy, it is necessary to understand the broader issues affecting adult literacy education in the United States. Therefore, this study begins by examining America's "literacy problem," shows how standards and requirements for literacy have increased over time, and documents the large number of Americans in need (chapter 2). Next, we show that adult learners have unique instructional needs (chapter 3) that are only partly being met by the patchwork of programs that provide adult literacy education (chapter 4). The study then analyzes how Federal policies have expanded adult literacy programs, but created a more fragmented system (chapter 5). The diverse web of adult literacy programs, however, faces common problems and needs that technology could help overcome (chapter 6). Nevertheless, the study shows that the potential of technology for both learners and programs is not being exploited, and significant barriers inhibit

wider or more sophisticated uses of technology (chapter 7). Finally, the study sketches a future vision in which better applications of technology make it possible to serve more adults and enable them to learn anyplace, anytime (chapter 8).

WHAT IS "LITERACY"?

Literacy is not a static concept. Almost 100 years ago, the proxy for literacy in the United States was being able to write one's name. Throughout this century literacy demands have become more complex and the standard for what constitutes literacy has risen (see figure 1-1). Despite considerable progress in raising the average level of educational attainment (today more than three-quarters of the adult population have completed high school), many believe that these gains have failed to meet the demands of a technological and global society. Scholars, educators, and policymakers are all struggling with how to redefine literacy to reflect changes in society, a global economy, higher educational standards for all students, and advances in technology. Technology, in all its forms, is having a profound effect on the ways people communicate with one another, shop, interact with social institutions, get information, and do their jobs. The current but evolving definition of what it means to be literate goes beyond the basic skills of reading, writing, and arithmetic. Other important skills being considered are higher order thinking and problem-solving skills, computer and other technology-related skills, literacy skills in the context of the workplace, and literacy skills as they relate to parenting and family life.

New Federal definitions of literacy incorporate some of these concepts: The 1991 National Adult Literacy Act defines literacy as: ". . . an individual's ability to read, write, and speak in English, and compute and solve problems at levels of proficiency necessary to function on the job and in society, to achieve one's goals, and develop

Figure 1-1—A Literacy Time Line: Rising Societal Standards for "Functional Literacy"

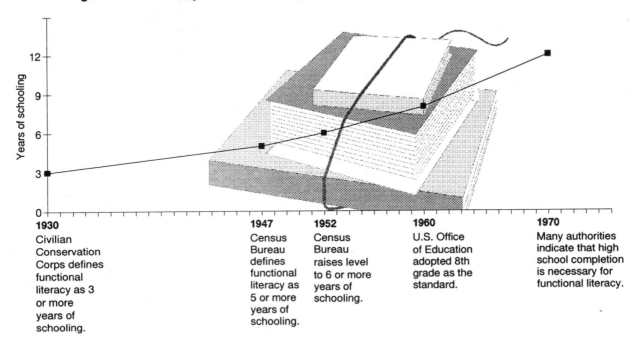

1930	1947	1952	1960	1970
Civilian Conservation Corps defines functional literacy as 3 or more years of schooling.	Census Bureau defines functional literacy as 5 or more years of schooling.	Census Bureau raises level to 6 or more years of schooling.	U.S. Office of Education adopted 8th grade as the standard.	Many authorities indicate that high school completion is necessary for functional literacy.

NOTE: This shows "literacy" in terms of years of schooling. OTA does not have data that allow comparison of average skill levels versus amount of schooling over this time period. The National Adult Literacy Survey (NALS) is expected to provide the first nationally representative data on the literacy skills of the Nation's adults (ages 16 and older). Data will include types of literacy skills, levels, and how these skills are distributed across the population. The first NALS report will be released September 1993.

SOURCE: Lawrence C. Stedman and Carl F. Kaestle, "Literacy and Reading Performance in the United States From 1880 to the Present," *Literacy in the United States,* Carl F. Kaestle et al. (eds.) (New Haven, CT: Yale University Press, 1991), p. 77.

one's knowledge and potential.''[5] The National Adult Literacy Survey, conducted by the Educational Testing Service for the National Center for Education Statistics, has adopted the following definition of literacy: ''... using printed and written information to function in society, to achieve one's goals, and to develop one's knowledge and potential.''[6] Clearly, then, being literate means more than just being able to read.

The way in which literacy is defined affects any estimates of the Nation's literacy problem—how many people lack adequate literacy skills—which in turn affects how the Nation perceives its literacy problem. Depending on which definition is chosen and which measurement method is employed, the problem can appear bigger or smaller. Those who want a quick estimate or simple yardstick are frustrated—literacy is not something that people either do or do not have, rather it is a continuum of skills that people possess in varying amounts. No single test or indicator can adequately discriminate between the literate and the nonliterate.

Nevertheless, whether the yardstick includes the performance of various literacy-related tasks, self-reported literacy problems, or educational attainment, the data suggest that a very large portion of the U.S. population is in

[5] Public Law 102-73, Sec. 3, National Literacy Act of 1991.

[6] Anne Campbell et al., Educational Testing Service, *Assessing Literacy: The Framework for the National Adult Literacy Survey,* prepared for the U.S. Department of Education (Washington, DC: U.S. Government Printing Office, October 1992), p. 9.

BASIC PROBLEM SOLVING TOOLS

klmnopqrstuvw

UIC University of Illinois at Chicago School of Art and Design

This project is a public service message from Pactrick Media Group, Inc. Design: Brooke Multack

As this public service message suggests, literacy today goes beyond the basic skills of reading, writing, and arithmetic to include problem-solving and other technology-related skills.

need of improving their literacy skills. OTA finds that at least 35 million adults have difficulties with common literacy tasks (see box 1-A). Although many of these adults can read at rudimentary levels, many need higher levels of literacy in order to function effectively in society, to find employment, or to be retrained for new jobs.

From all indications, only a small proportion of those in need of literacy education are receiving it. Government-sponsored literacy programs—the largest sector of literacy providers—currently serve about 4 million people.

OTA finds that the problem of inadequate literacy skills among adults is likely to grow over the next several decades. High rates of immigration and rising rates of poverty indicate that the number of children and families who are educationally at risk will continue to rise. These and other indicators suggest that literacy can be most effectively addressed through a "life-span" perspective that embraces both remediation and prevention. Literacy levels cannot be raised for the long term solely by remediation. **Educational efforts aimed at adults with low literacy skills today, however, can have important intergenerational effects; in addition to improving the**

life chances of the adult, they can increase the likelihood of positive educational outcomes for that adult's children.

WHO ARE THE LEARNERS AND WHAT DO THEY NEED?

Adults do not stop learning when they end their formal schooling. Whether they finish high school or college, or drop out somewhere along the way, adults face changing roles and life choices, and as a result, continue to acquire new skills and knowledge throughout their lives. More and more adults are choosing or being required to return to formal education—to relearn skills they have lost, to acquire skills they never obtained, or to learn new skills that were not taught when they attended school.

Learning and going to school have most often been associated with childhood and youth; most current ideas about learning and teaching are based on educating children. Educating adults is very different from educating children, however. Adults bring a wealth of knowledge and experience that can serve as a foundation for new learning. At the same time, adults have many competing demands in their lives that reduce the time available for education. And while most

Box 1-A—How Many Adults Have Literacy Needs? Estimating the Numbers

Surveying the Whole Adult Population

Estimates of literacy rates depend on the standard of literacy used to define who is literate and who is not. A number of different methods have been used, each of which has its weaknesses.[1] Nevertheless some method is needed for estimating the size of the literacy problem across the entire U.S. adult population. Some of the common estimates are presented below; all are calculated for a 1989 adult population ages 20 and over which numbered about 172 million people.[2]

Adults (in 1989) with:

• 8 years or less of schooling	19 million
• Classified as illiterate in the Census Bureau's 1982 English Language Proficiency Survey	22 million
• Classified as functionally incompetent on literacy tasks National Adult Performance Level Study (1975)	35 million
• Less than 12 years of schooling	38 million

Literacy Target Groups

Another way to attempt to estimate the size of the literacy problem is to look at different subgroups of the total population with a high likelihood of having inadequate literacy skills. Several such groups, and available estimates of their size, are presented below.

Adults not proficient in English[3]

• Those who report speaking a language other than English at home	26 million
• Those who report speaking English not well or not at all	6 million

Job seekers [4]

• Those whose literacy skills test below adequate level	8 million
• Those who perceive a need for better literacy skills	11 to 15 million

---

[1] The National Adult Literacy Survey (NALS) is expected to provide the first nationally representative data on the literacy skills of the Nation's adults (ages 16 and older). Data will include types of literacy skills, levels, and how these skills are distributed across the population. The first NALS report will be released in September 1993.

[2] Total population figures and data on school completion rates are from Robert Kominski, *Educational Attainment in the United States: March 1988 and 1989* (Washington, DC: U.S. Department of Commerce, Bureau of the Census, August 1991), tb. 2. The rates obtained in the English Language Proficiency Survey and the Adult Performance Level studies are projected forward and calculated for this 1989 population; this assumes that the rates have stayed the same, an untested assumption but one that others have also used to project these literacy rates forward. See U.S. Department of Education, Adult Learning and Literacy Clearinghouse, "Adult Literacy in the U.S.: A Little or a Lot?," unpublished report, 1989.

[3] U.S. Department of Commerce, Bureau of the Census, 1990 Census, unpublished data, tbs. ED 90-4 and ED 90-5.

[4] Based on a survey of the 20 million adults participating in Department of Labor programs. See Irwin Kirsch et al., *Beyond the School Doors: The Literacy Needs of Job Seekers Served by the U.S. Department of Labor*, prepared for the U.S. Department of Labor (Princeton, NJ: Educational Testing Service, September 1992). "Below adequate level" includes all persons scoring at Levels 1 and 2. See ch. 2 of this report.

---

adults participate in literacy programs voluntarily, their motives for learning vary widely. Getting a better job is only one goal; others might include becoming more independent or being able to help one's children. **Addressing the literacy needs of the Nation must begin, therefore, with the adults themselves—what resources they** **bring, what skills they may need or want, how they use literacy in their lives, how they learn, and what motivates them to want to learn more.**

Adults with low literacy skills form a very diverse group; few fit common stereotypes. For example, many adults with low literacy skills are successful in the workplace, and have found alternative strategies for learning and surviving in a print-based culture. Often their lack of literacy skills is masked by other competencies, so that colleagues and peers remain unaware of their hidden problem. For others, low literacy skills go hand in hand with poverty, unemployment, poor health, and educational failure, creating roadblocks to productive, satisfying lives. People like Eraclia spend much of their lives getting by. But they are survivors, self-reliant and determined to be independent. While society may label them ''illiterate,'' each has developed sophisticated coping skills. They are also motivated by a desire to learn and the hope that becoming literate will help them guide their children toward a richer life than they have known.

People use literacy in their lives for many different reasons. Moreover, a person's literacy skills may vary depending on the context. For example, a carpenter might be able to read and comprehend much more difficult material in a job-related manual than on a reading test. OTA finds that no one set of skills can be used to ''certify'' a person as literate, and no ''necessary'' amounts can be established. Needs vary and change according to the circumstances people face. These characteristics of adult learners suggest that the Nation needs a system of adult education that provides all adults with opportunities for lifelong learning as the world and their personal circumstances change, and that particularly encourages those whose limited literacy skills pose the greatest challenge.

Literacy programs should also recognize that people learn best when they are active participants in the learning process, when they are motivated by their own goals and interests, and when knowledge is presented in a context that is meaningful to them. To a large extent the present ''system'' of programs and services is designed

In this Los Angeles County jails educational program, inmates work on real literacy tasks designed to increase their chances of success following release.

for voluntary learners who come for assistance when they are ready. However, this segment of the population represents a very small proportion of those who could benefit from improved levels of literacy. The growing number of workplace and family literacy programs may be a way to bring more adults into literacy programs, by linking instruction and skills to immediate concerns and real life contexts.

There is a trend toward mandating participation of certain populations in literacy services (e.g., programs targeted at mothers on welfare and those in prison). This fundamental change may call for new instructional paradigms, but there is not enough data yet to know how these populations challenge traditional approaches to learning and measures of success. With an even more diverse learner population, research must focus on the learning strategies of adults, motivation and incentives, and development of approaches, learning materials, and technology tools.[7]

Adult learners also face special external and internal obstacles. Competing roles and responsibilities, situational barriers such as childcare or transportation, prior negative educational experi-

---

[7] The newly created National Institute for Literacy is expected to play a major role in research. By law, the Institute is charged with providing a ''. . . focal point for research, technical assistance and research dissemination, policy analysis and program evaluation in the area of literacy. . . .'' Public Law 102-73, Title I, Sec. 102, National Institute for Literacy.

Box 1-B—Advantages of Technology for Adult Learners

Reaching Learners Outside of Classrooms

- With portable technology, adults can learn almost anywhere, any time, and can use small parcels of time more efficiently.
- Technology can carry instruction to nonschool settings—workplaces, homes, prisons, or the community.
- Adults can be served who would otherwise be left out because of barriers such as inconvenient class scheduling or lack of childcare or transportation.
- Learning at home can be more convenient and private for those who would feel stigmatized by attending a literacy program.

Using Learning Time Efficiently

- Learners can move at their own pace, have greater control over their own learning, and make better use of their learning time.
- Learners can handle some routine tasks more quickly through such processes as computer spell checking.
- Many learners advance more quickly with computers or interactive videodiscs than with conventional teaching methods.

Sustaining Motivation

- Novelty factor can be a "drawing card."
- Technology can be more engaging, can add interest to repetitive learning tasks.
- Importance of computers in society can enhance the status of literacy instruction.
- Privacy and confidentiality are added to the learning environment, reducing embarrassment adults often experience.
- Technology-based learning environments do not resemble those of past school failures.
- Intense, nonjudgmental drill-and-practice is available for those who need it.
- Instantaneous feedback and assessment are provided.

Individualizing Instruction

- Computers can serve as "personal tutors"—instruction and scheduling can be individualized without one-on-one staffing; suitable for open-entry, open-exit programs.
- Materials and presentation formats can be customized to suit different learning styles, interests, or workplace needs.
- Images and sound can help some adults learn better, especially those who cannot read text well.
- Computers with digitized and synthesized speech can help with pronunciation and vocabulary.
- Adults with learning disabilities and certain physical disabilities can be accommodated.

Providing Access to Information Tools

- Adults need to learn to use today's electronic tools for accessing information.
- Adults believe familiarity with computers will make them more employable.

SOURCE: Office of Technology Assessment, 1993.

ences, and learning disabilities can easily deter all but the most motivated learners. Learners may need social and emotional support as well as flexible systems that match their schedules, pace, and learning style. **Finding better ways to match adult learners to services, removing barriers to participation, creating incentives for attending programs, and designing new strategies to** deliver services and support learning are all necessary if we are to improve the system. Technology has the potential to eliminate some barriers to participation and address some of the unique needs of adult learners (see box 1-B), but the current uses of technology in adult literacy programs have barely scratched the surface.

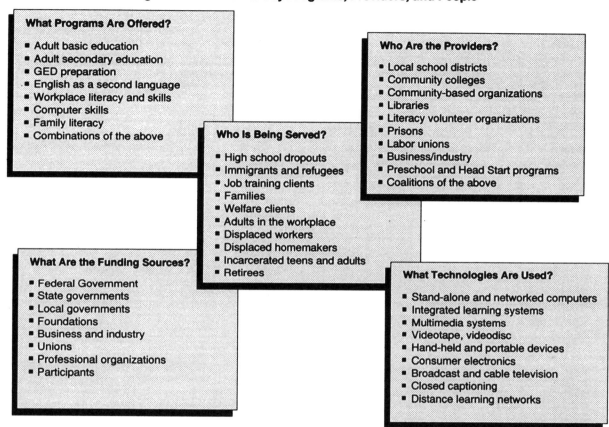

Figure 1-2—Adult Literacy Programs, Providers, and People

What Programs Are Offered?

- Adult basic education
- Adult secondary education
- GED preparation
- English as a second language
- Workplace literacy and skills
- Computer skills
- Family literacy
- Combinations of the above

Who Are the Providers?

- Local school districts
- Community colleges
- Community-based organizations
- Libraries
- Literacy volunteer organizations
- Prisons
- Labor unions
- Business/industry
- Preschool and Head Start programs
- Coalitions of the above

Who Is Being Served?

- High school dropouts
- Immigrants and refugees
- Job training clients
- Families
- Welfare clients
- Adults in the workplace
- Displaced workers
- Displaced homemakers
- Incarcerated teens and adults
- Retirees

What Are the Funding Sources?

- Federal Government
- State governments
- Local governments
- Foundations
- Business and industry
- Unions
- Professional organizations
- Participants

What Technologies Are Used?

- Stand-alone and networked computers
- Integrated learning systems
- Multimedia systems
- Videotape, videodisc
- Hand-held and portable devices
- Consumer electronics
- Broadcast and cable television
- Closed captioning
- Distance learning networks

SOURCE: Office of Technology Assessment, 1993.

WHAT PROBLEMS DO LITERACY PROGRAMS AND PROVIDERS FACE?

The numbers of adult literacy programs and providers are growing, prompted by increased Federal, State, community, and philanthropic awareness of literacy as an economic and social issue. Public programs are the largest sector, serving an estimated 80 to 90 percent of those who sign up for adult literacy instruction. Although data on total funding for literacy are not available, statistics from the U.S. Department of Education indicate that State and local support for adult literacy has grown more than eightfold since 1980, and Federal funding has doubled.[8] These increases have spurred the expansion of programs and services. **But despite this growth, adult literacy education operates at the margin.** Unlike elementary and secondary education, with a clearly defined and long-established tradition of control by State departments of education and local school districts, adult education has no "system." A patchwork of adult literacy services is provided in schools, community colleges, libraries, community centers, churches, housing projects, workplaces, and prisons (see figure 1-2). Although local school districts continue to be primary providers of adult literacy education, programs operated by community-based organi-

[8] See chs. 4 and 5 for further details.

zations have expanded and there has been a slight shift away from school-based programs. Even so, much of the content is remarkably similar across the variety of sponsors. Adult basic education, general equivalency diploma (GED) preparation, and English as a second language (ESL) are among the most popular offerings, but interest is growing in family and workplace literacy. The availability of services to learners is not uniform, however; it is a function of where the learner lives and works, more than of what his or her needs are.

Just as the definition of adult literacy is complicated by the multiple needs of learners at various points in their lives, so too is the web of services complicated by multiple funding sources, administering agencies, and service providers. While this diversity may have advantages, it makes it difficult to address critical but common issues that plague many programs. The lack of coherent referral among programs, problems with recruitment and retention, a high dependence on

volunteers and part-time teachers (and consequently high turnover of staff), and a lack of adequate tools to measure program effectiveness cut across all programs and providers.

OTA finds that funding is a constant concern that affects all of the above. Many programs have waiting lists, especially for such popular services as ESL. For most programs, unstable and short-term funding patterns make it difficult to plan, purchase necessary materials or equipment, or develop professional staffing ladders.

Fragmentation of effort is another ongoing problem. At least seven Federal agencies, and often many more State offices, administer adult literacy programs; each has its own rules, reporting requirements, and funding channels. Some States and localities have sought to overcome fragmentation and make the most of limited resources by improving coordination among education, training, and social and employment services and eliminating duplication of effort.

Adult literacy services have changed dramatically since the Federal Government's 1930s efforts to supply books to Work Progress Administration employees. Today, government is entering into joint ventures with private industry to provide computer-based literacy programs to employees at work, like this one at General Electric's Aircraft Engine Factory (right).

Some have also encouraged partnerships across local communities that link schools, businesses, churches, libraries, or other institutions to increase the level of support and marshal every available resource.[9] Such efforts are not easily accomplished, however—programs need information on what is available in their communities so they can fill in gaps; they need help with administration and accounting; and they need long-term funding to overcome the high turnover of staff and learners.

Key and critical resources in every program are the people who work with learners and manage programs. The dedication and involvement of staff—whether paid or volunteer, full or part time—are extraordinary in most cases. But the demands placed on staff are also extremely high, and turnover is persistent. Most programs rely on volunteers to carry a heavy burden of instruction—one-on-one tutoring is the most common instructional format—and the majority of paid teachers are part time. Specific training in teaching literacy for adults is limited. Volunteers, while dedicated, may not have the grounding necessary for effective teaching, diagnosing learning disabilities, and helping learners find critical auxiliary services. Even licensed teachers need more training since few are specialists in adult literacy. Furthermore, teachers, administrators, and volunteers would gain from professional standards, graduate-level programs, certification guidelines, and career ladders similar to those found in other educational environments.

Technology could help alleviate some of the problems of administration, fragmented service delivery, recruitment and retention of clients, and

high turnover of staff and volunteers (see box 1-C). Electronic databases could help maintain information, track funds, and match learners to support services. Programs could use telecommunications technology to train volunteers and staff and connect them with one another to share information and reduce isolation. And technology could help programs move their resources beyond their physical location to reach learners wherever they are.

WHAT IS THE IMPACT OF FEDERAL EFFORTS?

Since the founding of the Republic, the literacy of adult Americans has been an abiding Federal concern. Up until the mid-1960s the Federal response was very limited. The passage of the Adult Education Act in 1966 changed the Federal role, creating a categorical grant program for adult literacy and basic skills education. This act and subsequent legislative initiatives have helped build and define key features of the delivery system today.

Legislation enacted since 1986 has expanded and transformed the Federal role in adult literacy, increasing appropriations, creating new programs, attempting to build capacity and coordination among existing programs, and assigning new literacy-related missions to programs with broader goals, such as welfare reform, immigration reform, and job training. **The Federal Government currently spends at least $362 million for adult literacy and basic skills education, more than double the amount of 5 years ago.**[10] Federal dollars have an important leveraging effect and are critical sources of sustenance for

---

[9] The New York City Literacy Assistance Center and Baltimore Reads are two examples of how communities can pull together, build on existing educational capacity, involve businesses, bring in volunteers, and create entities that sustain these efforts by providing leadership, technical assistance, and financial support.

[10] This conservative estimate is far from a complete accounting of Federal spending on adult literacy and basic skills. Some important programs—including the Job Training Partnership Act, Job Opportunities and Basic Skills Training, State Legalization Impact Assistance Grants, Refugee Resettlement, and Even Start—have been omitted because the data needed to make a reasonable estimate of expenditures on adult basic skills is not available. The $362 million was calculated by totaling appropriations for programs with identifiable adult education and literacy obligations in 19 of the 29 ''core'' programs on which OTA focused. Almost 90 percent of this total comes from Department of Education programs. For more detail see ch. 5 and app. B.

Box 1-C—Advantages of Technology for Literacy Programs

Recruiting and Retaining Learners

- Technology can be a magnet, attracting learners.
- More learners can be served and teachers used more productively.
- Programs can broaden their reach, serving those in remote locations.
- Teachers and counselors can maintain regular contact with learners.

Improving Curriculum

- Teachers can create individualized, engaging instructional materials related to learners' needs and interests.
- Programs can share "what works" in terms of instructional materials and techniques.

Meeting Staff Development Challenges

- Teachers, volunteers, and administrators can be trained via video, distance learning, and self-study computer modules.
- Career ladders can be developed and information about vacancies can be posted nationwide.
- Staff can collaborate with their peers across town or country about problems, solutions, resources, and opportunities.

Enhancing Assessment and Evaluation

- Technology can track student progress continually, minimizing the need for "high anxiety" testing.
- Technology can provide diagnostic assistance for the teacher.
- Video and audiotape records, portfolio collections of writings, and other performance assessment measures can give more complete evidence of student progress.
- Program evaluation can be simplified by more systematic evaluation procedures and common data elements.

Streamlining Administration and Management

- Technology can more efficiently handle routine administrative tasks, freeing staff for instruction and providing comprehensive services to clients.
- Computer-based systems provide more efficient, accessible records on attendance, scheduling, personnel, budgeting, evaluation, and client tracking.

Augmenting Funding and Coordination

- Technology can serve as a magnet for fundraising and business contributions.
- Programs can pool resources and coordinate services, including social services, to serve learners better and avoid duplication of effort.
- Programs can share and access experts, databases, curriculum, public access software, government information, and national pools of literacy expertise.

SOURCE: Office of Technology Assessment, 1993.

many State and local efforts. Still the Federal literacy expenditure is small in comparison with overall State expenditures for literacy and for other major Federal education programs (see figure 1-3), meager in terms of the total population in need, and low as a national priority (see figure 1-4). There has been a proliferation of categorical grant programs with literacy-related missions. All this is at odds with the sort of large-scale, coordinated Federal offensive that some feel is necessary to address the literacy challenge.

Among the new Federal emphases since 1991 is a focus on workplace literacy programs for employed adults. These programs are intended to meet the literacy demands of the job market and create new workplace/education partnerships that stimulate private sector literacy efforts. While many leaders in business, labor, and local and State government support this direction for literacy, current efforts (both public and private) reach a very small number of workers. Thus far, Federal dollars have supported demonstration projects and limited "seed" development. Further expansion of the system of education and training has been proposed; how to accomplish the expansion is controversial.[11]

Another important emphasis has been on creating intergenerational family literacy programs. With their focus on prevention and remediation, they represent a small but significant shift in the Federal approach to the problem of literacy. Congress has begun to link family literacy initiatives with Federal Head Start and Even Start programs, as well as Chapter 1. Effective parenting strategies that foster young children's language development and school readiness are common concerns of all these programs. Similarly, expertise in adult learning is something that

Figure 1-3—Funding for Adult Education Compared With Other Federal Education Initiatives, Fiscal Year 1992

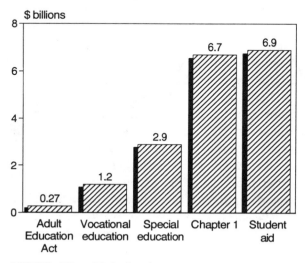

SOURCE: Office of Technology Assessment, 1993.

Figure 1-4—Funding for Select Federal Domestic Priorities, Fiscal Year 1992

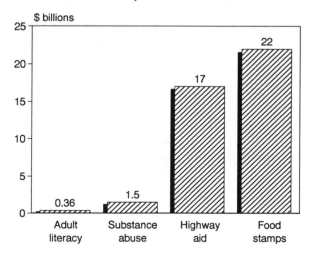

SOURCE: Office of Technology Assessment, 1993.

teachers need whether they are in Head Start or adult education programs.

Targeted Federal programs have encouraged States and local providers to reach out to groups of adults, such as the homeless and welfare mothers, whose access to basic education has been limited. By channeling more funding through programs with restricted eligibility, however, the Federal Government may be limiting opportunities for the millions of adult learners, including many limited English proficient adults who do not meet special criteria but have the potential to quickly become functionally literate, self-supporting citizens.

New Federal requirements and policies are shaping State and local responses. For example mandatory participation and minimum hours of instruction in the Job Opportunities and Basic Skills (JOBS) training program and the literacy program for Federal prisoners represent a marked shift away from the traditional model of voluntary, open-entry, open-exit programs. Other pol-

[11] Federal and State tax incentives to business, a national levy for education and training, and other mechanisms could be utilized. See U.S. Congress, Office of Technology Assessment, *Worker Training: Competing in the New International Economy*, OTA-ITE-457 (Washington, DC: U.S. Government Printing Office, September 1990).

In North Carolina at the Carver Family Literacy Program, an intergenerational approach to literacy seeks to provide the parent with literacy and parenting skills, and enhance the child's learning opportunities.

icy directives include efforts to improve the quality of services for learners through better coordination across programs, requirements for training and professional development of educational staff and volunteers, and moving toward learning assessments that are outcome-based. It is too soon to know how these "new requirements" for literacy programs will affect what is offered and who participates, but these are areas that should be followed closely.

The limited but promising use of technology is not surprising given the fact that the major Federal adult literacy laws[12] contain no provisions explicitly authorizing the use of technology; the exception is the Job Training Partnership Act (JTPA) and its authorization of the use of "advanced learning technologies." However, no programs contain capital budgets for equipment purchase or explicit funding for teacher training in technology. Most statutory and regulatory provisions regarding use of technology are op-

tions, not mandates.[13] The Department of Labor, the Department of Education, and the Small Business Innovation Research program have supported a handful of literacy-related technology demonstrations with discretionary money. The newly created National Institute for Literacy funded only three technology projects in its first round of awards. Taken together, the message about use of technology in adult literacy and basic skills programs from the Federal establishment, with the exception of the Department of Defense, has been "go slowly, if at all."

HOW COULD TECHNOLOGY MAKE A DIFFERENCE?

Today's technology offers enormous potential for substantially changing the field of adult literacy. It could provide an alternative to the labor-intensive, tutorial-based teaching that makes up the bulk of today's literacy training. For instance, multimedia technologies with speech, video, and graphics could offer a new hope for those who have experienced repeated failures in paper-and-pencil-based educational activities. Computer-assisted instruction could enable learners to proceed at their own speed with materials relevant to their lives, tailored to their personal interests, and compatible with their individual learning styles. Hand-held electronics, such as pocket language translators, could allow adults to learn on the bus or during coffee breaks— whenever they are able to study. Electronic networks could remove the isolation and stigma of low literacy by enabling adults to share experiences in small group discussions. With closed captioning as a standard feature, learners will be able to see and hear the words on broadcast or cable television to reinforce language and

---

12 For example, the Adult Education Act basic grant program, Even Start, State Legalization Impact Assistance Grants, Refugee Resettlement, and Adult Education for the Homeless.

13 The mandates that do exist, relating to the National Institute for Literacy and the Department of Labor National Workforce Literacy Collaborative, generally affect decisions at the Federal level, not programs in the field.

reading development.[14] Interactive telecommunications networks could bring the best teachers from around the country to the most remote learners (see box 1-D). All this is possible in technologies available today; much more will be possible in the next decade.

Yet the full range of capabilities has hardly been touched. **OTA finds that technology is not a central consideration for most literacy programs. By the same token, adult literacy applications are not high priorities for most vendors and developers in the technology industry.**

Computers are the most prevalent technology for literacy, but no more than 15 percent of literacy providers use them regularly for instruction, and many do not use them at all. Much of the available software provides drill and practice, not problem solving; many choices are geared for children, not adults. Advanced capabilities, such as speech recognition, speech generation, or interactive multimedia, are only beginning to be tested. Few literacy providers have sufficient technology for broad usage, or awareness of available software. More serious is the limited knowledge and training among staff and volunteers in the use of technology as a teaching tool.

Despite an explosion in cable, public, and commercial television channels and widespread ownership of television sets, there are only a handful of instructional television programs targeted to adult literacy that harness the power of the media. In fact, video technologies are surprisingly underused given their familiarity and availability.

A significant amount of hardware and software in businesses, homes, schools, and colleges is underutilized for literacy education. For example, common electronic devices, such as home video game machines, are largely ignored as technologies for literacy.

Box 1-D—Distance Learning in Vermont

In Vermont, where icy roads can cancel classes and long distances can keep others away, learners from across the State have been working toward their general equivalency diploma (GED) through a series of courses held over Vermont Interactive Television (VIT). *The Lou & Dave Show*, a 10-week GED mathematics course, enrolled 30 learners gathered at local sites throughout the State. They had a great time learning mathematics, thanks to a blend of show business and team teaching from two of the best adult education instructors in the State, Lou Dorwaldt at one site and Dave Shapiro at another. They use video and on-the-air high jinks to bring mathematics to life, using real-life Vermont situations and people the students know as subjects for mathematics problems, playing custom-made videos that present problem-solving activities in entertaining ways, and even having "the spirit of Pythagoras" make an appearance to talk about his renowned mathematical theories. Learners in remote locations who feel isolated by their low literacy skills found interacting with other adult learners across the State an important psychological boost. The program coordinator suggests some of the other benefits of doing courses over VIT: "It cuts down on the tutors' regular work time and also frees up more money, not only from the tutors' workload but by creating our own texts. Students found themselves working in large groups, becoming more self-reliant, while learning how to work and help each other. These are important skills for all adults hoping to function in today's world."[1]

---

[1] "Adult Basic Education: Expanding Horizons Over VIT," *Online*, The Newsletter of Vermont Interactive Television, vol. 2, No. 1, August 1991.

Why is there such a wide gap between practice and promise? While the barriers to more effective use of technology are similar to those faced in other arenas (most specifically elementary and secondary education), they are more severe in adult literacy programs. These barriers include needs for an expanded technology base, appropri-

---

[14] The Television Decoder Circuitry Act of 1990 requires that all television sets with screen sizes 13 inches or larger, whether manufactured or imported for use in the United States after June 30, 1993, will have captioning capability built directly into the television receiver.

Learning Technology Center, Vanderbilt University

In this Vanderbilt University multimedia project, researchers are exploring how video, graphics, audio, and text can support the acquisition of reading skills.

ate software, staff training, and stable funding and continuing support. In addition, the literacy market is fragmented and underdeveloped; not particularly attractive to vendors and software developers. Even so, there are encouraging signs on the horizon as the technology infrastructure expands, investment in literacy education increases, and recognition of the importance of lifelong learning grows.

POLICY ISSUES AND OPTIONS

The Federal Government has attempted to attack the large, multifaceted problem of low adult literacy skills in a piecemeal fashion. The current array of modest to small programs provides something for almost every type of literacy need but not very much for any, with inefficiencies for all.

Although existing literacy programs have helped millions of adults lead richer lives, there are many steps that would expand and improve services for adults with limited literacy skills and lead toward an integrated national strategy for adult literacy. These steps include both major initiatives and smaller, short-term strategies.

The first approach is a dramatic refashioning of the Federal role into a new scale of effort with greatly increased funding and higher visibility. The new program would expand, subsume, or replace existing piecemeal efforts. If Congress wants to bring adult literacy up to the level of other Federal programs that offer equal educational opportunities for those most in need (e.g., Chapter 1 and special education at the K-12 level, and Pell grants for higher education), a more comprehensive service delivery system will be necessary. This option is discussed at the conclusion of this section.

A more immediate strategy focuses on options for working within the existing system, while giving special attention to technology as a lever for change and as a resource to benefit learners and programs. OTA has identified three major areas in which congressional action would make a real difference:

- building the base of technology (hardware and software) for literacy,
- improving the system of literacy programs and services, and
- experimenting with new alternatives, both within and outside of the current system to reach more learners.

Building a Base of Technology for Literacy

To accomplish this goal, two broad strategies are considered: increasing access to technologies and stimulating development of literacy software and programming.

Increase Access to Technologies

Having access to hardware is the first, most obvious gateway to using technology. If there is to be more technology use in adult literacy programs, the Federal Government must take legislative and regulatory steps that will stimulate and legitimize the use of technology in adult literacy programs and eliminate provisions that inhibit it. This can be done deliberately as Federal program reauthorizations come up, by taking special care to eliminate impediments to use of technology in existing laws and regulations, adding new provisions explicitly encouraging technology, and enacting directives for inter-agency cooperation on technology in literacy-related programs. The sooner this is done, the sooner the benefits will appear.

Remove Legislative and Administrative Barriers. OTA's analysis suggests that while there are few if any direct prohibitions against technology in literacy programs (e.g., legislative language prohibiting use of funds to acquire technology), there are several ''indirect'' but real impediments. Among them are antisupplanting and eligibility requirements that restrict the use of

equipment to a single target group, such as legalized aliens, even though a program might be providing instruction to a mix of clients including displaced workers, recent immigrants, welfare recipients, or high school dropouts. In addition, separate funding streams and accountability requirements discourage integrated planning, purchase, and use of technology. In some cases, technology is underutilized and certain learners are unable to benefit because courses of instruction or equipment purchases were funded by a program that will not or cannot share these resources with other programs (see box 1-E).

Other barriers include evaluation or performance standards that emphasize immediate learning gains or employment outcomes, subtly discouraging long-term equipment investments or experimentation with technology-based instruction. Investment in technology is further inhibited by the absence of multiyear contracts in some Federal programs, the small size of most Federal discretionary grants, and a general suspicion among Federal policymakers and program administrators about the use of Federal funds for capital expenditures.

Although some States and local communities are finding ways around the maze of regulations, funding streams, and accountability requirements of multiple Federal programs, the Administration could lower the barriers and make it easier for literacy programs to acquire the technology they need. There are critical administrative actions the Federal Government could initiate now, including interagency efforts for planning, implementation, and regulatory revisions to allow cost-sharing for technology installation and applications.

In addition, the Federal Government can improve interagency coordination and thus increase the effectiveness of its adult literacy programs by developing a consistent governmentwide policy on technology for adult literacy and by using the tools of technology—such as integrated databases or teleconferencing—to promote coordina-

---

Box 1-E—Learn, Earn and Prosper: Mississippi's Project LEAP

Mississippi's Project LEAP (Learn, Earn and Prosper) is a satellite-based education and training program for Job Opportunities and Basic Skills (JOBS) recipients in 50 sites across the State. The distance learning courses recently developed by LEAP include reading, GED preparation, workplace readiness, and life-coping skills. These courses are restricted to JOBS clients only, because JOBS funding supports the instruction (five teleteachers and the teachers and aides at the local sites). Instruction is offered 4 days a week, 5 hours a day, and approximately 1,000 JOBS recipients are enrolled.

Although in only its early stages of development, Project LEAP has been inundated by requests from adult education programs to allow their students to watch the programs, since in many cases the downlink is located at a site where a mix of adult education programs are offered. Mississippi officials are attempting to cost-share the Federal program to allow greater use of these newly developed instructional materials.[1] Mississippi officials believe that they should be able to deliver these distance learning resources to many other learners—to inmates in correctional facilities, adults in adult basic education centers, and adults in their home.

Most of the satellite downlinks, it should be noted, were installed by the K-12 Federal Star Schools Program, and LEAP programming airs after school hours (from 4 to 9 pm). Mississippi has some 200 operational downlinks in schools across the State. In addition to Star Schools and Project LEAP, there are plans to use these distance learning facilities to offer an alternative high school program beginning in September 1993.[2] Plans are also under way to create a satellite-based training program for Head Start staff that will operate nationwide.

---

[1] Judy Williams, director, Governor's Office for Literacy and Workplace Enhancement, State of Mississippi, personal communication, Apr. 18, 1993.

[2] Ed Meek, director of resource development, Project LEAP, The University of Mississippi, personal communication, Apr. 19, 1993.

---

tion and improve program administration among agencies.

Encourage Technology Use Through New Regulations and Authorizing Language. Most Federal literacy programs lack explicit legislative language encouraging use of technology. Those provisions that do exist are options, rather than mandates to use technology or set-asides requiring a minimum investment in technology. In fact, the Adult Education Act (AEA) takes the opposite approach, capping the amount that may be used by the State resource centers for hardware and software at 10 percent. Congress could establish a set-aside for technology in the AEA (as it already has for other new initiatives, such as institutional corrections programs). Such a provision would likely gain some support among State adult education directors, who have recently recommended that in the next reauthorization "... the AEA should encourage a percentage of adult education allocation for innovation and technology in education."[15] A set-aside would give programs "permission" to fund technology acquisition; without this explicit policy, many may not make this investment. The signal to hardware and software developers from such a set-aside and the degree to which it would stimulate the market for adult literacy technology development would depend on its size. OTA estimates that a 10 percent set-aside would put $25 million into the marketplace.

A fixed percentage of set-aside funds for technology acquisition would probably be insufficient for small programs. It is important, therefore, that Congress take parallel steps to allow Federal funds to be pooled with other funding sources.

---

[15] U.S. Department of Education, Division of Adult Education and Literacy and Office of Policy and Planning, "Summary of State Adult Education Directors Forum, Feb. 18-19, 1993," unpublished document, p. 12.

Provide Direct Funding for Technology. Congress could provide capital funds for hardware and software acquisition for adult literacy programs directly through new Federal grants to local literacy programs. The amount of funding could vary with program size and scope.[16] To leverage the Federal investment, Congress could require a match with local, State, or private funds. Grants could require communitywide technology planning and cooperation across Federal programs. For example, if the major Federal programs (AEA JTPA, Head Start, and Chapter 1) were combined, it would have a substantial effect, increasing the pool of dollars available for technology. Technology resources could be located centrally or dispersed. The point is that the involvement of an entire community would aggregate demand and drive down the costs of hardware and software.

Planning and cooperation on a regional or State level would increase the effectiveness of available funds. Statewide technology initiatives in K-12 education in Florida and Texas, for example, have made it possible for schools to acquire computers, multimedia technology, and telecommunications capacity at lower cost than if each school or district made purchases separately—a good model for adult literacy.

Stimulate Development of Adult Literacy Software and Programming

Effective use of technologies requires quality software and programming tailored to the needs of adult learners. Available computer software is inadequate for the demands of literacy programs, and programming for video and other technologies is even more limited. The Federal Government has provided millions of dollars of research and development (R&D) support to develop educational television programming for the elementary, secondary, and college levels, software tools and networking applications for science and mathematics, and distance learning systems for K-12 education. By contrast, the Federal investment in programming, software, and networking applications for adult literacy has been almost nonexistent, except for the military's development of computer-based materials in basic skills.

Create an Adult Literacy Software/Programming Initiative. A targeted initiative is one way to speed development of a broad base of high-quality and effective applications of video, computer, and telecommunications technology for literacy. Congress could provide seed funding and encourage public/private partnerships among literacy educators, State agencies, software developers, and telecommunications providers, as it has done for K-12 distance learning through the Star Schools program. An appropriation of about $20 million per year for the next 5 years would serve as a significant stimulant to the field.[17]

Any such development should include stand-alone video courses and modules, interactive distance learning programs, and computer software and multimedia learning materials that address high-priority needs, especially:[18]

- English as a second language,
- high school completion and GED,
- workplace literacy,
- materials and resources designed for learners with very low literacy skills (especially those

---

[16] In plans for the new $7 million citywide St. Paul, Minnesota Center for Lifelong Learning, $500,000 has been budgeted for technology, including hardware, software, and telecommunications networking. Terilyn Turner, director, Center for Lifelong Learning, St. Paul, MN, personal communication, Apr. 24, 1993.

[17] By way of comparison, Congress originally authorized the Star Schools program for 5 years, setting an overall funding limit of $100 million. The National Science Foundation's application of advanced technology development is currently budgeted at approximately $12.5 million annually for research and development in mathematics, science, and technology for all levels of education.

[18] An adult literacy initiative could concentrate development of software and video programming in the areas of highest need. New data from the National Adult Literacy Survey of adults 16 years and older will become available later this year (September 1993). This data should help clarify the instructional needs of adults and which segments of the population are most in need of assistance.

By enabling adult learners to write in Spanish or English, this software program helps them learn English as they improve writing, thinking, and reasoning skills.

that make use of advances in digitized speech, graphics, and animation), and

- programs designed to reach both adults and young children in family literacy contexts.

Funding development of software and programming alone is not enough; the Federal Government would have to place equal priority on achieving broad distribution—making software and programming available across the range of literacy programs and providers, and bringing these resources to unserved learners in their homes and communities. Congress could require that rights and marketing strategies promote the widest possible distribution through cable, broad-cast television, video rental stores, software and music stores, and other less traditional outlets—such as welfare offices, post offices, public health clinics, libraries, and the workplace.

Fund Software and Programming Through Existing Technology Programs. Another option is to use existing Federal technology program authority to fund development of literacy applications, rather than initiate a separate software effort. The Federal Star Schools program already authorizes instruction for literacy, as does the Ready to Learn Children's Television Act. The National Science Foundation's (NSF) educational technology programs, the National Telecommunications and Information Administration's National Information Infrastructure program, and the technology programs at the Advanced Research Projects Agency (ARPA—Department of Defense) all have expertise in technology that could be applied to literacy. Without a specific allocation for adult literacy or a congressional mandate, however, literacy development will be largely left to chance and continue to exist at the margin.[19] This approach also makes it difficult to address literacy needs systematically and avoid duplication of effort.

Improving the System

Two broad policy strategies are considered for improving the system of literacy services. The first strategy focuses on helping administrators, teachers, and volunteers become more effective. The second strategy focuses on strengthening the connections among literacy providers, social services, and the private sector.

Expand Training and Professional Development

It is one of the sad ironies of adult literacy education that often those with the least professional training are asked to help the learners with the greatest educational needs. The system is unlikely to get better without strengthening the professional status and expertise of those who teach, administer, and volunteer in literacy programs. Professional development should involve several parallel improvements: continuing training for adult literacy educators, curriculum development and graduate-level programs in adult literacy instruction, more rigorous standards and certification requirements, and strategies for recruiting highly qualified personnel to teach and administer adult literacy programs. Technology can be a resource in all these efforts.

Coordinate and Expand Inservice Training. Teacher training and professional development efforts are new objectives of the National Literacy Act of 1991. Training is one of the missions of the newly established State resource centers. The act also increases the State set-aside for training and resource development from 10 to 15 percent of the AEA State grants under Section 353. Even so, funding from these sources will be insufficient to support systematic training activities for many States. Section 353 funds amount to no more than $25 million nationwide, and the $5 million appropriated for State resource centers in fiscal year 1993 is spread across every State and the outlying areas.[20]

One option for making the most of available funding is for Congress, through legislation, to allow States to pool Section 353 set-asides, along with State resource center grants, to create multistate or regional teacher training centers. Local adult literacy training funds could also be channeled into these centers. Similarly, training activities supported by other Federal and State programs involved in literacy training could be aggregated. Regulations should facilitate, not inhibit, training efforts that address common needs of adult literacy educators serving clients from JOBS, JTPA, Head Start, Corrections, Drug and Alcohol Rehabilitation, and other programs.

Collaborative training activities could also encourage cross fertilization of staff expertise. For example, teachers of young children in family literacy programs could study the learning problems of the children's parents; those who traditionally teach adults could learn about child development and early childhood education. The result would broaden the base of expertise in intergenerational literacy programs. Collaborations between those with training expertise in the workplace and those skilled in teaching reading and writing could encourage richer, more comprehen-

---

[19] Thus far, only two of the Star Schools projects have begun to experiment with adult literacy in a limited way.

[20] On a formula basis some States or territories receive as little as $2,500, and over half the States receive less than $50,000, which supports several other activities beyond teacher training.

Kirkwood Community College

Telecommunications technologies can be used to expand adult literacy services and programs.

sive workplace literacy programs. Social services counselors and ESL instructors might also benefit from joint training, as they learn more about the multiple needs and concerns of their clients. Collaborative professional development efforts could help to break down walls that exist between service providers funded from different sources, possibly creating a broader base for the profession.

Distance learning technologies could greatly facilitate multistate and multiagency training efforts by serving teachers and trainers in different locations and small programs. Federal Star Schools legislation now authorizes adult literacy instruction, and the telecommunications partnerships formed to serve adult learners could also provide training to literacy staff and volunteers. The most highly skilled teacher trainers, whether in community colleges, universities, or workplace programs, could train literacy instructors, counselors, and volunteers over interactive networks. Materials, strategies, and lesson plans could be created and shared over computer networks.

Support Adult Literacy Curricula and Graduate-Level Programs. Most adult literacy teachers and staff have received very limited specialized training in their field, and few universities offer advanced degree programs in adult literacy edu-

cation. Yet the challenges of adult literacy demand expertise in a range of areas: diagnosing and teaching adults with learning disabilities, creating curricula to meet the needs of culturally diverse populations, applying adult learning theory, and using technology—all in addition to acquiring the substantive knowledge to teach reading, writing, mathematics, GED subjects, and so forth.

Developing master's level programs and curricula is an essential step for producing a cadre of professional staff. Through the National Institute for Literacy (NIL), the National Center for Adult Literacy (NCAL), or the State resource centers, the Department of Education could work with universities to develop graduate programs. Another approach is to use distance learning technologies to pull together the resources and expertise of universities or regional consortia. One interesting prototype is the National Technological University—a consortium of engineering colleges and universities that provides advanced training and courses to engineers. This consortium was supported by the Department of Commerce's Public Telecommunications Facilities Program—a resource that could be tapped by the literacy community to bring together the necessary mix of faculty and programs. Additional Federal support can be channeled through the Department of Education's Fund for Improvement in Post Secondary Education, NIL grants, or new specialized grant competitions.

These programs could also target the development and distribution of innovative educational materials that bring instructional research, strategies, and resources to prospective and current teachers. Materials developed with this support should be made available in a range of technological formats, from tapes that can be taken home for review to state-of-the-art multimedia materials that can be distributed over networks.

Assist States With Their Professional Standards and Certification Guidelines. Almost one-half of the States have no special certification requirements for adult literacy teachers, and this has contributed to the low professional status of adult literacy education. If program quality is to be improved, more rigorous standards must be established for all adult literacy educators.

Certification is traditionally a State responsibility, but the Department of Education could assist by disseminating model standards. States such as New York, Connecticut, California, and Massachusetts are leaders in this area, and their experience could guide others. The Federal Government might also support efforts to develop regional or national teacher certification guidelines, or ask the National Board for Professional Teaching Standards to include a special assessment for adult education instructors.

Similar approaches at the State level could be developed for increasing the professional standards for volunteer tutors. Working from the models developed for tutor training by Literacy Volunteers of America or Laubach Literacy Action, States could develop certificate programs for volunteer training that would enhance the status, confidence, and effectiveness of volunteers. States could support volunteer agencies in their efforts to systematize standards for volunteer recruitment, training, and supervision.

Recruit More Teachers. If adult literacy programs hope to serve more than 10 percent of the target population, they will surely need more teachers. One potential source of new staff is military trainers being released as bases are closed and force levels are cut. Trainers from military basic skills education programs already have expertise in teaching adults, and many have extensive experience in technology-based instruction. To the extent that Congress establishes programs and provides funding to speed the conversion from military to civilian employment, it could capitalize on these trainers' skills by providing incentives for work in adult basic education, workplace literacy, and family literacy programs. Increased funding for additional literacy teachers could also be provided in other

Federal literacy-related programs such as VISTA (Volunteers in Service to America). If enacted, the new proposal for a Volunteer Service Corps for college students could be structured to include training of volunteers for adult literacy.

Encourage Coordination, Integrated Services, and Partnerships

Although some argue that the multitude of service providers and funding sources offers a rich variety of options and approaches, most agree that this disparate system creates problems for learners and diminishes program efficiency. There is often a mismatch between learner needs and program offerings; services are further restricted by a program's source of funding, target population requirements, location, and other factors. Many small programs are unable to aggregate the kinds of resources needed for planning, staffing, training, technology, and comprehensive services.

Better coordination would leverage resources more effectively and improve services to clients. Coordination must begin at the Federal level; mandates for State and local coordination are undercut when the Federal house is not in order.

Expand Federal Interagency Coordination. The National Literacy Act provisions for interagency coordination are a starting point for bringing coherence to the adult literacy field. The act mandates that NIL enlist cooperation among the Departments of Education, Labor, and Health and Human Services. If it is to reduce the fragmentation of literacy efforts, this interagency group should be expanded to involve the Department of Agriculture (Food Stamp program), ACTION (VISTA literacy volunteers), the Department of the Interior (Indian adult education), the Department of Housing and Urban Development (programs for public housing residents and the homeless), the Department of Justice (correctional education), the Department of Defense (basic skills training), and NSF (educational technology R&D and teacher training). All have a stake in adult literacy, and experience and resources to contribute. Given the ease with which other such interagency coordination groups slip into oblivion, Congress would be well advised to exercise oversight to ensure that NIL is fulfilling its mandate to work with the Federal agencies and serve as a link between the State resource centers, local programs, and the private sector.

An immediate priority for this interagency group would be to coordinate definitions, funding cycles, and accountability, reporting, evaluation, and eligibility requirements. This group could begin with a focus on actions that do not require changes in legislation, while working to assist Congress in removing legislative impediments to cooperative efforts—particularly those concerning technology (see above).

Reward State and Local Coordination. Recent legislation and executive initiatives all call for coordination at the State and local level. Congress may wish to back up these requirements with "glue money"—incentives to help States and local providers develop, extend, and improve effective models of coordination. The approaches recently taken by California, Oregon, Georgia, New York, and Michigan share several important ingredients: formal cooperation among State agencies through interagency agreements; centralization of those elements that can be implemented on a statewide basis, including staff development and certification; development of common definitions, program standards, and evaluation measures; and systems for collecting common data elements and sharing information. The impact of these efforts will be greatly enhanced if they are disseminated to other States through information networks created by State resource centers. If Congress wanted to mandate coordination, it could require evidence of working partnerships among programs as a criteria for funding.

Coordinated efforts do not come about easily. Many programs fear a loss of independence, and turf is jealously guarded. Incentives must be provided to assuage these fears and reward participation by making it easier, not harder, for programs to serve their clients. Furthermore, confidentiality is a serious concern when client data is coordinated and common records maintained. Issues regarding confidentiality—access to data, restrictions on personnel at various agencies, client oversight of personal records, and limitations of the use of records—must be addressed in this process.

Model Interagency Partnerships. If coordinated service delivery is to become more prevalent, we need better working models. Demonstrations of State and local systems of interagency coordinated service delivery should be part of federally supported R&D for adult literacy. These demonstrations should include evaluations of the difficulties encountered and analyses of the costs and benefits of coordinated services. Demonstrations of coordinated service delivery should integrate technology including client tracking systems such as "smart cards," databases that update course offerings and space availability, and multi-service information kiosks for public use.

Partnerships between public and private programs should also be encouraged or required in regulations or funding plans. Offering tax credits to entities that provide space, facilities (e.g., work site technologies for literacy instruction), curriculum development, or teachers' salaries is one way to encourage partnerships with private industry. While industries are usually willing to train their own employees, some incentives may be needed to encourage them to include other learners in their classes, whether they be "future employees" or members of the community in which industries are located.

Encourage Technology-Based Coordination and Dissemination. Technology can contribute to program coordination and effectiveness. Databases of program funding sources and their requirements could help programs seeking support from multiple sources. Technology could also ease recordkeeping and reporting requirements when multiple funding sources are involved.

Technology can help improve program quality by facilitating evaluation. Computer tools can simplify data collection, track the progress of learners, and analyze outcomes.

To effect change the adult literacy community must have easy access to information about successful programs, new technologies, and effective strategies. Recognizing this need, Congress allocated funding for State resource centers, and charged NIL with disseminating information on promising approaches. Both of these entities have many tasks to perform, however, and are just getting under way.

The problem is not a lack of good information, rather the problem is good access to information. One of the most pressing needs centers around use of technology: How are computers being used? What software applications are effective? How can technology support the learning needs of specific groups such as ESL learners? What are the pitfalls to be avoided? One model might be found in the Outreach and Technical Assistance Network (OTAN) developed to serve programs in California. OTAN has a wealth of information on technology that could be useful to other States. Similarly, the growing base of technology information at NCAL is needed by programs across the country. The experience and expertise of the New York Literacy Assistance Center and other similar efforts can be tapped. The newsletters and reports of the Business Council for Effective Literacy are key resources for workplace literacy programs. Thus, a key strategy for NIL and the State centers is to tap into the resources that are already working and broaden access to them. Electronic networking, teleconferencing, and information databases are ways that technology can facilitate dissemination of information and provide support to people in the field.

Congress may wish to expand dissemination activities at the State and regional level. It is at this level that practitioners can play a key role by helping programs and providers screen and evaluate computer software, sharing models of program coordination, and developing teacher training resources.

Experimenting With New Alternatives

In addition to expanding the base of technology and improving the system of existing adult literacy systems, it is time to step outside the constraints of the current system and ask some fundamental questions about adult literacy policy in the United States. How can the visionary applications of technology be made a reality? How can personal access to learning resources be extended to all adults, especially those who are not being reached by the current system? How could the Federal role in adult literacy be shaped into a coherent national strategy?

Technology has the promise to provide people with personal access to learning resources through computer tools that are portable and easy to use, video courses and modules, electronic libraries, and information services. Several questions should be explored to move in this direction: How would adults with low literacy skills use pocket electronic learning devices? How might they learn with a mix of courses and modules in video or multimedia formats? How could electronic networks (e-mail, voice mail, two-way interactive distance learning systems) be used for learning? If personal learning tools and telecommunications networks create new alternatives for learners, can they also create new alternatives for the larger system of programs and services?

Make Experimentation With Technology a Research Priority

If these alternatives are to be explored, the institutions currently charged with literacy R&D (NIL and NCAL) should take the lead, making experimentation with personal learning technology a priority for research. In the case of NIL, this must become a major commitment, particularly as funding levels increase. NCAL has already

Will we be able to exploit the versatility of new interactive technologies for learning and literacy?

taken first steps toward making technology a central research theme by conducting forums on technology and adult literacy. As one of the Federal education research centers, NCAL should seek connections with others, particularly the Center for Technology in Education, to share knowledge and collaborate on research proposals.

Include Adult Literacy in Advanced Technology Initiatives

As Congress considers initiatives to spur advanced technology development, including a high-speed information highway for research and education, it can significantly increase the benefits by adding R&D focused on adult literacy programs and adult learners. Congress may also wish to include funding for partnerships between

software developers, telecommunications providers, hardware companies, and literacy providers; this would bring the right people to the table to reach every part of society.

Rethink the Federal Role

If Congress wishes to rethink Federal literacy efforts, particularly to significantly increase funding, raise visibility, and unify piecemeal efforts, it must focus on those with the highest priority needs. Current attempts to clarify the changing requirements for literacy and survey the literacy skills of the adult population are important first steps. Data from the National Adult Literacy Survey is expected to provide much more precise information on the level of literacy skills possessed by various segments of the adult population and the impact of limited literacy on their employment and well-being. The real challenge will be to serve people who *can read*, but not well enough to function fully in the workplace and as members of society. Reaching this large group will require drawing people to education and training, and removing the stigma attached to adult schooling. It will also involve creating opportunities for adults to build learning into their lives, for employers to build learning into the workplace, and for other social institutions (e.g., libraries and medical centers) to build learning into everyday life.

In the long term, an integrated, nationwide learning system that reaches learners throughout their lifetime needs to be developed as part of the Nation's literacy policy. We are a long way from creating an interconnected and integrated system of K-12 education, adult education, vocational and technical education, higher education, and training, but technology, particularly telecommunications, is helping to link institutions and programs in new and important ways. Congress may wish to enlist telecommunications, improved learning and management tools, and information systems to create a comprehensive system for adult literacy.

The Changing Character of Literacy | 2

homas Jefferson believed that education in a republic served three important functions: "... to prepare some citizens to be public leaders, to enable all citizens to exercise the common rights of self-government, and to ready all citizens for the pursuit of happiness in the society's private sphere."[1] The skills required for citizenship and individual development were different in Jefferson's time than they are today or than they will be 10 or 20 years from now. "The main literacy problem, over the long run, has not been that people's literacy skills have been slipping, but that literacy demands keep rising."[2] Understanding what it means to be literate in American society today is an important part of the overall literacy challenge.

There are many different definitions of literacy, some broad and inclusive, others more narrow. For this report, the Office of Technology Assessment (OTA) adopts the definition of literacy that appears in the National Literacy Act of 1991: "... an individual's ability to read, write, and speak in English, and compute and solve problems at levels of proficiency necessary to function on the job and in society, to achieve one's goals, and develop one's knowledge and potential."[3] As this definition suggests, being literate today means more than just being able to read. Similarly, this definition suggests that literacy is relative and will be defined differently for different people; thus, no score on a test can adequately describe any individual's "level" of

[1] Robert D. Heslep, *Thomas Jefferson and Education* (New York, NY: Random House, 1969), p. 88.

[2] Richard L. Venezky et al., *The Subtle Danger: Reflections on the Literacy Abilities of America's Young Adults* (Princeton, NJ: Educational Testing Service, January 1987), p. 5.

[3] Public Law 102-73, sec. 3, National Literacy Act of 1991.

literacy. OTA considers inappropriate those definitions of literacy that specify thresholds above which one is literate. However, tests and other assessment tools can serve as proxies for estimating literacy in specific areas such as reading, writing, or mathematics when measurement of an individual's progress over time or the effectiveness of literacy programs is needed.

FINDINGS

- Changes occurring in society today are raising questions about the skills and knowledge essential to the education of all Americans. Along with the traditional components of literacy, citizens may need higher order thinking and problem-solving skills, computer and other technology-related skills, literacy skills necessary for the workplace, and literacy skills appropriate for family life.

- The Nation faces a sizable literacy challenge: a very large portion of the U.S. population is in need of improving their literacy skills. While numbers are difficult to fix, as many as 20 to 30 percent of the adult population (35 to 50 million people) have difficulties with common literacy tasks such as following written directions or locating and using information contained in documents, maps, and tables. Although many of these adults can read at rudimentary levels, they need higher levels of reading, writing, and mathematical proficiency to function effectively in society.

- The literacy needs of this large group are very diverse. Literacy services need to be targeted to meet specific needs. There are at least three segments of the adult population whose numbers are large enough to merit special attention in policy and educational planning: those who lack high school diplomas, those whose native language is not English, and those seeking jobs or better employment. Given their large numbers, these groups may be efficiently served by

new approaches and improved use of technology.

- Each year immigrants, high school dropouts, displaced workers, and others swell the already large numbers of those in the "literacy pool" who need improved skills. OTA estimates that somewhere between 1.0 and 2.3 million adults are currently added to this pool annually.

- Educational programs serving adults who are parents are likely to have two important outcomes: improving the skills and the life outcomes for the adult, and increasing the chances of school success for that adult's children. Special benefits are, therefore, likely when parents, especially mothers, are assisted by literacy programs.

- Dramatic demographic trends are changing the composition of the U.S. population, and the numbers of adults with literacy needs may grow even larger in the future. A challenge for policymakers is to develop long-range plans that anticipate the literacy needs of tomorrow while addressing an already large and difficult problem today.

- Just as the definition of literacy has expanded to include both workplace and family contexts, so too must the delivery system move beyond a school-based, institutional model to reach people in the workplace and help them learn while on the job, and to reach people in their homes and help them learn in new ways.

WHAT IS LITERACY?

Frequently cited estimates of the population of "functionally illiterate" adults in the United States range anywhere from 1 to 80 million.[4] Most of the discrepancies in the estimates can be explained by examining which definition of "literacy" is chosen and which measurement tool is used to represent that definition. Depending on the definition, the problem can appear big or small. And even if a seemingly straightforward

---

[4] U.S. Department of Education, Adult Learning and Literacy Clearinghouse, "Adult Illiteracy in the U.S.: A Little or a Lot?" unpublished document, n.d.; and Margaret Genovese, "Ill Feelings About Measuring Illiteracy," *Presstime*, September 1986, pp. 18-19.

Naturalization class for immigrants in the early 1900s. Throughout this century the skills required to participate fully in society have become more complex. The task of helping new immigrants acquire these skills has also changed dramatically.

definition is chosen—for example, ability to read—the estimates of how many people can read will vary depending on whether the researcher asks people *if they can read*, asks them *how much school* they have completed, or gives them *a reading test.*

> People often think of literacy as a hierarchical, measurable skill, but recent work by linguists and anthropologists suggests otherwise. Literacy is elusive, complex. Its study requires careful definitions.[5]

Public sense of what literacy is has changed dramatically over time. Early in this century the proxy for literacy was the ability to write one's name; by this historical indicator, most adults living in the United States today would be considered literate. Throughout this century the skills required for citizenship and individual development have become more complex and the expectations for what constitutes literacy have risen. On many measures—including years of schooling or acquisition of basic reading skill—literacy in America has improved. However, despite this improvement, more is needed to meet the demands of a technological society. Furthermore, experts contend that any ''standard'' for literacy—be it the equivalent of a high school education or a certificate of vocational competence—will need to be continually raised and

---

[5] Lawrence C. Stedman and Carl F. Kaestle, ''Literacy and Reading Performance in the United States From 1880 to the Present,'' *Literacy in the United States,* Carl F. Kaestle et al. (eds.) (New Haven, CT: Yale University Press, 1991), p. 77.

changed as the rate of technological innovation continues to accelerate.

Defining Basic Skills

The question of which skills are necessary for literacy becomes even more complicated if one tries to anticipate what skills might be required in 10 or 20 years. For many years, the notion of literacy usually meant reading; literacy proficiency was determined by a person's grade-level reading ability. Over time that notion has expanded to include reading, writing, and arithmetic.

Most models of elementary and secondary education are built on the assumption that these "basic" skills are developed in a sequential, hierarchical manner and can be associated with established grade-level equivalents.[6] Similarly, most adult literacy programs assume that adult education should replicate the school grades and eventually lead to the set of skills expected of a high school graduate;[7] these skills are understood to be useful for all adults and in a wide variety of settings.

During the 1970s, a number of literacy providers began to expand the notion of literacy to include "functional competencies" or "life skills" that all adults should have. This approach was first popularized by the Adult Performance Level Project, which focused on identifying the ". . . competencies which are functional to economic and educational success in today's society."[8] Their model of functional competency

expanded the requisite academic skills to include problem solving, speaking, and listening. In addition, these investigators conceived of competence partly in terms of knowledge areas (e.g., consumer economics and occupational knowledge) and thus focused on information that adults need to know, in addition to skills they need to have (see box 2-A).[9]

This competency-oriented approach has continued to gain acceptance. It emphasizes learning as ". . . the ability to perform specific literacy-related tasks in the context of work, family and other 'real-life' situations."[10] Since these tasks are different for every adult, this orientation leads to a more individualized set of "requisite skills."

Today most literacy programs teach some combination of academic basics and life skills. The approach chosen reflects a larger set of beliefs about the ends that adult literacy education should serve. "The goal of academically-oriented programs is to develop general abilities that presumably can be applied across situations depending on the goals of the learner. In contrast, competency-oriented instruction is intended to help learners handle specific tasks in their immediate life situation."[11]

One important issue in this debate is that of generalizability—some argue that focusing on a specific set of skills may not prepare learners to cope with new tasks or changing literacy demands.[12] Some educators further argue that literacy programs need to provide learners with a general set of skills that will allow them to gather and use information and continue learning through-

---

[6] Elizabeth Hayes, University of Wisconsin-Madison, "Beyond Skills Versus Competencies: Issues and Strategies in the Evaluation of Adult Literacy Instructional Programs," unpublished manuscript, March 1992.

[7] Thomas G. Sticht, Applied Behavioral and Cognitive Sciences, Inc., "Testing and Assessment in Adult Basic Education and English as a Second Language Programs," unpublished manuscript, January 1990.

[8] Norvell Northcutt, The University of Texas at Austin, "Adult Functional Competency: A Summary," unpublished manuscript, March 1975, p. 1.

[9] Stedman and Kaestle, op. cit., footnote 5.

[10] Hayes, op. cit., footnote 6, p. 1.

[11] Ibid., p. 4.

[12] Ibid.

out their lifetimes—to become "competent novices." For example, in the workplace:

> . . . being a competent novice means learning how to manage oneself effectively in a novel situation by noticing procedures and social interactions, copying experts, asking for explanations and guidance, getting a mentor, and taking extra time . . . to study the layout, devices, tools, and other artifacts . . . that make up the work setting.[13]

Beyond the Basics: Changing Views of Essential Skills

Changes occurring in society today, as well as projected future trends, suggest that any definition of what it means to be literate will need to change. Elementary- and secondary-level educators have begun to reexamine and redefine the skills and knowledge considered essential to the education of all Americans. Many of today's adults do not have these skills and knowledge. Technological advances will continue to change the ways people communicate with one another, shop, interact with social institutions, get information, and do their jobs. Projections about the changing nature of work suggest that a somewhat different profile of skills may be needed by high school graduates entering the workforce in the future. Changing economic and technological forces will continue to create displaced workers who need to relearn basic skills, upgrade those skills, or learn new skills. These trends suggest that adults cannot rely on a limited period of formal schooling during youth to carry them through the next 50 to 70 years of life.

There are many competing ideas about which new skills are the *most* important ones people need, but little empirical evidence exists to support any particular viewpoint. Throughout the education community today, there are many lively and productive debates going on about new goals, new skills, and new visions of what schooling should provide to all Americans. Similarly, there are many competing visions of what additional skills deserve room on the "literacy plate." Several of these new efforts are discussed below.

Portable Skills: Literacy as Problem Solving

Research in cognitive science suggests ways of understanding the underlying information-processing and problem-solving skills common to a wide variety of reading, writing, computational, and communication tasks.[14]

> The cognitive science conception of literacy orients us to think about literacy as a tool for knowledge construction, a tool for learning. This view of literacy takes us beyond routine acts of decoding or calculation, and even beyond fairly complex acts of filling out bureaucratic forms or following job instructions. . . . The goal is to educate a citizenry who are able to use print to learn, in new and changing environments. Citizens must learn how to learn from texts, rather than merely interpret them and memorize facts. They must be able to critically evaluate what they read, to express themselves clearly and cogently in written and oral form, and to use various forms of computer technology as tools for learning. Within cognitive science, literacy has been reconceptualized as reasoning or problem solving in order to generate new knowledge.[15]

Although this work is still under development, its most prominent application is the National Assessment of Educational Progress (NAEP) Literacy Assessment, which has grouped literacy skills into three areas—prose, document, and quantitative—each thought to represent distinct and important aspects of literacy. The NAEP

---

[13] Senta A. Raizen, *Reforming Education for Work: A Cognitive Science Perspective* (Berkeley, CA: National Center for Research in Vocational Education, December 1989), p. 61.

[14] Hayes, op. cit., footnote 6.

[15] Sarah Michaels and Mary Catherine O'Connor, "Literacy as Reasoning Within Multiple Discourses: Implications for Policy and Educational Reform," paper presented at the Council of Chief State School Officers 1990 Summer Institute, Newton, MA, p. 5.

Box 2-A—Life Skills and Competencies: Two Examples

Adult Performance Level Project: Competencies

Funded by the U.S. Office of Education in 1971, the Adult Performance Level (APL) Project was designed to define "functional competency." The original goal of the project was to: "... foster through every means the ability to read, write and compute with the functional competence needed for meeting the requirements of adult living."[1] In order to establish a comprehensive basis for defining important skills, the APL study held conferences on adults' needs, surveyed Federal, State, and foundation officials as to what should be taught in adult education classes, conducted a literature review, and interviewed undereducated adults.

This process generated a two-dimensional definition of functional competence "... best described as the application of a set of skills to a set of general knowledge areas ... which result from the requirements imposed upon members of a society."[2] Five general knowledge areas were identified: consumer economics, occupational knowledge, community resources, government and law, and health. In addition, four primary skills were identified that "... seemed to account for the vast majority of requirements placed on adults."[3] The four skills were called communication skills (reading, writing, speaking, and listening), computation skills, problem-solving skills, and interpersonal relations skills.

---

[1] Anabel Powell Newman and Caroline Beverstock, *Adult Literacy: Contexts and Challenges* (Newark, DE: International Reading Association, 1990), p. 68.

[2] Norvell Northcutt, The University of Texas at Austin, "Adult Functional Competency: A Summary," unpublished manuscript, March 1975, p. 2.

[3] Ibid., p. 2.

---

study is attempting to identify the information-processing skills that underlie competent performance in each area and develop ways to teach those skills.[16]

Technology Skills

New technologies, especially those that are computer-based, are viewed as increasingly important tools. Most recent high school graduates have some experience with computers. In addition to being used in schools as instructional aids, computers provide students with valuable skills for the labor market and other aspects of their lives. As early as 1983, the National Commission on Excellence in Education saw the need for all students to receive instruction in the use of computers as part of a basic high school education, along with English, mathematics, science, and social studies. Their report, *A Nation at Risk*, recommended that high schools equip graduates to:

> (a) understand the computer as an information, computation, and communication device; (b) use the computer in the study of the other Basics and for personal and work-related purposes; and (c) understand the world of computers, electronics, and related technologies.[17]

Similarly, the most recent revision (1991) of the Comprehensive Adult Student Assessment System (CASAS) competencies used in adult

---

[16] Irwin Kirsch et al., *Beyond the School Doors: The Literacy Needs of Job Seekers Served by the U.S. Department of Labor*, prepared for the U.S. Department of Labor (Princeton, NJ: Educational Testing Service, September 1992).

[17] U.S. Department of Education, National Commission on Excellence, *A Nation at Risk* (Washington, DC: U.S. Government Printing Office, April 1983), p. 26.

CASAS Competency List

A recent attempt to define the range of possible competencies for adult basic education efforts is the Comprehensive Adult Student Assessment System (CASAS). CASAS is based on a competency list that has been drawn up by adult basic education programs throughout California and other States; these skills represent the ''. . . basic and life skills necessary for an adult to function proficiently in society.''[4] To be included on the list, a competency must be rated as appropriate and relevant by at least 80 percent of the participating consortium agencies. (CASAS then allows programs to tailor their curriculum and their assessment to the populations they serve by selecting relevant competencies from the list.) Each year the participating organizations meet to revise and update the competency list. The list that follows gives examples of competencies that have been identified within seven content areas.[5]

1. Consumer Economics—includes skills such as:
   * uses weights, measures, measurement scales, and money;
   * understands methods and procedures to obtain housing and services; and
   * uses banking and financial services in the community.
2. Community Resources—includes skills such as:
   * understands how to locate and use different types of transportation and interpret related travel information;
   * uses the services provided by the Post Office; and
   * uses published or broadcast information.
3. Health—includes skills such as:
   * understands common ailments and seeks appropriate medical assistance;
   * understands medical and dental forms and related information; and
   * understands basic health and safety procedures.
4. Occupational Knowledge—includes skills such as:
   * understands basic principles of getting a job;
   * understands wages, benefits, and concepts of employee organizations; and
   * understands materials and concepts related to job training, employment, keeping a job, and getting a promotion.
5. Government and Law—includes skills such as:
   * understands voting and political process;
   * understands historical information; and
   * understands the concepts of taxation.
6. Computation—includes skills such as:
   * uses measurement;
   * interprets data from graphs or computes averages; and
   * uses estimation and mental arithmetic.
7. Domestic Skills—includes skills such as:
   * performs self-care skills; and
   * performs home-care skills.

---

[4] Comprehensive Adult Student Assessment System, *CASAS Statewide Accountability System for Federally Funded 321 Adult Basic Education Programs, Executive Summary* (San Diego, CA: 1991), p. 1.

[5] Comprehensive Adult Student Assessment System, *CASAS Competency List* (San Diego, CA: 1992); and Comprehensive Adult Student Assessment System, *ABE 321 Test Administrators Manual* (San Diego, CA: 1991).

basic education programs added the following new skills to their competency list:

- Interpret operating instructions and directions for use of a computer,
- Read or interpret computer generated print-outs, and
- Demonstrate use of business machines such as cash registers and calculators.[18]

Although directly educating people about computers is important, researchers have stressed that reading, comprehension, and reasoning skills are fundamental for computer use. One survey of small businesses found that employers feel they can train workers in computer-related skills relatively quickly if those workers have good general educational skills with reasoning and communication proficiencies.[19] While confirming the place of computer competence in a secondary school curriculum, *A Nation at Risk* recommended a brief period of computer education ($1/2$ year) compared with subjects such as English (4 years), mathematics (3 years), social studies (3 years), and science (3 years). Available data suggest that long periods of training in computer use are not necessary for most jobs. The National Commission for Employment Policy has predicted that as of 1995 only about 1 percent of all workers will have jobs that require long-term training in computer use, while about 23 percent of the labor force will have jobs with computer-related demands that require a minimal amount of training.[20]

These trends suggest that it will be increasingly important for adult education efforts to offer learners opportunities to use computers, gain familiarity with them as personal tools, and understand their role in society as communication and information devices. Since the software and hardware are constantly changing, these efforts will probably be most effective if they give students an underlying set of ''user skills'' that will enable them to understand and use new technologies, rather than train students in any specific software or application. Further research is needed to identify which cognitive skills underlie effective use of technology.

Literacy Skills for the Workplace

In recent years, a growing number of policy reports have suggested that workers will need new skills to perform jobs in the workplace of the future. Many of these reports have attempted to list the skills necessary for productive, entry-level workers. The most recent report of the Secretary's Commission on Achieving Necessary Skills (SCANS) proposed a three-part foundation of skills and personal qualities, as well as five competencies that ''. . . lie at the heart of job performance. . . . These eight requirements are essential preparation for all students, both those going directly to work and those planning future education.''[21] The three foundation skill areas are:

- *Basic skills*—reading, writing, arithmetic and mathematics, speaking, and listening;
- *Thinking skills*—be able to learn, reason, think creatively, make decisions, and solve problems; and
- *Personal qualities*—individual responsibility, self-esteem and self-management, sociability, and integrity.

The five workplace competencies that workers should productively use are:

---

[18] Comprehensive Adult Student Assessment System, *CASAS Competency List* (San Diego, CA: 1991), p. 10.

[19] Henry M. Levin and Russell W. Rumberger, ''Education and Training Needs for Using Computers in Small Businesses,'' *Educational Evaluation and Policy Analysis*, vol. 8, No. 4, winter 1986, pp. 423-434.

[20] See ibid.

[21] U.S. Department of Labor, The Secretary's Commission on Achieving Necessary Skills, *What Work Requires of Schools: A SCANS Report for America 2000* (Washington, DC: June 1991), p. xv.

El Barrio Popular Education Program, NY; photo by Jeff Heger

Changes occurring in society today suggest that any definition of what it means to be literate will also need to change. For example, although most recent high school graduates have received instruction in computers, many older adults have never had the chance to develop technology skills.

- *Resources*—know how to allocate time, money, materials, space, and staff;
- *Interpersonal skills*—be able to work on teams, teach others, serve customers, lead, negotiate, and work well with people from culturally diverse backgrounds;
- *Information*—be able to acquire and evaluate data, organize and maintain files, interpret and communicate, and use computers to process information;
- *Systems*—understand social, organizational, and technological systems, monitor and correct performance, and design or improve systems; and

- *Technology*—be able to select equipment and tools, apply technology to specific tasks, and maintain and troubleshoot equipment.

Table 2-1 lists the eight SCANS requirements along with the lists of workplace skills from three other selected reports. Although some of the skills and competencies differ, there is a fair degree of overlap and consensus. Broadly speaking, the skills fall into four groups: academic skills (e.g., reading and writing), social skills (e.g., oral communication and teamwork), organizational skills (e.g., problem solving and leadership), and attitudinal skills (e.g., motivation and good work habits).[22]

---

[22] Russell W. Rumberger, "The Definition and Measurement of Workplace Literacy," *California's Workforce for the Year 2000: Improving Productivity by Expanding Opportunities for the Education and Training of Underserved Youth and Adults*, study papers, California Workforce Literacy Task Force (Sacramento, CA: January 1991).

Table 2-1—Workplace Skills and Competencies: Some Examples From Selected Reports

Skill areas	SCANS	American Society for Training and Development	National Academy of Sciences	Stanford study
Academic	• Basic skills • Thinking skills	• Reading, writing • Computation • Learning to learn	• Reading, writing • Computation • Reasoning • Science and technology • Social and economic studies	• Written communication • Numeracy • Reasoning • Learning
Social	• Interpersonal skills	• Communication • Interpersonal skills • Teamwork • Negotiation	• Oral communication • Interpersonal relationships	• Oral communication • Cooperation • Working in groups • Peer training • Multicultural skills
Organizational	• Resources • Information • Systems	• Problem solving • Creative thinking • Organizational effectiveness • Leadership	• Problem solving	• Problem solving • Decisionmaking • Evaluation • Planning • Obtaining and using information
Attitudinal	• Personal qualities	• Self-esteem • Goal-setting/motivation • Personal/career development	• Personal work habits and attitudes	• Initiative
Other	• Technology	—	—	—

KEY: SCANS=Secretary's Commission on Achieving Necessary Skills.

SOURCES: Russell W. Rumberger et al., *Educational Requirements for New Technologies and Work Organization: Research Plan* (Stanford, CA: Stanford University, 1989); Anthony P. Carnevale et al., *Workplace Basics: The Skills Employers Want* (Washington, DC: The American Society for Training and Development, 1988); National Academy of Sciences, Report of the Panel on Secondary Education for the Changing Workplace, *High Schools and the Changing Workplace: The Employers' View* (Washington, DC: National Academy Press, 1984); and Secretary's Commission on Achieving Necessary Skills, *What Work Requires of Schools* (Washington, DC: U.S. Department of Labor, June 1991).

No research defines which skills are a prerequisite for all types of work. Similarly, there is little concrete information on the ''basic'' skill requirements of various jobs in the United States.[23] Nonetheless, the consensus represented in these and other reports seems to be that ''workplace basics'' should be expanded to include more than just academic and technical skills; organizational skills, social skills, and attitudinal qualities all may contribute to employability.

Literacy Skills for Family Life

Another area of literacy that has received increased attention in recent years focuses on families. Parents of young children are faced with new demands as their children prepare for and enter school. Many of these parents are unable to participate actively in their children's education. This parental interest and motivation, coupled with evidence that higher levels of parental education are related to better educational outcomes for children, has led to a growing focus on family or intergenerational literacy efforts. These programs aim to help parents (or other caregivers) improve their own basic skills while they learn new ways to incorporate reading, writing, and communication skills into the lives of their children. The benefits are thought to be twofold:

[23] Ibid.

as they improve their own life chances through increased education, caregivers also improve the chances that their children will be successful in school.

Box 2-B provides some examples of the kinds of skills and competencies family literacy programs seek to provide. Beyond basic skills, parents often gain skills and knowledge related to improving parent-child relationships, understanding child development, providing supervision, setting positive expectations, using written materials at home, and becoming involved in the child's school and other community organizations.

Scientific Literacy

Throughout this century enormous advances have been made in science and technology, and many of the serious problems of today's world require an understanding of scientific and technological concepts—e.g., acid rain, shrinking tropical rainforests, pollution, disease, population growth, and proliferation of nuclear technologies. Some educators have argued that the future depends in large measure on the wisdom with which people use science and technology. Many believe that all U.S. citizens need a better grasp of science. For example, the American Association for the Advancement of Science has recently launched a major initiative to define what constitutes scientific literacy in a modern society and outline a plan for achieving it.[24]

Another initiative focuses on how the Federal Government can increase public understanding of science.[25] A working committee reporting to the presidential Office of Science and Technology Policy has adopted the following goal: "By the year 2000, all segments of the American population will show improvement in scientific literacy and will display increases in the knowledge and skills necessary to make informed decisions."[26] They describe a scientifically literate American as one who can:

> . . . participate in discussions of contemporary scientific issues, apply scientific information in personal decision making, locate scientific information when needed, and distinguish valid information and sources from those that are not. To be scientifically literate, an individual should possess the skills necessary to understand and evaluate publicly disseminated information on science and technology and interpret graphic displays of scientific information.[27]

So What Skills *Do* People Need?

Although it would be nice to be able to answer this question by stating a clear, concrete set of skills that a person needs to acquire to be considered "literate," the answer has to be "it depends." As the discussion shows, literacy involves not one or two skills but a wide and diverse profile of skills and knowledge. Moreover, ". . . literacy is not an all-or-nothing state like small pox or pregnancy. It is instead a continuum of skills that are acquired both in and outside of formal schooling and that relate directly to the ability to function within society."[28] There is no absolute threshold of skill or competency above which people can be certified as literate and below which they can be said to have a literacy problem.

---

[24] F. James Rutherford and Andrew Ahlgren, *Science for All Americans* (New York, NY: Oxford University Press, 1990).

[25] Office of Science and Technology Policy, Federal Coordinating Council for Science Engineering, and Technology: Committee on Education and Human Resources, Public Understanding of Science Subgroup, "Report on the Expert Forum on Public Understanding of Science," Alexandria, VA, Aug. 20-21, 1992, unpublished report, 1992.

[26] Office of Science and Technology Policy, Committee on Education and Human Resources, Subcommittee on Public Understanding of Science, "Strategic Plan for Public Understanding of Science," unpublished report, Sept. 15, 1992.

[27] Ibid., p. 1-2.

[28] Venezky et al., op cit., footnote 2, p. 3.

Box 2-B—Family Literacy Skills: Some Examples

A number of programs have begun to adopt an intergenerational approach to literacy that recognizes the importance of viewing each adult not simply as an individual with literacy needs, but as part of a larger family network that includes children, spouses, and others. The focus is not solely on improving the basic skills of participants, but also on increasing their use of reading and writing in their everyday lives and with their children. The adult and child skills central to the goals of two family literacy programs are described here.

Even Start

Focusing on parents and children as a unit, Even Start projects have three interrelated goals: to help parents become full partners in the education of their children, to assist children in reaching their full potential as learners, and to provide literacy training for their parents.

Goals for children: [1]
- School Readiness:
    Age-appropriate cognitive and language skills
    Age-appropriate social skills
- School Achievement:
    Age-appropriate language skills
    Age-appropriate social skills
    Improved school attendance
    Low incidence special education, remedial placement and retention in grade
    Satisfactory school performance

Goals for parents:
- Literacy Behaviors:
    Shared literacy events with children
    Increased use of literacy materials
    Literacy resources in home
- Parenting Behavior and Skills:
    Positive parent-child relationships
    Home environment to foster child development
    Positive expectations for child
    Adequate supervision
- Education Skills and Expectations:
    Increased basic skills/English language ability
    Higher educational attainment
    Improved job skills and employment status
- Personal Skills:
    Increased self-esteem
    Increased self-efficacy
    Increased personal well-being
- Community Involvement
    Increased involvement in schools
    Access to social services

Kenan Trust Family Literacy Program

The primary goal of the program is to break the intergenerational cycle of undereducation and poverty by improving parents' skills and attitudes toward education, improving children's learning skills, improving parents' childcare skills, and uniting parents and children in a positive educational experience.

Goals for children: [2]
- Change the system of meaning within the home so children receive messages conveying the importance of education, the value of schooling, the importance of personal responsibility, and hope of achieving education, employment, and a successful adult life.
- Increase the development skills of preschool children to prepare them better for academic and social success in school.

Goals for parents:
- Provide a role model for the child of parental interest in education.
- Improve the relationship of the parent and child through planned, structured interaction which:
    a) Demonstrates to parents their power to influence their child's ability to learn;
    b) Increases the influence of literacy in the home so parents can help their children continue to learn;
    c) Identifies and encourages treatment for physical or mental handicaps of children in the program.
- Improve parenting skills of the adult participants.
- Enable parents to become familiar with, and comfortable in school settings.
- Raise the education level of parents of preschool children through instruction in basic skills.
- Help parents gain the motivation, skills, and knowledge needed to become employed or to pursue further education or training.

---

[1] Program goals are quoted from Robert St.Pierre et al., *National Evaluation of the Even Start Family Literacy Program: First Year Report*, prepared for U.S. Department of Education (Cambridge, MA: Abt Associates, Inc., Oct. 28, 1991), p. 6.

[2] Program goals are quoted from Sharon Darling and Andrew E. Hayes, *Breaking the Cycle of Illiteracy: The Kenan Family Literacy Model Program, Final Project Report 1988-89* (Louisville, KY: The National Center for Family Literacy, n.d.), pp. 19-35.

Literacy is not an on/off characteristic, and it is more than the ability to read and write a little. Literacy describes a wide variety of communicative acts, interpersonal strategies, and survival skills. It is more appropriate to picture a spectrum of literacies across a variety of specific needs and communities, from barely able to write or recognize your own name to highly and multiculturally educated. It is more accurate to ask whether people are *sufficiently* literate to meet their own needs and what society expects of them than to ask if they are literate.[29]

DEMOGRAPHICS OF ADULT LITERACY

Despite all the complexities, addressing the literacy needs of the Nation ultimately requires some way to understand the size and scope of the problem. Who is affected? Who should receive educational services? What resources are needed to meet the literacy needs of U.S. adults effectively? What literacy skills does today's technological society require for adults to function effectively? What skills might be required to meet societal demands 10 or 20 years from now? Answers to these and other questions require some method of defining and measuring the dimension of "adult literacy." This section examines some common ways of defining and measuring "literacy," and presents some estimates of the number of U.S. adults who lack adequate skills.

School Completion Rates

School attainment has been the most commonly used "measure" of literacy for the Nation. In the 1930s, the Civilian Conservation Corps defined "functional literacy" as 3 or more years of schooling, assuming that a person with that much schooling could read the essential print materials of daily life. Over time, the number of years of schooling thought to equal adequate

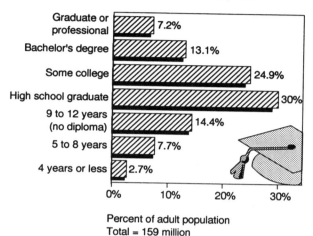

Figure 2-1—Highest Level of Education Attained by U.S. Adults Ages 25 and Over, 1990

- Graduate or professional: 7.2%
- Bachelor's degree: 13.1%
- Some college: 24.9%
- High school graduate: 30%
- 9 to 12 years (no diploma): 14.4%
- 5 to 8 years: 7.7%
- 4 years or less: 2.7%

Percent of adult population
Total = 159 million

SOURCE: U.S. Department of Commerce, Bureau of the Census, 1990 Census, unpublished data, tb. ED90-1.

literacy has increased. During World War II, the Army defined functional literacy as equivalent to a 4th-grade education. In 1947, the Census Bureau applied the term "functional illiterates" to anyone with less than 5 years of schooling; 5 years later, in 1952, they raised it to the 6th grade. By 1960, the U.S. Office of Education had adopted 8th grade as the standard and ". . . finally, by the late 1970s, some noted authorities were describing functional literacy in terms of high school completion."[30]

Figure 2-1 presents the school completion rates as surveyed in the 1990 census. If the completion of 4 years of schooling is considered a sufficient literacy goal, then 97.3 percent of today's adult population meet this standard. However, if the much higher standard of a high school diploma is used, then only 75.2 percent of adults would be considered "literate"—this means over 39 million adults have inadequate schooling.

School attainment figures show literacy rates vary considerably for different age cohorts. Over-

---

[29] Anabel P. Newman and Caroline Beverstock, *Adult Literacy: Contexts and Challenges* (Newark, DE: International Reading Association, 1990), p. 49.

[30] Stedman and Kaestle, op. cit., footnote 5, p. 92.

Figure 2-2—Dropout Rates for Persons Ages 16 to 24, 1972-91

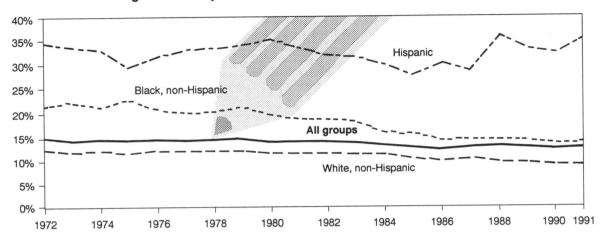

Since 1970, considerable progress has been made in decreasing the number of black dropouts. White dropout rates have decreased slightly. The Hispanic rate has remained high.

NOTE: Figure includes persons ages 16 to 24 who were not enrolled in and had not graduated from high school. The racial-ethnic group categories used here are those defined by the Bureau of the Census.

SOURCE: Data from U.S. Department of Commerce, Bureau of the Census, Current Population Survey presented in U.S. Department of Education, National Center for Education Statistics, *Dropout Rates in the United States, 1991* (Washington, DC: U.S. Government Printing Office, September 1992), fig. 5.

all, high school graduation rates are much lower among older Americans. While less than one-half of adults over age 75 are high school graduates, 86.6 percent of those between 25 and 44 have attained this level.

Nationally, dropout rates have been declining for blacks and whites, but not for Hispanics (see figure 2-2). Between 1972 and 1991, rates for blacks dropped from 21 to 14 percent and for whites from 12 to 9 percent.[31] Rates for Hispanics have shown no consistent trend, but have remained high. However, Hispanics make up an increasing proportion of all dropouts, because the total population of Hispanics ages 16 to 24 increased during this time period while the

populations of whites and blacks did not. In 1991, 16- to 24-year-old dropouts were 50 percent white, 32 percent Hispanic, and 16 percent black (see table 2-2, column d).[32]

Other demographic data, shown in table 2-2, indicate that in 1991, there were similar numbers of male and female dropouts between ages 16 and 24. Dropout rates were higher in homes with low-incomes (26 percent) than in middle- (12 percent) or high-income homes (3 percent). People between the ages of 16 and 24 were more likely to be dropouts if they lived in central cities (16 percent), than in suburban (9 percent) or nonmetropolitan areas (11 percent). However, using absolute numbers of 16- to 24-year-old

---

[31] Figures presented here are status dropout rates, which represent the proportion of individuals at any given time who are not enrolled in school and have not completed high school. There are a number of different ways of measuring dropout rates; for further discussion of these measures and some of the methodological issues involved, see U.S. Department of Education, National Center for Education Statistics, *Dropout Rates in the United States: 1991* (Washington, DC: U.S. Government Printing Office, September 1992).

[32] Ibid., p. 21. The population of whites ages 16 to 24 has decreased from approximately 28 million in 1980 to around 22 million in 1991. The black population of 16- to 24-year-olds has held relatively constant during this time period at about 4 million. The population of Hispanics ages 16 to 24 has increased from approximately 2.5 million in 1980 to around 3.5 million in 1991.

Table 2-2—High School Dropouts Ages 16 to 24, by Sex, Race-Ethnicity, Income, Region, and Metropolitan Status, 1991

	(a) Population (in millions)	(b) Number of status dropouts (in millions)	(c) Status dropout rate (percent)	(d) Percent of all dropouts	(e) Percent of population
Sex					
Male	15.4	2.0	13.0%	51.6%	49.4%
Female	15.8	1.9	11.9	48.4	50.6
Race-ethnicity[a]					
White, non-Hispanic	21.9	2.0	8.9	50.3	70.2
Black, non-Hispanic	4.5	.6	13.6	15.7	14.4
Hispanic	3.5	1.2	35.3	32.0	11.3
Family income[b]					
Low-income level	5.9	1.6	26.5	40.1	18.9
Middle-income level	18.1	2.1	11.8	55.0	58.2
High-income level	7.1	.2	2.7	4.9	22.9
Region[c]					
Northeast	5.9	.5	9.1	13.7	18.8
Midwest	7.8	.8	9.7	19.5	24.9
South	10.8	1.5	14.1	39.3	34.7
West	6.7	1.1	15.9	27.5	21.5
Metropolitan status					
Central city	10.5	1.7	16.3	45.4	33.8
Suburban	14.1	1.3	9.4	34.9	45.1
Nonmetropolitan.........	6.6	.7	11.3	19.7	21.1
Total	31.2	3.9	12.5	100.0	100.0

[a] Not shown separately are non-Hispanics who are neither black nor white, but who are included in the total. These racial-ethnic group categories are those defined by the Census Bureau.

[b] Family income in current residence. Low income is defined as the bottom 20 percent of all family incomes for 1991; middle income is between 20 and 80 percent of all family incomes; and high income is the top 20 percent of all family incomes.

[c] The Northeast consists of Connecticut, Maine, Massachusetts, New Hampshire, New Jersey, New York, Pennsylvania, Rhode Island, and Vermont. The Midwest consists of Illinois, Indiana, Iowa, Kansas, Michigan, Minnesota, Missouri, Nebraska, North Dakota, Ohio, South Dakota, and Wisconsin. The South consists of Alabama, Arkansas, Delaware, Florida, Georgia, Kentucky, Louisiana, Maryland, Mississippi, North Carolina, Oklahoma, South Carolina, Tennessee, Texas, Virginia, Washington, DC, and West Virginia. The West consists of Alaska, Arizona, California, Colorado, Hawaii, Idaho, Montana, Nevada, New Mexico, Oregon, Utah, Washington, and Wyoming.

NOTE: Percentages may not sum to 100 percent due to rounding.

SOURCE: U.S. Department of Commerce, Bureau of the Census, Current Population Survey 1991 data in National Center for Education Statistics, *Dropout Rates in the United States: 1991* (Washington, DC: U.S. Department of Education, September 1992).

dropouts (column b), 1.7 million lived in central cities, 1.3 million in suburbs, and 0.7 million in nonmetropolitan areas, indicating that substantial numbers of dropouts live in suburbs as well as central cities.

Data from the 1990 census also allow a regional examination of recent dropout rates. In 1990, about 1.6 million, or 11.2 percent, of all 16- to 19-year-olds were high school dropouts. When dropout rates were computed for each State, the rates ranged from 4.3 percent in North Dakota to 14.9 percent in Nevada and 19.1 percent in the District of Columbia. A total of 25 States had rates between 9 and 12 percent, while 14 States had rates below 9 percent; 11 States plus the District of Columbia fell above 12 percent (see figure 2-3).

Data on school attainment and dropout rates confirm that since the turn of the century, significant progress has been achieved in

Figure 2-3—Percentage of High School Dropouts Ages 16 to 19, by State, 1990

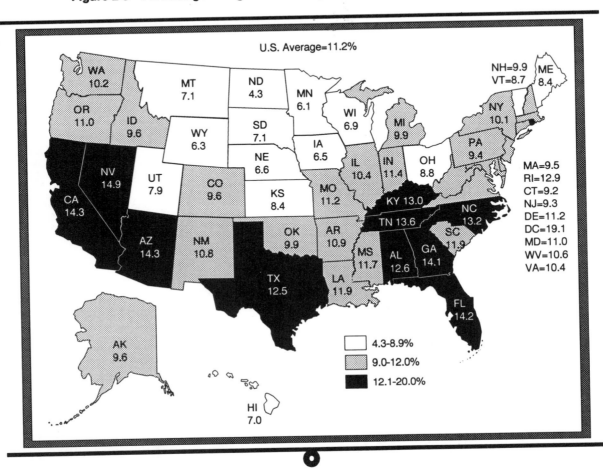

NOTE: All persons ages 16 to 19 who were not enrolled and had not graduated from high school were counted as dropouts.

SOURCE: U.S. Department of Education, National Center for Education Statistics, *Dropout Rates in the United States: 1991* (Washington, DC: U.S. Government Printing Office, September 1992), fig. 4.

increasing the numbers of Americans who complete secondary school.[33] Even with no change in the high school dropout rate, high school completion levels will rise for the Nation as a whole as the population ages and the cohort of older, less-educated adults becomes a smaller portion of the population.

The most significant problem with using school attainment as an index of literacy is that it reveals very little about actual knowledge and skills possessed by adults. The skills of adults with the same level of educational attainment vary widely. Indeed, there are many knowledgeable and skilled adults whose formal levels of schooling are not high.

Furthermore, although most analyses of employment and earnings demonstrate better outcomes for high school graduates than for drop-

---

[33] Harold L. Hodgkinson, *All One System: Demographics of Education—Kindergarten Through Graduate School* (Washington, DC: Institute of Educational Leadership, 1985).

outs, academic skill levels also influence these outcomes. Within each group—high school graduates and high school dropouts—those with better academic skills earn more.[34] In addition, lower levels of basic skills are associated with the increased likelihood that young adults (ages 18 to 23) will experience other difficulties such as joblessness, poverty, dropping out of school, and unwed pregnancies.[35]

Tests of Literacy Skills

One response to these arguments is to try to estimate literacy rates by testing people's skills directly. Beginning in the 1970s, survey researchers began to assess people's

> ... ability to read bureaucratic forms, instructions, and advertisements that are encountered in most adults' lives.... The 1970s estimates of functional illiteracy ranged from 15 percent to over 50 percent of the American population.... Not only did the studies produce varying estimates of illiteracy, but each single report contained estimates that differed depending on which cut-off point was used.[36]

One of the most popular, and seemingly straightforward, methods of measuring "literacy" is to assess the difficulty of the reading material a person (or a group of people) can read. For example, it is common to hear reports of high school graduates who read at an 8th-grade level or large numbers of adults unable to read newspaper stories written at the 11th-grade level.

Many attempts have been made to try to rate common "real-life" reading materials assumed necessary for everyday functioning. Although these methods depend on readability formulas, which can give widely disparate results, some interesting findings have been reported. For example, newspaper articles are reported to vary between 9th and 12th grade, while newspaper election coverage tends to be written at the college level. Best sellers, in contrast, have averaged around the 7th-grade level for the past 50 years. Some reports have suggested that many societal tasks are quite difficult:

> An apartment lease and food-stamp notices, for example, are at the college level, an insurance policy is at the twelfth-grade level, and an aspirin bottle is at the tenth-grade level. Antidote instructions on a bottle of corrosive kitchen lye are at the ninth-grade level, while tax forms and directions on how to prepare a T.V. dinner are at the eighth-grade level. Only a driver's license manual, estimated to be written at a sixth-grade reading level, falls within the grasp of many in the bottom 30 percent.[37]

The use of reading level estimates is fraught with technical and conceptual problems.[38] The primary difficulties include the following:

Determining what it means—Technically, reading level means "... that grade at which the average student can understand 75 percent of what is presented."[39] Thus materials assigned an 8th-grade reading level may not be fully understood by all persons reading at that level. An individual's reading skills also vary a great deal depending on such factors as background knowledge, interest, and familiarity with particular written materials (see chapter 3).

Conceptual limitations—Most modern definitions of literacy include much more than reading,

---

[34] Gordon Berlin and Andrew Sum, *Toward a More Perfect Union: Basic Skills, Poor Families, and Our Economic Future* (New York, NY: Ford Foundation, February 1988).

[35] Ibid.

[36] Richard Venezky et al., op. cit., footnote 2, pp. 13-15. See also Stedman and Kaestle, op. cit., footnote 5, for a more complete description of some of these survey efforts.

[37] Stedman and Kaestle, op. cit., footnote 5, p. 115.

[38] See also Kenneth Cadenhead, "Reading Level: A Metaphor That Shapes Practice," *Phi Delta Kappan*, February 1987, pp. 436-441.

[39] Stedman and Kaestle, op. cit., footnote 5, p. 113.

encompassing such skills as oral communication, writing, problem solving, reasoning, and computation. By focusing exclusively on reading level scores, many argue, we ignore these and other critical literacy domains.

Technical problems—Determining reading levels depends heavily on the particular test used, the types of reading skills tested and the difficulty of the items. In addition, readability formulas, used to determine difficulty, are not widely agreed on, and so give different results.

In the 1970s, survey researchers began to focus on a broader view of literacy and to test people directly for their ability to read a wide range of everyday materials and complete associated tasks. For example, in the Survival Literacy Test, adults were asked to complete five forms: a Social Security number request, a bank loan application, a driver's license application, a public assistance form, and a Medicaid form.[40] National studies conducted in the 1970s and early 1980s attempted to set some criteria to distinguish "functional literates" from "illiterates." Many of these studies were criticized for using arbitrary cutoff points or for ranking all people on a single scale—implying that literacy is one-dimensional, rather than a more complex set of skills.[41]

The most recent national survey of "literacy" has attempted to correct some of the limitations of earlier studies. In 1984, NAEP began the Young Adult Literacy Assessment to examine the abilities of young adults ages 21 to 25. Instead of trying to produce a single estimate of functional illiteracy, this study attempted to emphasize the multiple nature of literacy skills and to report how many young adults had reached various skill levels on different kinds of tasks. To do so, the NAEP Young Adult Study adopted the following

definition of literacy based on the advice of panels of experts: "Using printed and written information to function in society, to achieve one's goals, and to develop one's knowledge and potential."[42]

The NAEP study characterized literacy skills in terms of the following three "literacy scales":

- **prose literacy**—the knowledge and skills needed to understand and use information from texts that include editorials, news stories, poems, and the like;
- **document literacy**—the knowledge and skills required to locate and use information contained in job applications or payroll forms, bus schedules, maps, tables, indexes, and so forth; and
- **quantitative literacy**—the knowledge and skills needed to apply arithmetic operations, either alone or sequentially, that are embedded in printed materials, such as in balancing a checkbook, figuring out a tip, completing an order form, or determining the amount of interest from a loan advertisement.[43]

Performance in each of these areas is described in terms of a proficiency scale that extends from 0 to 500.[44] Tasks are placed along the scale to describe various levels of proficiency; increasingly difficult tasks characterize higher levels on the proficiency scales. Literacy skills can then be described in terms of the numbers of young adults who successfully complete tasks at each proficiency level. (See figure 2-4 for examples of document literacy tasks at different proficiency levels.)

The conclusions of this study include the following:

1. Most young adults demonstrate the skills and strategies necessary to complete tasks at the lower end of all three literacy scales. Such tasks

---

[40] Louis Harris and Associates, *Survival Literacy Study* (Washington, DC: National Reading Council, 1970).

[41] Stedman and Kaestle, op. cit., footnote 5.

[42] Irwin S. Kirsch and Ann Jungeblut, *Literacy: Profiles of America's Young Adults*, No. 16-PL-02 (Princeton, NJ: National Assessment of Educational Progress, 1986), p. 3.

[43] Ibid., p. 4.

[44] The mean of this scale was set at 305 with a standard deviation of about 50.

include writing a brief description about a job, locating a fact in a sports article, matching grocery coupons to a shopping list, entering personal information on a job application, and filling in information on a phone message form. ''The overwhelming majority of America's young adults are able to use printed information to accomplish many tasks that are either routine or uncomplicated.''[45] The authors conclude that ''. . . it is clear from these data that 'illiteracy' is not a major problem for this population.''[46]

2. Sizable numbers of young adults have difficulty with tasks of moderate complexity.

Basic skills in uncomplicated applications show high mastery. But in more complex contexts where judgments of relevance and similarity must be made and several dependent steps or matches done, abilities decline dramatically. . . . There can be no doubt from these data that problem-solving skills are weak, that even college graduates often fail to consider all relevant information in a literacy task, or are confused by logical/mathematical data.[47]

3. White young adults obtained the highest scores on all three scales while black young adults scored one full standard deviation lower; the mean scores of Hispanic young adults tended to fall halfway between black and white adults. Although some of this difference is explained by the lower school attainment of blacks and Hispanics, the gap is reduced only slightly when attainment is controlled.[48] It is important to note, however, that although black and Hispanic young adults are overrepresented among the young adults with low literacy skills, the majority of this group is white, since whites make up 77 percent of young adults.

4. The above findings were further substantiated when the reading proficiency of these young adults was compared with NAEP samples of 4th-, 8th-, and 11th-grade students. Further evidence that ''illiteracy'' is not a major problem is demonstrated by the finding that 94 percent of young adults read at or above the level of the average 4th grader. Roughly 80 percent reached or exceeded the average 8th-grade level, while 62 percent read as well or better than the average 11th grader.

The results of studies that have attempted to assess literacy skills directly are complex and difficult to summarize. One group of researchers, having reviewed the major studies of functional literacy rates, concluded the following:

Based on these studies, we find it reasonable to estimate that about 20 percent of the adult population, or around 35 million people, have serious difficulties with common reading tasks. An additional 10 percent are probably marginal in their functional-literacy skills.[49]

Literacy Target Groups

One of the reasons the size of the literacy problem is difficult to estimate is that literacy skills are not easy to observe or to measure. In addition, adults with low literacy skills have widely different needs. Thus another way to characterize the literacy problem is to examine target groups of the total population likely to have low literacy skills. The section that follows discusses three such groups: those without a high school diploma, immigrants/nonnative English

---

[45] Kirsch and Jungeblut, op. cit., footnote 42, p. 6

[46] Ibid., p. 5. These authors note that about 2 percent of the young adult population were estimated to have such limited literacy skills that they could not complete the tasks. ''Roughly one percent (or about half) of this group reported being unable to speak English. . . . The English speaking one percent . . . responded to a set of oral-language tasks. The comparatively low performance indicates that this group (about 225,000 people) may have a language problem that extends beyond processing printed information.''

[47] Venezky et al., op. cit., footnote 2, p. 28.

[48] Ibid., pp. 31-32. Racial-ethnic group categories used here are those used by the National Assessment of Educational Progress researchers.

[49] Stedman and Kaestle, op. cit., footnote 5, p. 109.

Figure 2-4—Assessing Literacy Skills Used in Everyday Life: The Young Adult Literacy Assessment

The Young Adult Literacy Assessment was conducted in 1984 to survey the literacy abilities of young adults ages 21 to 25. Each participant was interviewed and asked to complete tasks similar to those encountered by adults in everyday life. Tasks were presented in each of three literacy domains: prose, document, and quantitative. Tasks of varying difficulty levels were used in each area; performance was scored on a proficiency scale that extends from 0 to 500. More difficult items characterize higher levels on the proficiency scale. The figure shows the Document Literacy Scale and some sample tasks of varying difficulty that participants were asked to complete.

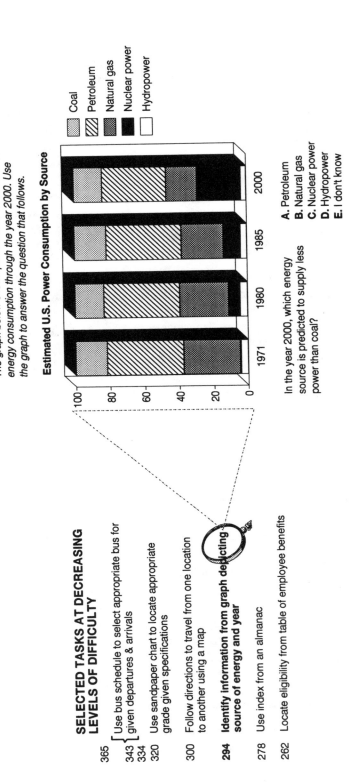

The graph below shows prediction of United States energy consumption through the year 2000. Use the graph to answer the question that follows.

Estimated U.S. Power Consumption by Source

Coal
Petroleum
Natural gas
Nuclear power
Hydropower

In the year 2000, which energy source is predicted to supply less power than coal?

A. Petroleum
B. Natural gas
C. Nuclear power
D. Hydropower
E. I don't know

SELECTED TASKS AT DECREASING LEVELS OF DIFFICULTY

365 ⎱ Use bus schedule to select appropriate bus for
343 ⎰ given departures & arrivals
334

320 Use sandpaper chart to locate appropriate grade given specifications

300 Follow directions to travel from one location to another using a map

294 Identify information from graph depicting source of energy and year

278 Use index from an almanac

262 Locate eligibility from table of employee benefits

	HOURS			
	REGULAR	2ND SHIFT	OVERTIME	TOTAL
	50 0			50 0

PERIOD ENDING 03/15/85

	FED WH	STATE WH	CITY WH	FICA
CURRENT	108 94	13 75		38 31
YEAR TO DATE	734 98	82 50		261 67

	REGULAR	OVERTIME	GROSS	DEF ANN	NET PAY
CURRENT	625 00		625 00		459 88
YEAR TO DATE			4268 85		

OTHER DEDUCTIONS — UNITED FD PERS IN MISC

CR UNION

CODE	TYPE	AMOUNT
07	DEN	4 12

OTHER DEDUCTIONS

CODE	TYPE	AMOUNT	MISC CODE

NON-NEGOTIABLE

Here is a wage and tax statement that comes with a paycheck.
What is the current net pay? _____
What is the gross pay for this year to date? _____

Here is a Social Security card.
Sign your name on the line that reads "signature."

257 **Locate gross pay-to-date on pay stub**
255 Complete a check given information on a bill
253 Complete an address on order form
249 Locate intersection on street map
221 Enter date on a deposit slip
219 Identify cost of theatre trip from notice
211 Match items on shopping list to coupons
196 Enter personal information on job application
192 Locate movie in TV listing in newspaper
181 Enter caller's number on phone message form
169 Locate time of meeting on a form
160 Locate expiration date on driver's license
110 **Sign your name**

SOURCE: Irwin S. Kirsch et al., *Literacy: Profiles of America's Young Adults—Final Report*, No. 16-PL-01 (Princeton, NJ: National Assessment of Educational Progress, September 1986).

speakers, and those seeking jobs or better employment. These groups are not independent of one another—an individual who is counted in one group (e.g., no high school diploma) is often a member of another (e.g., nonnative English speaker).

Adults Without a High School Diploma

Because people can be identified fairly easily as either holding or not holding a credential such as a diploma, this group can be counted and identified. As figure 2-1 illustrates, 25 percent of Americans age 25 and over (39 million people) do not hold a high school diploma. In addition, about 4 million persons ages 16 to 24 had not graduated from high school and were not enrolled in 1991.[50]

Although this is the group that most conventional adult education programs target, people within this group have widely differing levels of basic skills. Although some of these individuals may be unable to read at the most rudimentary levels, most have already achieved some level of competence in reading and writing. For example, data from the Young Adult Survey indicate that approximately 75 percent of 21- to 25-year-olds who have no diploma can read at least as well as the average 4th grader.[51] Of those who stayed in school beyond the 8th grade, 54 percent read as well as the average 8th grader and 27 percent as well as the average 11th grader. Among those with lower educational attainment (0 to 8 years), the figures were somewhat lower (37 percent for 8th grade and 15 percent for 11th grade).

Immigrants and Nonnative English Speakers

Another population of considerable interest in literacy efforts is immigrants and other adults not proficient in speaking English. As of 1989, approximately 16.5 million foreign-born people were legally residing in the United States; another 2 million undocumented immigrants were also thought to be living in the United States at that time.[52]

Immigration rates during the 1980s rank among the highest levels in U.S. history, surpassed only by the first two decades of this century (see figure 2-5). Approximately 6 million legal immigrants entered the United States during the 1980s. In addition, recent decades have shown a shift in the composition of immigrant populations.

> As recently as the 1950s, two-thirds of the legal immigrants to the U.S. came from Europe and Canada. By the 1980s, that percentage had dropped to 14 percent. In the '80s, 44 percent of the nation's legal immigrants came from Asia and 40 percent came from Mexico and other Latin American countries.[53]

It is difficult to estimate the literacy needs of this foreign-born population. Available data on the amount of schooling immigrants have received in their native countries reveal some interesting trends. For example, those immigrants entering the United States between 1975 and 1980 have completed the same number of years of school on average as the U.S.-born population (12.4 years, foreign born; 12.5 years, U.S.-born). However, these immigrants are concentrated at both the high and the low ends of the schooling distribution. A higher proportion of these immigrants have attended college (38 percent) than have people born here (32 percent). But a greater proportion of these immigrants are also found at the lowest education levels (31 percent have less than 9 years of schooling compared with 17 percent of U.S.-born). In contrast to this bimodal distribution for these immigrants, the largest proportion of the U.S. population clusters toward

---

[50] National Center for Education Statistics, op. cit., footnote 31.

[51] As tested by the National Assessment of Educational Progress in 1984. See Kirsch and Jungeblut, op. cit., footnote 42.

[52] Karen A. Woodrow, *Undocumented Immigrants Living in the United States* (Washington, DC: U.S. Department of Commerce, Bureau of the Census, August 1990).

[53] "Illegal Immigration," *CQ Researcher*, vol. 2, No. 16, Apr. 24, 1992, p. 368.

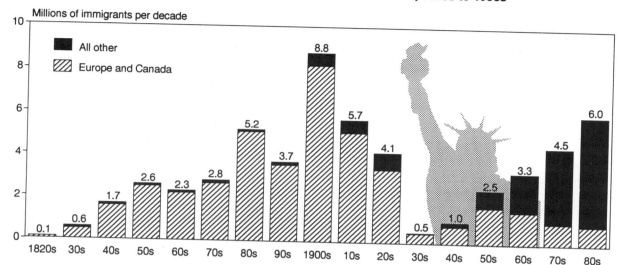

Figure 2-5—Legal Immigration to the United States, 1820s to 1980s

SOURCE: Data from the Immigration and Naturalization Service presented in "Illegal Immigration," *CQ Researcher*, vol. 2, No. 16, Apr. 24, 1992, p. 370.

the middle of the distribution at the high school completion level.[54]

Those immigrants at the lowest levels of education often have varying experiences with print materials and written languages as well as limited proficiency in speaking English. Many come from rural villages and tend to fall into three categories:

> . . . nonliterates, who cannot read or write in any language; semiliterates, who have the equivalent of a few years of formal education and minimal literacy skills; and non-Roman alphabetic literates, who are fully literate in their own language (such as Lao or Chinese) but who need to learn the Roman alphabet.[55]

Estimates of the total number of adults who have limited English proficiency are difficult to obtain. Most are based on self-reported answers to surveys conducted by the Bureau of the Census;

such self-report data probably show lower numbers than a direct test of English language proficiency would indicate.

The 1990 census indicates that 25.5 million adults (13.8 percent of all adults ages 18 and over) speak a language other than English at home (see figure 2-6). Of these adults, about 75 percent report speaking English well or very well. However, a total of 5.8 million adults report that they speak English not well or not at all. These are self-reports of *spoken* language proficiency and tell us little about people's skills at reading or writing English.

People who do not speak English at home are heavily concentrated in several regions of the United States (see figure 2-7). California, with 8.6 million, has more than twice as many as any other State. Five States (California, Texas, New York, Florida, and Illinois) account for 63 percent of those adults who speak a non-English language at

---

[54] U.S. Department of Labor, *The Effects of Immigration on the U.S. Economy and Labor Market* (Washington, DC: U.S. Government Printing Office, 1989). Data on the educational attainment of immigrants entering the United States in the 1980s were collected in the 1990 census, but will not be available until 1993.

[55] U.S. Department of Education, Office of Vocational and Adult Education, *Teaching Adults With Limited English Skills: Progress and Challenges* (Washington, DC: U.S. Government Printing Office, October 1991), p. 13.

Figure 2-6—Ability to Speak English in Non-English Speaking Homes: 1990 Census

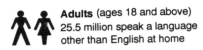

Adults (ages 18 and above)
25.5 million speak a language
other than English at home

When asked how well they spoke English:

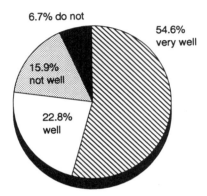

6.7% do not

54.6% very well

15.9% not well

22.8% well

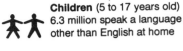

Children (5 to 17 years old)
6.3 million speak a language
other than English at home

When asked how well they spoke English:

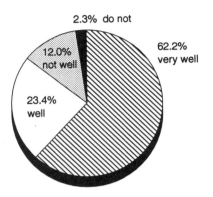

2.3% do not

62.2% very well

12.0% not well

23.4% well

SOURCE: U.S. Department of Commerce, Bureau of the Census, 1990 Census, unpublished data, tbs. ED90-4 and ED90-5.

home. Ten more States have over 400,000 such individuals; these 15 States combined account for 84 percent of the nationwide population.

There are a number of States that have high proportions of non-English speakers, even though the absolute numbers are not particularly high. For example, New Mexico ranks highest among the States with 35.5 percent of its population reported to be non-English speakers at home. However, New Mexico has far fewer people who are non-English speaking than does California, which is second at 31.5 percent (0.5 million as compared with 8.6 million in California). Other States that have relatively high proportions of non-English speakers but comparatively low absolute numbers include Hawaii, Rhode Island, Nevada, Alaska, and the District of Columbia (see table 2-3 for proportions by State).

Those Seeking Jobs or Better Employment

There has been increasing interest in understanding the relationship between literacy skills and employment. Many experts today argue that there is a growing job-literacy gap—a discrepancy between the skills of our population and those required to perform most of society's jobs. Estimates of the extent of this job-literacy gap have been very difficult to obtain, but the results that are available indicate that two different kinds of trends—"... dumbing down and rising literacy demands—are occurring at different levels in the occupational pyramid and in different sectors."[56] (See box 2-C.)

Nonetheless, it seems useful, as another method of describing the literacy problem, to attempt to estimate the number of individuals who have difficulty finding or keeping employment because of literacy difficulties. The Department of Labor (DOL) has recently commissioned a study of the literacy skills of three groups served by DOL programs: persons enrolling in the Job Training Partnership Act (JTPA) programs, persons applying for jobs through the Employment System (ES), and persons filing claims for

---

[56] Stedman and Kaestle, op. cit., footnote 5, p. 121.

**Figure 2-7—Number of People, Ages 5 and Above,
Speaking a Non-English Language at Home, by State, 1990**

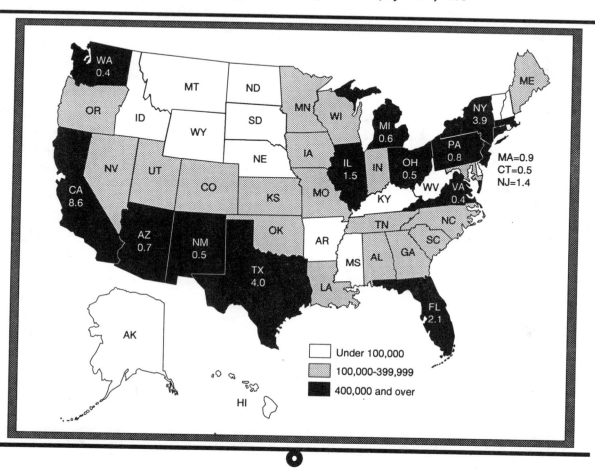

NOTE: The actual numbers (in millions) are given for States with 400,000 or more people speaking a non-English language at home.
SOURCE: U.S. Department of Commerce, Bureau of the Census, 1990 Census, unpublished data, tb. ED 90-6.

Unemployment Insurance (UI). This population, totaling about 20 million people, represents individuals who have experienced persistent difficulty finding jobs, who are unemployed and looking for work, or who are seeking better employment opportunities. "These groups include a significant segment of Americans who, with proper assistance, could enhance their liter-acy skills and in turn contribute in large measure to the growth of our nation."[57]

Building on the framework established in the NAEP Young Adult Literacy Assessment, a sample of the DOL program participants completed literacy tasks in three areas: prose, document, and quantitative literacy. This assessment goes beyond the Young Adult study, however, in

[57] Educational Testing Service, "Workplace Literacy: A Project Conducted by ETS for the Department of Labor," informational pamphlet, n.d., p. 3.

Table 2-3—States With 5 Percent or More of the Population (Ages 5 and Above) Speaking a Non-English Language at Home, 1990

Rank	State	Percentage
1.	New Mexico	35.5%
2.	California	31.5
3.	Texas	25.4
4.	Hawaii	24.8
5.	New York	23.3
6.	Arizona	20.8
7.	New Jersey	19.5
8.	Florida	17.3
9.	Rhode Island	17.0
10.	Connecticut	15.2
	Massachusetts	15.2
12.	Illinois	14.2
13.	Nevada	13.2
14.	District of Columbia	12.5
15.	Alaska	12.1
16.	Colorado	10.5
17.	Louisiana	10.1
18.	Maine	9.2
19.	Washington	9.0
20.	Maryland	8.9
21.	New Hampshire	8.7
22.	North Dakota	7.9
23.	Utah	7.8
24.	Oregon	7.3
	Pennsylvania	7.3
	Virginia	7.3
27.	Delaware	6.9
28.	Michigan	6.6
29.	South Dakota	6.5
30.	Idaho	6.4
31.	Vermont	5.8
	Wisconsin	5.8
33.	Kansas	5.7
	Wyoming	5.7
35.	Minnesota	5.6
36.	Ohio	5.4
37.	Montana	5.0
38.	Oklahoma	5.0

SOURCE: U.S. Department of Commerce, Bureau of the Census, 1990 Census, unpublished data, tb. ED 90-6.

setting five levels of literacy proficiency within each area, and describing the information-processing skills required for successful performance at each level.

The findings of this assessment show that large proportions of the DOL population demonstrate limited literacy skills. Overall, tasks at levels 1 and 2 (the lowest two of the five defined levels) were found to "... require relatively low-level information processing skills and it seems likely that skills evident at these levels would place severe restrictions on full participation in our increasingly complex society, including the workplace."[58] Approximately 40 to 50 percent of the JTPA and 40 percent of the ES/UI populations demonstrated literacy skills at these two lowest levels compared with slightly over 30 percent of the NAEP sample of young adults.[59] Of the total population of roughly 1 million JTPA and 19 million ES/UI participants, approximately 7.5 to 8.5 million are estimated to have significant literacy limitations. Regarding those adults who demonstrated skills at levels 1 and 2, the authors concluded:

> Unless an attempt is made to upgrade the level of literacy skills of these individuals, their success in job training programs may be limited, thus denying them access to the job market. Moreover, for those individuals who do succeed in a job training program without a concomitant increase in their literacy skills, the question remains whether a demonstrated low level of proficiency will enable them to avoid future employment difficulties that may arise from projected increases in skill requirements.[60]

Even more striking are findings regarding these adults' responses to questions about their own

---

[58] Kirsch et al., op. cit., footnote 16.

[59] When data for DOL populations were compared with the performance of the young adult sample, many significant differences were found (p <.05). Both DOL populations had significantly more people at the two lowest proficiency levels for document literacy. For quantitative literacy, both DOL groups were more heavily represented at level 1, while only the JTPA group was significantly larger at level 2. The only significant difference for prose literacy was the larger representation of JTPA clients at level 1.

[60] Kirsch et al., op. cit., footnote 16, pp. 9-10.

Box 2-C—The Future of Workplace Skills[1]

Changing workplace practices and related demand for technical training are elevating the level of basic skills needed for many jobs. Some industries with workforces of many low skill employees are confronting a need to upgrade their workers' basic skills as they adopt new technology and work practices. For example, the textile industry increasingly encourages employees to take advantage of workplace literacy programs offered by State and local agencies. Far from de-skilling work, the industry's investment in automated equipment has created a demand for more maintenance and repair people. While some low skill jobs have been eliminated by automation, many new jobs require greater skill.

Of course, not all jobs are changing in ways that require more skill of workers. Some jobs continue to be de-skilled or eliminated by automation, just as others are upgraded. There is disagreement about the overall direction of skill change, and how fast and pervasive the change is likely to be in the years to come. A recent study concluded that skills upgrading was limited primarily to best-practice firms. The study found no evidence to support the notion that there would be explosive growth in skill requirements in this decade. While occupational upgrading is occurring, the overall rate is slowing down compared with the 1960s and 1970s.[2]

The *Workforce 2000* report, by contrast, sees a major increase in occupational skill and education requirements by the year 2000. It found that more than one-half of the *new* jobs created between 1984 and 2000 would require people with some education past high school, and 30 percent of the new jobs would require a college degree.[3] But it is easy to overstate the implications of these projections. It is not clear how much of the projected increase in education would reflect skills needed by workers to perform their jobs versus other factors. For example, some employers use educational background as a way to screen job applicants. Moreover, the projected growth in education requirements only pertains to the one in six jobs that will be new in the year 2000; the educational background needed for all jobs will not change as dramatically.[4] Also, there are jobs in well-paid occupations (e.g., several construction trades, mechanics, repairers, and many sales and marketing jobs) that do not require college degrees that are projected to grow faster than average, although some of these may entail postsecondary education or apprenticeship.

In the end, there are several points that have come out of the debate about upskilling and de-skilling:

- The economy will continue to create many lower skill jobs. It seems unlikely that skill requirements for these jobs will change greatly over the next decade; some may be de-skilled, a few may be upskilled. These jobs also will not require much formal education beyond high school.
- Some jobs in some industries that have traditionally been defined as low or medium skilled will be upgraded as companies adopt new technologies and work practices. Current workers in these jobs will need retraining to develop new job skills; outside applicants will find the hiring process more demanding than in the past.
- The fastest rate of job growth will be in high skill professional, technical, and managerial jobs—jobs that traditionally have required postsecondary education or college degrees.
- In many industries it has become more difficult for people without postsecondary education to progress from lower level positions within firms to higher level positions.
- Many of the workers who will join the laborforce between now and the year 2000 will not be well matched to the better jobs created by the economy. Roughly one-third of the new entrants will come from minority groups that have traditionally received less and poorer quality education. Immigrants, many of whom need to develop English language skills, also will be a more important source of laborforce growth.

---

[1] This box is adapted from U.S. Congress, Office of Technology Assessment, *Worker Training: Competing in the New International Economy*, OTA-ITE 457 (Washington, DC: U.S. Government Printing Office, September 1990), pp. 155-157.

[2] Lawrence Mishel and Ruy A. Teixeira, *The Myth of the Coming Labor Shortage: Jobs, Skills and Incomes of America's Workforce 2000* (Washington, DC: Economic Policy Institute, 1990), pp. 65-67.

[3] William B. Johnston and Arnold H. Packer, *Workforce 2000: Work and Workers for the 21st Century* (Indianapolis, IN: The Hudson Institute, June 1987), p. 97.

[4] See Russell W. Rumberger and Henry M. Levin, "Schooling for the Modern Workplace," *Investing in People: A Strategy to Address America's Workforce Crises*, background papers, vol. 1, prepared for the Secretary of Labor's Commission on Workforce Quality and Labor Market Efficiency (Washington, DC: U.S. Department of Labor, September 1989), pp. 95-98.

perceptions of the adequacy of their literacy skills.

Some 65 and 60 percent of the JTPA and ES/UI client groups, respectively, perceive that they could get a better job if their reading or writing skills were improved and roughly 80 and 70 percent, respectively, report that their job opportunities would improve with increased skill in mathematics.[61]

Overall this translates into approximately 11.6 million DOL jobseekers who perceive their inadequate reading and writing skills to be a barrier to better employment and 14.9 million who perceive so for their mathematics skills. **Taken together, these findings indicate there is a significant need for adult education programs aimed at improving the literacy skills of jobseekers.**

Another method of anticipating needs for education is to examine what proportion of the current workforce has literacy skill limitations. Many workers are employed at jobs for which their skills seem adequate. But what would happen if their jobs changed substantially? Major national and global economic changes are driving labor market changes. For example, a special 1986 Bureau of the Census survey estimated that, between 1979 and 1984, about 5.1 million workers were displaced by major layoffs or plant closings from jobs they had held for more than 3 years.[62] How much of the current workforce might require improved literacy skills to benefit from retraining, keep a job with changing skill demands, or get a new job?

There is no clear answer to this question. Available data are usually based on specific companies that have surveyed the "basic" skills (reading, writing, arithmetic, and oral communication) of their workers or examined the skill levels of displaced workers. OTA's earlier work bearing on these topics has concluded that most estimates of basic skills levels among employed workers have been based on data from only a few companies.[63] For example, in one manufacturing firm, about 20 percent of the hourly workers were unable to cope with technical training because of deficient basic skills. Most of these workers had high school diplomas and did not think they had a basic skills problem.[64] OTA's 1986 analysis of displaced workers found that 20 to 30 percent of adults entering displaced worker programs in the mid-1980s needed to improve their basic skills.[65]

Seeking Better Information

The task of defining and estimating literacy—knowing the magnitude and character of the problem—is not straightforward. Definitions of what literacy is and what it means to be literate have changed and continue to change. Studies of literacy rates become rapidly outdated. In addition, because literacy is a "hidden" problem, it is easy to underestimate and difficult to study. Literacy skills are more easily assessed for identifiable groups, such as those in job training programs or those graduating from high school, than for the population as a whole. Yet it is difficult to determine optimal policy directions without some sense of the size and scope of the Nation's literacy needs.

Another problem plaguing attempts to survey a nationally representative population is that of

---

61 Ibid., p. 8.

62 U.S. Congress, Office of Technology Assessment, *Technology and Structural Unemployment: Reemploying Displaced Adults,* OTA-ITE-250 (Washington, DC: U.S. Government Printing Office, February 1986), pp. 105-109.

63 U.S. Congress, Office of Technology Assessment, *Worker Training: Competing in the New International Economy,* OTA-ITE 457 (Washington, DC: U.S. Government Printing Office, September 1990).

64 Larry Mikulecky, "Second Chance Basic Skills Education," *Investing in People: A Strategy to Address America's Workforce Crisis,* background papers, vol. 1, U.S. Department of Labor, Commission on Workforce Quality and Labor Market Efficiency (ed.) (Washington, DC: U.S. Government Printing Office, September 1989), p. 236.

65 Office of Technology Assessment, op. cit., footnote 62.

those who remain "uncounted." Many surveys have to exclude those individuals who cannot complete the forms or answer the questions. For example, the NAEP Young Adult Survey found that about 2 percent of the population had "... such limited literacy skills that it was judged that the simulation tasks would unduly frustrate or embarrass them."[66] Thus the NAEP conclusions about the literacy proficiencies of young adults are based on the 98 percent of the sample who were English-speaking and who were able to respond to the printed task. Similarly, during the base-year survey of the National Education Longitudinal Study of 1988, 5.4 percent of the students were excluded from the sample because they were unable to complete the questionnaire "... owing to limitations in their language proficiency or their mental or physical disabilities."[67]

Many surveys also sample only the noninstitutionalized population. This policy, while practical, may also contribute to further underestimation of the size of the total problem. For example, over 1 million adults were in prisons in 1990. Approximately 80 percent of U.S. prisoners are estimated to be high school dropouts.[68] These examples illustrate that those excluded from national samples may have some of the highest literacy needs.

The Adult Education Amendments of 1988 required the Department of Education to submit a report to Congress defining literacy and estimating the extent of adult literacy in the Nation. A nationally representative household survey of adults over 16 is currently being conducted by the Department under contract to the Educational Testing Service; inmates of Federal and State prisons are also included. The definition of literacy used in the NAEP Young Adult Literacy Assessment has been adopted. This approach will not yield a single number of "illiterates," but will "... produce a variety of estimates that show the percentages of adults performing tasks at different levels of difficulty."[69]

Among the goals of the survey are the following:

- Describe the types and levels of literacy demonstrated by the total adult population, adults within specified age ranges, and adults comprising "at-risk" subgroups;
- Characterize and help explain demonstrated literacy skills in terms of demographic and personal background characteristics;
- For the first time, profile the prose, document, and quantitative literacy skills of the American workforce;
- Relate literacy skills to current labor-market indices as well as occupational categories; and
- Compare assessment results from this survey with those from the 1985 literacy assessment of young adults conducted by NAEP and with those from the Workplace Literacy Assessment being conducted for the U.S. Department of Labor.[70]

The information obtained from this survey should help educational planners, policymakers, and researchers understand the literacy needs of various populations, improve and design effective educational programs, and make decisions

---

[66] Kirsch and Jungeblut, op. cit., footnote 42, p. 5. About one-half of those who could not complete the survey were estimated to be Spanish-speaking. The other one-half were administered oral-language tasks; results suggested that many of these adults have a general problem with language not limited solely to the use of printed materials.

[67] Philip Kaufman and Denise Bradby, *Characteristics of At-Risk Students in NELS:88* (Washington, DC: U.S. Department of Education, National Center for Education Statistics, July 1992), p. 5.

[68] Harold L. Hodgkinson, *A Demographic Look at Tomorrow* (Washington, DC: Institute for Educational Leadership, Inc., Center for Demographic Policy, June 1992).

[69] U.S. Department of Education, "Report to Congress on Defining Literacy and the National Adult Literacy Survey," unpublished report, July 1990, p. 4.

[70] Educational Testing Service, "National Adult Literacy Survey," brochure, n.d., p. 8.

about the best ways to use technology to reach larger segments of the population in need.

LITERACY NEEDS: GROWING OR SHRINKING?

As these estimates suggest, a large number of U.S. adults need to improve their literacy skills. As many as 20 to 30 percent of the adult population (35 to 50 million people) have difficulties with common literacy tasks. **However, to understand the Nations's literacy ''problem'' more completely, one must consider not only the pool of people in need today, but also look at factors that may increase or decrease the numbers of people needing literacy services tomorrow.**

New people will continue to enter the pool of those with literacy needs. Each year new immigrants, high school dropouts, displaced workers, and others will be added to the already large number of those who need to be served. Recent Census Bureau projections for the years 1992 to 2050 predict that new immigrants alone will total about 1 million each year.[71] In its strategic plan for adult education, the State of California has estimated that the number of people with literacy deficiencies will grow by about 3 percent per year.[72] Applying this figure to the entire U.S. literacy pool produces an estimate of 1 to 1.5 million new entrants each year. One national estimate puts the number of new entrants to the

adult basic education pool at 2.3 million.[73] Related factors such as rising or falling immigration or dropout rates will affect the numbers of adults who will enter the pool each year, and the effectiveness of adult literacy programs will influence the number of those who leave it.[74]

Any change in national goals for what a high school education should provide could also dramatically affect the number of adults who will require literacy services to reach those goals. If the average amount of schooling seen as necessary continues to rise, as it has throughout this century, and if the definition of skills essential to literacy continues to broaden, the number of adults needing literacy services could grow much larger. Demographic data also suggest that literacy needs are higher in some regions of the United States. Furthermore, projections of population growth indicate that the South and West will experience most of the growth in the Nation in the next decade.[75] These are the same regions that tend to have higher dropout rates and higher numbers of non-English speaking homes (see figures 2-3 and 2-7). Strategies for adult literacy education need to consider these regional differences.

One strategy for reducing the pool of those with literacy needs is to try to lessen the number of new entrants. Such a preventive approach would seek to assure that today's children are successful in school and obtain the literacy skills they need. Although the absolute number of children in the

---

[71] U.S. Department of Commerce, Bureau of the Census, *Population Projections of the United States, by Age, Sex, Race and Hispanic Origin: 1992 to 2050* (Washington, DC: U.S. Government Printing Office, October 1992). This estimate represents a middle range projection and reflects 1990 immigration law changes, as well as current knowledge of emigration, undocumented migration, and movement to and from Puerto Rico. Higher assumptions about immigration would put the expected yearly totals at about 1.3 million, lower range assumptions at about 600,000 per year.

[72] California State Department of Education, Adult Education Unit, *Adult Education for the 21st Century: Strategic Plan to Meet California's Long-Term Adult Education Needs*, 1989 ed. (Sacramento, CA: May 15, 1989).

[73] Paul Delker, ''Defining Adult Functional Literacy,'' *Functional Literacy and the Workplace: Proceedings of a National Invitational Conference, Washington, DC, May 6, 1983* (Washington, DC: American Council of Life Insurance, Education Services, 1983). This total is based on estimates of 1 million dropouts and nonfunctional graduates, 400,000 legal immigrants, 100,000 refugees, and 800,000 illegal entrants. Other estimates of illegal entrants are more conservative than this. The Bureau of the Census' best estimate adds about 200,000 net undocumented immigration to the United States each year. See Bureau of the Census, op. cit., footnote 71.

[74] See ch. 4 for a discussion of the adult education providers and programs.

[75] Hodgkinson, op. cit., footnote 68. See also U.S. Department of Commerce, Bureau of the Census, *Projections of the Population of States by Age, Sex and Race: 1989 to 2010* (Washington, DC: U.S. Government Printing Office, January 1990).

population has remained relatively constant over the last two decades, their proportion of the population has declined dramatically and should continue to do so. In 1960, children under age 18 accounted for 36 percent of all Americans; by 2010, they are expected to comprise only 23 percent. Thus the pool of new entrants to the future workforce will grow smaller. Minorities, particularly Hispanic and Asian children, are expected to make up an increasing proportion of the population under age 18.[76]

The number of children living in homes where a language other than English is spoken is also increasing dramatically; while the 1980 census reported that 9 percent of 5- to 17-year-olds fell in this category, the 1990 figures have risen to 14 percent—an increase of almost 1.8 million school-age children over the previous decade.

These and related demographic trends suggest the following educational consequences:[77]

- The number of children entering school from poverty-level households is expected to increase.
- The number and proportion of minority school children will increase.
- More children will enter school from single-parent households.
- A larger number of children who were premature babies will enter school; these children are more likely to experience learning difficulties in school.
- There will be more school children who were born to teenage mothers and mothers who have not completed high school.
- More children will enter school from homes where a language other than English is spoken.

Education has important intergenerational effects. When parents are assisted by literacy programs, they not only improve their own skills but also increase the chances of school success for their children.

Taken together, these projections suggest that the number of children entering school with one or more factors that put them at risk for educational difficulties will rise. The chances of any one child experiencing multiple risk factors is likely to increase as well.[78] Thus, the burden on an already resource-depleted school system is growing, not declining. Programs focused on optimizing early development, promoting school-readiness, and preventing school failure and school dropouts are extremely important interventions.[79]

Research findings have suggested another fruitful policy avenue for improving the future educational attainment of today's children. One of the most consistent findings of the research on positive educational outcomes for children is the influence of mothers' education level. This suggests the potential effectiveness of educational

---

[76] National Commission on Children, *Beyond Rhetoric: A New American Agenda for Children and Families* (Washington, DC: U.S. Government Printing Office, 1991).

[77] Hodgkinson, op. cit., footnote 33; and Aaron M. Pallas et al., "The Changing Nature of the Disadvantaged Population: Current Dimensions and Future Trends," *Educational Researcher*, vol. 18, No. 5, June-July 1989, pp. 16-22.

[78] For a discussion of educational risk factors, see Pallas et al., op. cit., footnote 77, pp. 16-22.

[79] See, for example, R.E. Slavin et al. (eds.), *Effective Programs for Students At Risk* (Boston, MA: Allyn and Bacon, 1989).

interventions focused on mothers (or primary caretakers). One study, for example, found that:

> ... having a mother who completed high school was a significantly more important determinant of the school enrollment of sixteen- to seventeen-year old youth than whether the mother was married or whether she had an additional $10,000 in family income per year, although both of these factors were also important.... Similarly ... [another group of researchers] used data from the National Longitudinal Survey of Youth Market Experience to predict young people's test scores on the basis of their mothers' and fathers' education and other variables. They found that an extra grade of attainment for the mother—when father's education, race and region of the nation were constant—was associated with an extra half-grade equivalent of achievement for her children. Because of this intergenerational effect of the parent's education on the child's, it is unlikely that we will be able to make a major difference for the child unless we place equal priority on education and academic remediation for the parent.[80]

Educational efforts aimed at adults with low literacy skills today are likely to have two important outcomes: improving the skills and the life outcomes for adults, and at the same time increasing the likelihood of positive educational outcomes for those adults' children or future children.[81] As yet very little research evidence is available to document the direct effects on children of raising a parent's education level. Research in this area is needed in order to design programs that can optimize the direct benefits for children as well as parents. **Existing evidence is compelling enough, however, to recommend that parents (especially mothers) of small children receive high priority in literacy policy and planning.**

A comprehensive literacy policy must consider the changing needs of people throughout the life cycle. The challenge of adult literacy is to develop a long-range policy that anticipates the literacy needs of tomorrow while addressing what is already a large and demanding problem today.

---

[80] Berlin and Sum, op. cit., footnote 34, p. 36.

[81] See, for example, Catherine E. Snow et al., *Unfulfilled Expectations: Home and School Influences on Literacy* (Cambridge, MA: Harvard University Press, 1991); and Thomas G. Sticht et al., *The Intergenerational Transfer of Cognitive Skills*, vols. 1 and 2 (Norwood, NJ: Ablex Publishing Corp., 1992).

Adults
as
Learners 3

Learning and going to school have most often been associated with childhood and youth; most of our ideas about learning and teaching are based on educating children. Adults, however, do not stop learning when they end their formal schooling. Whether they finish high school, college, or neither of these, adults find themselves faced with changing roles and life choices and, as a result, need new skills and knowledge throughout their lives. More and more, adults are seeking out educational opportunities—to relearn skills they have forgotten, to acquire skills they never got, or to learn new skills that were not even taught when they attended school. But adults are not children; their diverse needs, goals, and life situations would challenge even the best system of adult education. Thus, a discussion of how best to address the literacy needs of the Nation must include a careful look at the adults themselves—how they use literacy in their lives, how they learn, and what motivates them to improve their skills or gain new knowledge.

FINDINGS

- Adults with low literacy skills do not fit common patterns and stereotypes. They are at all ages and stages of the life cycle and have many different backgrounds, many different lifestyles, many different experiences and skills.
- A person's literacy skills vary in the different contexts of their lives, such as home, work, or school. For example, people are often more skilled at reading job-related materials than they are at reading unfamiliar materials. Each person can be thought of as having a profile of literacy skills adapted to that person's life situation and circumstances.

- Traditional school-based approaches used to provide education for children do not work well for adults because:
  - adults have many roles and responsibilities and thus many competing demands for their time;
  - adults bring with them a wealth of concepts, knowledge, and experience on which to build new learning;
  - adults have little time for learning, so they must often seek to learn things that are meaningful and can be applied immediately in their daily lives;
  - for the most part, adults seek education because they choose to do so—participation is voluntary, dropping out and re-entering are common.
- The people most likely to benefit from adult education are least likely to participate in it. Situational barriers such as work schedules, childcare responsibilities, transportation, and cost often prevent participation in formal education. In addition to these situational barriers, adults also have attitudes and feelings about school and learning that affect their decisions about further education.
- Taken together, these findings suggest that adults are more likely to invest the time and energy in opportunities to learn if those opportunities:
  - are provided in supportive environments that reduce the stigma attached to low literacy;
  - utilize materials and methods that respect the strengths, experiences and goals of learners;
  - offer content and materials that build on daily life experiences; and
  - can be delivered in ways that allow flexibility and choice—so that individuals can learn at their own pace, on their own time schedules, and under conditions that work best for different individuals.
- Technologies offer considerable promise for meeting the needs of adult learners, because they can deliver learning in places other than classrooms, facilitate the efficient use of precious learning time, sustain the motivation of adult learners, and reach many different types of learners in the ways they learn best.

LITERACY IN EVERYDAY LIFE: ADULTS WITH LOW LITERACY SKILLS[1]

The world of adults with low literacy skills in the United States is unknown territory for most of us. The research base is slim indeed. Little is known about what most adults read, how they use literacy in the various domains of their everyday lives, and how literacy interacts with technology. Still less is known about how adults with low literacy skills lead their lives in a print-based society, especially the great majority of those adults who are not enrolled in literacy programs.

A large number of adults with limited literacy skills have found a variety of ways to survive in a print-based culture, as shown by a few ethnographic studies. They have talents and skills in social relationships and in practical life skills. Many adults with low literacy skills are successful in the workplace; lack of such skills is often masked by other competencies so that colleagues and peers are unaware of these workers' "hidden problem." In contrast, some new immigrants may suddenly find themselves perceived as nonliterate because they lack written and communication skills necessary to function effectively in English, despite being highly literate in their native language. Whatever their current life circumstances, however, most adults with low literacy skills are aware that society places a great deal of value and status on literacy.

Although research on the literacy demands of everyday life is limited, several studies provide insights into literacy uses in diverse communities.

---

[1] Except where noted, this section draws on Center for Literacy Studies, University of Tennessee, Knoxville, "Life at the Margins: Profiles of Adults With Low Literacy Skills," OTA contractor report, March 1992. The names of individuals have been changed in order to guarantee anonymity.

Some studies have used ethnographic methods that provide rich, descriptive data about the contexts and activities of participants. Some of these studies address the literacy practices of adults with low literacy skills, and others address everyday literacy of non-native English speaking families. Other researchers have investigated how workers deal with the literacy demands of their jobs. These studies offer some important insights and conclusions; most are based on small samples of people who have been studied intensively and thus their generalizability is limited.

Profiles of Diversity

Adults with low literacy skills do not fit common patterns and stereotypes. They have many different backgrounds, lifestyles, experiences, and skills. Consider the following adults:

Fred Kruck is a 50-year-old steelworker who has recently been laid off because the plant where he had worked for 19 years closed. Last year he enrolled in truck-driving school as part of a Federal program to train laid-off workers in new skills; he dropped out of the program, however, because of a well-kept secret—he can barely read and write. He was "... the top laborer in the blast furnace, the meanest, most dangerous furnace in the mill, where he hollered orders to a dozen subordinates, deploying equipment the size of buildings. It never mattered, never even was mentioned, that he had graduated from high school without really learning to read and write. Now, with his furnace gone, it does."[2]

Lisa Bogan, aged 37, was born in rural Mississippi and lived there until she came to Knoxville, Tennessee, with her first husband in 1973. Separated now from her second husband, Lisa is struggling to overcome the effects of an abusive second marriage and provide for her two children with a job as a sales clerk in a department store. Although she has a high school diploma, she says she stopped learning in 6th grade and her

Although literacy is an important part of everyday life, individuals vary greatly in their purposes for reading and writing.

reading level is at 5th- or 6th-grade level. Both literacy and technology present some difficulties for her, and she has tried adult basic education classes to upgrade her skills. She is very active outside the home and family; she votes, attends PTA meetings, talks with teachers, and is active in her church.

Alicia Lopez, age 47, migrated alone and undocumented from her native Mexico to the San Francisco Bay Area in 1981. In 1986, she became a legal resident of the United States through the Immigration Reform and Control Act. Six years ago she brought her daughter and infant granddaughter to the United States. Alicia now lives in a home with her sister's family and raises her 6-year-old grandchild as if she were her own daughter. Although she dropped out of school in Mexico at age 13, she can read and write Spanish quite well; her written and oral language skills in English are, however, quite limited. Until 5 months ago, Alicia worked as a cook in several food preparation factories. Since nearly all of the employees were Spanish-speaking, she was able to function with very limited English. Alicia recently enrolled in an employment training

---

[2] Dale Russakoff, "Lives Once Solid as Steel Shatter in Changed World," *The Washington Post*, Apr. 13, 1992, p. A1.

program where she is learning facility maintenance skills and studying English. Her goal is to find stable employment that will enable her to adopt her two youngest grandchildren, currently in the foster care system because of their mother's drug addiction. While she is determined and capable of mastering new skills and systems, her limited English presents significant barriers to her ability to advance, particularly in the employment arena.

As these and other profiles in the literature suggest, there is no one type of person nor one universal characteristic that defines people with literacy needs. Adults with low literacy skills

... appear to embody a range of attributes, rather than presenting a homogeneous picture. Some are ambitious, others content; some approach life positively, while others are fatalistic and depressed. The same range of characteristics may be found in the population at large or among literate, educated adults.[3]

Similarly,

... individuals can be expected to vary greatly in their purposes for reading and writing, in the texts they choose to read and write, as well as in the contexts for performance of reading and writing abilities. A person's literacy profile might be conceptualized as a contemporary quilt in progress whose configuration is closely linked to specific settings characterized by specific opportunities and constraints.[4]

Those in need of literacy education, or "second chance" basic skills education,[5] can be almost anyone:

- Women who need to re-enter the workforce in the wake of divorce or teenage mothers who dropped out of school when they became pregnant.
- Refugees with college degrees who speak no English or children of Hispanic migrant workers whose itinerant way of life limited the time they spent in school.
- A recent high school graduate who is having difficulty entering the workforce or a 50-year-old auto worker whose plant recently closed.
- A mother at home who wants to be able to help her children with their homework or a working mother who needs to improve her mathematics skills in order to get a promotion.
- A truck driver who needs to pass a newly mandated written examination in order to keep his job or an inmate at a prison who is required to meet a minimum standard of literacy.

"The target population encompasses Americans who are employed, underemployed, and unemployed."[6]

Adult learners vary on a multitude of dimensions. **If the children in our public schools present a picture of remarkable diversity, adults do so even more.** Adults learners vary in age from 18 to over 80—with a corresponding wide variety of life experience. When children are in school, those of the same age will have approximately the same skill levels. Not so with adults, however; all levels of skill—from little or none to the highest levels—can be found at any age. Adults also vary in the amount of experience they have had in the workforce and the literacy demands of the jobs they have held. Learners come from all cultural and ethnic groups, urban and rural. Some live in poverty, some are middle-class. Adults who need to learn English can have extremely diverse experiences with

---

[3] Hanna Arlene Fingeret, "Social Network: A New Perspective on Independence and Illiterate Adults," *Adult Education Quarterly*, vol. 33, No. 3, spring 1983, p. 142.

[4] Susan L. Lytle, "Living Literacy: Rethinking Development in Adulthood," unpublished manuscript, n.d., p. 8.

[5] Larry Mikulecky, "Second Chance Basic Skills Education," *Investing in People: A Strategy to Address America's Workforce Crisis*, background papers, vol. 1, U.S. Department of Labor, Commission on Workforce Quality and Labor Market Efficiency (ed.) (Washington, DC: U.S. Government Printing Office, February 1986).

[6] Ibid., p. 218.

ON PARLE FRANÇAIS
SE HABLA ESPAÑOL
SI PARLA ITALIANO
MAN SPRICHT DEUTSCH
MÓWIMY PO POLSKU
WE ALSO SPEAK ENGLISH

New immigrants may often find themselves perceived as nonliterate because they do not speak English.

reading and writing in their native language—from no experience with the written word to highly proficient (see box 3-A). In addition, adults vary in their cognitive abilities; some significant portion of adults with low literacy skills probably have undiagnosed learning disabilities (see box 3-B).

Competence and Strength

Research reveals that adults with low literacy skills are strong and resourceful, skilled and knowledgeable. It is often assumed that such adults live impoverished lives, socially and culturally as well as in terms of literacy. In contrast, the research suggests that to lack reading skills is not necessarily to lack other skills: indeed the adults who have been studied had many other skills, full social lives, and much cultural knowledge. They were respected and ''functional'' members of their communities.[7]

A common theme among the profiles of adults with low literacy skills is that of self-reliance and independence. Many are determined to be independent, dislike having to rely on others, even family members, and do not want to live on welfare. They want and expect to have control of their own lives (see box 3-C).

Many also are faced with pressing issues of survival. Their lives have a fragile stability that can be easily overturned by life events such as poor health, accidents, or job changes. The following case provides a telling example.

Les Willard is a 36-year-old man who lives with his wife and two children in one of the poorest neighborhoods in Knoxville, Tennessee. Les puts in long hours of work, including extra jobs on weekends and fixing things around his own house. He needs to work these hours to support his extended family, which includes a disabled brother and an elderly father. If he could get his electrician's license, he would earn higher wages and perhaps need fewer working hours, but he cannot get the license because his reading skills are too low to pass the required test. He cannot improve his literacy because he needs to work such long hours. He has been physically ill off and on over the past several years with an undetermined stomach ailment. He does not seek medical help because he has no medical coverage. When he fell off a roof and broke some ribs, he bound them up himself, and went on with his life. He sees himself as someone who ''holds up,'' who takes pride in managing his family responsibilities and taking care of his ''kin.'' He and his wife have managed to build a solid marriage as well as a supportive environment for their children and extended family. They want their children to be better educated and have more opportunities than they had and have taken

---

[7] Hanna Arlene Fingeret, Syracuse University, ''The Illiterate Underclass: Demythologizing an American Stigma,'' unpublished Ph.D. dissertation, 1982; ''Social Network: A New Perspective on Independence and Illiterate Adults,'' *Adult Education Quarterly*, vol. 33, No. 3, spring, 1983, pp. 133-146; Linda Zeigahn, ''The Formation of Literacy Perspective,'' *Adult Learning in the Community*, Robert A. Fellenz and Gary J. Conti (eds.) (Bozeman, MT: Center for Adult Learning Research, Montana State University, 1990); and Linda Zeighan, ''Conceptual Framework for a Study of Community and Competence,'' paper presented at the 29th Annual Adult Education Research Conference, Calgary, Alberta, Canada, May 6-8, 1988.

Box 3-A—Literacy Needs Among Those Who Speak
English as a Second Language

Imagine being the teacher in a class that includes:[1]

Paulo, age 49, who came to the United States from Mexico 12 years ago. He went to school through the 6th grade and can read and write in Spanish at an elementary level. In the United States, he lives and works in a community that speaks Spanish almost exclusively, and consequently he still speaks English at a beginning level.

Chuob, age 30, who grew up in a small village in Cambodia and has had no formal education. She speaks only her native tribal language, which until recently had no alphabet or written form. She cannot read or write in any language.

Tien, age 24, who recently immigrated from Vietnam. He can read and write well in Vietnamese, having completed several years of post-high school technical training there. Although he speaks English at a beginning level, he does not yet know the English alphabet and thus cannot read or write any English.

Marta, age 35, who was an elementary school teacher in a city in El Salvador. There she read and wrote fluently in Spanish and had an intermediate proficiency with spoken English. Since her arrival in the United States 1 year ago, she has lived and worked in a largely English-speaking community and her spoken English proficiency has improved to an advanced level. Her ability to read and write English is still quite limited.

Carmelita, age 19, who was born in the United States to parents who had immigrated from Mexico. She grew up in an urban neighborhood that was exclusively Spanish speaking. Although she learned to speak English in school, she had difficulty keeping up in her academic work. She dropped out of school in the 8th grade because she could not understand her classwork well enough. Although her spoken English proficiency is quite high, she does not read or write well in either English or Spanish.

The needs of these five learners exemplify the widely divergent population often known as limited-English-proficient (LEP). LEP learners can vary by age, by socioeconomic status, and by legal resident status. Some other important characteristics that vary across LEP populations include:[2]

Language and educational background. Levels of education can vary from those who are completely unschooled and lack rudimentary learning tools to those who are highly educated. While some LEP persons read and write extremely well in their native languages, others may not read or write at all, or may speak a nonwritten language. Some speak and write a language with a Latin alphabet or other linguistic features similar to those of English, and therefore face an easier transition to English proficiency. Others speak and write languages with non-Latin characters, or with a phonology that differs from the English phonic sounds, and thus may take longer to make the transition to English proficiency.

Occupational skills. Some LEP persons have professional or technical skills, but need proficiency in spoken and written English before they can use their skills in the U.S. job market. Many have skills that will not transfer into the U.S. job market, or have no job skills. Those with education or occupational skills are often underemployed if their proficiency in English is low.

Cultural backgrounds. LEP populations have a diverse array of cultural backgrounds. Some were born in the United States or have lived here for a long time, although many LEP people live in urban barrios or migrant camps and consequently are still immersed in a nonmainstream subculture. Others arrived in the United States recently, either by choice as migrants or immigrants, or by necessity, as refugees. Of the recent immigrants, some are from urban industrialized environments while others come from traditional rural settings totally unlike modernized U.S. society. The cultural diversity among LEP persons presents a broad array of language groups, as well as a myriad of different values about time, world view, interpersonal relations, learning style, and attitudes toward education, family, age, and occupations.

---

[1] These examples are adapted from Kathleen Troy, ''ESL Literacy Program Planning: Looking for Common Ground,'' *TESL Talk*, vol. 20, No. 1, 1990, pp. 318-329; and California Advisory Council on Vocational Education, *Horizon: An Overview of Vocational Education and Employment Training Services for Limited-English Proficient Persons in California* (Sacramento, CA: n.d.).

[2] These descriptions adapted from California Advisory Council on Vocational Education, op. cit., footnote 1, p. 30.

Box 3-B—Learning Disabilities Among Adults

A typical volunteer literacy tutor might spend 1 or 2 hours a week helping an adult learn to read. But how many tutors, like this one, feel baffled by the lack of progress their student is making?

I've been working with Marty for 8 months now. He tries really hard, remembers to bring his books, and is faithful about meeting me at the library for our weekly sessions. I keep wondering though, it's like I'm not sure if he's making that much progress. . . . He rubs his eyes a bit and sometimes I have to repeat directions. I thought Marty would be doing much better by now, maybe even reading the newspaper. What can I do to really see where Marty is and where he can go?[1]

Chances are Marty is one of many adults who have a learning disability that interferes with learning to read. The term "learning disabilities" did not become popularly used until the 1970s when Public Law 94-142 (The Education for All Handicapped Children Act of 1975) established guidelines for serving learning disabled children in the public schools. But little is known about what happens to learning disabled children when they become adults and how learning disabilities affect people throughout their lives. Many adults in the general population went through the school system before learning disabilities were diagnosed and services provided. There is growing agreement that literacy providers need to understand learning disabilities, not only in order to plan programs for these students, but also to be able to make appropriate referrals to other agencies and resources.

Although there is no universally recognized definition of learning disability, the most commonly accepted definitions all refer to a substantial discrepancy between an individual's intellectual ability and his or her academic achievement for which there is no other basis such as sensory or motor disabilities. Many definitions also refer to difficulties with basic learning processes such as attention, memory, and integration. Learning disabilities can affect reading, writing, language, and/or mathematical abilities.[2]

Most research on learning disabilities has focused on children, and estimates of the size of the population vary because of problems associated with defining and diagnosing this problem. In a 1987 report summarizing available data, the Interagency Committee on Learning Disabilities concluded that 5 to 10 percent is a reasonable estimate of the portion of the general population affected by learning disabilities.[3] Learning disabilities are not uniformly distributed across the population; evidence suggests that they are found more often in males and in socioeconomically disadvantaged populations.

The rate of learning disabilities could be quite high among certain segments of the population. Some experts have suggested that the rate of learning disabilities may be especially high in adults whose reading skills are below the 8th-grade level. These estimates suggest that anywhere from 30 to 80 percent of these "poor readers" who enter literacy programs may have learning disabilities.[4]

Large numbers of adults who attend literacy programs, therefore, may have unrecognized learning disabilities. Some point out that, for adults, learning disabilities can make adjustment to other aspects of life—such as work and social relationships—especially difficult. However there is also ". . . considerable knowledge accumulating about (1) how to assess for learning disabilities and (2) how to create positive learning environments for the learning disabled . . . it is generally felt that learning disabled persons can be taught basic skills and can learn to overcome (but not eliminate) their disabilities."[5]

---

[1] Donald Keefe and Valerie Meyer, "Profiles of and Instructional Strategies for Adult Disabled Readers," *Journal of Reading*, vol. 31, No. 7, April 1988, p. 614.

[2] Jovita Martin Ross, "Learning Disabled Adults: Who Are They and What Do We Do With Them?" *Lifelong Learning: An Omnibus of Practice and Research*, vol. 11, No. 3, 1987, pp. 4-7, 11.

[3] Interagency Committee on Learning Disabilities, *Learning Disabilities: A Report to the U.S. Congress* (Washington, DC: Department of Health and Human Services, August 1987), cited in U.S. Department of Labor, Office of Strategic Planning and Policy Development, *The Learning Disabled in Employment and Training Programs*, Research and Evaluation Report Series 91-E (Washington, DC: U.S. Department of Labor, 1991).

[4] U.S. Department of Labor, op. cit., footnote 3, p. 28.

[5] Ibid., p. 54.

Box 3-C—Profile of Yuvette Evans[1]

Yuvette Evans is a 26-year-old single parent of 9-year-old Jessica and 5-year-old Jarvis. They live in a public housing project in an inner-city neighborhood of Knoxville, Tennessee. Her apartment is small and sparsely furnished. She does not like the community, chooses not to have contact with her neighbors, and keeps her family in the house most of the time. Except for one or two friends and her boyfriend, Yuvette has little social interaction or support.

Yuvette works 20 to 30 hours a week as a waitress at a chain restaurant from 5 p.m. until 9 p.m. or sometimes until midnight. Her children go to a babysitter while she works. She is proud of being able to work and earn money for the things the family needs, to "... pay out of (my) pocket instead of somebody else doing it." Her AFDC payment is small, and Yuvette works hard to try to lift her family out of poverty.

Yuvette spends much effort meeting the needs of her children. Jessica is in elementary school and Jarvis attends a Head Start program in the afternoons. Both children have experienced speech problems; Yuvette has sought help for these problems and is supportive of the children's schools. Although she feels that she was not as involved as she should have been in the early years of her daughter's schooling, she is working hard to stay involved now. Yuvette has dreams for her children; more than anything, she wants them to be free from the need for government assistance. Yuvette pins that hope on education, believing that graduation will mean a good job.

Although she liked elementary school and got good grades, Yuvette reports that her later school years were characterized by social isolation and disconnectedness. She completed most of the 12th grade and got grades that were "ok" despite having had Jessica at age 16. However, because she moved to Atlanta with her mother during the 12th grade, Yuvette never completed requirements for a diploma.

In the past 8 years, Yuvette has enrolled in three separate adult education programs, but has not gotten her general equivalency diploma (GED). Multiple moves interfered with completion of the first program; in the second, a Job Training Partnership Act program, she reports not feeling integrated or engaged with the teacher or other students. The third program was an Even Start class, provided to parents of young children. Yuvette enjoyed this class which emphasized group work and cooperation. However because it met every morning from 9:30 to 12:30, Yuvette found she had little or no time with her children. "I tried to do both of them (work and go to school). If it was just me I'd do both. But I've got Jarvis and Jessica. If I do both, I'm not gonna be having time for them." She quit the program, but hopes to find a way to go back and remains confident that she can succeed in a GED program: "I like math and I am good at spelling. I can read, I made it to the 12th grade!"

Although Yuvette says she does not particularly like to read, she does read when necessary; she readily uses mathematics in shopping activities and on the job. Literacy skills do not appear to be a barrier to the things she attempts in her life. Yuvette does not have a car or a driver's license. She usually depends on herself to figure things out in her own life and sees herself as having little power to affect what happens in the "outside" world. Although she occasionally watches the news on television, Yuvette does not read books, newspapers, or magazines. She has never voted and does not seem interested in current events.

Yuvette's most immediate dream has been to purchase a few things for her bare apartment. She has acquired a new couch, chair, and television through a rent-to-buy program and hopes to be able to follow through until she owns them. Her heartfelt desire to have this couch and chair has, however, saddled her with a debt and with the decreased ability to stop working long enough to participate in a program that will help her prepare for her GED. Raising her children in a positive and loving way, completing her GED, and finding skilled employment that pays above survival wages are important goals for Yuvette. Despite her social isolation and poverty, she has managed to hang on to these dreams and is working to make a better life for her children.

---

[1] Adapted from Center for Literacy Studies, University of Tennessee, Knoxville, "Life at the Margins: Profiles of Adults With Low Literacy Skills," OTA contractor report, March 1992. The names of individuals have been changed.

deliberate and time-consuming steps to try to secure good schooling for them.

Strategies for Literacy

Despite their low literacy skills, many adults have developed a rich and diverse array of strategies for adapting to the literacy demands of a print-based society and for learning new skills in their daily lives. The Office of Technology Assessment's (OTA) profiles of adults suggest a number of strategies that adults with low literacy skills use to cope with daily life. Some people rely on others to help, and develop social networks based on reciprocal exchange. Many people have worked out a variety of ways of managing in which they do not depend on others; such strategies of self-reliance include learning the routine formats of bills and forms, making educated guesses, and using written text for specific purposes such as writing down words to look up in a dictionary (see box 3-D). Avoidance of situations where literacy or language demands exceed skills is an important strategy for many. Still others, particularly non-native speakers of English, use technology for information and communication.

LEARNING IN ADULTHOOD

Much of what is known about learning comes from studying children in schools. In contrast, little is known about the process of learning that continues once a person leaves school. Adults continue to learn throughout their lives. Transitions in life stages and changing life conditions often provide the impetus for much of this learning.

Some researchers have examined how adults learn in the various arenas of their lives, particu-larly the workplace. One of the most consistent findings of the research on literacy acquisition among adults is that a person's literacy skills vary as a function of different settings (e.g., work, school, and home) in which he or she develops and uses those skills. Evidence indicates that work-related literacy demands and uses are very different from school-related ones, and that experienced workers are much more skilled at on-the-job problem solving using reading, writing, and mathematical skills than at pencil-and-paper tests measuring the ''same'' operations. One line of research has looked at on-the-job reading and writing demands.[8] This research has several consistent findings.

- Workers in most types of employment do considerable job-related reading. The average times reported in different studies range from 30 minutes to 2 hours per day. When workers' literacy activities were compared with those of high school and technical school students, workers' average daily reading time of 113 minutes was found to be higher than that of students in school.[9]
- Job-related reading is primarily ''reading-to-do'' (as opposed to ''reading-to-learn,'' which is the primary purpose of school-based reading).

Workers read and write to accomplish tasks, solve problems, and make evaluations about the useful-ness of material. . . . Students in secondary schools read primarily to obtain information needed to answer teacher questions.[10]

Work-related literacy demands are strongly repetitive and contextualized, and related to knowledge that the worker already has. Workers have repeated opportunities for reading and

---

[8] See, for example, Thomas G. Sticht et al., Human Resources Research Organization, ''Project REALISTIC: Determination of Adult Functional Literacy Skill Levels,'' *Reading Research Quarterly*, vol. 7, No. 3, 1972, pp. 424-465.

[9] Larry Mikulecky, ''Job Literacy: The Relationship Between School Preparation and Workplace Actuality,'' *Reading Research Quarterly*, vol. 17, No. 3, 1982, p. 418.

[10] Larry Mikulecky and Jeanne Ehlinger, Institute for the Study of Adult Literacy, Pennsylvania State University, ''Training for Job Literacy Demands: What Research Applies to Practice,'' unpublished report, 1987, p. 4.

Box 3-D—Profile of Sokhhoeun[1]

Sokhhoeun is a 38-year-old Cambodian refugee who arrived in the United States in 1981 after a grueling 6-year odyssey with his family through Cambodia and northern Thailand. He now lives in Oakland, California, with his wife and three children, ages 13, 11, and 9. Members of his extended family, as well as many other Cambodians, live in the area. Most Cambodian immigrants in the area are members of a formally structured community mutual support system; Sokhhoeun is the designated leader for his neighborhood, 1 of 15 in Oakland.

Sokhhoeun grew up in rural areas of Cambodia and spent most of his childhood helping his father who was a rice farmer. He had no formal schooling until the age of 13, when he was sent for 2 years to a Buddhist temple to study as a monk. Formal instruction in Buddhist doctrine was conducted by oral transmission, followed by exposure to the corresponding written texts. After a few months time, Sokhhoeun learned to read and write the Cambodian (Khmer) language.

At age 15, his education ended when Sokhhoeun moved with his family to a region of Cambodia known for its diamonds; they worked as diamond prospectors in isolated forested areas for 8 years. Sokhhoeun was married at 18; his first child was born several years later. In 1975, when the Khmer Rouge took control, Sokhhoeun and his family were forced to become laborers in a sugar cane plantation. After 1979, the family began traveling in search of food and eventually reached a refugee camp in Thailand where they applied for resettlement in the United States. Once Sokhhoeun found out they had been selected, he began to study English—paying for lessons from another refugee in the camps for 3 months until they left for San Francisco.

Sokhhoeun enrolled in a refugee English as a second language (ESL) literacy program when he first came to the United States, and stayed in it for 6 months. This experience added considerably to the very limited English speaking and listening skills he had acquired in the refugee camp. A year later, he enrolled in a bilingual (Chinese-English) vocational training program in electronic assembly. Because he does not speak Chinese, the program was not very helpful; before the end of the program he found a job as a stock handler in a warehouse. After being laid off and falling ill, he volunteered with a refugee resettlement agency, helping newly arrived refugees connect to social service agencies. He was soon invited to work at the agency as a bilingual teacher's aide in the ESL literacy program. He has held this job for 6 years.

When he first arrived in this country, Sokhhoeun relied heavily on a Cambodian friend to apply for identification papers, a Social Security number, refugee cash assistance, and medical care. In order to become self-sufficient as quickly as possible, Sokhhoeun developed an important strategy: he decided to make copies of all forms that were filled out for him before turning in the forms. ''I have to watch them (his friends). How can they do . . . the word they use . . . or whatever. Then, after he help me to fill out the form . . . I take it home . . . I just make a copy first. That's my idea. . . . Then later on . . . if I want to do that again, I know, oh, maybe I can make copy from the old one. . . . Because I didn't know the English, I cannot read the English. But if I have a copy, I can follow, I can copy do the same thing.''

Sokhhoeun does not read much for pleasure; most of the written materials he encounters are in English. His English reading at home is limited to a Cambodian-English medical dictionary that he studies to expand his medical vocabulary. Although he hopes one day to become a medical translator in a hospital, he does not seem to have clear ideas about the educational steps necessary to achieve these goals. He watches the television news regularly but seldom reads newspapers. Within 6 months of his arrival, he had learned to drive a car and purchased one. He has a bank account and has recently mastered the use of the bank teller machine.

When learning new skills, such as using the bank machine or driving a car, he reports a consistent pattern that helps him master new skills. First he asks someone to describe the procedure and demonstrate it. Then he performs the task, under their supervision, usually several times. He then writes down the steps. Next he performs the task repeatedly on his own, until he is comfortable with it. The next time he must perform the task, he uses the written text to refresh his memory. Thus, for Sokhhoeun, text serves a very practical purpose: to make information permanent and to retain it for future retrieval.

---

[1] Adapted from Center for Literacy Studies, University of Tennessee, Knoxville, ''Life at the Margins: Profiles of Adults With Low Literacy Skills,'' OTA contractor report, March 1992. The names of individuals have been changed.

re-reading the material, and their job experience provides them with knowledge that helps them understand the written material.

- When researchers administered general reading tests and job-related reading tests, they consistently found that workers score two or more grade levels higher on the job-related reading.[11] Workers' skills at reading on the job are affected by factors other than general reading skill: e.g., knowledge of concepts, familiarity with vocabulary, and a need to know key terms.

- General literacy skill is only one small factor in job performance. Several studies have found that literacy skills did not account for differences among those who were more or less skilled at their jobs.[12] Results suggest that thinking and organizational skills are more important than reading and writing skills per se:

... superior job performers differ from their less able counterparts in their ability to think through what is needed on the job and then to apply reading and writing abilities to complete these job tasks efficiently. Superior workers know when to skim, when to look for new information, how to decide which information to jot down, how to compose meaningful messages to co-workers, when to check a reference, and how to find ways to organize notes and information to better do their jobs.[13]

A lot has been learned about cognitive and literacy activities on the job from detailed and systematic observations of workers in a milk processing plant.[14] How do workers develop strategies for solving familiar job problems? In one example, researchers recorded observations of product assemblers filling mixed case and unit orders. Assemblers often did not literally follow the written order. Instead they found efficient mathematical solutions to solve the problem even though these solutions required that the workers switch from one base number system to another. Errors were virtually nonexistent for experienced assemblers. In contrast, novices and students made more mistakes and often followed literal solutions that involved many more transfers.

The researchers found that experienced workers had creative and sophisticated solutions to commonplace problems. Workers found new ways to solve old problems. The investigators conclude:

> Since creativity is a term ordinarily reserved for exceptional individuals and extraordinary accomplishments, recognizing it in the practical problem-solving activities of ordinary people introduces a new perspective from which to grasp the challenge of the ordinary.[15]

But when the same workers who were so accurate and sophisticated in their mathematical skills on the job were administered paper-and-pencil arithmetic tests, they made many errors on problems similar in format to those they solved so well on the job.

This research identifies some of the ways skills such as reading, writing, and mathematics are commonly used in everyday settings to solve problems (see box 3-E). It also suggests that the difference between skilled and effective workers and novices may lie more in their ability to

---

[11] William Allan Diehl, Indiana University, ''Functional Literacy as a Variable Construct: An Examination of Attitudes, Behaviors, and Strategies Related to Functional Literacy,'' unpublished Ed.D. dissertation, 1980, p. 251.

[12] Larry Mikulecky, ''Literacy Task Analysis: Defining and Measuring Occupational Literacy Demands,'' paper presented at the Adult Education Research Conference, Chicago, IL, 1985, p. 12.

[13] Mikulecky and Ehlinger, op. cit., footnote 10, p. 11.

[14] Sylvia Scribner, ''Studying Working Intelligence,'' *Everyday Cognition: Its Development in Social Context*, Barbara Rogoff and Jean Lave (eds.) (Cambridge, MA: Harvard University Press, 1984), pp. 9-40; and Sylvia Scribner, ''Thinking in Action: Some Characteristics of Practical Thought,'' *Practical Intelligence: Nature and Origins of Competence in the Everyday World*, Robert F. Sternberg and R.K. Wagner (eds.) (Cambridge, England: Cambridge University Press, 1986), pp. 13-30.

[15] Scribner, ''Thinking in Action,'' op. cit., footnote 14, p. 28.

Box 3-E—Profile of Tom Addington[1]

Tom Addington is a 27-year-old farm laborer who lives with his wife and three young children in a rented four-room frame house in rural Virginia. He describes himself as a family man and his children, ages 5, 3, and 2, are very important to him. Tom works as a member of a crew that hires out for tobacco farming. He also does other seasonal farm work and gathers ginseng for sale. At present, he is paid by the hour or in exchange for rent but next year he hopes to raise his own crop of tobacco ''on shares'' (since he owns no land of his own).

Tom's home has few amenities—there is no water and no bathroom in the house. He operates largely in a cash economy. He has never had a bank account and does not file a tax return, except to get low-income credit if he has been paid by someone who withholds. The family receives Food Stamps and help from the Women, Infants, and Children (WIC) program, a U.S. Department of Agriculture supplemental food program. Although Tom has owned vehicles, he traded them because he has never been able to get a driver's license due to his low reading skills. In an area where the only public transportation is school buses and the shopping town is 20 miles away, not being able to pass the driver's license test is a serious problem. To shop, go to the doctor, or visit their child's school, Tom and his wife must catch a ride with family members who live nearby.

Most of Tom's life is taken up with work and he seems particularly motivated to meet the needs of his children: ''I love my kids, very much. . . . And I guess the biggest majority is taking care of them. I don't mind that too bad 'cause if a man's gonna amount to anything he's got to get out here and work for it. . . . It's kinda hard on me every day 'cause, you know, I never know where I'm gonna get ahold of the next penny at.''

Tom has lived in rural Scott County most of his life. He dropped out of school when he was 17 and ''taking 9th, 10th-grade subjects.'' Tom feels resentment toward school because he never learned to read well: ''. . . they just passed me to get rid of me . . . they wouldn't try to learn me nothing so I just quit goin'. . . . I was willin' to learn how to read, grow up to be you know maybe something better than what I am now besides doin' farm work, maybe you know be on a public job makin' good money, something like that, doin' carpenter work or something.''

Tom's reading is limited to recognizing key words such as those he encounters on food labels, familiar bills, prices, and road signs. He cannot read the newspaper. The only writing he does is when he signs his name. He relies on his wife to read the mail and read to the children. When he encounters situations where reading would be helpful, he relies on others to explain and demonstrate what he needs to know. Tom feels more confident about his mathematical skills and uses mathematics in practical problem solving. He explains how he estimated his bid for cutting a field of tobacco: ''You count one row . . . and if you got, say, 100 sticks in a row, and you got 20 stick rows, that'd be 2,000 sticks . . . some rows might have a stick shorter or somethin' like that, and we guess at it a little bit.''

Tom also estimates the rate to apply soda and fertilizer to a piece of land for tobacco at the rate of 500 pounds of soda and 1,500 pounds of fertilizer to the acre. Since plots of farm land are often irregular, it requires a good eye and a lot of practice to make good estimates. The agricultural extension agent confirmed the practical problem-solving abilities of farmers like Tom: ''They've got it upstairs, using human computers.''

Tom's work involves skills such as driving a tractor and spearing tobacco. It also involves technical knowledge. He knows what needs to be done to grow tobacco and in what sequence. He uses agricultural chemicals and determines how much is needed. He has skills as a mechanic. He gardens and knows his environment as a hunter and an herb digger. In none of these areas did his knowledge come from literacy and schooling.

Tom's only schooling as an adult occurred when he spent 7 months in Richmond in a correctional institution after he was ''in a little bit of trouble.'' There he had classes in mathematics, English, science, and spelling. He felt pleased with the experience, but was surprised to learn he was only at the 3rd-grade level. Although he thinks about getting more education, he feels he does not have the time; in addition he feels: ''I'm kinda bashful you know 'cause I just won't let anybody come in and try to learn me to read, something like that, 'cause I know it makes them angry and I get angry and just don't want to do nothing.''

---

[1] Adapted from Center for Literacy Studies, University of Tennessee, Knoxville, ''Life at the Margins: Profiles of Adults With Low Literacy Skills,'' OTA contractor report, March 1992. The names of individuals have been changed.

Common everyday literacy tasks include making sense of a school report card, a bank deposit slip, a bus map, and dosage information on a medicine bottle.

Directions: SHAKE WELL BEFORE USING (CLIP INSIDE)

Squeeze bottle to accurately dispense medicine into dosage cup provided.

Dosage-

Age	Weight	Dose
Under 2 yrs.	Under 28 lbs.	Consult physician
2-5 yrs.	28-47 lbs.	Fill cup to ½ Tbs.
6-11 yrs.	48-95 lbs.	Fill cup to 1 Tbs.
12 yrs. and over	96 lbs. and over	2 Tbs. or Try one of the Adult Formula 44® medicines

Repeat every 6 hours. No more than 4 doses in 24 hours, or as directed by a doctor.

WARNING: A persistent cough may be a sign of a serious condition. If cough persists for more than 1 week, tends to recur, or is accompanied by fever, rash, or persistent headache, consult a doctor. Do not take this product for persistent or chronic cough such as occurs with smoking, asthma, emphysema, or if cough is accompanied by excessive phlegm (mucus) unless directed by a doctor. Do not exceed recommended dosage because at higher doses nervousness, dizziness, or sleeplessness may occur. Do not take this product for more than 7 days. If symptoms do not improve or are accompanied by fever, consult a doctor. Do not take this product if you have heart disease, high blood pressure, thyroid disease, diabetes, or difficulty in urination due to enlargement of the prostate gland unless directed by a doctor. *Drug Interaction Precaution:* Do not take this product if you are presently taking a prescription drug for high blood pressure or depression without first consulting your doctor. KEEP THIS AND ALL DRUGS OUT OF REACH OF CHILDREN. In case of accidental overdose, seek professional assistance or contact a poison control center immediately. As with any drug, if you are pregnant or nursing a baby, seek the advice of a health professional before using this product.

3903 BC105 11374

STORE AT ROOM TEMPERATURE. AVOID EXCESSIVE HEAT.

RICHARDSON-VICKS INC.
SHELTON, CT 06484 U.S.A.
A PROCTER & GAMBLE COMPANY

Questions? Comments? Call toll free at 1-800-843-9657.

DREW MODEL SCHOOL
TEAM I

NAME: Benjamin Brokaw   GRADE: 1
TEACHER: A. Devlin

SCHOOL YEAR 91-92 GRADE PLACEMENT NEXT YEAR

Marking Code - Symbols used to evaluate academic subject areas:

M = Mastered skills/concepts
W = Worked satisfactorily on skills/concepts
H = Had difficulty with skills/concepts

READING
Level of instructional materials
Reads with understanding
Shows growth in vocabulary
Reads independently
Uses word recognition skills
Effort

ORAL COMMUNICATION
Uses listening skills
Expresses ideas clearly
Shows growth in vocabulary
Effort

WRITTEN
Expres...
Shows...
Write...
Use o...
Spell...
Applie...
Effort

MATHEMA...
Level o...
Under...
Compu...
Use p...
Effort

Lee Highway Line
Routes 3A,B,C,E,F
Westpark-West Falls Church Line
Routes 3W,Z

Legend
M — Metrorail Station
★ — Terminal Stands
□ — Fare Zone Limits
■ — Rush Hour service
■ — Base service

N ←

WESTPARK

NOTES: RTS. 3A,B,C,E
Passengers will be permitted to board bus in Revenue or Non-Revenue Service Along Americana Dr. for Eastbound trip.

Passengers will be permitted to stay on bus and alight at any bus stop in Revenue or Non-Revenue Service from Patriot Dr. & Americana Dr. to Heritage Dr. & McWhorter Pl.

Passengers will be permitted to stay on bus at Rosslyn Metro Station and alight at any Metro bus stop from Rosslyn Metro Station to Lee Hwy. & Scott Street in the Westbound direction Revenue Service.

Metrobus Routes 3W,Z
SPECIAL 50¢ FARE AND TRANSFER REGULATIONS
EFFECTIVE JUNE 29, 1991

● 50 Cent Fare
● Valid bus transfers will be accepted for full fare
● Bus transfers issued on these routes will be good for a 50 cent discount toward regular fare on next line
● Rail to bus transfers will not be accepted on these routes
● Valid Flash Passes will be accepted for the full fare (All Virginia Passes and the Maryland/D.C. Pass)

CHECKING DE...

ACCOUNT NAME(S)
STREET ADDRESS
CITY, STATE, ZIP

ACCOUNT NUMBER

All items are received subject to the terms and conditions of your account agreement and are credited for deposit only after they are verified by the institution for cash receipt or payment.

⑊500B⑊0000⑊

CURRENCY
COIN
CHECKS
LESS CASH RECEIVED
TOTAL DEPOSIT

2B

Box 3-F—Assessing Progress: Learners and Tests

Tests and other evaluation tools are used in literacy programs for many different purposes. The most stringent evaluation requirements—often requiring the administration of standardized tests to all learners before and after participation in the program—are usually imposed by funding agencies who want to know what they are getting for their money. "Accountability is seen by many as the principal driving force behind the surge of interest in evaluating literacy projects."[1]

Evaluation serves many other important functions. Teachers and administrators can benefit from program evaluation and the opportunity to examine what works and what does not within the program. Tests often are used as a basis for decisions about admitting or placing learners—helping to match learners to programs at the right skill level. In addition, tests are sometimes used to make "discharge" decisions—certifying that a student has successfully completed a program and is ready to move on to the next step. Credentials such as the general equivalency diploma, which may be required by some employers, require a test in order to certify the learner's achievements.[2]

But probably the most important reason for conducting evaluations in literacy programs is that learners want to know how they are progressing. At the Technology for Literacy Center in Minnesota, learners were asked on their initial visit: "What will keep you coming back to this program?" Over 80 percent of the learners said: "I know I'm making progress."[3]

Unfortunately the types of information that can be most valuable to the learner are often not the kinds of information collected for accountability and program evaluation. For one thing, the kinds of progress that may be most significant to learners—an increased sense of self-esteem or self-sufficiency, for example—are hard to measure concretely. In addition, because different learners have different goals, the one or two measures chosen by the program may not cover important gains made in other areas.

For many adults with low literacy skills, taking standardized tests can be an experience fraught with anxiety and memories of past school failures. One learner described the experience of taking the Test of Adult Basic Education (TABE) before entering a program:

... we had maybe 40 people [taking the TABE at the same time]. There was a break in the middle and maybe only half came back. That was so sad. They didn't feel they could finish that."[4]

---

[1] Terilyn C. Turner, "Conducting Evaluation in Adult Literacy Programs: Issues and Recommendations," paper presented at the Midwest Research-to-Practice Conference, St. Paul, MN, Oct. 3-4, 1991.

[2] For further discussion of the roles of literacy tests see Richard L. Venezky, "Matching Literacy Testing With Social Policy: What Are the Alternatives?" policy brief PB 92-1 (Philadelphia, PA: National Center on Adult Literacy, May 22, 1992).

[3] Turner, op. cit., footnote 1, p. 3.

[4] Terilyn C. Turner and Stacey Hueftle Stockdill (eds.), *The Technology for Literacy Project Evaluation* (St. Paul, MN: The Saint Paul Foundation, Inc., December 1987), p. 171.

---

perform practical problem solving than in their reading or computational ability per se.

Other studies of problem solving in everyday situations also show selective and creative approaches. One group of researchers studied problem-solving activities as people did their grocery shopping.[16] "Expert" shoppers (who ranged in formal education level from the 8th grade upward) used a variety of complex and fairly sophisticated mathematical calculations to aid in their decisionmaking in grocery stores. However, these same shoppers were then tested with a paper-and-pencil test on the same mathematical operations they had used in grocery shopping. Average scores were 59 percent on the arithmetic test, "... compared with a startling 98 percent—

---

[16] Jean Lave et al., "The Dialectic of Arithmetic in Grocery Shopping," in Rogoff and Lave, op. cit., footnote 14, pp. 67-94.

Because standardized tests are designed to be used across many programs and types of learners, their content is often quite broad and general. "The nationally standardized and normed tests are not sensitive enough to the specifics of what is being taught in the program."[5] Because many learners have little time to attend programs and because individual goals are not necessarily covered by standardized tests, there is often very little increase in the standardized test scores of most adult learners. In addition, evaluators have noticed that participants often feel that they *have* made considerable improvement in their skills, despite the minimal gains that might register on the tests.[6] This can be a source of frustration for learners—programs allow them to set individual goals and stress learning in context, yet the tests do not reflect these same goals and emphases.[7]

Several recent developments offer new promise for meeting the assessment needs of adult learners. First has been a growing interest, throughout all levels of education, in alternatives to existing tests for assessing the learner's progress. Often called "performance assessment," these methods can range from interviews about goals and progress, self-evaluations, portfolios of works over time, oral performances, writing assignments, or projects. These methods offer the promise of providing rich information that is directly tied to the learner's goals and program of instruction. These methods can help make the evaluation of a learner's progress an integral part of the learning process and can help to sustain the motivation of learners. Whether such methods can also be adapted for use in program evaluation, accountability, or student certification is still an open question and will require considerably more research and development.[8]

A second promising development is the use of technology to administer tests. Computer-administered tests show considerable promise in reducing the anxiety associated with testing because of the privacy they offer. And because they are usually scored immediately, such tests can also reduce or eliminate the stresses associated with waiting for test results. In addition, computers can be used to administer "adaptive" tests, which adjust the questions to the skill level of the test taker, thus reducing the frustration caused by answering many questions that are too difficult. Perhaps all 40 students taking the TABE in the above example would have stayed to complete the test (and enroll in the literacy program) had they been able to take such an individualized test!

---

[5] Thomas G. Sticht, Applied Behavioral and Cognitive Sciences, Inc., "Testing and Assessment in Adult Basic Education and English as a Second Language Programs," report prepared for the U.S. Department of Education, Division of Adult Education and Literacy, January 1990, p. 11.

[6] See, for example, Janice Lee Albert and Deborah D'Amico-Samuels, *Adult Learners' Perceptions of Literacy Programs and the Impact of Participation on Their Lives* (New York, NY: Literacy Assistance Center, Inc., August 1991).

[7] See Hanna A. Fingeret and Susan T. Danin, *"They Really Put a Hurtin' on My Brain": Learning in Literacy Volunteers of New York City* (Raleigh, NC: Literacy South, January 1991).

[8] For further discussion of these issues, see U.S. Congress, Office of Technology Assessment, *Testing in American Schools: Asking the Right Questions*, OTA-SET-519 (Washington, DC: U.S. Government Printing Office, March 1992).

virtually error free—arithmetic in the supermarket."[17]

Results of these studies suggest that available methods for assessing people's literacy do not give the full picture of what people can do. Just as research in cognitive science has indicated that knowledge and processes are intertwined, the research on everyday uses of literacy confirms that when the process (literacy as skill) is separated from the knowledge (everyday context), everyone looks much less skilled than they really are. This suggests that many people who perform poorly on paper-and-pencil tests may nevertheless be functioning adequately, or to their own satisfaction, in their everyday lives. These results also suggest the need for new kinds of literacy assessment methods; the trend toward developing performance assessments in education offers the promise of providing a broader and more complex picture of individual accomplishment (see box 3-F).

---

[17] Ibid., pp. 82-83.

These findings about the importance of context in learning are highly congruent with the view of learning that has emerged from the cognitive sciences. This approach, which applies to both children and adults, challenges many of the traditional assumptions about learning on which most classrooms have been based.[18] The traditional model assumes that complex skills can be broken down into simple skills, each of which can be mastered independently and out of context. Not until all components are mastered can more complex thinking skills develop. Moreover, in this model, the teacher is the active partner in the educational process, imparting knowledge to a passive student as though filling an empty jug.

In contrast, the "constructivist" view of learning underscores the importance of the student actively constructing his or her own knowledge. This view of learning suggests the following principles to guide the design of effective learning environments:[19]

- People do not easily or predictably transfer learning—either from school to "real life," from real life to classrooms, or from one subject to another. Educational experiences should help students transfer skills, concepts, and knowledge they have learned to new situations.
- Learners are not passive vessels into which knowledge can be poured, but rather active participants in their own learning. "The student needs chances to engage in choice, judgment, control process, problem formulation; s/he needs the chance to make mistakes. We have an adage in our culture, 'Experience is the best teacher.' In other words, you learn when you

do, a popular observation borne out by the research. Although not sufficient for effective learning, doing is necessary."[20]

- Knowledge is acquired from experience with complex, meaningful problems rather than from practicing subskills and learning isolated bits of knowledge. "Human beings—even the small child—are quintessentially sense-making, problem-solving animals. . . . As a species, we wonder, we are curious, we want to understand. . . . Fractionated and decontextualized instruction fails to mobilize this powerful property of human beings in the service of learning."[21]
- Learners are not blank slates, but rather carry concepts and knowledge they have acquired elsewhere into the learning situation. "In other words, the teaching challenge is not to write on a clean slate. It is to confirm, disconfirm, modify, replace, and add to what is already written there."[22]
- Skills and knowledge are best acquired in context. Previously it was thought that in order to make skills and knowledge more generalizable, most learning should be general and separated from the context of everyday life. "Context, however, turns out to be critical for understanding and thus for learning. . . . The importance of context lies in the meaning that it gives to learning."[23]

ADULTS SEEKING LEARNING OPPORTUNITIES

Adults learn all the time, in all the arenas of their lives. For some adults, new roles and life transitions—becoming a parent, moving to a new

---

[18] For further discussion see Lauren B. Resnick and Daniel P. Resnick, "Assessing the Thinking Curriculum: New Tools for Educational Reform," paper prepared at the National Commission on Testing and Public Policy, August 1989.

[19] These five principles and their discussion are drawn from Sue E. Berryman, Teachers College, Columbia University, "Cognitive Science: Indicting Today's Schools and Designing Effective Learning Environments," unpublished manuscript, Apr. 24, 1991.

[20] Ibid., p. 4.

[21] Ibid., p. 8.

[22] Ibid., p. 9.

[23] Ibid., p. iii.

Box 3-G—Profile of Michela Stone[1]

Michela Stone is a 32-year-old single white woman refugee from Byleorussia in the western part of the former Soviet Union. Two years ago she emigrated with her father to San Francisco. In Russia she had completed a bachelor's degree in accounting and a master's degree in accountancy teaching. She had been teaching accounting and statistics in a college there.

Michela lives alone in a small apartment and she knows few of her neighbors. Her father lives nearby in government-subsidized housing. She currently works as a bookkeeper with a nonprofit community center for Russian emigres; although she speaks English with her coworkers, much of her job involves working with Russian emigres with whom she speaks Russian. Most of the people she knows are Russian and she feels part of the wider Russian community network. To supplement her income, she works 7 hours a week (one night and Saturday mornings) as a bookkeeper for a small dental practice. In addition, she still cooks and cleans for her father, leaving her little free time for community activities or education. Most of her free time is spent reading, both in Russian and in English.

When she first came to the United States, Michela spoke no English. At first, she made herself read English for 1 hour a day. She has also enrolled in several adult education classes: a basic literacy course focusing on developing skills in everyday situations, accounting, and two English classes. Initially, Michela carried a dictionary with her, "... always with me. For 2 years, in my purse." In general, she has little difficulty with written English. What she does not understand immediately, she remembers or writes down to look up when she gets home. She has had much greater difficulty learning to speak and understand spoken English.

When she first arrived in San Francisco, Michela worked as a cleaner in an apartment building and then did office work in a hotel. "People would tell me that I couldn't get a job as an accountant. You can get a job at a hotel or cleaning up someone's mess. Why they did that I don't know. It was mis-instruction. It made me think I was nothing." Her current job utilizes only some of her considerable job skills. Michela's goal is to improve her English so that she can pass the Test of English for Foreign Learners (TOEFL)—a test that non-native speakers must pass in order to enroll in college. "I'd like to be able to go to college here. Enroll in a business program. Get an MBA. Nobody thinks my MA from Russia is worth much. I took TOEFL once and scored only 10 below. . . . I'll certainly take it again when I have time to study."

Michela uses a number of strategies for improving her English and feeling more assimilated into American life. She watches television in order to gain cultural information about American life and to get ideas for conversation topics; although she doesn't have a VCR she thinks it would be nice to have one so that she could tape programs to discuss with her father and friends. Michela has also begun to teach Russian to three Americans: "We read and write and speak Russian and English. Maybe 1 hour, 2 hour a week. Then I learn something about American lifestyle. Cultural exchange. To meet American people, to learn something from them."

---

[1] Adapted from Center for Literacy Studies, University of Tennessee, Knoxville, "Life at the Margins: Profiles of Adults With Low Literacy Skills," OTA contractor report, March 1992. The names of individuals have been changed.

part of the country, taking a new job, developing a medical problem—precipitate new learning and the acquisition of new skills. Most people desiring to gain new knowledge or improve their skills probably do so informally, e.g., by reading books or listening to books on tape, watching television, setting up informal tutoring exchanges with a friend or relative, observing others, doing volunteer work, using the library, or attending lectures at community centers (see box 3-G). But some adults seek formal education through enrolling in courses or engaging a tutor.

Evidence shows that people most likely to benefit from adult education are least likely to participate in it. In 1990-91, a large-scale, nationally representative survey was conducted about the educational activities of adults in the United States. Thirty-eight percent of adults ages

17 and over reported participating in some educational activity during the 12-month period.[24] Findings included the following:

- People with jobs were more likely to participate than those who were unemployed or not in the labor force (41 percent as compared to 21 percent and 14 percent respectively);
- People with higher levels of education were more likely to attend (see figure 3-1);
- People with higher incomes had higher participation rates;
- Adults between the ages of 35 and 44 had the highest rates of any age group;
- Adults with children under 16 had higher rates than those with no children (37 percent as compared to 28 percent); and
- Men and women participated at the same rate.

These findings suggest that ''...those who would benefit greatly from participation in some part-time educational activity seemed less likely to do so—that is, adults with a 12th-grade education or less, who were not employed, or whose households were at the lowest income levels.''[25]

The Decision to Participate in Adult Literacy Education

Adults entering literacy programs are significantly different from children in school. They are, for the most part, ''schooled.'' Most of them have had at least 7 years of schooling, many have had some high school, and some have graduated from high school, but without proficiency in reading or other basic skills. Furthermore, these adults enter the classroom with a wealth of life experiences that reframe and often screen both their perceptions and their participation in the learning experience. They usually are volunteer learners, and face issues of entry and commitment many

Figure 3-1—Percentage of Adults (17 and Over) Participating in Educational Activities During 1990-91, by Current Education Level

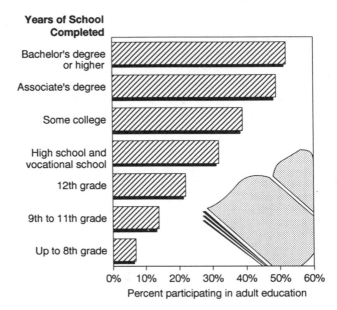

Percent participating in adult education

NOTE: "Educational activities" include all full- and part-time formal and informal educational experiences in which adults participated over the 12-month period preceding the survey. This includes enrollment in college, vocational training, GED instruction, English as a second language, and any other type of education or training provided by any type of provider including colleges and universities, employers, community organizations (e.g. library, museum), and State and local agencies. Those still attending elementary or secondary school were excluded from the survey.

SOURCE: Roslyn Korb et al., U.S. Department of Education, National Center for Education Statistics, "Adult Education Profile for 1990-91," NCES #91-222, September 1991.

times in their adult lives as they drop out of and reenter programs. These adults have a strong sense of self, an emotionally laden history of past learning experiences, and a complex set of motivations.

Why do more adults not enter literacy programs? What factors affect their decisions to seek educational opportunities?

---

[24] The survey did not include those enrolled full time in high school.

[25] Roslyn Korb et al., U.S. Department of Education, National Center for Education Statistics, "Adult Education Profile for 1990-91," NCES 91-222, unpublished report, September 1991, p. 2.

There was . . . a period of waiting to hear where and when to go to class, telephone calls and letters back and forth between Ms. Altman and the program, before she was finally told where to come to begin instruction. That first night, Ms. Altman remembers, ''I sat in my car. I was supposed to be in at 5:30. I sat in my car until 6:00 because I was afraid to go in. Finally, I got enough nerve to go in and when I walk in [the center director] was very nice and she says, 'Rose your tutor is not here. You're gonna have to wait another two weeks before you can attend class.' ''[26]

Making the initial decision to visit a literacy program or attend the first class can often be a very difficult hurdle for adults with low literacy skills. Several interview studies suggest that a tremendous amount of courage, as well as social support from others, is required.

Making the call and entering the program was stressful for everyone we talked with; it required great courage, trust, and, sometimes, overcoming obstacles such as finding money for carfare or childcare, negotiating with spouses and maneuvering through unfamiliar subway and bus routes. Family members and close friends are often key to students moving forward.[27]

A number of researchers have underscored the importance of the first meeting in determining whether or not adults continue in adult education. One researcher states: ''This is the stage when many under-educated participants drop out . . . and it calls for assurance that the first class session will be a positive experience.''[28] Many programs have begun to change how they de-

scribe and advertise their programs in order to encourage people to enter. The workplace literacy program started by the United Auto Workers and Ford, for example, has discovered the importance of physically leaving the classroom door open at all times, despite considerable noise from the machinery in the plant. Prospective students, they discovered, were reluctant to venture into the program when they could not see what they were walking into.[29]

Several factors that make it difficult to enter into learning programs include:

Shame and embarrassment about revealing a long kept secret. ''Illiteracy'' in this country is a stigma that carries with it many negative stereotypes.[30] Many adults have learned to compensate for their lack of reading skill by covering up and passing as literate. Enrolling in a literacy program effectively ''blows one's cover'' since it requires public disclosure. For example, one participant challenged her interviewer:

I don't know if you remember the first time you ever met somebody that didn't know how to read. First they were speaking to you like anybody and all of a sudden they say ''You know I can't read.'' Did your expression change? Did you think differently about them? A lot of people do when you tell them I can't read. All of a sudden . . . now you're a dumb idiot. Before you were someone to have a conversation with, but after you told them that they totally changed their opinion and you could hear it in their voice, you could see it in their face.[31]

Painful past experiences with schools and teachers. Most people with low literacy skills

---

[26] Hanna Arlene Fingeret and Susan Tuck Danin, *They Really Put a Hurtin' on My Brain: Learning in Literacy Volunteers of New York City* (Raleigh, NC: Literacy South, January 1991), p. 41. Fortunately, the center director worked out an arrangement so that Ms. Altman could begin more quickly.

[27] Ibid., p. 39.

[28] Linda K. Bock, ''Participation,'' *Developing, Administering and Evaluating Adult Education*, Alan B. Knox and Associates (eds.) (San Francisco, CA: Jossey-Bass, 1980), p. 127.

[29] See ch. 4 for further description of the United Auto Workers/Ford workplace learning program.

[30] Hal Beder, ''The Stigma of Illiteracy,'' *Adult Basic Education*, vol. 1, No. 2, summer 1991, pp. 67-78.

[31] Fingeret and Danin, op. cit., footnote 26, p. 151.

have not experienced success in school situations. "For many, public school is associated with shame and pain from the time they were young."[32] Some, like Tom, describe not being able to learn or understand but being passed on through the system:

> I wasn't learning nothing, they just passed me to get rid of me. They'd send me down on the ball field, rake the ball field off or tell me to go to sleep or something or other.... Seemed like they didn't have enough patience so I just quit goin'. I wasn't learnin' nothin'. They wouldn't try to learn me nothing so I just quit goin'.... They ought to took their time 'cause I was willing to learn. They ought to took their time to learn me but they didn't seem like they cared that much.[33]

Although most students have painful past experiences with schooling, they are affected in different ways: some retain negative self-evaluations of themselves as learners, some do not believe in the usefulness of education, and some remain reluctant to subject themselves to schools and teachers once again.

The threatening nature of change. The decision to enter a literacy program often is the culmination of a long period of personal struggle. "Even after they have admitted to themselves that they need to develop better literacy skills, it can be years before someone enters a program."[34] Deciding to come usually means the participant is deciding to change something about their life—to be different than they are now.

> In the future I would like to go to school because I would like to have something more meaningful

than a factory job. If I go to the school, I want to try to find some interesting job—you know—to learn how to get some more money doing something different because I need to be some other woman, you know. I don't want to be the same all the time.[35]

Often the decision to enter a program cannot be attributed to a single event, but is part of a larger process of change or life transition. Losing a job, confronting alcoholism, breaking up an intimate relationship, or having one's children begin school can lead to changing roles and life choices. "As adults move through the life cycle, new motivations to learn are constantly being generated by the need to perform new roles."[36] While deciding to address a literacy problem can be associated with a sense of hope and empowerment, it can also trigger fear of failure or of being incapable of realizing one's dreams. Researchers have also suggested that improved literacy can be a threat to the balance of power in a family or between a couple.[37] Improved literacy can alter the stability of the person's current life situation. One learner describes it in this way:

> At first my husband didn't approve. He would say, "You're always going out; you read too much; you think you know everything." ... Because I couldn't read, I was more dependent on him. When I learned to read he lost something because I didn't need him so much. I think it was something like what can happen when an alcoholic stops drinking.[38]

Fear of job loss. Many prospective learners express a fear of reprisal such as job loss if employers learn about their true literacy skills.

---

[32] Ibid., p. 31.

[33] Center for Literacy Studies, op. cit., footnote 1, p. 19.

[34] Fingeret and Danin, op. cit., footnote 26, p. 35.

[35] Kathleen Rockhill, "Literacy as Threat/Desire: Longing to be SOMEBODY," *ESL Literacy: Theme Issue of TESL Talk*, Jill Bell (ed.), vol. 20, No. 1, 1990, p. 104.

[36] Hal Beder, *Adult Literacy: Issues for Policy and Practice* (Malabar, FL: Krieger Publishing Co., 1991), p. 50.

[37] Rockhill, op. cit., footnote 35.

[38] Kathleen A. Fitzsimmons, "African-American Women Who Persist in Literacy Programs: An Exploratory Study," *The Urban Review*, vol. 23, No. 4, December 1991, pp. 245.

Fear of supervisor punishment has been identified as a deterrent to participation in a number of workplace literacy programs.[39] Some of these programs have had to offer offsite classes or enlist union support to encourage employees to attend.

> I was kinda scared the first time when I couldn't read really. . . . I was kinda scared to talk to my boss actually about that because I thought she was going to fire me. So one day I told her I wanted to talk to her. So she was willing to listen and I tell her I have a reading problem. And actually she was very sympathetic with me. She helped me.[40]

The Importance of Motivation

An adult's motivation is often quite high by the time they walk in the door of a literacy program.

> Motivation is the force which impels voluntary adult learners toward literacy education. When it is strong, adults can be expected to overcome the barriers to participation that life imposes. When motivation is weak, participation is highly unlikely. It follows that if literacy programs can develop recruitment and instruction which is congruent with learners' motivations, success in attracting and retaining students will be considerably enhanced.[41]

A number of theorists and researchers have studied the motivations of adult learners. Although findings vary from study to study depending on populations studied and methods used, several general principles have emerged from this research.[42] Adults give a variety of reasons for participating in adult education. These motiva-

Adults turn to education for many reasons including helping their children with homework, getting a new job, reading for fun, or learning something new.

tions go well beyond a simple desire to improve basic skills or get a high school diploma. One review of the literature suggests that the goals reported in most studies can be grouped into three broad types: employment goals (to gain or upgrade employment), hopes related to children, and self-improvement.[43] In fact, one of the most frequently cited motivators for attending adult education is self-improvement, which includes reasons such as becoming a better person, wanting to learn new things, being more independent, becoming better informed. These self-improvement reasons appear to be equally, if not more, important than vocational motivators (e.g., getting a better job, making more money).[44] Motiva-

---

[39] Larry Mikulecky, "Workplace Literacy Programs: Organization and Incentives," paper presented at "Adult Learning and Work: A Focus on Incentives," a conference sponsored by the U.S. National Center on Adult Literacy, Nov. 4-5, 1991.

[40] Fingeret and Danin, op. cit., footnote 26, p. 39.

[41] Beder, op. cit., footnote 36, p. 39.

[42] For a more complete review of the research see ibid.

[43] Miriam Balmuth, Kingsborough Community College, City University of New York, "Essential Characteristics of Effective Adult Literacy Programs: A Review and Analysis of the Research," unpublished paper, 1986.

[44] Beder, op. cit., footnote 36. See also Clifford Adelman, U.S. Department of Education, *The Way We Are: The Community College as American Thermometer* (Washington, DC: U.S. Government Printing Office, February 1992), p. 31. This report suggests that adults who attend community colleges ". . . are more interested in learning, in acquiring new skills, and in completing . . . basic general education than in advanced credentials, even if those credentials yield greater economic rewards."

tion also seems to be influenced by age and the learner's place in the life cycle. For example, diversion (a desire to dispel boredom) is given as a reason for participating by younger and older. people, but less so for those in middle age. Concerns about professional advancement, in contrast, were highly motivating to those in middle age, less so in later years.[45]

Why People Do Not Participate

Most estimates suggest that somewhere between 5 and 10 percent of eligible adults have enrolled in federally sponsored literacy programs within the last year.[46] As the above section has demonstrated, the adult who shows up at an adult education program is likely to be highly motivated and has managed to overcome or set aside other potential barriers to participation. But what of the adults who never come? What do we know about those who do not participate in literacy programs? It is much easier to survey, observe, and interview adults who come to programs than the much larger part of the population who do not. Lack of information about nonparticipants is a major problem facing those who would increase participation rates.[47]

Some researchers have attempted to find out what the common barriers are to attending adult education classes. Most of these efforts are surveys that provide a list of possible reasons for not attending classes and ask adults to select the ones that apply to them.[48] This research is of limited generalizability, however, because it tells us only what people *say* keeps them from participating, which can be greatly affected by social desirability (e.g., it is easier and more acceptable to say cost and time are deterrents than to admit one is too anxious to try it or that one thinks education is worthless). Nevertheless this work has helped to illuminate the commonly cited reasons that people give for not attending.

Most of the research on barriers or deterrents to participation in adult education has been conducted with a broad range of adults, and does not focus on those with few skills. A synthesis of this general research suggests eight major types of deterrents:

"1. Individual, family or home-related problems (e.g., child care, poor health, transportation difficulties)

2. Cost concerns, including opportunity costs and lack of financial assistance

3. Questionable worth, relevance, or quality of available educational opportunities

4. Negative perceptions regarding the value of education in general, including those related to prior unfavorable experience

5. Lack of motivation or indifference toward learning (e.g., anomie, apathy)

6. Lack of self-confidence in one's learning abilities, including lack of social support/encouragement

7. A general proclivity toward nonaffiliation (e.g., marginal involvement in social activities)

8. Incompatibilities of time and/or place, especially those associated with conflicting demands of work."[49]

---

[45] Beder, op. cit., footnote 36. See also K. Patricia Cross, *Adults as Learners* (San Francisco, CA: Jossey-Bass, 1981).

[46] For example, see Hal Beder, "Nonparticipation in Adult Education," *NCAL Connections*, newsletter, winter 1992, pp. 4-5.

[47] Gordon G. Darkenwald, Literacy Assistance Center, Inc., "Adult Literacy Education: A Review of the Research and Priorities for Future Inquiry," unpublished report, 1986.

[48] For example, survey items include statements such as: "I would feel strange going back to school," "I don't have enough free time to go back to school," "School is too hard," "I haven't known where there are any classes," "I don't need a diploma," "My friends would laugh at me if I went back to school." Hal Beder, "Reasons for Nonparticipation in Adult Basic Education," *Adult Education Quarterly*, vol. 40, No. 4, summer 1990, pp. 207-218. For a review of these survey attempts see Beder, op. cit., footnote 36.

[49] C.L. Scanlan, *Deterrents to Participation: An Adult Education Dilemma* (Columbus, OH: ERIC Clearinghouse on Adult, Career, and Vocational Education, 1986), p. 35.

Table 3-1—Factors Affecting an Individual's Decision to Participate in Adult Education

Internal factors	External factors
• Self-evaluation (especially beliefs about self as a learner)	• Attitudes of family and peers
• Attitudes toward education and school	• Life-cycle transitions/role changes
• Motivation and importance of personal goals	• Access to information about relevant educational opportunities
• Expectation that education can help with goals	• Situational barriers to participation: (e.g., time, money, transportation, childcare needs)
• Perceptions about the amount of effort required	• Institutional barriers (e.g., fixed schedules, registration requirements, course prerequisites)

SOURCE: Office of Technology Assessment, 1993.

Reasons for nonparticipation thus fall into two major groupings: reasons internal to the person and those that are external or in the environment (see table 3-1). Internal reasons (which have also been called dispositional or psychosocial) include attitudes and feelings about the usefulness and value of adult education and evaluations about oneself as a learner.[50] External reasons can be situational (cost, time, transportation), informational (not knowing about relevant opportunities) and institutional (issues under the control of the schooling institution such as scheduling, registration procedures, course prerequisites, and location of the classes).

Different barriers are likely to be more or less important to different kinds of people. For example, situational barriers tend to be associated with those who are married, have children, and hold a job. Cost factors tend to be cited by younger age groups, and adults of lower socioeconomic status tend to be more deterred by lack of information.[51] However, very little is known about which deterrents are most important and whether the elimination of those barriers would actually increase participation.

Of the situational barriers, lack of time seems to be most often and consistently cited by adults as a deterrent. "Clearly, such proven strategies as varied and flexible scheduling, distance learning, and provisions for self-pacing will make education more accessible to adult learners."[52] Other strategies for removing situational barriers might include providing childcare or transportation costs, locating learning sites near the workplace, providing better information about available resources, and so forth. Decisions about which situational barriers to remove—for example, by providing childcare—will depend on the specific groups being served by programs.

Because they are more concrete, situational barriers are often the easiest to remove or change through policy decisions. Attitudinal barriers may prove to be far more difficult and complex to address. Dislike for school, low perception of the need for education, and perceptions that a large amount of effort is required to make gains in adult education all reduce participation of those most in need. Strategies for removing some of these attitudinal barriers might include developing ways to encourage or motivate those who do not perceive a need or to convince learners that progress is possible and leads to desired outcomes. If dislike for school is a substantial deterrent to adults with low literacy skills, then educational programs may need to be "deschooled" and removed from some of the institu-

---

[50] G. Darkenwald and S. Merriam, *Adult Education: Foundations of Practice* (New York, NY: Harper and Row, 1982).

[51] Beder, op. cit., footnote 36.

[52] Thomas Valentine and Gordon C. Darkenwald, "Deterrents to Participation in Adult Education: Profiles of Potential Learners," *Adult Education Quarterly*, vol. 41, No. 1, fall 1990, p. 40.

A lack of time or transportation prevents many adults from attending literacy classes. This classroom on wheels travels throughout Los Angeles bringing learning resources to adults in their own neighborhoods.

tional trappings of schools. Although these are all strategies worth exploring, no one really knows which, if any, will have the greatest impact on increasing participation rates.

MEETING ADULT LEARNER NEEDS: THE ROLE OF TECHNOLOGY

New technologies offer considerable promise in addressing the special concerns faced by adult learners who wish to improve their literacy skills. Technology can deliver instruction to learners in many new and different ways, whether they are computer-based, video-based (e.g., television and videotapes), or audio-based (e.g., radio, audiotape, and telephone). Some of the promise of new technologies reflects effects on increasing and sustaining motivation. Another plus is the possibility that instruction delivered via technologies may directly influence cognitive understanding—that is, help learners master new information better, more comprehensively, or more quickly. Other advantages come from the flexibility and efficiencies these new technologies offer to adults who have very small amounts of time to devote to learning.

Although those using technology to teach literacy have considerable anecdotal evidence of its effectiveness, very little empirical evidence is available to substantiate these claims. Some research evidence has accumulated about the effects of technology on learning,[53] but much of it is based on studies done with children. The research that has been done with adults comes primarily from higher education and military settings.

With these caveats in mind, then, the promise of technology for adults with low literacy skills can be described in a number of areas.

Reaching Learners Outside of Classrooms

Technology can facilitate the delivery of learning experiences in places other than classrooms. Adults can learn at times and places convenient for them; many situational barriers such as lack of transportation or childcare can be overcome by bringing instruction into homes and communities. Similarly, for many adults with low literacy skills privacy is important; learning in their own homes may offer a less stigmatizing way to obtain further education. Because of painful past experiences with classroom-based learning, some adults with low literacy skills may be more motivated to give education a ''second chance'' if it can be delivered in nonschool-based settings, such as the home, libraries, or community centers.

Attempts to offer adults instruction that is more convenient has its roots in the correspondence course—a method invented in the late 19th century to provide instruction to learners unable to attend a class.[54] Communications media such as broadcast television and audio recording have long been used in corporate, military, and university continuing education sectors as a means to offer education at a distance. More recently new forms of telecommunications have offered new possibilities for reaching learners.[55]

But do adults learn as well or as effectively when taught at a distance? Is face-to-face instruction an inherently superior way of teaching or can other methods be just as effective? Most studies that have compared face-to-face instruction with other methods such as teleconferencing, video-based instruction, or instruction via radio and audiotapes have found that achievement gains made by students exposed to the technologies were at least equal to those made by students receiving face-to-face instruction.[56] In addition, although the research findings indicate that the absence of face-to-face contact is not detrimental to learning, the literature suggests that a requirement for successful distance education may be a carefully designed learner support system. In such a system students are supported by teachers who do things such as help students organize study time and develop study skills, provide diagnostic counseling and tutorial assistance when necessary, and monitor and help sustain student involvement and motivation for learning.[57]

Using Learning Time Efficiently

Technologies can facilitate more efficient use of precious learning time. Because they must juggle multiple roles and responsibilities, most adults have very little time to devote to learning. Many adults who have tried to participate in literacy programs find themselves unable to sustain their participation because of conflicting job schedules, family responsibilities, or transportation problems. Although they may have precious parcels of free time, these do not always occur when classes are scheduled. To sustain their motivation, many adults may need to take advan-

---

[53] See, for example, Jerome Johnston, *Electronic Learning: From Audiotape to Videodisc* (Hillsdale, NJ: Lawrence Erlbaum, 1987).

[54] Michael G. Moore, ''Effects of Distance Learning: A Summary of the Literature,'' OTA contractor report, May 31, 1989.

[55] See U.S. Congress, Office of Technology Assessment, *Linking for Learning: A New Course for Education*, OTA-SET-430 (Washington, DC: U.S. Government Printing Office, November 1989). Available from the U.S. Department of Commerce, National Technical Information Service (NTIS), 5285 Port Royal Road, Springfield, VA 22161 (703) 487-4650; order #PB90-156969.

[56] Johnston, op. cit., footnote 53; Moore, op. cit., footnote 54; and Saul Rockman, ''Learning From Technologies: A Perspective on the Research Literature,'' OTA contractor report, December 1992.

[57] Moore, op. cit., footnote 54.

tage of these small segments of time or may be drawn to opportunities that offer other efficiencies such as learning while commuting, waiting in the doctor's office, or on a lunch break. Technology offers ways to deliver education at times and places that can maximize the efficient use of free time.

There are a number of other ways that technology can make learning more efficient. When a group of students sits in a classroom and learns from a teacher, the pace of instruction is set by the teacher. Some students could move at a faster pace, while other students, perhaps with less prior knowledge or with other needs, could benefit from a slower pace. Technology can allow students to master content at the pace that suits them best. For example, audio and videotapes of lectures allow students who need repetition to revisit the material until it is mastered, while other students move on to new materials. Features of computers and multimedia technologies can allow the learner to set the pace at which text is read or materials are presented. People can spend more time on things they do not understand, while moving quickly through those they have already mastered. A lecture or a broadcast presented at a fixed rate is understood by some learners but leaves some bored and others confused. Allowing the learner to control features such as pace, the need for repetition, and the need for extra explanation or feedback helps optimize time spent learning. This capacity of the technology is particularly important for adults, since they come to educational settings with an extremely wide range of life experience, knowledge, and formal schooling.

A review of adult education studies comparing computer-based education (CBE) to conventional instruction methods found positive effects on adult learners.[58] First, these CBE methods raised achievement scores by an average of 0.42 standard deviations—or the equivalent of an increase from the 50th to the 66th percentile. In addition, in 12 of the 13 studies that reported instructional time, the computer methods were faster; i.e., adults learners typically required about 70 percent of the time required by conventional teaching methods. These results suggest that, at least in general adult education, the learner can learn as much or more of the material in a shorter amount of time than with conventional methods.

A more recent review of interactive videodisc methods in the military, higher education, and industrial training suggests a very similar pattern.[59] Across 47 studies reviewed, results suggested that interactive videodisc instruction increased achievement an average of 0.5 standard deviations over conventional instruction, an increase from the 50th percentile to about the 69th percentile of achievement. Results also suggested that the more the interactive features were used, the more effective was the instruction. The average amount of student time saved across eight studies that looked at this factor was 31 percent. These results suggest that adults (in military, higher education, and training settings) learn more in less time with interactive videodisc methods. Studies to date are not detailed enough, however, to allow conclusions about whether factors such as self-pacing account for these efficiencies.

Sustaining Motivation

Technologies can enhance and sustain the motivation of adult learners. Many factors can deter an otherwise motivated adult from participating in a literacy program. Technology offers ways of protecting the privacy of learners. In addition to its capacity to deliver instruction outside of classrooms, technology offers other

---

[58] C.C. Kulik et al., ''The Effectiveness of Computer-Based Adult Education: A Meta-Analysis,'' *Journal of Educational Computing Research*, vol. 2, No. 2, 1986, pp. 235-252. See also Rockman, op. cit., footnote 56.

[59] J.D. Fletcher, *Effectiveness and Cost of Interactive Videodisc Instruction in Defense Training and Education* (Alexandria, VA: Institute for Defense Analyses, July 1990).

Los Angeles Times Learning Center

Computers offer privacy, self-paced instruction, and patient feedback—features that adult learners value.

privacy options. Working on computers, for example, learners no longer have to worry about making mistakes or feeling evaluated by teachers and peers. Computers are patient, nonevaluative tutors. But privacy need not mean isolation. Learners can use electronic networks, fax, telephones, and other distance technologies to share information and communicate with learners or tutors in other locations—still retaining their anonymity but participating in new kinds of "schools" and "communities."[60]

Educators working with technology have long been aware of a kind of "novelty" factor that improves the motivation of students working with technology. Learners, it seems, find technology a "fun" way to learn and may also find it rewarding to master "new machines." Adults with low literacy skills may particularly enjoy the opportunity to work with computers and gain experience with this important and pervasive technology. Some educators have also argued that computer methods also sustain motivation, because they can allow learning materials to be customized to meet the interests of individual learners. For example, a learner could scan a newspaper article of her choice into the computer; she could practice various assignments using content in which she is interested.

Multimedia technologies allow learners to branch off and explore ideas of particular interest.

---

[60] Terilyn Turner, "Literacy & Machines: An Overview of the Use of Technology in Adult Literacy Programs," unpublished manuscript, 1993, p. 7.

The computer's capacity to allow learners choices over content as well as provide immediate feedback on the learner's responses makes it particularly well-suited to maintaining the motivation of a student as he or she progresses. These features are particularly important for adult learners who often feel that learning is difficult and may need to re-experience themselves as successful learners.

Research on attitudes and motivation in relation to technology-based instruction is fairly limited, though many of the published conclusions seem to be positive. Some of the positive effects associated with computers may be novelty effects of using technology rather than the instructional potential of the delivery system itself.[61] Research with students from elementary to college age indicates that students enjoy using computers for several reasons: they like being able to make mistakes without embarrassment; they enjoy immediate, helpful feedback; and they like graphics and game formats. Some studies have suggested that computers are motivating because they give students the feeling of being in control. Other studies have suggested that computers contribute to students spending more time on a task, which in turn can contribute to higher levels of achievement.[62]

The benefits on motivation of factors such as immediate feedback, encouragement for correct answers, and being able to work on content of personal interest has long been known. The design of software that incorporates these features is likely to influence motivation and learning more than the effects of the technology alone. Good instructional software that builds on what is known about adult learning is likely to influence achievement and attitudes. Most available research cannot, however, distinguish among the various explanations for the motivating effects of technologies.

Individualizing Instruction

Technologies can offer opportunities to individualize instruction, reaching all types of learners in ways they learn best. Different media offer different modalities for presenting material: some materials may be understood better if they can be heard (e.g., a persuasive speech) or seen demonstrated (e.g., the steps involved in cardiopulmonary resuscitation). Information presented in two modalities at the same time can sometimes facilitate learning; e.g., beginning readers often benefit from hearing text read to them while they follow along with the text.

Audio and video technologies have long been used in classrooms to supplement print-based materials. The expanding capacities of new multimedia technologies offer opportunities for learners to access materials in many different forms—text, graphics, moving video, still video, digitized audio—and to combine these modes in unique ways. Thus, the new technologies offer ways of individualizing instruction to meet the needs of different types of learners.

The research on this topic is not extensive but it suggests that individuals do differ in their responsiveness to different media. Several studies have suggested that lower achieving students benefit more from the availability of audio and videotaped versions of courses. In one study, university students in the lowest quartile of achievement who received their psychology course via audiotape outperformed the live lecture students; in addition, fewer of the lower achieving tape students dropped the course.[63]

---

[61] Rockman, op. cit., footnote 56.

[62] Jay P. Sivin and Ellen R. Bialo, Interactive Educational Systems Design, Inc., ''Microcomputers and Related Learning Technologies: Overview,'' unpublished manuscript, n.d. See also Kathy A. Krendl and Debra A. Lieberman, ''Computers and Learning: A Review of Recent Research,'' *Journal of Educational Computing Research*, vol. 4, No. 4, 1988, pp. 367-389.

[63] See Johnston, op. cit., footnote 53.

Some of the most pertinent evidence comes from the British Open University, which in the 1970s and 1980s created a large number of multimedia courses (i.e., these courses included components of printed text, television, radio, and audiotape). These were higher education courses designed to be completed primarily at home. Research on the use of the various media in these courses indicated strong individual differences between students in their ability to learn from different media.

> Whereas most students on most courses do seem to make an effort to watch the majority of television programmes, there is no coherent pattern for radio. Some students listen to none. Others listen to them all. Some listen to half. . . . Although radio may not be used a great deal by a lot of students, those students who do use it regularly find it extremely valuable. . . . The *weaker* students who do watch or listen rate the broadcasts as *more* helpful than do the more successful students.[64]

Having examined other possible explanations, the researchers concluded that some students have difficulty with text, as they have not been successful readers in their past academic experiences. These students are likely to rely on audio and video for a simplification of the material.

One group of researchers working with adult literacy learners developed an inventory to distinguish between auditory learners and visual learners. Results suggest that those learners who read at lower levels (junior high and below) have a strong preference for auditory-based instructional materials.[65] These researchers argue for the importance of including clear digital audio components in effective literacy courseware.

Providing Access to Information Tools

For many years, printed text was the primary medium through which people gained information. Schools and libraries provided access to books and other texts, and taught people how to use these resources to get needed information. Today a whole new information infrastructure is emerging; access to it depends on understanding and using a variety of technologies.

> As individuals, those of us already equipped with a computer and a modem on our desks do not represent the Americans who have the most to gain by greater access to information. We already have the means to find out most of what we want to know, electronically or through books, magazines, and, most importantly, through telephone calls to fellow members of the informed. Moreover, our basic needs (e.g., for health, education, and a job) are largely met.[66]

Just as the inability to read has often isolated people from the mainstream of society, technological "illiteracy" threatens to marginalize those who lack technology access. Helping adults learn to use information tools promotes lifelong learning and independence. Everyone is entitled to know how to make effective use of the variety, quality, and quantity of information available as well as the powerful tools for creating and manipulating information (see box 3-H).

CONCLUSIONS

The findings of this chapter on adults and learning have several important implications for literacy policy planning. Contrary to stereotype, adults with low literacy skills are strong and resourceful, skilled and knowledgeable. Each brings a wealth of concepts, knowledge, and experience as a base for new learning. These

---

[64] Anthony W. Bates, "Adult Learning From Educational Television: The Open University Experience," *Learning From Television: Psychological and Educational Research*, Michael J.A. Howe (ed.) (London, England: Academic Press, 1983), pp. 73-74.

[65] John A. Gretes, "Using Interactive Videodisc for the Assessment of Adult Learning Styles," paper present at the NATO Advanced Research Workshop "Item Banking: Interactive Testing and Self-Assessment," Liege, Belgium, Oct. 27-31, 1992.

[66] Francis D. Fisher, "What the Coming Telecommunications Infrastructure Could Mean to Our Family," *The Aspen Institute Quarterly*, vol. 5, No. 1, winter 1993, p. 121.

Box 3-H—Television as Everyday Teacher: The Importance of Media Literacy[1]

Television is everywhere. Over 98 percent of all households own at least one television set. After work and sleep, television viewing is reported to be the most frequent activity for adults. John Goodlad, in his book, *A Place Called School*, concludes that television has become the "common school" in contemporary society—more so than the public schools.[2]

Television has become the primary source of information for many Americans— particularly those for whom reading print is difficult. Less educated and poorer citizens spend more time viewing television than the better educated and more affluent.[3] OTA's case studies suggest that many immigrants value television as an important information source—a way to find out about American culture, to obtain news, and to improve their English skills. Many also use it as a means of encountering, albeit electronically, native speakers of English, a feat that most cannot accomplish otherwise. In the words of one immigrant: "I watch the news and soap operas. 'Young and Restless' is a favorite. There's a lot of stories. It helps me find out about American life."[4] After almost 50 years, television's impact on people's everyday understanding, as well as its capacity to educate, may still be seriously underestimated.

Television, like print in the past, is now our major medium of communication. Yet the idea that television has also created the need for a different literacy has not been widely recognized. After all, print literacy only became a desirable goal of society after the invention of the printing press. The problem may be that television is so pervasive and, in its broadcast form, so accessible and available to all with such little effort, that it seems everyone is fluent in its language. But just because most people have achieved a minimum level of proficiency does not mean that higher levels are not possible or necessary.

The distinction between information and entertainment on television has become increasingly blurred. "News is entertainment and entertainment is news . . . (Viewers) know as much about police stations and emergency wards from television drama as from information programming or their own experience."[5] The "language" of television is hard to recognize because the information received from watching TV looks and sounds real. But just because it presents moving images, natural sounds, and spoken language does not mean it is real life. Television is just as artificial and symbolic as the printed word. People can understand it, just as they can understand their native language without reading or writing it, but their relationship to it is likely to be passive not active.

Technology is now available to foster the mass proliferation of video "literacy." Small format camcorders and VCRs are to video literacy what the printing press was to written literacy. There could be a camcorder in every classroom. Children and adults could learn how to "read and write" fluently in the language of their time.

With this in mind, Charles Brover of York College in New York City asked some professional video producers to teach his adult literacy class about basic production. Then he challenged his students to create a video program of their own and they accepted enthusiastically. Not only did his students do a lot of writing and reading as they planned the production but ". . . there are some secondary advantages as well," says Brover. "They're thinking of television differently, they're paying more attention to what they see on television and are more critical about it. . . . I think that it's taken out some of the magic of it, but mainly I think it's made them agents of literacy and so it's very exciting for me."

---

[1] Adapted from Christine Holland and Jim St.Lawrence, "Does Video Instruction Have a Part to Play in Adult Literacy Programs," unpublished manuscript, 1993.

[2] John I. Goodlad, *A Place Called School: Prospects for the Future* (New York, NY: McGraw-Hill, 1984).

[3] Barbara A. Marchilonis and Herman Niebuhr, *Television Technologies in Combatting Illiteracy: A Monograph*, ED 253 772 (Washington, DC: National Institute of Education, 1985).

[4] Center for Literacy Studies, University of Tennessee, Knoxville, "Life at the Margins: Profiles of Adults With Low Literacy Skills," OTA contractor report, March 1992, p. 138.

[5] Tamar Liebes, "Television, Parents and the Political Socialization of Children," *Teachers College Record*, vol. 94, No. 1, fall 1992, p. 74.

adults are not passive vessels into which learning should be poured, but active builders of their own skills and knowledge—participants in the educational process. These adults are capable of making choices, of mastering their own learning tools, and of becoming competent consumers of learning opportunities. The delivery of literacy services must consider these learners as potential consumers exercising choice over available options.

The great majority of adults needing literacy skills do not participate in educational programs for which they are eligible. The problem of nonparticipation—what causes it and how factors such as culture and life history may affect it—needs to be better understood. New models of education, tools of instruction, and methods for delivery need to be developed that will appeal to nonparticipants.

Adult learners participate in learning opportunities for a wide variety of reasons, which include, but are not limited to, employment and workforce participation. ''Adult literacy education must focus on meeting learners' goals, for as long as participation is voluntary society can reap its benefits only if learners are able to reap their own.''[67] Literacy policy and planning needs to recognize that learners have a broad range of learning goals and outcomes. Adult literacy education can be viewed as an investment in an educated citizenry. To paraphrase Thomas Jefferson, education should enable all citizens to exercise the rights of self-government and to pursue happiness and individual development within society. Literacy policy and practice can be developed to build on the goals and motivations of individual learners.

---

[67] Beder, op. cit., footnote 36, p. 161.

The Literacy System: A Patchwork of Programs and Resources | 4

The literacy service delivery ''system'' is a heterogeneous and eclectic mix of funding sources, programs, administrative agencies, and service providers. Literacy programs range from individual tutors working one-on-one with learners in small voluntary programs to federally sponsored research efforts affecting thousands of learners. Instruction and services are provided by school districts, community colleges, employers, labor unions, community-based organizations, libraries, and churches. Programs take many different approaches: some focus on basic reading and writing skills; others on family-based literacy, workplace literacy, or on daily living skills; and some tackle literacy as an element of job training. This complex, diverse system is frequently criticized for being fragmented and inadequate. There is an almost universal sense that more can and should be done, and that it can and should be done better.

FINDINGS

- The providers of adult literacy services are diverse and do not form a comprehensive system for addressing the literacy needs of the Nation. Students seeking literacy assistance are confronted with a web of disconnected, often overlapping programs.
- There is no one best approach to providing adult literacy services, but some programs have been more successful in meeting learners' needs than others. Success seems to reflect greater resources, secure funding, and a philosophy that responds to the learner's individual needs.
- Data do not currently exist to enable the Office of Technology Assessment (OTA) to make any reasonable estimate of the

total funding devoted to adult literacy education. Public support is the most identifiable source. Federal funding has grown significantly in the last few years, and has provided leadership, leveraging other dollars toward adult literacy. However, the greatest growth over the last decade has been in State support, now outstripping Federal funding for literacy. As the major funders, Federal and State programs and policies largely define who is served and how and where they are served.

- The overall amount spent by business and industry on literacy training for their workers is expanding due to union and public perception of the links between literacy and economic competitiveness, but there is no aggregate data on these programs.

- A number of factors, including new Federal and State laws, a diverse population of learners, and changing technologies have combined to increase the variety of learning sites and public and private agencies funding and administering programs. Most importantly, new opportunities go beyond the traditional school-based programs run by local education agencies (LEAs).

- The content of adult basic education (ABE), adult secondary education, preparation for the general equivalency diploma (GED) examination, and English as a second language (ESL) instruction shows little variation across program sponsors. An increasing emphasis on matching curriculum to the learner's daily needs has led to more contextualized content, especially as workforce and family literacy programs gain in popularity.

- Most programs have been based on an open-entry/open-exit model, allowing students to proceed at their own pace and leave when they choose. While this approach is important for adults and assumes different motivational factors than those of schoolchildren, it also means that many adults do not remain in programs long enough to receive the full benefit of instruction.

Rapid turnover and high dropout rates lead to limited learning gains.

- Most instruction is provided by part-time or volunteer teachers. Certified teachers are generally K-12 educators without special training in the art and science of teaching adults. Volunteers receive little training and support for the challenges they are expected to meet.

- Funding is a constant concern. For most programs, unstable and short-term funding make it difficult to plan, to purchase necessary equipment or materials, or to develop professional staffing ladders. The instability of funding also gives a negative message to the clients.

- The use of technology in adult literacy programs is limited, but growing. Technology can offer benefits for individual learners and for program management. For today's labor-intensive system, technology is an alternative for overburdened programs unable to provide comprehensive individualized instruction to large numbers of students.

- The barriers to more effective use of technology are similar to those faced in K-12 education, but more severe in adult literacy programs. These barriers include funding limitations, staff unschooled in teaching with technological tools, administrators unaware of technology's potential, and uneven curriculum coverage in current software.

THE DELIVERY SYSTEM

The patchwork of the present system is best understood by answering these questions: who provides the funds, who administers the programs, who is being served, what kind of instruction do they receive, and who are the teachers?

Who Provides the Funds?

Money for programs comes from many sources: Federal, State, regional, and local government agencies on the public side and businesses, unions, foundations, charitable institutions, and individual donors on the private side. Estimating a total amount of literacy funding is complicated because most programs receive support from multiple public and private sources, literacy services may be subsumed under broader funding categories, and data collection requirements of sponsors do not necessarily complement one another. OTA finds that it is impossible to specify the total amount spent on adult literacy services across the Nation.

It is clear, however, that the public sector is the most identifiable and largest source of support. Consequently, the public sector has an enormous effect on program administration.

Federal Programs and Dollars

The Federal Government supports adult literacy education through an assortment of targeted programs administered by several Federal agencies. These programs not only provide a base of funding for local literacy efforts, but also greatly influence State and local funding, administrative structures, priorities, target populations, services, and instructional approaches. These efforts are explored in more detail in chapter 5.

At least 29 different Federal programs in 7 agencies support adult literacy and basic skills education as one of their primary purposes, and many more include adult literacy as a peripheral goal. Chief among the Federal literacy programs is the Adult Education Act (AEA), administered by the U.S. Department of Education (ED). In fiscal year 1992, the AEA provided $270 million for the following programs: State basic grants; State literacy resource centers; workplace literacy partnerships; English literacy programs; and national research, evaluation, and demonstration. ED also supports literacy education through special programs for adult prisoners, commercial drivers, homeless adults, Native American adults, and migrant adults, and through the Even Start Family Literacy Program, the Bilingual Family Literacy Program, the Library Services and Construction Act, and the Student Literacy Corps.

Although ED continues to have primary responsibility for adult education, the influence of other agencies, particularly the Departments of Health and Human Services (HHS) and Labor (DOL), is growing. HHS administers the new Federal $1-billion Job Opportunities and Basic Skills (JOBS) training program for welfare recipients, as well as programs for refugees and eligible legalized aliens and family literacy activities under the Head Start program. DOL has responsibility for the $4-billion Job Training Partnership Act (JTPA), which authorizes basic skills education as a means toward its primary goal of workforce development for disadvantaged youth and adults. Other Federal programs with adult literacy and basic skills education as a major purpose are spread across other agencies, including the Departments of Defense, Justice, and Interior, and ACTION.

Because many Federal programs authorizing multiple activities do not require that obligations or expenditures for adult education activities be reported separately, available data is limited for estimating Federal funding.[1] At best, one can arrive at a partial, low-end estimate by totaling identifiable adult education and literacy obligations. Using this method, OTA estimates the fiscal year 1992 spending for adult literacy to be *a minimum* of $362 million.[2]

State and Local Programs and Dollars

All States participate in the major Federal literacy-related programs, and most participate in several smaller Federal programs as well. In addition, States fund their own programs, both to fulfill their matching responsibilities under Federal programs and to carry out State-identified priorities. As a result, State-level activities and programs in support of literacy vary considerably.

---

[1] Judith A. Alamprese and Donna M. Hughes, *Study of Federal Funding Sources and Services for Adult Education* (Washington, DC: Cosmos Corp., 1990), p. vi.

[2] See ch. 5 for further discussion.

Box 4-A—Baltimore: The City That Reads[1]

Of all the things I might be able to accomplish as Mayor of our city, it would make me proudest if one day it could be said of Baltimore that this is the city that reads.[2]

"The City That Reads" is Baltimore's slogan, emblazoned on park benches, trash trucks, and billboards throughout the city. Moving from rhetoric to reality has been a major challenge in a city where an estimated 200,000 of its 736,000 residents live with functional illiteracy. The Mayor's first step was forming a collaboration with United Way of Central Maryland, creating two linked but significantly different organizations:

- *Baltimore City Literacy Corp. (BCLC):* A "quasi-governmental" agency under the mayor's office that works with other governmental agencies and is principally responsible for developing the city's literacy initiatives.
- *Baltimore Reads, Inc. (BRI):* a private, nonprofit corporation, with responsibility for fund-raising and coordinating the partnership. The director of BCLC also directs BRI, although it has its own independent board of directors drawn from the business community, United Way, schools, AFL-CIO, newspapers, the Junior League, YMCA, churches, social service agencies, and political leaders.

The political clout of the new mayor produced quick results. Within 6 months, a variety of agencies with literacy interests but no previous history of collaboration—the Job Training Partnership Act (JTPA), the Community College's adult basic education program, the public library, and community-based organizations—came together to create a strategic plan. BCLC would develop several new literacy centers that were to become self-sustaining, and BRI would coordinate the efforts of a number of existing community-based programs. The Mayor's Office and the United Way each contributed $75,000 to these efforts.

One early challenge was building consensus in the literacy provider community. It was helpful to have a director with skills in community organizing with no vested literacy interests; her "neutrality" helped create a working partnership among the many factions. The continuing support of the mayor, in combination with the United Way,

---

[1] This box is based on OTA site visits and a case study by J.D. Eveland et al., Claremont Graduate School, "Case Studies of Technology Use in Adult Literacy Programs," OTA contractor report, June 1991, pp. 77-101.

[2] Mayor Kurt Schmoke, Inaugural Address, 1987.

New Jersey, for example, administers 63 different basic skills and literacy programs through 6 different State agencies; Illinois reports 33 different funding sources.[3]

Many State agencies are involved in the administration of literacy-related programs. Although State administrative structures roughly track the Federal structure—ED funds flow to State education agencies, JOBS funds to welfare agencies, library funds to State libraries—there are important variations by State. In many States, the agency with responsibility for elementary and secondary education programs also administers adult education.[4] Other States place adult education in agencies responsible for vocational education, community colleges, or job training.

To bring coherence to literacy efforts, 40 States have created State-level coalitions to coordinate

---

[3] U.S. Department of Education, *A Summary Report: National Forums on the Adult Education Delivery System* (Washington, DC: U.S. Government Printing Office, 1991), p. 15.

[4] Critics have charged that this arrangement, which has historical precedent in the AEA, has contributed to the "second-class status" of the adult basic education program. See William F. Pierce, "A Redefined Role in Adult Literacy: Integrated Policies, Programs, and Procedures," background paper for the Project on Adult Literacy, Southport Institute, 1988, p. 16.

provided a strong foundation for the program to evolve. Baltimore Reads also received considerable publicity and financial support from the family of baseball star Cal Ripken.[3]

"Baltimore Reads" has become an integrated system of citywide literacy programs and includes a hotline, literacy hubs and satellites, technical support and assistance, and research into challenges faced by adult learners. The original six community-based literacy programs have expanded to 21 programs. Baltimore's literacy efforts leverage Federal, State, and local monies, as well as business and foundation support. The city's share of Federal Adult Education Act funds, administered at present through the community college, are supplemented by Federal library service funds, $800,000 from city-administered JTPA funds, State welfare reform, and a separate State Literacy Works Program.

The BCLC/BRI program provides curriculum expertise and technological support to local literacy efforts. A curriculum specialist helps programs identify useful materials and instructional approaches, and maintain contact with the professional literacy community. One of BRI's major goals is to experiment with and evaluate new technologies to provide technical assistance and a "technology vision" to local programs. Since most programs have neither the resources to acquire hardware and software nor the expertise to install and maintain it, BRI's technical specialist—"the Indiana Jones of used computers"—plays a variety of roles, from "computer guru," to part-time classroom teacher, to software evaluator. A used computer donation program has increased the installed hardware base; e.g., when a city department changed its system, BRI received the 10 computers that were being replaced.

Various technologies have been installed in different centers. For example, in the Ripken Center a computer laboratory with an integrated learning system supplements classroom instruction. Students can listen to lessons on headphones, which helps those with low reading skills. One student noted: "The headphones give instruction, put reading on the brain." Baltimore's public library system plans to open small computing centers in four of its local branches to allow computer access for area residents, with assistance from BRI's technical specialist. The Ripken Center is also a test site for software under development by the Educational Testing Service, an interactive video and computing system used to teach problem-solving strategies in the areas of document, text, and numerical literacy.

---

[3] Ripken, a Baltimore local and Orioles baseball team hero, appears in public service announcements, does baseball card signing to support BRI, and, through the program "Reading, Runs, and Ripken," money is donated to BRI based on the home runs hit by Ripken over the season. He and his wife have been leading financial backers and literacy advocates for the city. One of BRI's new literacy centers is named "The Cal Ripken, Jr. Literacy Center."

literacy agencies and organizations.[5] Some are placed under the Governor's Office,[6] while others are placed under the Department of Education[7] or another existing agency such as the Office of Community Colleges,[8] Public Library Office,[9] or Department of Commerce.[10] These coalitions serve predominantly as public information resources; few are able to coordinate programs and policy for all the relevant service providers in their State.

Many cities and localities also provide public funding for literacy services and solicit funding from local industry and philanthropic sources (see box 4-A). Most major cities have literacy councils

---

[5] Robert A. Silvanik, *Toward Integrated Adult Learning Systems: The Status of State Literacy Efforts* (Washington, DC: National Governors' Association, 1991), p. vii.

[6] Arkansas, Florida, Hawaii, Indiana, Maryland, Massachusetts, Mississippi, Nevada, New York, and North Carolina.

[7] Arizona, Colorado, Connecticut, Iowa, Maine, Michigan, Rhode Island, and Utah.

[8] Oregon.

[9] Alabama, District of Columbia, and Wyoming.

[10] Texas.

that provide public information on literacy resources, coordinate efforts to connect learners with programs, and provide technical assistance, training, and funding assistance.

It is difficult to determine how much funding for adult education comes from all State and local sources, especially as compared to the Federal share. States face the same problems as the Federal Government in accurately estimating contributions from all relevant sources, especially from programs in which basic skills education is just one of many allowable activities. Local literacy programs generally keep detailed data on receipts and expenditures, in categories defined for their own needs.

Statistics are available on State and local matching contributions under the AEA, the major source of Federal funding for adult literacy in many States. These statistics show that State and local matching expenditures for adult education have mushroomed in the past several years and now outstrip Federal AEA contributions. For example, while Federal expenditures for adult education rose from $100 to $158 million between 1980 and 1990, during the same time period State and local expenditures went from $74 to $622 million.[11] (See figure 4-1.)

Care must be taken in interpreting estimates of AEA matching funds. First, aggregate data mask wide variations among States and localities (see table 4-1). Most of the growth in State and local matching funds is attributable to large increases in a handful of States,[12] with several States providing only the minimum match required by law or slightly more.[13] One 1990 study of nine geographically diverse local programs found that in five sites, State and local dollars provided the majority of support, ranging from 67 to 95 percent of the total, while in the other four Federal funding predominated.[14] In addition, AEA matching funds may not be a reliable proxy for total State spending, since past studies have found that States may underreport their true AEA contributions.[15] Moreover, these AEA matching expenditures are only part of the picture. State and local matching under other Federal programs—such as JOBS, public library programs, and Even Start—is increasing the pool of total literacy funding, as are expenditures for State-initiated literacy programs. Finally, the growth in State funding may be slowing as some States confront fiscal crises.

In sum, while aggregate State and local funding has grown—and likely exceeds aggregate Federal funding from all sources—the Federal Government remains the leading partner in some States, an essential partner in the rest, and a catalyst for funding in all.

Private Support

Private support for literacy comes from many sources: foundations, United Way contributions, businesses, unions, and individuals. While there are a few corporations and foundations supporting literacy efforts nationwide—the United Par-

---

[11] Federal Basic Grants to States under the Adult Education Act were $100 million in fiscal year 1980 and $157.8 million in fiscal year 1990 (actual dollars). This represents a 57.8 percent increase since 1980. State and local expenditures were $74.3 million in fiscal year 1980 and $622.1 million (actual dollars) in fiscal year 1990, a 737.4 percent increase since 1980. Figure 4-1 shows this growth in adjusted dollars. R.S. Pugsley, Office of Vocational and Adult Education, Division of Adult Education and Literacy, U.S. Department of Education, personal communication, October 1992.

[12] Joan Y. Seamon, director, Division of Adult Education and Literacy, U.S. Department of Education, personal communication, Apr. 1, 1992.

[13] The State minimum acceptable match increased from 10 to 15 percent for fiscal year 1990, to 20 percent for fiscal year 1991, and to 25 percent for fiscal year 1992.

[14] Mark A. Kutner et al., *Adult Education Programs and Services: A View From Nine Programs* (Washington, DC: Pelavin Associates, 1990), p. iii.

[15] Ibid. The incentive to underreport likely stems from a desire to have more flexibility in the use of State funding, since funds that are not reported as matching are not governed by AEA planning and other requirements.

Figure 4-1—A Comparison of Federal[a] and State/Local[b] Expenditures for Adult Education, Fiscal Years 1980-93

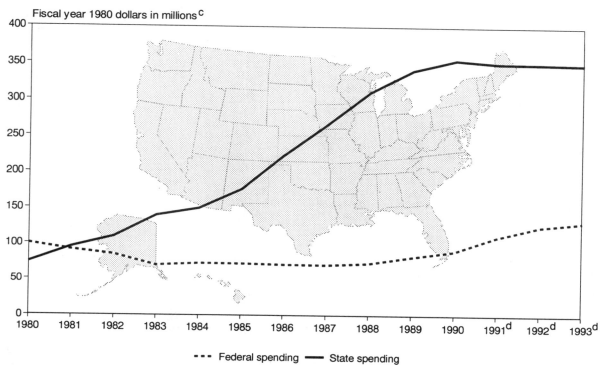

Fiscal year 1980 dollars in millions[c]

- - - Federal spending   —— State spending

[a] Federal dollars are Federal basic grants to States under the Adult Education Act.
[b] State/local expenditures for 1991, 1992, and 1993 are estimates by the U.S. Department of Education.
[c] Fiscal year 1980 dollars were calculated using the Congressional Research Service's Implicit Deflator for State and Local Government Purchases of Services.
[d] Estimated State/local expenditure.

SOURCE: R.S. Pugsley, U.S. Department of Education, Division of Adult Education and Literacy, Office of Vocational and Adult Education, unpublished data, October 1992.

cel Service Foundation, Coors Brewing Co., and Toyota Motor Corp., to name three of the largest efforts—many more companies support efforts benefiting literacy activities in the communities where their employees live and work (see table 4-2). Industries spend millions of dollars training their own employees in basic skills,[16] as well as supporting overall literacy efforts in their communities. Unions have provided support for literacy out of general dues or, in some cases, on a shared basis with industry (see box 4-B).

Who Administers Programs and Provides the Services?

In the literacy world, distinctions must be made among the entities that provide the funding, those that administer the programs, and those that deliver the actual services to adults. Often these entities are different. For example, a local service provider, such as a community-based organization (CBO), may receive funding from several different Federal and State programs and private

---

[16] The total spent by employers, government agencies, and unions on improving employee basic skills is not known precisely, but probably does not greatly exceed $1 billion per year. U.S. Congress, Office of Technology Assessment, *Worker Training: Competing in the New International Economy*, OTA-ITE-457 (Washington, DC: U.S. Government Printing Office, September 1990), p. 154.

Table 4-1—Fiscal Year 1990 Expenditures and Enrollments Under the Adult Education Act, State-by-State Comparison

State or other area	Total Federal expenditures	Total State/local expenditures	Total expenditures	State match	1990 total enrollment	Cost per student
Alabama	$2,777,200	$2,800,304	$5,577,504	50.21%	40,177	$159
Alaska	378,254	1,760,960	2,139,214	82.32	5,067	406
Arizona	1,487,000	2,725,057	4,212,057	64.70	33,805	90
Arkansas	1,782,390	7,442,486	9,224,876	80.68	29,065	305
California	9,196,782	216,952,480	226,149,262	95.93	1,021,227	238
Colorado	1,343,385	357,748	1,701,133	21.03	12,183	82
Connecticut	1,772,830	11,921,606	13,694,436	87.05	46,434	220
Delaware	544,735	230,091	774,826	29.70	2,662	260
District of Columbia	604,801	4,220,535	4,825,336	87.47	19,586	401
Florida	5,611,296	52,679,924	58,291,220	90.37	419,429	372
Georgia	3,742,737	2,601,315	6,344,052	41.00	69,580	54
Hawaii	571,644	1,388,706	1,960,350	70.84	52,012	53
Idaho	648,262	180,000	828,262	21.73	11,171	61
Illinois	6,290,817	7,304,958	13,595,775	53.73	87,121	151
Indiana	3,132,164	21,748,771	24,880,935	87.41	44,166	427
Iowa	1,588,770	3,329,586	4,918,356	67.70	41,507	103
Kansas	1,288,997	287,351	1,576,348	18.23	10,274	148
Kentucky	2,509,184	263,625	2,792,809	10.16	26,090	231
Louisiana	2,838,563	6,244,123	9,082,686	68.75	40,039	174
Maine	814,526	4,351,264	5,165,790	84.23	14,964	89
Maryland	2,458,855	3,601,401	6,060,256	59.43	41,230	100
Massachusetts	2,877,406	9,621,265	12,498,671	76.98	34,220	313
Michigan	4,904,768	123,452,005	128,356,773	96.18	194,178	1,415
Minnesota	2,025,941	10,714,081	12,740,022	84.10	45,648	493
Mississippi	1,902,422	335,722	2,238,144	15.00	18,957	101
Missouri	3,056,131	1,606,738	4,662,869	34.46	31,815	143
Montana	584,101	403,231	1,077,422	45.78	6,071	162
Nebraska	924,073	190,258	1,114,331	17.07	6,158	84
Nevada	591,838	465,856	1,057,694	44.04	17,262	331
New Hampshire	666,701	536,041	1,202,742	44.57	7,198	151
New Jersey	4,083,836	19,519,833	23,603,671	82.70	64,080	108
New Mexico	886,496	1,357,127	2,243,623	60.49	30,236	72
New York	9,719,848	26,777,640	36,497,488	73.37	156,611	231
North Carolina	4,219,967	19,311,736	23,531,703	82.07	109,740	235
North Dakota	574,554	257,777	832,331	30.97	3,587	394
Ohio	5,836,288	6,471,483	12,307,771	52.58	95,476	126
Oklahoma	1,830,980	285,600	2,116,580	13.49	24,307	73
Oregon	1,217,964	7,345,449	8,563,413	85.78	37,075	206
Pennsylvania	6,784,560	1,214,589	7,999,149	15.18	52,444	152
Rhode Island	821,483	1,400,943	2,222,426	63.04	7,347	240
South Carolina	2,351,279	7,789,840	10,141,119	76.81	81,200	121
South Dakota	590,200	164,098	754,298	21.76	3,184	166
Tennessee	3,113,800	525,977	3,369,777	14.45	41,721	90
Texas	8,437,165	7,608,691	16,045,856	47.42	218,747	70
Utah	722,932	3,484,000	4,206,932	82.82	24,841	169
Vermont	484,168	2,086,009	2,570,177	81.16	4,808	505
Virginia	3,394,170	3,210,757	6,604,927	48.61	31,649	203
Washington	1,631,503	5,208,345	6,839,848	76.15	31,776	201
West Virginia	1,528,239	1,286,216	2,814,455	45.70	21,186	106
Wisconsin	2,513,690	6,360,491	8,874,181	71.67	61,081	217
Wyoming	412,459	267,329	679,788	39.33	3,578	166
Puerto Rico	2,630,440	308,337	2,938,777	10.49	28,436	98
Guam	149,021	0	149,021	0.00	1,311	81
No. Marina Is.	99,943	0	99,943	0.00	160	382
United States	$132,951,650	$622,069,755	$755,021,405	82.39%[a]	3,565,877	$217[a]

[a] Average.

SOURCE: U.S. Department of Education, Division of Adult Education and Literacy, Office of Vocational and Adult Education, n.d.

Table 4-2—Examples of Private Sector Support for Literacy

Donor foundation or company	Recent grants (amount and date)	Description of literary support
Barbara Bush Foundation for Family Literacy	1990: $500,000 1991: $500,000 1992: $500,000	Grants to 10-15 organizations (for up to $50,000 each) to establish community family literacy programs, train teachers, and publish and disseminate materials documenting successful programs.
Bell Atlantic	1989-91: $595,000 1992-95: $500,000	In cooperation with American Library Association, establishes library-based family literacy programs in local libraries in mid-Atlantic States.
Black and Decker Stanley Tools	1991: $100,000 in tools, manuals, and other job materials	In partnership with HomeBuilders Institute and U.S. Department of Education, to upgrade education and skills for construction workers.
Coors Brewing Co.	1990: 5-year, $40-million grant	"Literacy. Pass It On" program commitment to provide literacy services to 500,000 adults through literacy hotline, support to volunteer organizations, and an advertising campaign to raise awareness of the literacy needs of women.
William H. Donner Foundation	1990: $336,000 1991: $96,500	Multiyear grants to support innovative literary projects in community-based organizations (CBOs), for young first offenders in a work camp in Tennessee, and for unemployed ex-offenders on release from correctional institutions.
John S. and James L. Knight Foundation	1990: $309,000 1991: $233,000 1992: $597,000	Supports projects in 26 urban and rural communities where Knight-Ridder newspapers operate. Recent grants supported hiring staff, creating computer labs, establishing hotlines, and purchasing and creating texts and software for a range of literacy programs.
Southland Corp. (7-Eleven Stores)	1991: $120,000	Grants to 77 community literacy organizations in Maryland, Virginia, West Virginia, and the District of Columbia.
Toyota Motor Corp.	1991: 3-year, $2-million grant	Grant to National Center for Family Literacy to establish intergenerational literacy programs in five cities under national grant competition.
United Parcel Service Foundation	Phase I—1989: $2.25 million Phase II—1992: $1.51 million	Grants to United Way of America, Association for Community Based Education, Literacy South, Manpower Demonstration Research Corp., U.S. Basics, and local literacy volunteer agencies for capacity building, training instructors and staff in CBOs, and developing new family literacy projects.

SOURCE: Office of Technology Assessment, 1993, based on reports from Business Council for Effective Literacy, U.S. Department of Education, Foundation and Corporate Grants Alert, and personal communications.

sources, and may have to adhere to the requirements of the several different agencies or organizations that administer these programs. Conversely, a Federal agency may channel funding to a State administrative institution, which in turn makes grants to several different types of local service providers.

Several different types of organizations administer local programs, including LEAs, CBOs, libraries, community colleges, regional administrative units, and others. Numerous entities also provide the actual literacy services, among them schools, community colleges, businesses and industries, correctional facilities, and community and volunteer agencies. Federal administrative structures and funding streams seem to have a major influence on who administers funds and provides services at the local level: JTPA services tend to be provided by CBOs, library literacy services by libraries, and AEA services by LEAs. Because AEA is the largest and most influential program, education agencies are the predominant

Box 4-B—Ford's Skills Enhancement Program[1]

"Doug" is typical of Ford Motor Company's 100,000 employees at over 80 sites. Fifty-two years old, he's worked at the Walton Hills stamping plant in northeast Ohio ever since dropping out of school after the 11th grade to go to work.[2] Although he's not far from retirement, Doug fears being laid off before then. "At my age, and with my seniority, where can I get a job with this pay?" ($35,000). Doug is unnerved by the technological changes in the plant, but when the union encouraged members to attend classes, he hesitated. "I spent 3 weeks coming up to the door, trying to build the courage to come in. I wasn't sure if maybe people would find out I can't read so great and then it might look bad for me on my job."

Ford's Skills Enhancement Program (SEP) was set up under a United Auto Workers-Ford collective-bargaining agreement in 1982. The program is funded under Ford's Education, Development and Training Program (EDTP) serving hourly employees nationwide. Company contributions, based on hours worked per employee, generate approximately $40 million per year for the program.

Since EDTP activities are on the employees' own time and supported by monies that would otherwise go to worker wages, the union is careful to distinguish the EDTP programs from job training activities that are Ford's responsibility to provide to employees during working hours. The SEP is one of the several EDTP "Avenues for Growth," including: 1) tuition for personal development courses; 2) college tuition assistance and onsite classes; 3) retirement counseling; 4) financial planning; and 5) advisers for general life/education planning. SEP began in 1983 as basic skills enhancement with offerings in adult basic education, general equivalency diploma (GED), high school completion, and English as a second language. In 1987, the word "basic" was dropped from the title because of the stigma it created; at the same time, more upper-level classes were added to improve the image of the program. Confidentiality is central to the program. "People see me in the lab and don't know if I'm learning basic fractions or math for statistical process control. There isn't the sense of being dumb if you are in there."

Central features of SEP include individual assessment, academic advising, open-entry/open-exit participation, competency-based instruction, and varied instructional techniques, using a considerable amount of computer-aided instruction. Having the program onsite reduces some of the negative associations with school that some workers have not shaken from their younger days, and makes it possible for workers to come in at breaks or before or after shifts. Using an integrated learning system, employees can pick up exactly where they left off, eliminating a lot of otherwise wasted time trying to get started. "It's totally pressure free. I can go back over and over the material until I get it. And besides, it's fun. You can't just pick up a history book and keep reading. You'd fall asleep. The computer keeps you interested, keeps you going."

Walton Hills is more heavily computer-oriented than other centers for another practical reason: space at the plant is at a premium. The 30- by 10-foot classroom has space for computers along three of the walls, a few cabinets, and two small tables that seat about six people each. There is very little group instruction; rather, students walk in, pick up their assignment sheets, and go to work on their own, using the teacher as a resource. Placement testing is available, but some learners, like Doug, are afraid of tests. "I'd rather start at the beginning and, if that's too easy, I can always move ahead."

Instruction is provided by the United Technologies Center (UTC), a self-supporting arm of nearby Cayahoga Community College. Walton Hills contracted with UTC because of its extensive resources and experience with computer-aided instruction. The UTC manager at Walton Hills is a full-time instructor and three other teachers, now retired, share two and one-half part-time positions in the program. The participants are typical of the 2,000 hourly employees at the plant, but there is a much higher participation rate among women than men.

Seven of Doug's fellow classmates have passed the GED, but, even though his teacher thinks he's ready, Doug's been hesitating. "I'm not sure—tests and I don't get along. It costs a lot more to take the test here at work, but I'm not sure about taking it at the high school. Just walking in the door there, the smells, everything about that place makes me feel bad all over again. But here at work I like being a student."

---

[1] This box is based on an OTA site visit and a case study by J.D. Eveland et al., Claremont Graduate School, "Case Studies of Technology Use in Adult Literacy Programs," OTA contractor report, June 1992, pp. 135-161. "Doug" is a fictious name.

[2] About half of Ford's hourly employees have completed only high school; the other half is equally divided between those with some college and those who never finished high school.

administering agency and also the primary service deliverer, and schools the most common site of service delivery. Currently, 60 percent of the funding under the AEA State grant program goes to LEAs; the remainder goes to higher education institutions (22 percent), and a mix of intermediate agencies, other State agencies, and CBOs.[17]

Within these general trends, States have developed various delivery systems, taking greater or lesser advantage of the latitude that exists in most Federal laws for using a range of local service providers. For example, Massachusetts distributes AEA funds through a direct competitive grant process that puts CBOs and other nonschool providers on equal footing with LEAs; as a result, CBOs receive about one-half the AEA funding.[18] Texas—a populous State covering a vast geographic area—has used a unique regional approach to deliver adult education services. Texas channels adult education funding from several sources (including the AEA, the State adult education program, State Legalization Impact Assistance Grants (SLIAG), and JOBS) through 60 regional cooperatives, headed by a locally designated fiscal agent. Most of the fiscal agents are independent school districts, but some are education service centers and public community colleges or universities. Each cooperative in turn arranges for services to be delivered through a network of public, private, and volunteer agencies and organizations in the local community.[19]

As a result of recent amendments to the AEA encouraging funding for nonschool providers and new emphases like workplace literacy and family literacy, a shift may be occurring from LEA and school-based programs to nontraditional and voluntary literacy providers. CBOs are playing a larger role. A recent study showed that, overall, CBOs receive about two-thirds of their funds from government sources[20] and the remaining one-third from nongovernment sources.[21] Many are affiliated with another organization—the public library, public school system, volunteer organization, or other institution—with whom they may share space, tutors or teachers, instructional materials or training, fund-raising efforts, or other arrangements for joint program operation.[22]

Volunteer programs also play an important role, especially in reaching the most disadvantaged learners. The two major volunteer organizations, Literacy Volunteers of America (LVA) and the Laubach Literacy Action (LLA) are training more volunteer tutors and serving an increasing number of learners (see box 4-C). Together the two organizations serve over 200,000 learners in over 1,500 programs nationwide.[23] Some of their 150,000 volunteers work one-on-one with learners as private tutors, while others perform administrative assistance or assist teachers in ABE programs.[24] Both LVA and LLA support their efforts largely through sales of adult education

---

[17] U.S. Department of Education, *Distribution of State-Administered Federal Education Funds: Thirteenth Annual Report* (Washington, DC: 1989), p. 54.

[18] Robert Bickerton, director, Bureau of Adult Education, Massachusetts Department of Education, personal communication, January 1992.

[19] Pavlos Roussos, Texas Education Agency program director for adult education, notes that the cooperative system is an effective approach because it reduces duplication, paperwork, and costs; improves accountability and facilitates coordination of programs at the local level; and enables the State to provide some level of service in most communities. Personal communication, January 1992.

[20] An average of 50 percent from State sources; 30 percent from Federal sources, and 20 percent from local government sources. Association for Community Based Education, *National Directory of Community Based Adult Literacy Programs* (Washington, DC: 1989), p. 71.

[21] Averaging almost $20,000, of which 26 percent comes from foundations, 18 percent from corporations, 17 percent from United Way, 12 percent from religious organizations, 6 percent from tuition, and 22 percent from miscellaneous other sources. Ibid., p. 71.

[22] Ibid., p. 71.

[23] Ellen Tannenbaum and William Strang, *The Major National Adult Literacy Volunteer Organizations, Final Report, Volume 1: A Descriptive Review*, prepared for the U.S. Department of Education, (Rockville, MD: Westat, Inc., 1992), pp. 57-58.

[24] Ibid., p. vii.

Box 4-C—Literacy Volunteer Organizations

Volunteers are the lifeblood of many adult literacy programs. Without their commitment of time, talent, and support for adult learners on a one-to-one basis, the Nation's adult literacy efforts would be greatly impoverished.[1] Most volunteers are affiliated with one of the two major volunteer agencies, Literacy Volunteers of America (LVA) and Laubach Literacy Action (LLA) (see table).

The organizations have much in common. Both organizations have been strong advocates for adult literacy legislation and support. In many communities, volunteer programs and adult education service providers work together informally. Adult basic education (ABE) programs often refer students who need one-on-one tutoring to LVA or LLA; they in turn often send their "graduating" students on to ABE, job training, and other programs.

Volunteer tutors are given 10 to 21 hours of training in literacy instruction by the LVA or LLA and work with learners twice a week for 1 to 2 hours per session. When progress is slow, as it generally is with learners whose literacy skills are limited, it is not uncommon for either the volunteer or the learner to drop out. Many volunteers burn out and do not stay even a year.[2] Considerable effort and resources are devoted to recruiting, preparing, tracking, coordinating, and retaining volunteers. Although recruitment has become more difficult with greater numbers of women working outside the home, increased commitments of two-career families, and greater childcare and eldercare responsibilities, both LLA and LVA continue to grow. Both programs continue to seek better ways to match tutors to learners, in order to improve the learning outcomes.

Volunteers and professional staff need supervision, assistance, and evaluation, but monitoring is limited and evaluations take time, money, and expertise. LVA and LLA are working to increas professionalism in local programs through more structured training, data collection, and recordkeeping. They are creating joint training programs for trainers of tutors and local literacy program managers. One new training emphasis is tutoring in small groups, especially for ESL instruction.

Technology use is limited by lack of funding, limited technological expertise, and concern that technology could reduce personal contact between learners and tutors. While the number of LVA affiliates using computers is growing, many continue to use them for program management only. Several computer database management systems have been developed to help programs track volunteers and students.

Both organizations recognize technology's potential to extend the range of the tutor's expertise, give learners practice time beyond tutorial sessions, and train tutors. Videotapes are increasingly used to enable tutors to study professional teaching techniques on their own time. Programs are experimenting with teleconferences to link local affiliates for training and discussion.[3] Dedicated computer networks could expand connections between programs, as well as allow learners to share their writing or work in collaborative projects with learners across the room or across the country.[4] One rural program plans to make portable laptop computers available to students at home.[5] Handheld devices could be loaned to learners so they can extend their learning time to "downtime" at home, on public transportation, and during breaks on the job. Partnerships can extend the range of small programs; for example, an LVA affiliate joined with several other adult literacy agencies in their area to raise funds for a comprehensive integrated learning system. As a result of this collaboration, the LVA office gained visibility, and its expertise enabled it to become the central resource center for adult literacy in the region.[6]

---

[1] One study showed that 94 percent of local adult literacy programs used volunteers, as did 51 percent of federally funded State-administered adult education programs. U.S. Department of Education, National Center for Education Statistics, *Adult Literacy Programs: Services, Persons Served, and Volunteers*, OERI Bulletin (Washington, DC: 1986).

[2] V.K. Lawson et al., Literacy Volunteers of America, Syracuse, NY, "Evaluation Study of Program Effectiveness," January 1990, pp. 4-5.

[3] For example, the Correctional Education Association and the American Correctional Association, in cooperation with LVA and LLA, hosted several national interactive videoconferences on the subject of literacy progams for the incarcerated.

[4] An adult literacy forum, operated by the New York State LVA office on the private telecommunications link, "America Online," links volunteer programs throughout the State and participating programs around the country.

[5] Preston Miller, Literacy Volunteers of Franklin County, Malone, NY, personal communication, November 1992.

[6] Gaye Tolman, executive director, Literacy Volunteers of Maricopa County, AZ, personal communication, November 1992.

Organization	Laubach Literacy Action (LLA)	Literacy Volunteers of America (LVA)
Established	1968 in Syracuse, New York, by Frank C. Laubach	1962 in Syracuse, New York, by Ruth Colvin
Size:		
Number of local affiliates	1,023 (45 States)	434 (41 States)
Number of volunteers	98,271	51,437
Number of learners	147,087	52,338
Characteristics		
Volunteers	Not available	80% female, 50% are 45+ years of age, 75% white, 40% have attended or graduated from college, and 40% work full time.
Learners:	50% female, nearly all are over 18, two-thirds are literacy/basic reading and one-third are English as a second language (ESL) students.	50% female, most are under 45, 33% white, 21% black, 22% Hispanic, 40% report having a 9th- to 12th-grade education, and 10% report having less than a 5th-grade education.
Budget and sources	$8.7 million was received at the national level ($7.5 million from the sale of publications and $1.2 million in public or private support). Expenditures: of $8.5 million in national expenses, $5.6 million was spent on publications, $1.4 million on LLA operations, and the remainder went to international literacy operations.	$2.2 million was received at the national level; 40% from the sale of LVA publications and the remainder from public or private donations. Expenditures: of the $1.9 million in national expenses, one-half went to programs, services, and conferences; $662,000 was spent on publishing materials.
Philosophy and approach	Promotes local choices among instructional methods focusing on learners' personal goals, including the Laubach Way to Reading series of skill books based on a phonetic approach.	Eclectic, following the goals and interests of the individual student. Specific and uniform initial training of tutors is required.
Instructional method	One-on-one tutoring and some small-group instruction in basic literacy skills and ESL.	One-on-one tutoring and some small-group instruction in basic literacy skills and ESL.
Training content and commitment	10 to 18 hours of training over 3 to 4 sessions, nominal materials fee ($10), guidance and reference materials, in-service training.	18 to 21 hours of training over 4 to 6 sessions, nominal materials fee, and a 1-year commitment to tutor 2 1-hour sessions per week, inservice training, guidance and reference materials.
Retention and attrition		
Tutors	Information not available at this time.	About 50% stay a full year or more. 1988-89 data indicates that 32% left after less than 1 year.
Learners	Information under development	40% leave before 25 hours of instruction; about 25% of learners stay 50 or more hours.

NOTE: The Laubach Literacy Action profile is based on 1990 data and the Literacy Volunteers of America, Inc. profile is based on 1991 data.

SOURCE: Ellen Tenenbaum and William Strang, Westat, Inc. "The Major National Adult Literacy Volunteer Organizations—Draft Final Report, Volume 1: A Descriptive Review," prepared for the U.S. Department of Education, Office of Policy and Planning, 1992.

Many literacy programs have recognized the need to ''go where the learners are'' to attract participants. This learning center is in a shopping mall.

publications created to assist tutors and local programs.

Volunteer organizations face several significant challenges. LVA and LLA serve learners with very limited literacy skills. These clients tend to be ''. . . more needy, have more cognitive limitations, or have more traumatic learning histories that may have caused them to fail at ABE or shy away from the ABE system.''[25] Yet volunteers, who typically have 10 to 21 hours of preservice literacy training, are expected to teach these challenging students. While all programs seek to provide more training, they are often hindered by the lack of staff to develop or conduct training, resources to purchase commercially developed training packages, or money to send volunteers to conferences for continuing educa-

tion. Many also find it difficult to schedule training that meets the needs of volunteers who work and live throughout a large area.

Location of Services

Most programs[26] offer service at several sites; the most common sites are public high schools (70 percent) and adult learning centers (40 percent).[27] Approximately one-quarter of programs offer services at correctional facilities, workplaces, community colleges, and community centers. These AEA service delivery sites have shifted over the last decade, from locations at public high schools, vocational schools, libraries, and churches, toward a higher incidence of workplace sites, adult learning centers, commu-

---

[25] Ibid., p. 19.

[26] ''Programs'' are organizations that receive Federal literacy grants through a State; many programs distribute funds to subunits or grantees. Thus, there are many more literacy program sites (24,325) than programs (2,819). Malcolm Young, project director, Development Associates, Inc., personal communication, February 1993. Development Associates, Inc., ''National Evaluation of Adult Education Programs: Profiles of Service Providers,'' First Interim Report to the U.S. Department of Education, March 1992.

[27] An adult learning center refers to a building or section of a building used exclusively for adult education. Often these buildings are public schools no longer used for K-12 classes and converted for use as adult education facilities. Young, op. cit., footnote 26.

nity colleges, and correctional facilities[28] (see figure 4-2). (See box 4-D.)

Who Is Being Served?

Adult learners may be workers, job seekers, welfare recipients, immigrants, inmates, high school dropouts, or any others whose past skills do not match their current needs. They come from all ethnic and racial groups. As described further in chapter 5, targeted Federal and State programs have focused attention on new groups of learners served at new sites: e.g., welfare recipients in JOBS and JTPA programs, inmates in Federal prisons, the homeless in shelters and community centers, and workers at their job sites. For some of these learners—in particular, welfare recipients and incarcerated adults—participation may be mandated rather than voluntary. While the providers serving these new groups may remain the same, these new emphases affect the type of programs offered.

No count has been taken of the total number of learners served by combined Federal, State, local, and private sector efforts. Participant counts are confounded by the fact that many learners span several categories or are targeted by several program funding sources: e.g., a welfare recipient may be both a high school dropout and a recent immigrant; an incarcerated youth may also receive basic skills in a job training program. In addition, the same adult may enter and leave one or more programs several times over a period of years.

The most complete data have been collected through the AEA. These data suggest that the 2,800 programs supported by the AEA served a total of 3,565,877 clients in 1990.[29] Data on numbers of clients served is subject to debate, however. For Federal reporting purposes, clients

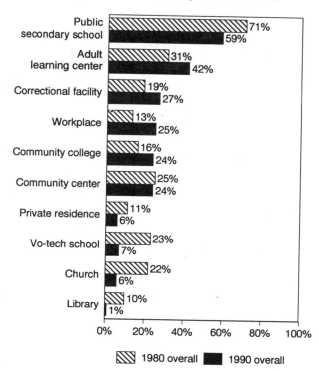

Figure 4-2—Percent of Adult Literacy Programs Using Various Locations, 1980 and 1990

- Public secondary school: 71% / 59%
- Adult learning center: 31% / 42%
- Correctional facility: 19% / 27%
- Workplace: 13% / 25%
- Community college: 16% / 24%
- Community center: 25% / 24%
- Private residence: 11% / 6%
- Vo-tech school: 23% / 7%
- Church: 22% / 6%
- Library: 10% / 1%

(▨ 1980 overall ■ 1990 overall)

NOTE: Totals exceed 100 percent because many programs use multiple sites to deliver services.

SOURCE: Development Associates, Inc., "National Evaluation of Adult Education Programs, Profiles of Service Providers," First Interim Report for the U.S. Department of Education, March 1992.

served are those who have completed 12 hours or more in an AEA-funded program; however, for State reporting purposes, many local programs count all who go through the intake process (testing and placement into appropriate classes) whether or not the learner attends for the minimum of 12 hours of instruction.

A recent study[30] indicates that between 15 and 20 percent of all clients who go through the intake process never actually receive any instruction.

---

[28] Development Associates, Inc., op. cit., footnote 26, p. 13.

[29] U.S. Department of Education, Division of Adult Education and Literacy, Office of Vocational and Adult Education, "Adult Education Program Facts—FY 1990," fact sheet, January 1992.

[30] Development Associates, Inc., "National Evaluation of Adult Education Programs: Second Interim Report, Profiles of Client Characteristics," draft report, 1993.

Box 4-D—New York Public Library Centers for Reading and Writing

"You know you go through life so long . . . bluffing," explains Winston,[1] *a 60-year-old maintenance worker who has become a regular at the Mott Haven Public Library's Center for Reading and Writing. "The average person around you don't know that you don't know [how to read well], but you've got enough street sense to bluff your way practically through anything." Last year, Winston finally gathered the courage to do something more for himself. "One day you decide, 'well, I'm an older man now. . . . I really don't have anything to bluff anymore for.'" Six months later, Winston says he's proud of meeting his goals. "I don't know if anybody else can see the progress,"* he states, *"but I can. I can see my progress."*

The Mott Haven Public Library is one of the Centers for Reading and Writing in the New York City Public Library system. Adults from many walks of life come there to spend afternoons, evenings, and Saturdays in literacy tutorials and classes. In groups of two to five, they use computer and video technologies to engage in collaborative reading exercises, share learning strategies, discuss current events, keep personal journals, and document life experiences. While practicing skills in the context of materials based around their daily activities, learners help each other work through their personal learning challenges.

For many participants, initial interest in the program was sparked by their desire to learn to use computers. They see technology around them in their everyday lives, but do not understand it, according to the Centers' learning technologies specialist. "They want to be a part of the Computer Age," she notes.[2]

At Mott Haven, computers and other technologies are an integral part of improving literacy. For example, learners use word processors to write and publish personal journals and stories. Through their writings, they communicate with peers at other library centers. They are encouraged to focus on key ideas, organize their writing, and think of effective ways to communicate with their audience. The reading and language skills required for writing are taught and practiced as needed. When learners leave the program, they often have a finished product—a portfolio of work to show friends, family, and potential employers.

Small group tutorials and workshops can be expensive, but the Library Centers have managed to turn small budgets into a goldmine of learning resources. In 1985, substantial funding came from a windfall from maturing bonds issued by the New York Municipal Assistance Corporation in the 1970s. A grant for $1.08 million was used to "beef up" the program. In each subsequent year, the city has budgeted about $75,000 for printed materials and $20,000 for software and video. The centers have stretched their dollars to enroll about 1,400 students every year: approximately 600 in the reading and writing classes and Saturday writing workshops, and 800 in tutorials. Some also participate in a federally funded training program. For a per-student expenditure of about $200, the program has dramatically changed the lives of participants, according to teachers, volunteer tutors, and learners themselves.

Public libraries have always played a pivotal role in self-directed learning. Like Mott Haven, many libraries want to provide access to information and learning with the new technologies. However, libraries' ability to continue to provide the services that the public expects is dependent on more costly resources—hardware as well as software—at a time when many local public budgets are shrinking. Serious budget cutbacks threaten expansion or even continued use of technology for New York's Library Reading and Writing Centers. The 12 Macintosh computers in 8 sites are falling into disrepair: 2 are broken with no money to fix them. The software, used by hundreds of students, is dated. Funding for technical assistance and equipment maintenance is in short supply. The lack of funds for dedicated phone lines has curtailed full implementation of an experiment in online communications between students and teachers that was piloted in two of the centers. Plans to purchase a scanner to input pictures, drawings, and text into the students' journals may never come to pass if current funding trends continue.

---

1 "Winston" is a fictional name. OTA site visit, Nov. 19, 1991.

2 Bryna Diamond, technologies specialist, New York Public Library Centers for Reading and Writing, personal communication, 1992.

Furthermore, after 40 weeks, only about 12.5 percent of those who actually begin attending are still active. When these adjustments are considered, the number of those actually served to any significant degree in AEA programs in fiscal year 1990 may be as low as 2.2 million. Participant counts for literacy activities reported by other Federal agencies may also be included in this total, since many individuals counted under other program categories actually receive literacy services through AEA programs. For example, in 1990, 313,671 adults in institutionalized settings (correctional institutions, rehabilitation facilities, hospitals, and mental institutions) received full-time adult education and literacy instruction through Federal and State funding.[31] DOL analysts estimate that 170,000 individuals received some basic skills instruction through DOL programs in 1991.[32] The HHS JOBS program reported 118,621 participants in education programs.[33] And 18,000 homeless individuals participated in basic educational services under the Stewart B. McKinney Homeless Assistance Act from summer 1988 to 1989.[34] Many of these learners are counted in the AEA totals.

An analysis of learners by program sponsor shows that different types of sponsors tend to reach different adult populations. For example,

data on entrants to programs supported under the AEA for the 1-year period ending April 1992 indicate that 42 percent of the learners were white, with the remaining 57 percent minorities.[35] CBOs serve a higher subset of minorities; nearly three-quarters of participants are minorities.[36] Gender distribution suggests that more women than men are served in both AEA-funded programs[37] and CBOs,[38] but volunteer programs serve men and women in equal numbers.[39]

What Kinds of Instruction Do They Receive?

Although adult literacy programs are often commonly referred to as ''adult basic education,'' this is a misnomer. Several types and levels of instruction are offered in these programs. Program levels generally correspond to elementary and secondary school grade levels; learners are placed into classes based on their literacy skills as measured on such tests as the Test of Adult Basic Education or the Adult Basic Learning Examination. These standardized norm-referenced tests provide norms for adults, and are used to interpret scores in grade levels (based on K-12 school norms) and in relation to test performance of other

---

[31] Funding for programs for adults in institutionalized settings was $24 million in 1990. U.S. Department of Education, *A.L.L. Points Bulletin*, vol. 4, No. 1, February 1992, p. 1.

[32] Actual figures have not been compiled. This estimate is taken from Marian Schwarz, ''Television and Adult Literacy: Potential for Access to Learning for an Unserved Population,'' report prepared for The Ford Foundation, June 1992, p. 6.

[33] Educational activities are those ''. . . directed at attaining a high school diploma or its equivalent, another basic education program, basic and remedial education or education in English proficiency.'' U.S. Department of Health and Human Services, Family Support Administration, ''Average Monthly Number of JOBS Participants by Component, FY 1991,'' instructions for completing Form FSA-104, 1990, p. 3.

[34] U.S. Department of Education, *Education for Homeless Adults: The First Year* (Washington, DC: December 1990), p. 1.

[35] Racial and ethnic identity of learners was: white, 42 percent; Hispanic, 31 percent; black, 15 percent; Asian or Pacific Islander, 9 percent; and Native American or Alaskan Native, 2 percent. Mark Morgan, Development Associates, Inc., personal communication, February 1993.

[36] A 1989 survey of CBOs reported that ethnic and racial identity of learners was: Hispanic, 30 percent; white, 26 percent; black, 26 percent; Asian, 13 percent; Native American, 3 percent; and other racial and ethnic groups, 4 percent. (The figure for whites was not given, but extrapolated from the other percentages listed.) Association for Community Based Education, op. cit., footnote 20, p. 69.

[37] Forty-two percent of participants were male; 58 percent, female. Morgan, op. cit., footnote 35.

[38] In the Association for Community Based Education survey, 56 percent of participants were female; 44 percent male. Association for Community Based Education, op. cit., footnote 20, p. 69.

[39] A 1991 LVA learner profile lists 49.2 percent female and 50.8 percent male; LLA data for 1990 report learners 50 percent male and 50 percent female.

adults.[40] Critics of this approach suggest that adults' learning ability is more complex than statistical grade-level measures reflected in standardized test scores.

The most common types of adult education include:

- *Adult Basic Education*: Sometimes referred to as ''below the 8th-grade level,''[41] ABE is typically divided into three levels: level 1 refers to students functioning at reading grade levels 0 to 3; level 2 for those at the 4th- to 6th-reading grade levels, and level 3 for the 6th- to 8th-reading grade level. Since most ABE instruction is roughly equivalent to the 4th-through 8th-grade levels, and the characteristics of programs serving level 1 students are different than those serving the level 2 and 3 students, OTA refers separately to level 1 as *Beginning Literacy*.
- *Adult Secondary Education*: ASE refers to instruction for adults whose skills are at the secondary (high school) level. The focus is generally on attaining a high school diploma either by completing course work or passing the GED examination.[42]
- *English as a Second Language*: ESL instruction teaches English (reading, writing, and speaking) to non-English speakers.[43] As will be discussed below, ESL is complicated by the fact that it includes learners with a range of literacy levels in their own language.

A majority (60 percent) of federally supported adult education programs provide at least some instruction of all three types—ABE, ASE, and ESL. The percentage of programs providing ABE (92.3 percent) and ASE (85 percent) is higher than those offering ESL (68.9 percent). Nevertheless, ESL students make up the largest group of clients (35.2 percent of clients are in ESL programs, versus 35 percent in ABE and 29.8 percent in ASE),[44] suggesting that ESL programs are those with the largest numbers of students, or the ones most likely to have waiting lists.

A range of learning environments is used in adult literacy instruction. As shown in figure 4-3, individual instruction and small group instruction are the most common. Computer-aided instruction or learning laboratories are used in only 14 percent of federally supported ABE programs.[45]

Beginning Literacy

A sizable number of adults who seek literacy assistance function below the 4th-grade level. While some LEA programs serve learners at this level, volunteer programs and community-based programs traditionally concentrate their efforts on this group.[46]

Beginning literacy programs typically provide one-on-one private instruction by volunteer tutors who meet with learners 2 to 4 hours a week. Materials are developed locally or provided by

---

[40] Thomas G. Sticht, Applied Behavioral & Cognitive Sciences, Inc., ''Testing and Assessment in Adult Basic Education and English as a Second Language Programs,'' report for the U.S. Department of Education, January 1990, p. 6.

[41] Development Associates, op. cit., footnote 26, glossary, p. xi.

[42] Ibid., glossary, p. xi.

[43] Ibid., glossary, p. xi.

[44] Ibid., pp. 14-15.

[45] Today, the total number of computers in elementary and secondary school instruction is over 3 million, with over 90 percent of all elementary and secondary schools using computers for instruction. Although the total number of computers used in adult basic education is unknown, it is clearly far behind comparable use for K-12 education.

[46] One study of CBOs noted that 57 percent of students enter with reading skills at less than the 5th-grade level, and another 27 percent with skills at the 5th- or 6th-grade level. Association for Community Based Education, op. cit., footnote 20, p. 69.

Figure 4-3—Learning Environments Used in Adult Education Programs

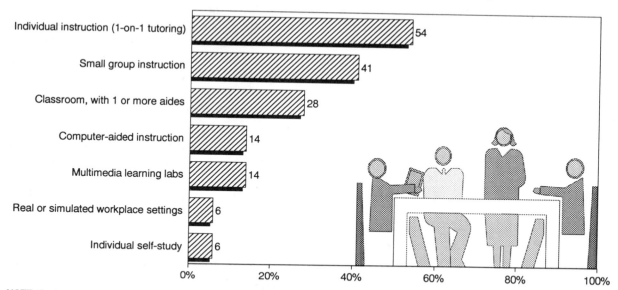

NOTE: Scale represents percentage of programs using specified learning environment for approximately one-third of instructional time or more. Totals exceed 100 percent because many programs use more than one type of learning environment.

SOURCE: Development Associates, Inc., "National Evaluation of Adult Education Programs, Profiles of Service Providers," First Interim Report to the U.S. Department of Education, March 1992.

literacy volunteer organizations or commercial publishers.[47] The Laubach Way to Reading series, for example, takes students through a series of levels based on a phonics approach. These levels correspond, in general, with levels measured on the Test of Adult Basic Education. Tutors supplement these materials with audiotapes, flash cards, word games, and beginning reading exercises. LLA encourages tutors to adopt flexible approaches in using their materials.

LVA programs use a "whole language" approach, focusing on material tied to a learner's goals and interests, or "language experience" where learners dictate or write paragraphs based on their lives and interests, using these words as the basis for developing a vocabulary. Decoding skills (learning symbol and sound relationships and word patterns) are taught in the context of printed materials meaningful to the learner.

Computer use in beginning literacy programs is limited. Although the number of adult literacy software titles is quite extensive, there is very little software aimed at beginning readers. Few software applications use audio, an essential feature for nonreaders.[48] Moreover, most early reading programs are geared explicitly to children and include features that may "turn off" many adults.[49]

---

[47] The Association for Community Based Education study showed 61 percent of CBOs use materials developed by their own program and 46 percent use material developed by other literacy programs. Furthermore, 25 percent use other materials such as newspapers, letters, and life-skills materials. Ibid., p. 69.

[48] Only 23 of all ABE level 1 products (9.3 percent) take advantage of human speech. Jay Sivin-Kachala and Ellen Bialo, Interactive Educational Systems Design, Inc., "Software for Adult Literacy," OTA contractor report, June 1992, p. 6.

[49] Ibid., p. 6.

Adult Basic Education

ABE programs focus on learners who have some reading skills. Instructors are certified in elementary and secondary education and generally teach part time. Students typically participate in small classes several hours a week. Volunteer tutors often assist as classroom aides or provide supplemental personal tutoring to accompany ABE instruction. Courseware includes textbooks developed by commercial publishers, LVA or LLA materials, or materials created by teachers to fit the needs and interests of their students. A small but growing number of ABE programs use computer software, often networked integrated learning systems allowing a student to move through a range of instructional content and levels. ABE programs use a vast range of software titles, some created for children and others created especially for adult learners.[50]

Adult Secondary Education Programs: High School Completion and the GED

Some people believe that the most important goal for adult literacy students at all levels is to attain high school certification in one form or another.[51] A high school degree has become a necessary passport to many jobs, as well as to vocational and higher education programs. The 1970 amendments to the AEA added adult secondary education as a part of the AEA grants to States. Although the AEA has traditionally emphasized programs for adults with a 5th-grade equivalency level or lower, State ABE programs have tried to get the most "bang for the buck" by concentrating funds on the learners who were easiest to reach and serve—those with a base of skills to build on in seeking the more easily attainable GED or high school diploma. Therefore, although the act stipulates that not more than 20 percent of each State's basic grant may be used for programs of equivalency for a certificate of graduation from secondary school,[52] States continue to emphasize ASE programs with their own money.

While enrollment in ABE remained relatively constant from 1980 to 1990, ASE growth was more dramatic. In 1990, ASE students numbered 1.1 million, more than 30 percent of the total 3.6 million adults enrolled in adult education,[53] and 103 percent higher than the comparable percentage of a decade earlier.[54]

There are three types of ASE programs: high school completion programs, the external diploma program, and preparation for the GED examination. Of the ASE students in fiscal year 1990 programs funded by the AEA, 206,952 passed the GED and another 67,000 obtained adult high school diplomas.[55]

High school completion programs are most like a traditional high school program and are designed and offered through local school systems. The requirements are based on the number of Carnegie Units required for graduation in the particular State where the learner resides. Classes are usually offered through the local school districts, in schools and after hours, and must be taught by certified teachers. Students must attend for the prescribed number of hours of instruction and testing is often the measure of satisfactory completion.

---

[50] Ibid., p. 6.

[51] Hal Beder, *Adult Literacy: Issues for Policy and Practice* (Melbourne, FL: Krieger Publishing Co., 1991), p. 114.

[52] Section 322 of the AEA.

[53] U.S. Department of Education, op. cit., footnote 29, "State Administered Adult Education Program 1990 Enrollment," table.

[54] U.S. Department of Education, *A.L.L. Points Bulletin*, vol. 4, No. 2, April 1992, p. 1. This number barely touches the total of potential clients—39 million U.S. adults ages 25 or older who lack a high school diploma. In addition, there are about 4 million people ages 16 to 24 who had not graduated from high school and were not enrolled in 1991 in any school. U.S. Department of Education, National Center for Education Statistics, *Dropout Rates in the United States: 1991* (Washington, DC: U.S. Government Printing Office, September 1992).

[55] U.S. Department of Education, op. cit., footnote 29, p. 2.

The *External Diploma Program* is administered by the American Council on Education, the professional organization also responsible for the GED. External diplomas are granted based on a combination of demonstrated capabilities including oral and written communication, computation, and the analysis and manipulation of data in context. Assessment does not include standardized paper-and-pencil tests, but rather is based on performance in simulations that parallel situations found on the job or in personal life. This is the smallest of the high school credentialing programs; in 1990, 3,000 adults received external diplomas from local schools in 10 States.[56]

The *GED Certificate Program* is the most common vehicle for ASE students to obtain a high school diploma. GED content corresponds to what graduating high school seniors are expected to know in the areas of writing, social studies, science, literature, the arts, and mathematics.[57] The minimum score required for passing each of the five subtests is set by each State. Most participants in GED preparation courses are targeted at the 7th- to 9th-grade reading level, although participants range from the 6th- to the 11th-grade reading level. GED preparation classes focus on language and computational skills, but also cover test-taking skills and other subjects. Because the content of these classes is test driven, classes tend to be structured and use commercially published materials. Programs often use computers to provide additional independent practice for GED students. As students may be weak in one area and strong in others, software

More than 750,000 learners took the GED examination in 1991. Odelia Cantu celebrates her success at a graduation ceremony.

programs offer students an opportunity to concentrate on a specific area of the test, and practice and move at their own speed until mastery is achieved.[58]

Over 800,000 students took the GED tests in 1991, a 6-percent increase from the previous year; the percent passing also increased, from 70 to 72 percent. There was also an 8-percent rise in the number taking the Spanish-language GED tests.[59] Not all adults working toward the GED certificate are enrolled in GED preparation classes. One of the largest GED preparation programs in the country is offered over public television. GED on TV, sponsored by Kentucky Educational Television (KET), offers assistance and encouragement to students both in classes and at home as they prepare for the examination. An estimated 1.2 million students in Kentucky and throughout the Nation have passed the GED examination after viewing the KET/GED series.[60]

---

[56] U.S. Department of Education, *A.L.L. Points Bulletin*, op. cit., footnote 54, p. 3.

[57] Janet Baldwin, "Schooling, Study, and Academic Goals: The Education of GED Candidates," *GED Profiles: Adults in Transition*, No. 2, January 1991, p. 5.

[58] A review of adult literacy software found that the smallest percentage (19.3 percent) of titles are suitable for the GED submarket. However, unlike many of those in the larger category of ABE (81.8 percent of all adult literacy titles), GED preparation software is popular among students and programs because these products are written for adults and not children. See Sivin-Kachala and Bialo, op. cit., footnote 48, p. 6.

[59] GED Testing Service of the American Council on Education, *1991 Statistical Report* (Washington, DC: 1992), p. 2.

[60] KET, The Kentucky Network, *1991 Annual Report* (Lexington, KY: n.d.), p. 5. See also ch. 7.

English as a Second Language

ESL is literacy's coat of many colors—a program that is offered in the workplace, community colleges, community programs, prisons, and LEAs. The learners have one thing in common—a need to learn how to speak, understand, read, and write in English. Beyond this, they range across the spectrum, from refugees[61] and recent immigrants[62] to long-term residents, including many non-English speakers who are U.S. citizens. ESL students span a range of languages, levels of English proficiency, and literacy in the native language. It can be a great challenge serving this diverse and complex audience of learners (see chapter 3, box 3-A). Computer software for ESL instruction offers great promise for individualizing instruction, especially when speech and audio are included to help students develop their English skills. However, ESL software for adults is limited despite great demand. Better instructional approaches and materials that provide bilingual assists to students across the curriculum, especially in writing skills, mathematics, vocational skills, and GED preparation, are needed.[63]

ESL accounts for the fastest growing and largest portion of the adult literacy program in the United States. ESL enrollment in Federal AEA programs nearly tripled between 1980 and 1989, when it exceeded 1 million students; currently one in every three students enrolled in adult education participates in ESL instruction.[64] It is estimated that, by the year 2000, 17.4 million limited-English-proficient (LEP) adults will be living in the United States, and immigrants will make up 29 percent of the new entrants into the labor force between now and then.[65] Many programs have waiting lists as long as several years, and could easily fill all their ABE slots with ESL students.

Two pieces of Federal legislation have been influential in creating this ESL demand. The Immigration Reform and Control Act provided amnesty for millions of illegal immigrants already living in the United States, and required that all applicants demonstrate minimal proficiency in English and U.S. history/government by taking a test or providing a certificate of enrollment in approved courses.[66] The second piece of legislation was the Immigration Act of 1990, which created a demand for ESL in adult literacy by allowing greater immigration.[67] ESL programs for adults are also supported by the AEA and several other Federal literacy programs (see chapter 5). Many ESL programs are offered in the workplace, often tied to vocational skill development, for those already employed but constrained in their advancement by limited English skills.

---

61 A "refugee" is defined as a person who is outside his or her native country and is unable or unwilling to return for fear of persecution on the basis of race, religion, nationality, membership in a particular social group, or political opinion. 8 U.S.C. 1101 (a) (42).

62 An "immigrant" is defined as any alien (including refugees) except those that belong to certain specified classes, such as foreign government officials, tourists, or students. 8 U.S.C. 1101 (a) (15).

63 Sivin-Kachala and Bialo, op. cit., footnote 48, p. 40.

64 U.S. Department of Education, Office of Vocational and Adult Education, *Teaching Adults With Limited English Skills: Progress and Challenges* (Washington, DC: 1991), p. 7. ESL instruction is more intensive than other AEA-funded programs; ESL clients average 5.9 hours of instruction per week versus 4.4 hours for ABE and 4.2 hours for ASE. Morgan, op. cit., footnote 35.

65 U.S. Department of Education, op. cit., footnote 64, p. 10.

66 There were 3 million applicants for legalization as a result of these amnesty provisions; about 55 percent live in California. Comprehensive Adult Student Assessment System, "A Survey of Newly Legalized Persons in California," report prepared for the California Health and Welfare Agency, 1989, pp. 1-2.

67 Except for several classes of immigrants, from 1980 to 1990 the number of immigrants admitted to the United States was limited to 270,000 per year, with a maximum of 20,000 from any one country. 8 U.S.C. 1151 (a), 1152 (a). The 1990 act provided for an increase in total immigration per year, starting with approximately 700,000 per year from fiscal years 1992-94 and leveling off at an annual total of at least 675,000 immigrants beginning in fiscal year 1995. Refugees are not included in this total. Joyce Vialet and Larry Eig, "Immigration Act of 1990 (P.L. 101-649)," CRS Report for Congress, Dec. 14, 1990, p. 2.

Who Are the Teachers?

The personnel who work in adult literacy programs are overwhelmingly volunteer rather than paid, and part time rather than full time. The ratio of volunteers to full-time professional teachers in federally supported AEA programs nationwide is almost 8-to-1[68] and only 1 in 4 paid staff members is full time. In community-based and volunteer programs, the ratio of volunteers to paid staff, and part-time to full-time instructors, is higher.

Most paid staff were, or still are, K-12 teachers. Slightly less than one-fifth of full-time instructors in AEA programs are certified in adult education; 13 percent of full-time instructors hold no teacher certification.[69] Furthermore, only 7 percent of part-time instructors in AEA programs are certified in adult education but 81 percent of part-time staff earned other types of teaching certificates.[70] Most States do not require special certification in adult education for those who teach in literacy programs; some States have no certification requirements of any kind (see chapter 6, figure 6-3). Forty-five percent of federally funded AEA programs do not have a single staff person certified in adult education, a single full-time instructor or administrator, or a directed inservice training effort.[71]

NEW EMPHASES IN LITERACY PROGRAMS

The delivery of services is changing as the definition of literacy expands, public awareness grows, new players enter the field, and new partnerships form. While ABE, ASE, and ESL instruction remain the ''meat and potatoes'' of adult literacy programs, several new types of literacy programs are growing in importance. Chief among these are workplace literacy and family literacy programs. These programs recognize that literacy needs are changing as the demands of the workplace and demands placed on families increase. A third type of program increasing in frequency is literacy for incarcerated adults.

Workplace Literacy

Literacy requirements change as employment demands change. In the past, when manufacturing, mining, farming, and forestry jobs formed the traditional base of the workforce, those who lacked a high school diploma could get by because of the jobs they had and the supervision they received. But workers' necessary skills are changing as the economy shifts from manufacturing to a service-based workforce.[72] Furthermore, new skills are needed as industries purchase new technologies and adopt statistical quality control, team-based work, and participatory management processes. A worker in a pulp and paper mill where modernization has changed his job sums up his anxiety:

> With computerization I am further away from my job than I have ever been before. I used to listen to the sounds the boiler makes and know just how it was running. I could look at the fire in the furnace and tell by its color how it was burning. I knew what kinds of adjustment were needed by the shades of color I saw. . . there were smells that told you different things about how it was running. I feel uncomfortable being away from those sights and smells. Now I have only numbers

---

[68] Development Associates, Inc., op. cit., footnote 26, p. 18.

[69] Ibid., p. 77.

[70] Ibid., p. 77.

[71] National Evaluation of Adult Education Programs, Bulletin No. 3, December 1991, p. 5.

[72] ''One telling measure of the change ahead is that the trade and service sectors will *add* more jobs between 1985 and the year 2000 than now exist in all U.S. manufacturing.'' William B. Johnston and Arnold H. Packer, *Workforce 2000: Work and Workers for the 21st Century* (Indianapolis, IN: Hudson Institute, 1987), p. 59.

to go by. I am scared of that boiler, and I feel that I should be closer to it in order to control it.[73]

As a host of studies have pointed out, the United States is unlikely to remain an economic power without improving the basic skills of its workers.[74] Companies may not realize the extent of their employees' basic skills deficiencies until they attempt to make a major change that requires training, then find that their employees lack the basic skills to read the texts or understand the computations required.

Schools have an important role to play, but with 75 percent of the workers for the year 2000 already out of school and on the job, the immediate task is up to the employer. Only a few employers have taken up this challenge; today only 1 in 10 employees receives formal training of any kind from his or her employer, and this training is typically focused on executives, managers, and highly skilled technicians, not front-line workers.[75] Helping employees acquire basic skills is not a priority with most companies.[76] The problem is particularly acute for small companies (under 100 employees), which together employ 35 percent of the total U.S. workforce.[77] Despite the fact that they are more likely to employ workers with less education, small companies do not have the expertise to offer training in-house, the resources to contract for training, or the numbers of employees to make a focused effort profitable.[78]

Workplace literacy programs are one response to the need for improved worker skills. These programs upgrade the job-related basic skills of employees or prepare job seekers for work in specific industries. Usually they are offered through partnerships of business, labor, unions, schools, private industry councils, and government agencies; partnerships are especially attractive for small businesses unable to mount programs alone[79] (see box 4-E). Workplace literacy programs, often conducted at or near job sites using work-related tasks and materials, can improve morale, customer satisfaction, error rates, productivity, and profits.[80]

States have been important sources of support for workplace literacy, using economic development funds or other State funds, or Federal AEA basic grants. The Federal Government also specifically encourages employer-sponsored workforce literacy programs through the National Workplace Literacy Partnerships Program of the U.S. Department of Education. An evaluation of this program concluded that these projects have maintained high student retention rates—higher

---

[73] S. Zuboff, *In the Age of the Smart Machine: The Future of Work and Power* (New York, NY: Basic Books, 1988), p. 63.

[74] National Center for Adult Literacy, *Adult Learning and Work: A Focus on Incentives*, conference papers (Philadelphia, PA: Nov. 4-5, 1991); Johnston and Packer, op. cit., footnote 72; U.S. Department of Labor and U.S. Department of Education, *The Bottom Line: Basic Skills in the Workplace* (Washington, DC: U.S. Department of Labor, 1988); National Center on Education and the Economy, *America's Choice: High Skills or Low Wages!* (Rochester, NY: 1990); Office of Technology Assessment, op. cit., footnote 16; and Anthony Carnevale, *America and the New Economy* (Alexandria, VA: American Society for Training and Development, 1991).

[75] Anthony Carnevale and Leiber Gainer, American Society for Training and Development, "The Learning Enterprise," prepared for the U.S. Department of Labor, February 1989, p. 48.

[76] Several studies of employer involvement in workplace basic literacy skills programs showed a range of from 3 to 26 percent of respondents saying they offered remedial education for their employees. Office of Technology Assessment, op. cit., footnote 16, p. 168.

[77] The Small Business Administration defines "small businesses" as under 500 employees. Using this figure, there are over 5 million small businesses in the United States; they employ 57 percent of the workforce. Forrest P. Chisman, *The Missing Link: Workplace Education in Small Business* (Washington, DC: Southport Institute for Policy Analysis, 1992), p. 1.

[78] Laurie J. Bassi, *Smart Workers, Smart Work: A Survey of Small Businesses on Workplace Education and the Reorganization of Work* (Washington, DC: The Southport Institute for Policy Analysis, 1992).

[79] A survey of 107 workplace literacy programs revealed that 92 percent involved 2 or more partners. Larry Mikulecky, "Workplace Literacy Programs: Organization and Incentives," in National Center for Adult Literacy, op. cit., footnote 74, p. 7.

[80] Bassi, op. cit., footnote 78, p. 52.

than any other type of adult education programs.[81] The program's success has been attributed to a number of factors, including the close involvement of public and private partners, convenient worksite locations, work-related content, incentives such as work-release time, and supportive, nonstigmatizing environments.[82] Many of these features are shared by privately sponsored workforce literacy programs.

Increasingly, unions are negotiating workplace education into labor contracts. Unions encourage voluntary programs with open-entry/open-exit approaches to increase worker flexibility and choice. Programs are rarely labeled "basic skills" because of the stigma attached; instead, most attempt to offer courses across a range of levels so that training is seen as important to all employees. Confidentiality is often tightly maintained, as employees fear that if their educational deficiencies are made public, they may be used against them by management. For example, in one program involving a coalition of local industries and educational providers, a difficult issue arose when the coalition offered GED courses to employees, many of whom, it was discovered, had lied on their original application forms about having a high school diploma. Ordinarily, this would be grounds for dismissal, but to overcome this dilemma, the employer offered an "amnesty" to those who agreed to take the GED.[83]

Technology in Workplace Literacy Programs

Several of the challenges faced by workplace literacy programs are particularly amenable to technological solutions. Computers are often selected for these programs because they offer self-pacing and confidential records of student progress. One employee need not be aware of what another employee is studying on the computer. Furthermore, when computer laboratories are a central component, a teacher need not

Workplace literacy and training programs are growing in importance as workers at all levels increasingly must use technology, analyze information, and work in teams.

always be present to enable an employee to study. During breaks or between shifts, students can "pick up where they left off," especially when integrated learning systems with recordkeeping capabilities allow easy entrance to the instructional system. Finally, the very use of computers attracts many students. Many enter programs that use computers with the assumption that technology training will help them keep current jobs or enable them to find other employment if necessary.

Research suggests that the most successful way of teaching adults literacy skills is to put the material into a meaningful context. Most workplace literacy programs conduct a job-site analysis to link literacy skills to actual on-the-job tasks. Typically, a local community college or school district conducts a learner and workplace analysis as a basis for the overall program. Curriculum materials incorporate worksite vo-

---

[81] U.S. Department of Education, *Workplace Literacy: Reshaping the American Workforce* (Washington, DC: May 1992), p. 9.

[82] Pelavin Associates, Inc., "A Review of the National Workplace Literacy Program," unpublished report, 1990, pp. 32-33.

[83] OTA site visit, Tulsa Training Coalition, Inc., Tulsa, OK, July 23, 1992.

Box 4-E—A Partnership for Literacy: Dalton, Georgia[1]

"Bobby" is typical of many of Dalton's workforce. He quit school after the 6th grade, married at 14, started working in the mills at 16, became a foreman at age 17, and has been a supervisor and valued worker for 40 years. His company, faced with increasing foreign competition, modernized and streamlined the manufacturing process, using a sophisticated computerized photospectrometer to monitor the production line activity. Workers are required to read the printouts and make on-the-spot adjustments. Bobby was offered a promotion to supervise the new system, but there was a problem: Bobby couldn't read the printouts, the manuals explaining the machinery, or memos sent by management to describe the new work he was supposed to supervise. He can't read at all, although no one ever knew it in the old job; he'd always carried a newspaper with him to work to mask his problem. "You gotta find someone else; I can't do this job," he told his boss, and said he'd quit rather than have people discover his secret.

Sixty-five percent of the carpet manufactured in the United States is produced in Dalton, Georgia, the "Carpet Capital of the World." The textile mills of Dalton-Whitfield County in southern Appalachia have traditionally made the area a mecca for high-wage, low-skills jobs. However, job skills requirements are changing rapidly as the carpet industry relies more on computer-aided technology. This "skills mismatch" is a real problem for the local community, where fewer than one-half of the adults in the county have a high school education.[2] One carpet manufacturer surveyed its hourly employees and found that only 8 percent had the skills the company projected it needed to remain competitive. Another small, family-owned company in the area had invested hundreds of thousands of dollars in state-of-the-art manufacturing equipment and saw productivity drop rather than improve. The owner discovered that all the hourly employees assigned to use the equipment were functionally illiterate.

Local industry could not survive without finding a way to keep the "Bobbys" of the workforce productive, but the problem was too large for the adult education program in the area to handle alone. In July 1990, the Dalton-Whitfield business community and the Chamber of Commerce created the nonprofit Education is Essential Foundation, Inc. (EIE). The goal of the foundation was to go beyond traditional "paper-and-pencil" literacy programs, already overbooked and meeting limited success in filling the educational needs of the community. Since computers were driving the changes in the workplace, they looked to computers to provide a solution to the learning gap. Initial grants of $30,000 from the Tennessee Valley Authority and $10,000 from the Appalachian Regional Commission leveraged another $120,000 in local contributions from the United Way, businesses, civic groups, and individuals.

The first year the foundation placed 12 multimedia personal computers using an integrated learning system (ILS)[3] in the public adult education literacy centers. Then, recognizing that 95 percent of the local welfare recipients lacked a high school degree, and noting that literacy program attendance had tripled at the sites where computer systems were installed, the foundation established a computer laboratory in the local welfare office in a joint project with the Department of Family and Children Services. Under Georgia's PEACH program (Positive Education and Community Health), welfare clients had previously attended mandated classes at the adult learning centers, but now meet as a class 4 hours every morning at the welfare office, a more convenient location. Attendance and gains are monitored on the computer, and one-half of the instructional time is computer-based. Attendance has improved, and learners are moving ahead more quickly, registering gains of one full grade level for every 18 hours logged on the system. The computers have been a real attraction for learners, who are proud to be "learning computers;" nowadays lines begin forming at the welfare office before the doors open—not people waiting for the checks, but learners wanting access to the learning system.

Heartened by experience with public sector programs, the foundation bought several ILSs and loaned them to companies, to make them available for employees on their own, before or after a workshift. "People are too tired

---

[1] Information in this box, except where noted, is from Janet Bolen, coordinator, Education is Essential Foundation, Inc., personal communication, December 1992. "Bobby" is a fictitious name.

[2] The 1980 census data indicated that 56 percent of the adults in the county did not have a high school diploma. By 1992, this figure had dropped to 40 percent. Bolen, op. cit., footnote 1.

[3] Computer Curriculum Corp. Integrated Learning System software includes 2,800 hours of multimedia instruction in K-12 and more than 3,000 hours of skills courseware.

after work to go to classes, and the one-on-one sessions with tutors were just too slow for most people."[4] By the fall of 1992, 10 companies had purchased their own units for workplace learning laboratories. Currently, 35 ILS workstations are in place at 21 business and community sites throughout the county, with an average of 2 new laboratory installations each month. "There's a healthy competitive spirit among the local businesses now. No one wants to be out of step," says the foundation coordinator. Participation now includes all sizes and types of industries, from the largest carpet manufacturer, with 7,500 employees, to a small catering company. EIE coordinates group classes and training on the system, assembles meetings among "users groups," and seeks new sites for setting up systems, like day-care centers where parents and children can take turns learning with a range of software.

By the fall of 1992, over $300,000 had been raised to support EIE literacy efforts. While the initial grants from national and regional public entities formed the basis on which the program has been built, private sector support and enthusiasm must carry the burden to keep the program viable. The State of Georgia encourages private support through a $150 per-employee tax credit to employers who provide or sponsor adult basic skills education for their employees. The foundation sponsored a luncheon to explain to employers how to apply for the tax credits, and described the workplace and computer-aided literacy programs currently available in the community, encouraging more to participate.

The number of learners passing the GED grew from 200 in 1990 to close to 350 in 1992, the equivalent of another high school class graduating each year.[5] The impact on the local K-12 system, which once had one of the highest dropout rates in the Nation, also has been positive. Adults attending school provide role models for their children, and high school dropout rates have been cut by 13 percent. And Bobby has that new job at the mill, but he no longer just carries a newspaper to work—now he reads it.

---

[4] Lynne Peer, director of Marketing Services, J&J Industries, Dalton, GA, personal communication, December 1992.

[5] While not all of these have used the computer-based instruction, the computers have been a big attraction, bringing people into programs.

cabulary, procedures, and context. While this can be accomplished with traditional training programs, computer-based systems make it easier to create customized materials and individualize learning plans that match basic skills content with workplace context.

Family Literacy

The hand that rocks the cradle also tells the family stories, reads the books, asks "What did you do at school today?"[84]

Another example of the shifting view of literacy is the growth in family literacy programs. Research has shown that the education level of the mother is the strongest variable affecting a child's school achievement;[85] parents can increase children's chances to succeed in school through such means as reading to children or modeling good reading habits.[86] But if the parents themselves are unable to read, the children miss this extra boost.

Family literacy or intergenerational literacy refers to the goal of reaching all members of a

---

[84] Anne C. Lewis, *Listening to Mothers' Voices: A Reporter's Guide to Family Literacy* (Washington, DC: Education Writers Association, 1992), p. 1.

[85] Some suggest that funds for compensatory education for children would be better spent if they directly focused on improving the literacy of mothers instead. Ibid., p. 1. Also see, for example, Sandra Van Fossen and Thomas G. Sticht, *Teach the Mother and Reach the Child: Results of the Intergenerational Literacy Action Project of Wider Opportunities for Women* (Washington, DC: Wider Opportunities for Women, July 1991).

[86] See, for example, T.G. Sticht and B.A. McDonald, *Making the Nation Smarter: The Intergenerational Transfer of Cognitive Ability* (San Diego, CA: Applied Behavioral and Cognitive Sciences, Inc., 1989); and Ruth Nikase, Boston University, "The Noises of Literacy: An Overview of Intergenerational and Family Literacy Programs," prepared for the U.S. Department of Education, Office of the Secretary, Mar. 3, 1989.

family with literacy activities. Program providers can be private or public or a combination of several sources. The major source of Federal support has been ED and HHS, which fund the Even Start Program, the Bilingual Family English Literacy Program, and the Head Start Family Literacy Initiatives. Many States have established family literacy programs using their 10-percent AEA set-aside for innovative and coordinated approaches.

Family literacy programs run the gamut from family story hours at the public library to comprehensive programs that offer instruction to both children and adults. One model—Parent and Child Education (PACE)—was developed in Kentucky and replicated nationally as the Kenan Trust Family Literacy Program. This program has four components: early childhood education; adult basic education and pre-vocational skills; a support group for parents to discuss common parenting issues and concerns; and an intergenerational activity called PACT—parent and child together time.[87] Over 50 sites nationwide have been trained in this model by the National Center for Family Literacy in Louisville, Kentucky.

Experiences with the Federal Even Start program suggest some of the challenges faced by family literacy programs.[88] One challenge is high turnover[89]: a family may move out of the service area or lose eligibility[90] or may be dissatisfied and drop out of the voluntary program. Additionally, some programs are structured for short-term interventions in order to recruit more eligible families in subsequent years. Finally, family literacy programs face the difficult choice of whether to focus resources on the "ready to learn" family in which parents attend ABE classes, children attend early childhood education programs, and parents learn about parenting; or on the families with the lowest skill levels and most severe problems, who may need crisis intervention and several months of extensive social services until the family is indeed "ready to learn."[91]

Technology in Family Literacy Programs

Some family literacy programs use the computer as a vehicle to draw parents and children together, attract participants, or make reluctant parents more comfortable in a school setting and more likely to connect with their child's education. For example, in programs supported under a partnership between Apple Computer and the National Center for Family Literacy, the computer was a used as a ". . . literacy tool: a pencil, typewriter, paint brush, crayon, recorder, scissors, and eraser (thank goodness!) all rolled into one easy-to-use machine."[92] Parents and children were encouraged to create materials to take home and share, using word processing and print capabilities to make posters, banners, greeting cards, and other items both children and parents could take pride in. Stories written by parents went home for reading aloud to children. Parents were also encouraged to preview children's software. These activities sought to help remove parents' fear of computers and help them consider ways to help their children learn. A telecommunications system linked the seven projects, enabling

---

[87] Rebecca King, *Using Computers in Family Literacy Programs* (Louisville, KY: National Center for Family Literacy, 1992).

[88] Robert G. St. Pierre, "Early Findings From the National Evaluation of the Even Start Family Literacy Program," paper presented at the First National Conference on Family Literacy, University of North Carolina, Chapel Hill, NC, Apr. 12-14, 1992, p. 2.

[89] Almost 74 percent of the families that participated in Even Start during 1989-90 did not continue in the second year of the project. Ibid., p. 6.

[90] To be eligible, a family must have an adult in need of adult basic skills training and eligible for adult basic education programs, have a child less than 8 years of age, and must live in a Chapter 1 elementary school attendance area. Ibid., p. 1.

[91] Ibid., p. 9.

[92] King, op. cit., footnote 87, p. 2.

Just Grandma and Me, by Mercer Mayer; Broderbund Software, Inc.

Family literacy programs encourage parents to read with their children. CD-ROM technology brings animation, music, and talking characters to the onscreen pages of this "living book," with Spanish and Japanese translations in the same program.

them to share lessons, products, and ideas with one another.[93]

Programs for Incarcerated Adults

On any given day, over 1.2 million Americans are behind bars. Their literacy problems are severe. Four out of five do not have a high school diploma, and more than 75 percent lack basic reading and mathematics skills.[94] Other estimates suggest that 85 percent of juveniles who come before the courts are functionally illiterate and 60 percent of incarcerated juveniles read below the 5th-grade level.[95] Overall, the literacy problems

of the criminal offender population are three times as severe as those of the general population.[96]

Although educational programs have long been offered in jails and prisons, these programs are becoming more important with new Federal and State directives mandating participation and with additional funding targeted specifically on literacy for prisoners. The literacy policy for Federal prisoners mandates minimum participation and provides economic incentives to continue beyond the minimum level. The Federal Bureau of Prisons now requires all inmates, regardless of

---

[93] Ibid., p. 3.

[94] U.S. Department of Education, op. cit., footnote 31, p. 1.

[95] Anabel Powell Newman et al., "Prison Literacy: A Survey of the Literature," *Final Report Year 1, Volume IV: Working Papers,* National Center on Adult Literacy at the University of Pennsylvania (ed.) (Philadelphia, PA: November 1991), p. 158.

[96] Ibid., p. 158.

their educational attainment, to be tested when they enter a Federal facility; with a few specific exemptions (e.g., deportable aliens), all who test below 8th-grade equivalency on any of the six subtests must enroll in adult education for 120 days or until a GED is achieved. Those with limited English skills must attend an ESL program until they function at the 8th-grade level of competency skills on the Comprehensive Adult Student Assessment System (CASAS) test. Although inmates may opt out of the ABE program after the minimum mandatory period, if they do not continue to the specified level they cannot be promoted in prison industries above the entry job level.

Mandated participation for inmates has required increased financial commitment to literacy. With implementation of mandated GED and ESL standards, the Federal Bureau of Prison's budget for literacy services jumped from 25 percent of its total budget in fiscal year 1988 to 40 percent in fiscal year 1991.[97] Teachers in Federal prisons are generally full-time civil service educators; they have either teaching degrees or college degrees plus teaching experience, or have passed the National Teachers Exam.[98]

These Federal policies directly affect only 5 percent of the inmate population.[99] Almost three-quarters of all incarcerated offenders—750,000—are in long-term prisons and reformatories run by States; another 424,000 are in jails run by cities, counties, and local law enforcement agencies.[100] In 1990, 944 (78 percent) State correctional facilities operated onsite ABE programs for inmates. Even more (962) operated secondary academic programs.[101] Many of these are mandated literacy programs: in 1992, 17 States and the District of Columbia required literacy programs in their prisons.[102] Most of the remaining States have nonmandatory literacy programs. Of the States reporting mandatory literacy programs, the level of literacy ranged from a low of the 4th grade to a high of 9th grade in all subjects. Staff in State and local facilities are generally part-time teachers from the K-12 sector, but some facilities hire their own full-time teaching staff.[103] Many inmate literacy programs use the services of volunteer groups like LVA and LLA.

Most State and local correctional education activities are supported predominantly by State and local funding. However, literacy programs in nonfederal facilities are also supported through two new Federal grant programs under the 1991 National Literacy Act. Although authorized at $10 million, appropriations were $5 million for fiscal year 1992. The legislation authorized competitive grants to State or local correctional agencies for either programs in functional literacy or programs to develop and improve prisoners' life skills to reduce recidivism.

While prisons provide a "captive" audience for literacy programs, they create unique challenges. The overcrowding found in many prisons reduces availability of classroom space. Classes are often overbooked, library resources are limited, and hours and space available to inmates for

---

[97] Nancy Kober, "Profiles of Major Federal Literacy Programs," OTA contractor report, July 1992.

[98] Sylvia McCollum, Federal Bureau of Prisons, U.S. Department of Justice, personal communication, February 1993.

[99] In 1991, an estimated 823,414 men and women were under the jurisdiction of State or Federal correctional authorities. U.S. Department of Justice, "Prisoners in 1991," Bureau of Justice Statistics Bulletin, May 1992, p. 2.

[100] Ibid.

[101] U.S. Department of Justice, Bureau of Justice Statistics, *Census of State and Federal Correctional Facilities, 1990* (Washington, DC: U.S. Government Printing Office, December 1992).

[102] Heidi Lawyer, *Survey of Mandatory Literacy Programs in State Prison Systems* (Richmond, VA: Virginia Department of Correctional Education, March 1992).

[103] For example, a study of education in California county jails found that 96 percent of teachers are part time. Barry Stern, "Baseline Study: Education in County Jails," report to the California State Department of Education, March 1990, p. 25.

study or tutoring in private are restricted. Prison routines and work time often conflict with class time. Students may be moved from one institution to another without regard for their academic programs and with few mechanisms for transferring educational records, credits, or maintaining continuity with teachers or tutors in new facilities. Disciplinary actions can remove a prisoner from an academic program and those housed in maximum security settings are often unable to participate in classes or tutoring. When crises occur, "lock downs" can mean the indefinite cancellation of classes for all inmates, with little or no notice to teachers.

The transient nature of jail populations creates special problems; most jail inmates are moved out within 2 weeks, and almost all within 6 months,[104] making education programs difficult to structure. However, many consider jails a critical time to reach offenders and start them on alternate paths before they become hardened criminals.

Technology in Literacy Programs for Inmates

Early applications of technology in prisons were disappointing. In the 1970s, mainframe computers were linked by telephone lines to "dumb" terminals onsite in several Federal correctional institutions, but the cost of leases and monthly telephone charges, the inflexibility of the system, and limited courseware all led to dissatisfaction.[105] However, more powerful, flexible, and engaging technologies have led to renewed interest in technology.

New mandates for literacy in prisons have made correctional institutions an appealing technology market for several reasons, including the collective purchasing power of large correctional systems and the opportunities they provide for

A series of interactive satellite teleconferences jointly produced by PBS, correctional educators, and literacy volunteer organizations provided information on literacy programs for incarcerated adults.

linking software across servers. In 1990, the Federal prison system initiated a competitive bidding process for an audio-based integrated learning system (ILS). The ILS that was selected[106] has been placed in 24 Federal facilities, with an average of 12 terminals at each site. Students typically spend approximately one-half hour of their 6-hour instructional day working on their own on the system. Teachers have found the range of software gives them an efficient way to manage and individualize instruction, since they typically have no two students working on the same subject at the same level at the same time.[107]

A number of State prison systems also have purchased various ILSs on a statewide basis to get a competitive price and to assure that teachers throughout the prison system will benefit from the technology training provided by the vendors.

---

[104] A survey of seven county jails in California found that approximately one-half the inmates are released within 3 days after booking, 57 percent within 1 week, 63 percent within 2 weeks, and 96 percent within 6 months. Ibid., p. 23.

[105] Sylvia McCollum, "Computers Can Help," *Federal Probation*, vol. 49, September 1985, p. 35.

[106] The Plato System, manufactured by The Roach Corp.

[107] McCollum, op. cit., footnote 98, 1993.

Box 4-F—Literacy in the Los Angeles County Jail System[1]

In the Santa Loma Women's facility, "Carole,"[2] four months pregnant and awaiting trial on a charge of cocaine distribution, sits in class staring at a video showing the transfer of drugs from a mother's bloodstream to that of her fetus. "What Mother Takes, Baby Gets" makes the private act of taking drugs no longer private. She's taking the parenting class because her public defender told her it might help her chances for parole. Carole's beginning to see that it also might help her chances of having a healthy baby.

The Los Angeles County jail system, ironically described as "the largest jail in the Free World," houses over 23,000 men and women in 11 facilities. Over the course of a year, more than 250,000 people pass through the system: most are awaiting trial, sentencing, or transfer but some are serving sentences of up to 1 year.

The Correctional Education Division (CED) of the Sheriff's Department contracts with the Hacienda-La Puente Unified School District to provide educational programs in each facility. Over 40 different courses, which vary from site to site, include general equivalency diploma (GED) preparation, course work for the high school diploma, English as a second language (ESL), employability skills, life skills, vocational training, parenting programs, and AIDS education, as well as rehabilitation counseling covering child abuse, substance abuse, and victim awareness. A special initiative under the Job Training Partnership Act expands job-readiness skills. Because many of the courses are limited in size, there are waiting lists for some classes. Many courses, like the AIDS awareness seminar, are designed as 1-day programs to accommodate the transient client population. Legislation limits instruction to 3 hours per day, and classes are scheduled whenever the sheriff indicates there is free time in the inmates' schedules, including late at night—for vocational education in office cleaning.

Instructors use a variety of methods, including videotapes with small group discussion and computer-based instruction, to meet the needs and preferences of students. A customized program of individual study is the only possible approach for some inmates. On first entering the schools, inmates are given an aptitude test and set up with a tutoring program on the computer. When inmates feel ready to move on, an instructor works with them to assess their progress before giving them additional learning materials. Most educational activities are voluntary and inmates can choose what to study—a manifestation of CED's philosophy of empowering the inmates.

CED can request students' transcripts from school districts in California and other custodial facilities. Many inmates take advantage of the opportunity to continue their education at other facilities when transferred: in 1990, approximately 4,000 transcripts were transferred in and out of the Los Angeles jail system.

The Media Services program, with about 180 computers installed in 12 sites and a VCR in each classroom, uses an approach described as "an open architecture in a closed environment." "Open architecture" refers to the use

---

[1] This box is based on an OTA site visit and a case study by J.D. Eveland et al., Claremont Graduate School, "Case Studies of Technology Use in Adult Literacy Programs," OTA contractor report, June 1992, pp. 57-75.

[2] "Carole" is a fictional composite of actual inmates.

Texas recently purchased a different ILS[108] for correctional facilities throughout the State; 36 prisons now have computer laboratories equipped with 20 workstations each. Included in the overall purchase price is a training package that supports several days of intensive instruction at a central training facility for two or three instructors; when they return they are "local experts" and train other prison instructors in technology use.[109]

Several other States have made or are considering similar systemwide technology purchases for these reasons.

Other technology configurations have also been adopted. For example, the computer training facility in the Los Angeles County jails uses an open architecture in a closed environment (see box 4-F). The 12 jail sites housing some 25,000 inmates contain about 180 computers, mainly

---

[108] INVEST, by Jostens Learning Corp.

[109] Margaret Smith, Texas Department of Corrections, personal communication, February 1993.

of stand-alone computers equipped with a variety of courseware packages. The "closed environment" refers both to the nature of jails and to the Sheriff's Department's concerns for data security. In one instance, an entire jail was "locked down," because a student prisoner had stolen a diskette on which he had written his life story. Media Services is trying to network all sites in a way that allays fears about possible data security, while at the same time providing internal connectivity.

In 1981, CED began an aggressive and innovative program of internal courseware development that has extended into newer multimedia technologies. The "Mac Literacy Project" developed reading materials for inmates at the 3rd- and 4th-grade reading levels using vocabulary, topics, and idioms frequently used in the jails. Another software development effort employs text, animation, and synthesized speech to help students use the "mouse" so they can become self-sufficient in using the computer. ESL lessons involve realistic adult living situations and students can record and playback their attempts to imitate the target sounds. CED has also produced innovative software for use in vocational training programs, including carpet laying, commercial painting, tile setting, and dog grooming. Most of these programs employ "hot text," so that learners can click the mouse on unfamiliar words and hear them spoken, a valuable assist for many learners.

Video instruction has always been the primary emphasis of the Media Services Laboratory, and CED's video production facilities are extensive. The laboratory produces short "single-concept videos" to illustrate a particular concept or skill—e.g., the safe use of hand tools—and longer videos for more general use. For example, a series on the successful ESL teaching methods has been used in teacher inservice training. The Media Services program supports itself through the sale of videos and courseware, some of which are developed under contract for other literacy organizations. Media Services also provides technology training and support to CED teachers. Video has been extensively used in teacher training, helping to overcome the difficulties associated with a large instructional service area.

Despite the high profile CED gives technology-based instruction and the consensus that it is the wave of the future, information technology is just one of many tools used by CED. Instruction is still provided primarily through traditional educational approaches and materials. High inmate turnover and prohibitions on contact with released inmates stymy evaluation efforts. The director maintains a positive outlook:

> The ultimate goal is to have the inmates leave the jail better than when they entered. . . . Many feel that county jail facilities provide the best opportunity to change people around, because the crimes and circumstances involving these inmates are not as bad as those in State and Federal facilities. There is a strong need to increase these individuals' self-esteem and motivation, and have them understand that they are in charge of their own destiny.[3]

[3] Ernestine Schnulle, Corrections Education Division, Hacienda-LaPuente Adult Education, LaPuente, CA.

Apple Macintoshes, a result of the educational coordinator's personal collaboration with Apple in developing program materials. Much of the software used at the jails has been developed by the teachers themselves, including literacy materials incorporating vocabulary and idioms frequently used at the jail.

Many of the features that make interactive technology viable for adult learners are especially useful for inmates. Allowing material to be individualized and paced at the learner's speed is important for prison populations with variable educational backgrounds and ranges of literacy needs. Working on a computer offers privacy for learning and a sense of control—features generally missing in prison life and therefore highly valued. Furthermore, group interaction with some applications develops important social skills that many inmates lack. Technology is seen as a tool for the future and using computers improves prisoners' sense of self-worth.

Prison walls can be scaled via the technology—telephone/computer links can connect inmates with teachers or tutors outside the walls of the prison, while prison libraries, often woefully understocked, can be upgraded through links with libraries on the outside, databases, and other information resources. In youth correctional facilities, incarcerated juveniles can finish high school programs and participate in classes through linkups with local high schools, community colleges, or technical institutes. For the inmate who must be isolated, education can still take place even though he or she cannot "attend" class—via personal lessons on a computer, watching a televised class or tapes, or participating in a distance learning class via audiographics, satellite, cable, or other available technology. Since teachers and tutors in prison are available on a part-time basis and are often affected by security restrictions, technology can be a personal "secure" tutor.

POLICY IMPLICATIONS

It is not surprising that this patchwork of programs and providers has been unable to meet the challenges of providing comprehensive, intensive, long-term adult literacy service to the growing numbers of adults in need. With their limited resources and capabilities, predominantly part-time or unpaid staff, unstable funding, and lack of coordination, America's adult literacy programs serve at best less than 10 percent of the target population each year with low-intensity services of quality ranging from excellent to poor. High-quality adult literacy programs, of which there are many, are all the more impressive for the limitations under which they must operate, and the difficulties of the multiple demands and pressures adult learners face.

Despite the diversity of programs and services, a number of common issues appear, including: the need to enhance the professional status of adult literacy staff; the problems of providing comprehensive services; concerns with accountability and assessment of progress; the need for a research base on effective practices; the potential for encouraging partnerships and vehicles for coordination; and the promise of technology as a tool for more intensive individualized instruction as well as for better teacher training, recordkeeping, and information sharing. These issues are described in chapter 6.

The Federal
Role in Adult
Literacy
Education | 5

Since the mid-1960s, the Federal Government has played a critical role in providing education services to adults with inadequate literacy skills.[1] Unlike elementary and secondary education, where a mature State and local infrastructure existed before the Federal Government entered the field, public adult education is in many ways a Federal creation.

The main engines of the Federal role in adult education are the categorical grant programs—chief among them the Adult Education Act (AEA)—that support adult literacy and basic skills education. The Federal role is more than the sum of its grant programs, however. The Federal Government influences adult literacy services in other important ways—through executive branch initiatives and regulations, Federal leadership and public awareness activities, census counts and studies documenting and defining illiteracy, research and development, and congressional and departmental budget decisions. This chapter traces the evolution of the Federal role in adult literacy over time, analyzes current Federal efforts, and considers Federal policy on technology in adult literacy.

FINDINGS

- The Federal response to the problem of adult illiteracy consists of many categorical programs—at least 29, perhaps many

---

[1] Federal programs use a variety of terms to describe educational services below the college level for adults who are not proficient in basic skills or the English language. "Adult education," "basic skills," "literacy skills," "English literacy," and "English language instruction" all appear in Federal law, sometimes undefined. In discussions of specific programs, this chapter employs the terms used in the relevant legislation. Otherwise, this chapter uses the term "adult literacy education" or "basic skills education" when referring to the broader OTA definition set forth in chapter 2 of this report.

more, depending on the definition used—that in some way aid adult literacy and basic skills education. Although the individual programs have solid records of accomplishment, together they create a Federal role that is complicated, fragmented, and insufficient, and which, by its very nature, works against development of a coordinated Federal adult literacy policy.

■ Legislation enacted since 1986 has increased appropriations, created new programs, attempted to build capacity and coordination among existing programs, and assigned new literacy-related missions to programs with broader goals, such as welfare reform, immigration reform, job training, and prisoner rehabilitation. Whether adult education providers will have adequate tools and resources to carry out their new jobs will depend on how well the new laws are implemented and funded.

■ Total Federal spending for adult literacy is hard to calculate because specific expenditures for literacy education are not available for the Job Training Partnership Act (JTPA), Job Opportunities and Basic Skills Training (JOBS), Even Start, and other key programs. However, the Federal Government currently spends at least $362 million for adult literacy and basic skills education, more than double the amount of 5 years ago. Although Federal literacy dollars are a critical source of sustenance for State and local programs, these dollars are small in comparison with other major Federal education expenditures and meager in terms of the total population in need.

■ Though the U.S. Department of Education (ED) remains the primary Federal player in the adult literacy field, new legislation has expanded the influence of the Department of Health and Human Services (HHS) and the Department of Labor (DOL) at the Federal level, and their counterpart agencies at the State level. These shifts in agency responsibilities portend changes in who is served, what services they receive, and what outcomes are expected of them.

■ New Federal initiatives are increasing the emphasis on workplace literacy, family literacy, and literacy for adults with special needs, such as the homeless, the incarcerated, welfare mothers, and certain refugees. By channeling more funding toward special groups, however, the Federal Government may be inadvertently limiting opportunities for millions of adult learners, including many limited-English-proficient (LEP) adults, who do not meet these criteria but have the potential to quickly become functionally literate, self-supporting citizens.

■ Different and sometimes incompatible Federal funding streams, eligibility restrictions, and accountability requirements are a considerable source of frustration for State and local literacy practitioners and drive State and local delivery systems in ways that may not always reflect adult learner needs or promote efficient management practices.

■ Congress has sought to improve the quality and effectiveness of federally funded adult education programs by instituting outcome-based evaluation, and by strengthening teacher training, research, dissemination, and other components of the adult literacy infrastructure. Further work is needed to improve the knowledge base about adult learning, and to ensure that evaluation standards and quality indicators are appropriate, measurable, and consistent with long-term program goals.

■ By sending mixed and sporadic messages about the use of technology in adult literacy programs, the Federal Government has failed to exert the leadership necessary to overcome a cautious attitude toward technology among some adult literacy practitioners and to realize the potential of technology to improve instruction and program management.

■ Congress has enacted several requirements and incentives aimed at fostering coordination across Federal, State, and local literacy programs. In addition, States and local service providers are undertaking their own coordination initiatives.

Although promising, these efforts can only accomplish so much without further changes in law and departmental policy to make programs and requirements more consistent and complementary.

GROWTH OF THE FEDERAL ROLE IN ADULT LITERACY

Since the founding of the republic, the literacy of adult Americans has been an abiding Federal concern. Although the nature of Federal involvement in adult education has changed considerably over two centuries, the rationale has remained much the same. **Our democratic system presumes an educated citizenry.** Literacy affects our economic prosperity, social welfare, national security, and the future of our children. And the persistence of illiteracy drains the public till.

Historical Perspective

Through most of our history (see box 5-A), the Federal Government demonstrated its concern about adult literacy in very limited ways.[2] From the 19th through the early 20th century, general literacy instruction, like the rest of education, was not considered a Federal responsibility. Adult education programs were conducted by religious groups, settlement houses, charitable organizations, public schools, and other private and public institutions.[3] The Federal role was limited mostly to documenting literacy and illiteracy rates through the decennial censuses and providing some adult education for selected civil servants.

In the first half of the 20th century—as waves of immigrants reached American shores, as mass Army testing revealed serious basic skills deficiencies among World War I recruits, and as Federal surveys and special commissions called attention to the plight of educationally disadvan-

World War I mass testing found that 25 percent of army recruits were illiterate and lacking basic skills. It was not until World War II that literacy materials were developed and distributed to military personnel in response to test results and public pressure.

taged adults—pressures for Federal action mounted. In response, the Federal Government took several steps that might be considered early uses of adult education as a social policy tool. Among these were the enactment of education programs for immigrants in 1918 and for adult Native Americans in 1921, the initiation of a literacy campaign under the Works Progress Administration in 1936, and the development of literacy materials for military personnel at the end of World War II.

The Modern Federal Role Takes Shape

In the early 1960s, as the Federal Government became more active in education, Congress paved the way for a stronger interventionist role in adult education. In 1963, Congress amended the Manpower Demonstration and Training Act to provide basic skills education for unemployed adults; then in 1964 it created a State adult education program under the Economic Opportunity Act, a

---

[2] The following historical discussion was drawn from an OTA analysis of Federal legislation and from National Advisory Council on Adult Education, *A History of the Adult Education Act* (Washington, DC: 1980); Marie Costa, *Adult Literacy/Illiteracy in the United States* (Santa Barbara, CA: ABC-CLIO, 1988); and U.S. Department of Education, *History of the Adult Education Act: An Overview* (Washington, DC: 1991).

[3] Carmen St. John Hunter with David Harman, *Adult Illiteracy in the United States* (New York, NY: McGraw-Hill, 1979), p. 13.

Box 5-A—Highlights of the Federal Role in Adult Literacy: 1777 to 1986

1777 First expenditure of Federal funds to provide instruction in mathematics and military skills to Continental Army soldiers.

1840 U.S. Census collects first literacy data by asking heads of families how many white persons over age 20 in household cannot read or write.

1879 Federal School for Engravers provides first education and training to civil servants.

1914 World War I testing reveals 25 percent of draftees are illiterate.

1917 Legislation requires potential immigrants over age 16 to pass a literacy test.

1918 Passage of Immigration and Nationality Act: funds to public schools for English language, history, government, and citizenship programs for naturalization candidates.

1921 Passage of On-Reservation Indian Adult Education Act: literacy training for Native Americans.

1929 President Herbert Hoover appoints Advisory Committee on National Illiteracy; committee spearheads privately funded campaign with goal of teaching 5 million adults to read and write.

1933 President Franklin Delano Roosevelt initiates three employment programs with basic skills components: Federal Emergency Relief Administration, Civilian Conservation Corps, and Works Progress Administration. In 1936, Works Progress Administration starts 4-year literacy campaign.

1945 The military develops literacy materials with functional approach based on military life.

1955 The U.S. Office of Education establishes an Adult Education section.

1963 Congress passes Library Services Act; amends Manpower Development and Training Act to support basic skills for unemployed adults and out-of-school youth; and passes Vocational Education Act.

1964 Passage of Economic Opportunity Act: establishes Adult Basic Education State grant program for adults 18 and over whose inability to read or write English impairs their employment opportunities. Program administered by Office of Economic Opportunity (OEO).
Congress also approves Library Services and Construction Act.

1966 Congress passes the Adult Education Act (AEA): establishes Adult Basic Education program with broader mission than OEO program. Shifts responsibility to U.S. Office of Education.

1969 U.S. Office of Education initiates Right to Read campaign. Its goal: eradicating illiteracy by 1980.

1970 Congress amends AEA to encourage States to establish secondary-school completion programs for adults without high school diploma.

1972 Amendments to AEA expand programs for Native American adults.

1974 Further amendments to AEA limit share for adult secondary programs, create special programs for limited-English-speaking adults and the elderly, reserve funds for experimental projects and teacher training, and require cooperation with other programs.

1975 Federally sponsored Adult Performance Level study declares that 20 percent of adult Americans are functionally incompetent and another 34 percent are marginally competent.

1978 Amendments to AEA seek to expand service delivery system, encourage support services, give special attention to adult immigrants, and authorize several new research activities.

1982 Census Bureau survey estimates between 17 and 21 million American adults—nearly 13 percent—are illiterate.

1983 U.S. Department of Education establishes the Adult Literacy Initiative.

1986 National Assessment of Educational Progress concludes that great majority of young adults ages 21 to 25 have basic literacy skills but sizable proportion lack ''critical thinking'' skills.

SOURCES: National Advisory Council on Adult Education, *A History of the Adult Education Act* (Washington, DC: 1980); Marie Costa, *Adult Literacy/Illiteracy in the United States* (Santa Barbara, CA: ABC-CLIO, 1988); and U.S. Department of Education, *History of the Adult Education Act: An Overview* (Washington, DC: 1991).

War on Poverty program overseen by a new Office of Economic Opportunity (OEO).

The modern Federal role really took shape in 1966 with passage of the Adult Education Act, still the cornerstone of the Federal role today. Prior to 1966, few States had invested in adult basic education on their own.[4] The AEA transferred administrative responsibility for the State grant program from OEO to the U.S. Office of Education in the Department of Health, Education, and Welfare, and broadened the program to encompass basic education, English as a second language (ESL), and citizenship education. States received funds based on their numbers of adults without a high school diploma, and demand for services soon exceeded expectations. In subsequent years, the act was amended several times to encourage secondary-school completion programs, place more emphasis on special populations, build teacher training capacity, and broaden the base of service providers.

Beginning in the mid-1960s and continuing through the 1980s, Congress also enacted several other laws with implications for literacy policy: e.g., the Vocational Education Act, the Library Services and Construction Act (LSCA), the JTPA, the Volunteers in Service to America (VISTA) literacy program, and the Indian Education Act.

Public Awareness, "Bully Pulpit," and National Leadership

President Herbert Hoover's 1929 advisory committee on national illiteracy was an early effort to publicize illiteracy problems and rally public, private, and volunteer support—the bully pulpit approach. The Right to Read initiative, begun in 1969 under President Richard Nixon, was another such campaign; 6 years later the effort was downgraded in the bureaucracy, its goal of eradicating illiteracy by 1980 far from

Library of Congress

Many approaches have been used to gain public support and stimulate action to improve literacy. This 1938 poster by Rockwell Kent was part of the Federal Government's effort to stress the importance of reading.

being achieved. In the 1980s, the Adult Literacy Initiative under the Reagan Administration once again sought to raise public awareness, promote volunteerism, and coordinate literacy activities across the Federal Government.[5]

The Federal Government also helped shape literacy policy through efforts to document and define adult competencies. The 1975 Adult Performance Level survey and the 1986 literacy survey of young adults conducted by the National

---

[4] James T. Parker, "Modeling a Future Basic Education," *Adult Learning*, vol. 1, No. 4, January 1990, p. 16.

[5] A persistent criticism of these kinds of public awareness campaigns was that they offered the "illusion of genuine commitment" without meaningful new funding or consistent programmatic support, and as such would only ". . . sedate some people with the notion that 'something important' was now going to be done." Jonathan Kozol, *Illiterate America* (Garden City, NY: Anchor Press/Doubleday, 1986), p. 51.

Assessment of Educational Progress helped call attention to the continuing problem of illiteracy and spur national efforts to rethink literacy in functional terms.

Congress "Discovers" Adult Literacy: 1986 to the Present

In the late 1980s, "Congress discovered adult literacy."[6] Passage of the 1986 Immigration Reform and Control Act, which authorized the State Legalization Impact Assistance Grants (SLIAG) program supporting English literacy instruction, set off a wave of legislative activity that continued into 1991[7] (see box 5-B). The wave of legislative activity crested in 1988, the year in which the AEA and other major education programs came up for reauthorization and also an election year.

The laws enacted since 1986 expanded existing literacy programs, created new programs, and attached new literacy mandates to programs with broader purposes. Many gave public adult literacy programs "new jobs to do": integrating immigrants into the mainstream through the Immigration Reform and Control Act; moving people off welfare through the Family Support Act; breaking the generational cycle of illiteracy through the Even Start Act; reducing recidivism among ex-offenders through the Crime Control Act; and increasing employability through the Omnibus Trade and Competitiveness Act, the Carl D. Perkins Vocational and Applied Technology Education Act, and amendments to the JTPA.[8]

The executive branch also launched new literacy initiatives. President George Bush's 1989 Education Summit with the Governors produced six ambitious education goals for the year 2000, including Goal #5:

> Every adult American will be literate and will possess the knowledge and skills necessary to compete in a global economy and exercise the rights and responsibilities of citizenship.[9]

HHS provided seed money to all Head Start grantees for family literacy activities. The Bureau of Prisons raised the compulsory education participation requirements for Federal prisoners to a high school diploma equivalency level. DOL channeled discretionary funding into workforce literacy projects.

These past 6 years of activity have transformed the Federal role in adult education. In one sense, Congress has ". . . tied the fortunes of the federal human service agenda to the effectiveness of the literacy system in performing the new jobs assigned to it."[10]

To improve existing literacy programs and provide resources to fulfill these heightened expectations, Congress in 1991 passed the National Literacy Act (NLA) (see box 5-C). The NLA set forth a capacity-building agenda aimed at providing more resources, more professional staff, better coordination, higher program quality, and a stronger research base. It also amended the AEA, created the National Institute for Literacy

---

[6] Forrest P. Chisman et al., *Leadership for Literacy: The Agenda for the 1990s* (San Francisco, CA: Jossey-Bass, 1990), p. 221.

[7] Many factors helped fuel this legislative vigor. Attention from the media, scholars, writers, and business people linked the issues of illiteracy and declining American competitiveness and kept them in the public eye. The elementary and secondary school reform movement helped highlight weaknesses at other levels of education. Public, private, and volunteer literacy organizations began forming coalitions and identifying common goals. Perhaps most important, the political climate of the first term of the Reagan Administration—characterized by domestic budget cuts and few new social programs—had begun to turn, and it could be argued that the Democrat-controlled Congress was anxious to take advantage of a legislative window of opportunity.

[8] Chisman et al., op. cit., footnote 6, pp. 225-226.

[9] U.S. Department of Education, *America 2000: An Education Strategy* (Washington, DC: 1991), p. 9.

[10] Chisman et al., op. cit., footnote 6, pp. 225-226.

Box 5-B—Key Legislation and Executive Actions: 1986 to 1991

1986 **Immigration Reform and Control Act:** amnesty to undocumented aliens living in the United States; State Legalization Impact Assistance Grants (SLIAG) cover public assistance, health, and education services for newly legalized aliens.

Job Training Partnership Act (JTPA) Amendments: remedial education in Title II-B program.

Volunteers in Service to America (VISTA) Literacy Corps: more VISTA volunteers assigned to literacy effort.

1987 **Stewart B. McKinney Homeless Assistance Act:** literacy programs for homeless adults.

1988 **Hawkins-Stafford School Improvement Amendments:** Adult Education Act revised to improve planning and evaluation and better serve special populations. New programs: workplace literacy partnerships, English literacy grants, Even Start program for educationally disadvantaged parents and preschool children, and bilingual family literacy program for limited-English-proficient families.

Omnibus Trade and Competitiveness Act: basic skills education for dislocated workers under JTPA Title III and a Student Literacy Corps of undergraduate volunteer tutors.

Family Support Act: overhaul of Federal welfare system; mandates literacy education for welfare recipients through new Job Opportunities and Basic Skills (JOBS) training program.

1989 **Education Summit:** President George Bush and Governors produce six National Education Goals, including goal that all adult Americans will be literate by year 2000.

1990 **Crime Control Act of 1990:** mandatory literacy (including English as a second language) for Federal inmates below 8th-grade literacy level.

Carl D. Perkins Vocational and Applied Technology Education Amendments: greater emphasis on basic academic skills as part of vocational training.

National and Community Service Act: Commission to spur volunteerism in literacy and other areas.

1991 **National Literacy Act of 1991:** improve Federal research, program quality, and coordination; authorizes several new programs.

Higher Education Act Technical Amendments: program to help commercial drivers pass mandated literacy test.

Federal Bureau of Prisons regulations: compulsory education requirements for Federal prisoners raised to high school diploma equivalency level.

Head Start Family Literacy Initiative: Department of Health and Human Services encourages all Head Start grantees to incorporate family literacy into their regular activities.

SOURCE: Office of Technology Assessment, 1993.

---

and several new programs, established a statutory definition of literacy. Whether the NLA will provide literacy programs with the additional funding and tools they need to fulfill the new demands remains to be seen. The Federal role is at a critical juncture.

CURRENT FEDERAL ROLE

What is the result of 25 years of direct Federal attention to the literacy problem? Few would deny that Federal seed money, especially the AEA, has encouraged the growth of public, State, and local programs and has benefited millions of

---

Box 5-C—Major Provisions of the National Literacy Act of 1991

New definition of literacy. "An individual's ability to read, write, and speak in English, and compute and solve problems at levels of proficiency necessary to function on the job and in society, to achieve one's goals, and develop one's knowledge and potential."

National Institute for Literacy. This new Institute will conduct research, develop a national database, provide training and technical assistance, and advise on policy. Administered jointly by Department of Education, Department of Labor (DOL), and Department of Health and Human Services.

State resource centers. States will establish centers to foster coordination of literacy resources, develop new teaching methods, promote innovation, and provide technical assistance.

New Programs

- National workforce demonstration grants for large-scale projects involving unions and businesses.
- National Workforce Literacy Collaborative in DOL for technical assistance on workforce literacy.
- Grants to improve functional literacy and life skills of State and local prisoners.
- Public broadcasting program to produce family literacy programming and materials. (Unfunded)
- Challenge grants for community or employee literacy programs using VISTA volunteers. (Unfunded)

Amendments to Adult Education Act

- Extends act through 1995 and increases authorization of appropriations.
- States must provide "direct and equitable access" to Federal funds by a range of service providers.
- States will make "Gateway Grants" to public housing authorities for literacy programs.
- Secretary of Education will develop quality indicators by July 25, 1992; States will develop similar indicators for State and local programs by July 25, 1993.
- State set-aside for innovative projects and teacher training increased from 10 to 15 percent.
- States must evaluate 20 percent of the grant recipients in the State each year.

SOURCES: Public Law 102-73; Paul M. Irwin, Congressional Research Service, Education and Public Welfare Division, "National Literacy Act of 1991: Major Provisions of P.L. 102-73," CRS Report for Congress 91-811 EPW, Nov. 8, 1991; and U.S. Department of Education, "The National Literacy Act of 1991," *A.L.L. Points Bulletin*, October 1991, pp. 1-2.

---

adults who otherwise would have remained unserved.[11] Yet all together, some observers contend, "... the Federal initiative in adult literacy has been minimal, inefficient, and ineffective."[12]

The Federal Government also has been a pervasive and powerful influence—arguably *the* most powerful influence—on the provision of adult education services at the State and local level. Federal programs and policies affect State and local funding, administrative structures, pri-orities, target populations, services, and instructional approaches.[13] Nevertheless, a picture emerges of a Federal partner whose influence can be both beneficial and counterproductive (with the difference not always readily apparent); a partnership with as yet untapped potential to improve the coordination and delivery of adult education services.

Some cautions are in order. The State and Federal roles in adult education have matured

---

[11] U.S. Congress, House Committee on Education and Labor, *House Report 100-95* (Washington, DC: U.S. Government Printing Office, 1987), pp. 87-88.

[12] William F. Pierce, "A Redefined Role in Adult Literacy: Integrated Policies, Programs, and Procedures," background paper for the Project on Adult Literacy, Southport Institute, 1988, p. 1.

[13] Some of the information in this chapter is based on OTA site visits to two States, Massachusetts and Texas, in January 1992. The site visits included interviews with State agency staff for education, welfare, employment and training, libraries, technology, and a literacy council; and with local educational agencies, community colleges, city agencies, and community-based organizations.

somewhat contemporaneously, so it can be hard sorting out where Federal influence ends and State influence begins. Moreover, States take very different approaches to the same set of laws, programs, and guidance coming out of Washington, with States often adding interpretations and requirements on top of Federal ones. These differences among States are attributable not only to such factors as size, demographics, wealth, history, and political climate, but also to State leadership and philosophy. Some States have charted their own courses in adult education, independent of Federal policy, and serve as beacons for the Nation.

To assess the Federal role in greater depth, the Office of Technology Assessment (OTA) has analyzed major Federal laws and regulations and found several significant themes and trends that cut across programs and agencies.

The Number of Federal Literacy Programs

As recent studies have shown, determining how many Federal programs support adult literacy is a difficult proposition.[14] Only a handful of Federal laws have adult literacy or basic skills education as their primary purpose. Others authorize literacy education as a means toward another end. Some Federal programs give State or local entities discretion over how much to spend on literacy activities. Should all of these be counted as Federal literacy programs? What about programs, such as those run by the military and the Bureau of Indian Affairs, that are not specifically authorized by law but have been established by the executive branch under general legislative authorities for education? And what about programs that seek to *prevent* illiteracy? Taken to the extreme, the entire gamut of elementary and secondary education programs could be considered illiteracy prevention.[15]

Regardless of the definitions and categorizations used, it is clear that the Federal role in adult literacy is composed of many separate programs in several different agencies. The most recent study, which took a very broad view, found 77 programs in 11 Federal agencies that provided some degree of support for adult literacy education in fiscal year 1989; 23 of these were what the study called ''primary'' programs, in which ''adult education is explicitly stated as a primary objective in the program's authorizing legislation.''[16] Any analysis of the Federal role must at some point draw distinctions that could be viewed as arbitrary, and therefore any count of Federal adult literacy programs should be viewed as just a broad indicator.

OTA's analysis of the Federal role relies on a somewhat smaller core group of programs that together comprise the bulk of the Federal effort in adult literacy and basic skills education (see appendix B). These programs include those with literacy as a primary, explicit mission, as well as a few others—like the JTPA, JOBS and refugee/immigrant programs—that have the potential for significantly influencing adult literacy and basic skills education.

---

[14] See Mary E. Kahn, *Literacy Management Information Project Report* (Washington, DC: Washington Consulting Group, Inc., 1986); U.S. Congress, House Committee on Education and Labor, Subcommittee on Elementary, Secondary, and Vocational Education, *An Assessment of the Federal Initiative in the Area of Adult Literacy* (Washington, DC: U.S. Government Printing Office, 1987); and Judith A. Alamprese and Donna M. Hughes, *Study of Federal Funding Sources and Services for Adult Education* (Washington, DC: Cosmos Corp., 1990). The problems associated with defining the Federal literacy effort were illustrated by controversy surrounding publication of the *Literacy Management Information Project Report* (LMIPR), which concluded that there were 79 literacy-related programs in 14 Federal agencies. The House Subcommittee on Elementary, Secondary, and Vocational Education accused the report of promoting ''misinformation'' and released its own report, concluding that 48 percent of the programs mentioned in the LMIPR were not conducting adult literacy activities at all, and 32 percent did not have literacy as a major function.

[15] Paul M. Irwin, Congressional Research Service, Education and Public Welfare Division, ''Adult Literacy Issues, Programs, and Options,'' CRS Issue Brief IB85167, Apr. 5, 1991, p. 2.

[16] Alamprese and Hughes, op. cit., footnote 14, p. 9.

OTA's analysis suggests three important findings about the number of Federal programs:

- Even a rather narrow approach to counting programs turns up 29 literacy-related programs in 7 Federal agencies—bolstering the contention that Federal literacy programs are fragmented and mismatched.[17]
- The separate categorical program remains the preferred congressional approach to addressing the national illiteracy problem, and the number of programs has increased in recent years.
- Most of the programs are relatively small (in Federal terms). Of the 19 programs with identifiable adult education funding, only AEA basic grants have appropriations over $100 million; while 16 programs have appropriations under $10 million.

How did the Federal role come to be characterized by multiple categorical programs spread across several agencies? This may reflect the multiple dimensions of the illiteracy problem—economic, occupational, social, cultural, and educational—that call for different responses. Federal legislation also tends to be "reactive," attacking urgent problems with narrow, self-contained responses. Furthermore, categorical programs are easier to track, audit, and evaluate—virtues in a climate with increasing demands for "accountability." Another reason may be the jurisdictional organization of Congress and the executive branch, which tends to discourage crosscutting legislation or broad, systematic policy development. A final set of factors is political.

Sponsoring a separate bill under one's own name is often a more attractive option for a member of Congress than offering an amendment to someone else's bill or refashioning an existing program.

Are there too many Federal programs? Many State administrators and local service providers feel that ". . . the proliferation of programs has too often resulted in a fragmented delivery system"[18] or in ". . . multiple delivery systems, none of which provide the comprehensive, long-term services needed to meet the challenge of improving the basic skills of millions of adults."[19] The problem, they say, is not so much with duplication of services—with such great need, additional funding sources are always welcome. Rather, the problem lies with duplicative administrative tasks, different funding streams, incompatible service criteria, and an abundance of paperwork.[20]

State and local administrators reserve particular complaints for the small categorical programs, which some view as "short-term, unstable, fragmented" funding sources.[21] Some Federal discretionary grants must be recompeted annually, which makes budgeting and staffing of local programs difficult and unstable. Under those Federal programs that seek to demonstrate new or innovative approaches, funding often ceases once the new approach is tested, which discourages some grantees from applying at all.

Agency Roles

Although program assignments to Federal agencies roughly follow jurisdictional lines,[22]

---

[17] Pierce, op. cit., footnote 12, pp. 25-26.

[18] Ibid.

[19] Ibid., p. 18.

[20] Ibid., pp. 15-16.

[21] The University of the State of New York, State Education Department, *Adult Literacy: The Key to Lifelong Learning* (Albany, NY: February 1992), p. 15.

[22] The placement of literacy programs *within* Federal agencies also affects the visibility and focus of the effort. For instance, the AEA is administered by an ED division two levels below the Secretary, under an assistant secretary who also has responsibility for vocational education—a placement that some have characterized as being ". . . buried among higher priority programs within the Department of Education." Similarly, in some States, the primary adult education coordinator or director reports directly to the Chief State School Officer, while in others the office is two or three levels deep within the bureaucracy. See Pierce, op. cit., footnote 12, p. 18.

there is overlap. Both ED and the Department of the Interior administer literacy programs for Native American adults. Basic skills training for the workforce is addressed by ED and DOL. Programs for incarcerated adults exist in ED and the Department of Justice. Programs fostering volunteerism for literacy can be found in ED, the ACTION agency, and the new Commission on National and Community Service.

New Federal programs have enhanced the roles of DOL and HHS in the delivery of adult literacy services, although ED remains the major Federal administering agency. The growing influence of other Federal agencies has brought a new set of State entities into the literacy mix alongside State education agencies (SEAs), most notably agencies for welfare and employment training, but also agencies for libraries, refugee services, corrections, and higher education, as well as the Governors' offices. This shift has increased the complexity and, some say, the fragmentation of administrative structures. Each Federal or State agency has its own mission, constituency, and rules and regulations—which may or may not be compatible—and each tends to address literacy education "... from the vantage point of [its] own legislative mandate."[23] Many of these entities also have their own funding streams. As figure 5-1 illustrates, complex relationships can arise from the interweaving of multiple Federal and State agencies, funding streams, and service providers.

Some literacy administrators, usually those representing traditional adult education providers, see the involvement of new agencies as a negative trend. Because education is not the primary mission of welfare, employment, and training agencies, they note, these agencies are not usually staffed by education professionals and may not be attuned to the structures and approaches of adult education organizations and institutions. Others see these new players as bringing a fresh perspective to service delivery and a whole new set of funding partners into the literacy mix.

In addition, a whole separate Federal-to-local funding stream exists, composed of programs in which the Federal Government makes direct grants to the local projects, bypassing the State. Whether these programs are duplicative funding sources, "... unlikely to leverage State financial organizational and administrative resources,"[24] or whether they cut out a layer of bureaucracy depends largely on one's vantage point.

Federal Dollars

At least $362 million was appropriated in fiscal year 1992 for adult literacy from the Federal Government (see table 5-1). This is more than double the $179 million appropriated in fiscal year 1988 for roughly the same group of programs (see figure 5-2). Closer examination of Federal funding reveals some interesting findings. Compensating for inflation, funding for literacy programs has grown 175 percent for the programs included in the $362 million. This growth has not been uniform: appropriations for the AEA more than doubled after a period of stagnant funding; other programs, such as AEA English literacy grants, were cut; and some current programs included did not exist in 1988.[25] It could be argued that much of the increase in spending merely restored purchasing power lost earlier in the 1980s, as a result of budget cuts and freezes. **Nevertheless, the increase is significant because it occurred during a period of limited growth in domestic programs and because even modest new dollars can bring meaningful benefits to the field.**

Total Federal literacy funding is likely much higher than $362 million. As the following

[23] Kahn, op. cit., footnote 14, p. 12.

[24] National Alliance of Business, *Shaping Tomorrow's Workforce: A Leadership Agenda for the 90's* (Washington, DC: 1988), p. viii.

[25] Nancy Kober, "Profiles of Major Federal Literacy Programs," OTA contractor report, July 1992.

Figure 5-1—Programs, Agencies, and Funding Streams: The Massachusetts Example

State participation in multiple Federal basic skills, workforce training, and related programs often produces complex interagency relationships and funding streams at the State and local levels, especially when the State funds its own programs with similar goals. The range of workforce development and basic skills programs in the State of Massachusetts, though far from the most complex State example, suggests the complex webs that arise from the interplay of different funding streams.

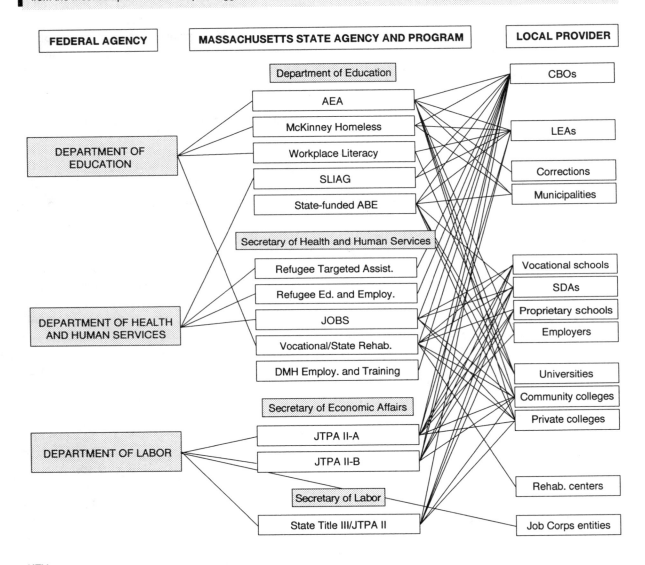

KEY
AEA = Adult Education Act
SLIAG = State Legalization Impact Assistance Grants
ABE = Adult Basic Education
JOBS = Job Opportunities and Basic Skills
JTPA = Job Training Partnership Act

CBO = Community-based organization
LEA = local education agencies
SDA = service delivery area
Rehab. = rehabilitation

SOURCE: Office of Technology Assessment, 1993, based on information developed by the Massachusetts Jobs Council.

Table 5-1—Appropriations for Major Federal Adult Literacy and Basic Skills Programs

	Fiscal year 1992 funding (in millions)		Fiscal year 1992 funding (in millions)
Department of Education		**Department of Labor**	
Adult Education Act (AEA) Basic Grants ....$	235.8	Job Training Partnership Act (JTPA) Title II-A, Training for Disadvantaged Youth and Adults ......$(1,773.5[a])	
AEA State Literacy Resource Centers	5.0	JTPA Title II-B, Summer Youth Employment	
AEA Workplace Literacy Partnerships	19.3	and Training	(495.2[a])
AEA English Literacy Grants	1.0	JTPA Title III, Dislocated Workers	(577.0[a])
AEA National Programs	9.0	JTPA Title IV-B, Job Corps	(846.5[a])
Literacy for State and Local Prisoners	5.0	National Workforce Literacy Collaborative	0
Commercial Drivers Program	2.5		
Adult Education for the Homeless	9.8	**Department of Defense**	
Special Programs for Indian Adults	4.3	Army Basic Skills Education Programs (BSEP):	
Even Start Family Literacy	(70.0[a])	BSEP I & II ....$	6.5[d]
Bilingual Family English Literacy	6.1	Navy Skills Enhancement Program	3.1[d]
Library Services and Construction Act (LSCA)		**Department of the Interior**	
Title VI, Library Literacy	8.2	Bureau of Indian Affairs Adult Education ....$	3.4
LSCA Title I, Public Library Services	(83.9[a])		
Student Literacy Corps	5.4	**Department of Justice**	
Migrant High School Equivalency (HEP)	8.3	Bureau of Prisons Literacy Program ....$	16.1[d]
Department of Health and Human Services		**ACTION**	
Job Opportunities and Basic Skills Training (JOBS) ...$	(1,000.0[a])	Volunteers in Service to America (VISTA) Literacy	
State Legalization Impact Assistance Grants (SLIAG) ..	(1,122.9[a] [b])	Corps ....$	4.8
Refugee Resettlement Program	83.0[a]	**Total FY 1992 funding** ....$	**362.4**
Head Start Family Literacy Initiative	9.0[c]		

NOTE: Amounts in parentheses are not included in Total FY 92 funding.

[a] Amounts are for entire program; specific expenditures for adult literacy are not available.

[b] Deferred.

[c] Minimum.

[d] Estimate.

SOURCE: Nancy Kober, "Profiles of Major Federal Literacy Programs," OTA contractor report, July 1992.

evidence suggests, even small percentages of expenditures for adult basic skills under such large programs as JTPA, JOBS, and SLIAG can be significant:

- A 1990 DOL report estimated that in 1986 8 percent of JTPA Title II-A enrollees and in 1984 6 percent of JTPA Title III enrollees received basic skills training.[26] If even 1 percent of the $2.35 billion currently appropriated for these two programs were used for basic skills, it would constitute in excess of $20 million.

- Under the Job Corps program (Title IV of JTPA), $40.8 million—or 7.2 percent of the appropriation for Job Corps center operations—was spent on basic education in program year 1990.[27]

- The 8-percent "Governors' set-aside" under JTPA totals $142 million nationwide; nearly all States offer some adult literacy programs with this money.[28]

- Under the JOBS program, States report spending a total of $14.5 million in *combined* Federal and State funding for adult basic and general equivalency diploma (GED) education, with

---

[26] U.S. Department of Labor, "Major Federal Programs Supporting Adult Literacy Efforts in the U.S. Department of Labor," unpublished report, 1990.

[27] Gerri Fiala, director, Division of Planning, Policy, and Legislation, U.S. Department of Labor, personal communication, May 15, 1992.

[28] Robert G. Ainsworth et al., *The JTPA Education-Coordination Set-Aside: States' Implementation of the Program* (Washington, DC: National Commission for Employment Policy, 1991), p. 8.

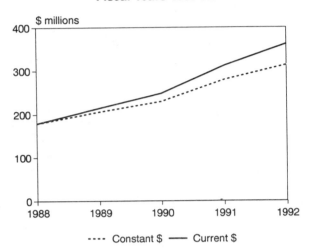

Figure 5-2—Identifiable Federal Funding for Adult Literacy and Basic Skills Education, Fiscal Years 1988-92

---- Constant $ —— Current $

NOTE: Constant dollars have been calculated using the Implicit Deflator for State and Local Government Purchases of Services. Separate computations were made for the forward-funded programs authorized by the AEA by applying the price index for the succeeding fiscal year in which funds are appropriated.

SOURCE: Office of Technology Assessment, 1993.

the amount from Federal sources alone unavailable.[29] Expenditures of JOBS money for education through the high school level vary widely by State; one study found a range from $0 to over $4.8 million in fiscal year 1991.[30]

■ JOBS expenditures on basic skills would be higher if States would "draw down" their full JOBS entitlements.[31]

■ The SLIAG program injected significant new money into the adult literacy stream. However, the fiscal year 1992 appropriations were deferred and the authorization is slated to expire.

Despite recent growth in Federal funding, the question remains as to whether the Federal Government is doing "enough" about the problem of adult illiteracy. Placing the Federal commitment in different contexts sheds some light on the issue. Although AEA funding has grown to $270 million, it still constitutes just 1 percent of the total ED budget. Compared with other multibillion-dollar programs—vocational education, special education, Chapter 1, or student aid—the AEA remains modest (see figure 5-3). And compared with the total Federal funding commitment to other multifaceted domestic problems—building the Interstate Highway System, providing Food Stamps, or preventing and treating drug abuse, to cite just a few—the $362 million in identifiable Federal expenditures for literacy appears disproportionately small (see figure 5-4).

Another way of looking at spending is in the context of need for services. From 1990 to 1991, the Federal AEA programs served 3.6 million[32]—between 5 and 10 percent of the illiterate population, depending on which definitions and estimates are used.[33] This is far less, for instance, than the percentage of eligible Chapter 1 children (60

---

[29] Wilbur Weder and Dennis Poe, Division of Program Evaluation, Office of Family Assistance, U.S. Department of Health and Human Services, personal communication, May 1, 1992. This figure does not include self-initiated education, or the $300 million HHS provides in childcare for JOBS participants.

[30] Jan L. Hagan and Irene Lurie, *Implementing JOBS: Initial State Choices* (Albany, NY: The Nelson A. Rockefeller Institute of Government, 1992).

[31] GAO estimated that in fiscal year 1992 about 38 percent of the Federal appropriation—or nearly $372 million—may have gone unspent because States were not meeting matching requirements. See U.S. General Accounting Office, *Welfare to Work: States Begin JOBS, But Fiscal and Other Problems May Impede Their Progress* (Washington, DC: U.S. Government Printing Office, 1991), p. 44. According to fiscal year 1993 HHS budget documents, $832 million of the $1 billion available for fiscal year 1992 was spent, leaving $168 million, or 17 percent, unspent from that year's budget authority.

[32] Joan Seamon, director, Division of Adult Education and Literacy, U.S. Department of Education, personal communication, Apr. 1, 1992. AEA participation counts are based on numbers of persons receiving 12 hours of services or more, and therefore include adults who are in the program for a relatively short time or who receive services of lesser intensity.

[33] U.S. Department of Education, *A Summary Report: National Forums on the Adult Education Delivery System* (Washington, DC: U.S. Government Printing Office, 1991), p. 27.

to 70 percent) or Head Start children (30 to 60 percent, depending on the age group used) estimated to be served.[34] As the pool of adults in need of services increases by an estimated 1 million annually due to legal and illegal immigration,[35] and perhaps another 1 million due to school dropouts, it must be asked whether Federal funding is running to stay in the same place.

A reliance on funding from multiple Federal sources may exacerbate the touch-and-go funding situation of many local literacy providers. Federal discretionary grants or contract letters sometimes do not arrive until well after the project period has begun, a particularly troublesome problem in competitive grant programs and in reimbursement-based programs such as JOBS and SLIAG. AEA, JOBS, and JTPA also pass through dollars on different timetables.

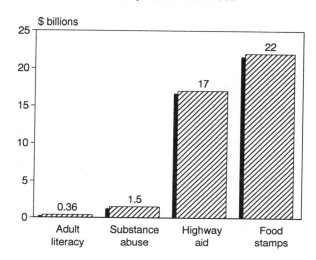

Figure 5-4—Funding for Select Federal Domestic Priorities, Fiscal Year 1992

SOURCE: Office of Technology Assessment, 1993.

The situation is further complicated because some Federal programs are forward-funded (grantees know the amount of their awards before the beginning of the year in which the funds are obligated); some are current-year funded (funds arrive during the fiscal year); and some operate on a reimbursement basis (agencies receive reimbursements for funds they have already spent). State programs may operate on a different fiscal year than the Federal fiscal year, confusing the situation still more.[36]

Finally, Federal programs have different provisions for carrying over unobligated funds. AEA funds can be carried over for 27 months and JTPA funds for an additional 2 years. JOBS does not allow funds to be carried over but permits obligated funds to be liquidated during the 12 months following the end of the fiscal year.

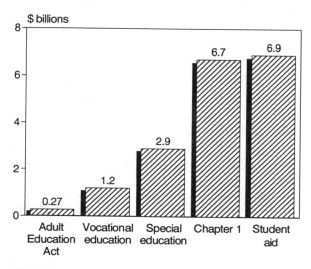

Figure 5-3—Funding for Select Department of Education Programs, Fiscal Year 1992

SOURCE: Office of Technology Assessment, 1993.

---

[34] Jeffrey McFarland, U.S. Congress, House Committee on Education and Labor, Subcommittee on Elementary, Secondary, and Vocational Education, personal communication, Dec. 5, 1991; and Terry Deshler, U.S. Congress, House Committee on Education and Labor, Subcommittee on Human Resources, personal communication, Dec. 5, 1991.

[35] "Illegal Immigration," *CQ Researcher*, vol. 2, No. 16, Apr. 24, 1992, pp. 363, 366.

[36] Some States, such as Texas, have put all their programs on the same planning cycle, regardless of when the State gets the dollars.

New Emphases

The past 6 years of legislative activity have produced marked changes in emphasis in Federal literacy programs. In general, the new emphases recognize that there are diverse types of "literacies" and that improved literacy can have a multiplier effect, in terms of better jobs, improved parenting, reduced welfare dependence, and less criminal recidivism.

One new emphasis is workplace literacy. Since 1988, several new Federal programs have focused on improving workers' basic skills, including the workplace literacy partnership program, national workplace literacy strategies, and a commercial drivers program[37]—all in ED; and a national workforce literacy collaborative in DOL.[38] In addition, workforce development efforts target those on the margins of the labor market. New amendments to the JTPA and Federal vocational education legislation emphasize basic skills instruction as a component of job preparation for unemployed adults, displaced workers, displaced homemakers, single parents, and disadvantaged youth. Federal workplace literacy efforts amounted to about $21 million in fiscal year 1992. It remains to be seen whether these efforts are sufficient to meet the educational needs of working adults with basic skills deficiencies—a

group some have called "... the most seriously neglected national priority in this [literacy] field."[39]

Family literacy is a second new emphasis in the Federal framework. The Even Start program,[40] the Head Start family literacy initiative,[41] the Bilingual Family English Literacy program,[42] and certain provisions of the Library Literacy program[43] give an intergenerational focus to the Federal role that was largely absent before 1988. The JOBS program, too, might be said to consider intergenerational issues by targeting Aid for Dependent Children (AFDC) parents of young children. In comparison to need, however, the total Federal family literacy effort is still in the budding stage.[44]

A third new emphasis is mandatory participation—a marked departure from the traditional adult basic education (ABE) approach, in which participants enroll voluntarily and set their own goals. The most far-reaching mandates are in the JOBS program, which directs States to require certain welfare recipients—primarily young custodial parents with inadequate basic skills—to participate in educational programs, if childcare is provided and to the extent that State resources permit. The full effect of this mandate has not been felt yet due to limited State funding and the ability of States to fulfill Federal participation requirements with volunteers.[45] A similar but

---

[37] The Motor Vehicle Safety Act of 1986 required commercial drivers to pass a written and oral knowledge test or risk losing their license. The deadline for compliance was April 1992.

[38] In cooperation with other agencies, DOL is developing a new initiative to provide technical assistance to small and medium-sized businesses to help them cope with a variety of work restructuring issues; this initiative will encompass the functions of the National Workforce Collaborative and several other related functions. Gerri Fiala, director, Division of Planning, Policy, and Legislation, U.S. Department of Labor, personal communication, Apr. 30, 1992.

[39] Forrest P. Chisman, *Jump Start: The Federal Role in Adult Literacy* (Southport, CT: The Southport Institute, 1989), pp. iv-v.

[40] The Even Start program under Chapter 1 of the Elementary and Secondary Education Act targets educationally disadvantaged parents and their children ages 0 to 7 who live in low-income Chapter 1 school attendance areas.

[41] HHS now requires all Head Start grantees to incorporate family literacy into their regular activities.

[42] Title III of the Elementary and Secondary Education Act authorizes this program for limited-English-proficient parents and children.

[43] Library Services and Construction Act, Titles I and VI.

[44] Funding for these programs totaled $85 million in fiscal year 1992, of which $70 million was for Even Start. The specific amount of Even Start money spent on adult literacy education (as opposed to children's education, parenting education, and other authorized activities) is not available, but it is unlikely to be high, since regulations encourage projects to use existing literacy resources in the community.

[45] Hagen and Lurie, op. cit., footnote 30, pp. 15-16.

In many States, AFDC clients are being placed in education programs to improve their literacy skills. The New Chances Multi Resource Center in Minneapolis provides GED and life-skills instruction to teenage mothers with Federal funding from the JOBS programs.

smaller program in the Department of Agriculture, the Food Stamp Employment and Training program, also mandates education and training for certain Food Stamp recipients. As noted in chapter 4, mandatory participation is becoming a trend in programs for incarcerated adults, as well.

A fourth new emphasis is improving the quality, effectiveness, and infrastructure of adult literacy programs. Over the years, Federal adult education programs have been criticized for devoting relatively little attention to teacher training, research, and data collection. The 1988 AEA amendments and the 1991 NLA set forth a new knowledge-acquiring, capacity-building, and

program improvement agenda for the Federal Government and the States. The 1991 act, in particular, authorizes a National Institute for Literacy, State resource centers, a National Adult Literacy Survey, and a national workplace strategies demonstration program, and requires indicators of program quality in AEA programs.

Many people in the field consider the new capacity-building provisions—particularly the National Institute and the State resource centers—to be the most significant provisions of the 1991 law.[46] Several new research and implementation issues have arisen as a result of legislation enacted since 1986 and could form the core of a

---

[46] Forrest P. Chisman, president, Southport Institute for Policy Analysis, personal communication, Jan. 8, 1992; Richard K. Long, Washington representative, International Reading Association, personal communication, Jan. 9, 1992; and Joan Y. Seamon, director, Division of Adult Education and Literacy, U.S. Department of Education, personal communication, Dec. 10, 1991.

research agenda for the National Institute and State resource centers. Areas for study include the effects of mandated participation, differences in learning styles among target groups, effective uses of technology for instruction and management, and the effects of competition for program slots when there are waiting lists.[47] Thus, the success of many of the new Federal programs hinges in part on how well and how expeditiously this ambitious new knowledge-acquiring and capacity-building agenda is implemented.

Definitions of Services

OTA finds that Federal literacy laws, collectively speaking, take a haphazard approach to defining key services and activities. Different terms are used to mean roughly the same thing, and many critical terms are not defined at all. For example, all the following terms are used to describe allowable services in different Federal laws: adult basic education, adult secondary education, literacy training, basic skills education, basic skills training, remedial education, English as a second language, English literacy instruction, and English language instruction. In many cases, these terms are not defined in law or regulation; where they are, they are sometimes defined differently across programs.[48] Vagueness is especially pronounced in the JTPA: the terms basic education, remedial education, and literacy training are used in ways that imply different meanings, yet none are defined.

This inconsistency and vagueness may be attributable to the pluralistic needs of the eligible population, to the different historical roots of the various Federal literacy efforts, or to ever-changing perceptions of what constitutes an adequate level of literacy. Nevertheless, with key terms left up to guesswork, the possibilities for multiple interpretations and misinterpretations abound, even as the chances of accurately assessing the extent of the problem diminish.

Section 3 of Public Law 102-73, the 1991 NLA, seeks to improve this situation by instituting a statutory definition of literacy with a functional orientation, one that ED intends to apply over the long term to all its programs:

> An individuals' ability to read, write, and speak in English, and compute and solve problems at levels of proficiency necessary to function on the job and in society, to achieve one's goals, and develop one's knowledge and potential.

Whether other agencies will follow suit and adopt this as a consistent Federal standard remains to be seen.[49]

Target Populations

Until fairly recently, most Federal aid to adult education was relatively untargeted. The bulk of funding was (and still is) distributed through AEA basic grants, open to any adult with educational need, regardless of income, country of origin, or other restrictions. Programs in other agencies dealt with a handful of special target groups, such as military personnel.

New Federal laws have increased the amount of Federal funding with restricted eligibility, shifting the Federal emphasis somewhat toward:

- Low-income adults, through the JOBS and JTPA programs;
- Parents of young children, through the family literacy and JOBS programs;
- Groups with special needs (i.e., State and local prisoners and the homeless); and

---

[47] The National Center for Adult Literacy, one of the Department of Education's federally funded research centers, can also contribute to the base of knowledge about program effectiveness, adult learning and motivation, and use of technology.

[48] For example, "literacy" is defined in functional terms in the new National Literacy Act definition, whereas the JOBS regulations define literacy as a grade-equivalent level of 8.9. Similarly, "limited English proficient" is defined in three slightly different ways in the AEA, family bilingual education, and JOBS regulations.

[49] Seamon, op. cit., footnote 46.

■ Highly defined subcategories of newcomers (eligible legalized aliens, refugees, and Cuban and Haitian entrants).

The general intent seems to be to drive more resources toward groups that Congress feels may have been neglected or underserved by traditional programs.[50]

Targeted Federal programs seem to be accomplishing their intended effect of channeling more funds toward adults with special needs and encouraging States and local providers to reach out to groups, such as the homeless and welfare mothers, whose access to general ABE programs has been limited.[51] As a result of the JOBS program, for example, more welfare clients are being referred to adult education programs and almost one-half of the States report shifting the emphasis of their welfare-to-work efforts away from immediate job placement toward basic skills and long-term education or training.[52]

An analysis of targeting provisions raises several issues, however. First, a question arises as to whether the growth of targeted programs means a diminished emphasis on other adults who may not fit into Federal "boxes"—working adults, certain LEP adults, educationally disadvantaged adults above the poverty line, adults with learning disabilities, and high school graduates who have not mastered basic skills. All of these groups must compete for spaces in AEA-funded programs, other public programs, or private/volunteer programs. Given current funding levels, it is unrealistic to imagine that they

will all be served. Yet the Federal laws appear to expect that literacy programs will be able to serve all of the new target populations without diminishing services to the groups traditionally enrolled in ABE. Some State and local practitioners feel that targeted programs require them to be more responsive to Federal guidelines than to the community needs.[53]

This inadequacy in the Federal framework is particularly pronounced regarding the LEP population, the fastest growing group in adult education. Here the Federal role is a ". . . combination of generosity and neglect."[54] Those eligible under SLIAG and the Refugee Resettlement program benefited from significant Federal funding. The rest of the LEP population—including most immigrants, undocumented aliens, and native-born Americans—must seek help through the AEA or nonfederal programs, unless they are fortunate enough to live in a community that has received a Federal LEP discretionary grant or a bilingual family literacy grant. Although ESL enrollments in Federal AEA programs now comprised 35 percent of the total,[55] services still fall far short of need. According to one local ESL director in Massachusetts, the number of slots available for working LEP adults—the majority of their waiting list—has decreased as the proportion of their budget coming from special Federal programs has gone up. Adults eligible for SLIAG, refugee programs, JOBS, and needs-based programs can "jump" the wait list, but this lengthens

---

[50] This trend must not be overstated. The majority of identifiable Federal literacy funding, provided through AEA basic grants, is still relatively unrestricted, as are such programs as library literacy and VISTA. And the new emphasis on workplace literacy for employed adults might be considered a trend in a very different direction, toward serving the least economically disadvantaged who are already in the job market.

[51] It should not be forgotten that some new Federal ideas, such as workplace literacy and welfare reform, were actually pioneered by the States.

[52] U.S. General Accounting Office, op. cit., footnote 31, p. 4.

[53] The University of the State of New York, op. cit., footnote 21, p. 15.

[54] Chisman et al., op. cit., footnote 6, p. 13.

[55] U.S. Department of Education, *Teaching Adults With Limited English Skills* (Washington, DC: U.S. Government Printing Office, 1991), p. 1.

the wait for those left behind and discourages them from seeking help.[56]

Recent legislation has not clearly resolved whether limited Federal resources should focus on those adults with the most severe educational needs, who incur the greatest social costs, or on those closest to functional literacy, with the greatest promise of becoming productive workers in the shortest time. The current mix of Federal programs leans somewhat in the direction of the former, but with enough departures in favor of the latter to suggest that the Federal Government is trying to be all things to all people. As many program people note, when the number of "priority" groups proliferates to a certain point, the whole concept of priority loses its meaning, and it becomes hard to distinguish the true priorities.

Are Federal JOBS requirements really expanding the total pool of resources for adult literacy education or merely changing the composition of adult classes by displacing "slots" available for nonwelfare adults? Many States, in compliance with HHS regulations[57] are placing JOBS clients in education services paid for by sources other than JOBS funds. In one 1991 study, 26 States reported that 40 percent or more of JOBS participants were placed in activities paid for by other providers.[58] Research also suggests that many States do not have enough program slots to fill the demand for JOBS services; over one-half of the States cited or expected shortages in alternative, basic, and remedial programs for JOBS clients, particularly in rural areas.[59]

Finally, the Federal concept of compartmentalization by target group is somewhat at odds with how most local programs prefer to operate,

accepting all comers and grouping by type and level of instruction.

Administrative Entities and Service Providers

The Federal Government has played an important role in the development of public infrastructure to serve illiterate adults. Until recently, SEAs and local education agencies (LEAs) dominated the scene. The creation of new programs, the rise of DOL and HHS as key players, and the revamping of AEA distribution requirements are bringing about changes in State roles, administrative structures, funding streams, and the mix of service providers.

The 1991 amendments to the AEA require a range of service providers to have "direct and equitable access" to Federal funds. In effect this change signals a shift away from LEAs and school-based models toward community-based organizations (CBOs) and other diverse providers.[60] These amendments have potentially far-reaching implications for service delivery, as States revise their allocation systems to comply and as previously unfunded organizations compete for direct grants. The Texas Education Agency, for example, has drafted amendments to its AEA State plan that allow all eligible grantees to apply directly to the State for competitive grants, but that also encourage eligible recipients to participate in a consortium, with a single fiscal agent applying on behalf of several service providers. Massachusetts, by contrast, is likely to make very few changes in its competitive process.

Broadening the base of service providers as required by law may also give rise to a whole new

---

[56] Betty Stone, ESL director, Somerville Center for Adult Learning Experiences, Somerville, MA, personal communication, Jan. 28, 1992.

[57] HHS regulations require States to ". . . identify existing resources . . . and assure that costs for these other services for which welfare recipients have been eligible are not incurred by the JOBS program." 45 CFR 250.12.

[58] U.S. General Accounting Office, op. cit., footnote 31, p. 23. Also see Hagen and Lurie, op. cit., footnote 30, p. 8.

[59] U.S. General Accounting Office, op. cit., footnote 31, p. 31.

[60] Many researchers, as well as CBO advocates, argue that school-based adult education programs, because of their outreach methods, institutional settings, locations, and teaching approaches, are less likely to serve the most disadvantaged adults than CBOs and other private nonprofit providers.

set of service delivery issues: how to guarantee quality control throughout a larger, more diverse network; how to establish economies of scale and efficient management practices; how to provide technical assistance to local organizations that have not worked with Federal requirements before; and how to assure coordination and avoid duplication.

New legislation also increases the role of the private sector. The workplace literacy program, for example, makes businesses and labor unions direct grantees and primary partners in delivering services. Other programs give private-sector groups responsibility for planning, advising, coordinating, developing curriculum, providing technology, and, in the case of JTPA, overseeing programs.

Finally, the Federal role affords greater recognition to volunteer literacy efforts through such programs as the VISTA literacy corps, the library literacy programs, the Student Literacy Corps, and the Commission on National and Community Service, and through AEA amendments requiring States to describe how they will use volunteers to expand the delivery system.

Services and Activities

Until recently the Federal Government has been cautious about prescribing the types of adult education services or the quality and intensity of those services. Aside from limiting the amount for adult secondary education and specifying which support services are allowable, the AEA has been relatively flexible. Critics have argued that the flexibility in the law regarding instructional services—together with limited Federal funding and an input-based evaluation system—has helped create an adult basic education model that provides low-intensity services for a short time to many people and that relies on part-time teachers and volunteers.

In general, the Federal framework seems to be edging toward greater prescription regarding activities and services. Under the refugee resettle-ment program, for example, English language instruction must be related to "obtaining and retaining a job" and must be provided outside normal working hours to the extent possible. The Even Start program requires each project to contain certain minimum elements—such as screening, support services, and home-based programs. In at least some cases, this type of Federal prescription seems aimed at ensuring quality control.

These more prescriptive service requirements seem to be having an effect at the State and local level. Many local providers have responded to JOBS' minimum 20-hour requirements by mounting a high-intensity program for JOBS and other clients who have time to devote to these programs. As implementation progresses, this program will provide a good case study of the effects of participation mandates and of a more intense level of services.

A related trend is toward specifying minimum levels of participation and a minimum intensity of services. For example, in the JOBS program, reimbursements are based on average numbers of clients who receive a minimum of 20 hours of service weekly, and individuals are deemed to be participating satisfactorily if they attend 75 percent of scheduled JOBS activities. The Bureau of Prisons also mandates a minimum of 120 hours of literacy instruction for inmates below the GED level. Although the AEA remains relatively nonprescriptive, the newly mandated indicators of program quality being developed by the Secretary of Education could also have an impact on modes of instruction and intensity of services.

Federal laws are also becoming somewhat more open about funding support services, such as childcare, transportation, outreach, and counseling. New Federal programs have also helped move services to nontraditional locations, such as job sites and homeless shelters. Federal family literacy programs, which emphasize services for both parents and children at a single site, are also helping to change traditional assumptions about how and where services are delivered.

Public Broadcasting Service

Regulations have raised the compulsory education requirements for Federal prisoners to high school diploma equivalency level. At the Maryland State Penitentiary, inmates use the library to expand their skills and pursue personal interests.

Accountability Requirements

Most Federal adult literacy programs contain a range of fiscal, reporting, and evaluation requirements aimed at ensuring that programs serve the intended clients and use sound financial and management practices. The most common fiscal requirements call for State and local matching, limit administrative costs, require maintenance of effort, and prohibit supplanting of State and local funds. Of particular significance are matching requirements. These vary considerably across programs. JTPA, for example, is 100 percent federally funded; other programs are 50 percent or less. This means that the Federal Government has "... a differing locus of leverage ..." for each program—"[o]bviously an agency can push harder when it kicks in the lion's share of the money."[61]

Most programs also have annual reporting and recordkeeping requirements, each of which may seem sensible in context, but which cumulatively may produce a substantial burden for participating agencies. State and local providers often find multiple Federal accountability requirements "... cumbersome, confusing, and costly ..."[62] and a considerable source of frustration. Several State and local administrators report that because accountability is so different from one funding source to another, a program that gets three or four different discretionary grants must have as many accountability systems. One formal evaluation concluded that when local programs obtain funds from multiple sources, they pay an information burden price, since they often must collect the same information in slightly different forms to satisfy different reporting requirements. Further frustration occurs when Federal requirements change in midstream, even after a law is well in place.[63]

Needs-based programs and reimbursement-based programs, such as JOBS, SLIAG, and JTPA, seem to generate the most criticisms from local providers,[64] and programs administered by HHS and DOL seem to breed more complaints about requirements and paperwork than ED programs. Some of this may be attributable to the sheer size of the HHS and DOL formula grant programs. Another likely reason is that Congress,

---

[61] Christopher King, "Commonalities Among Education, Training and Human Service Programs," *Making the Connection: Coordinating Education and Training for a Skilled Workforce* (Washington, DC: U.S. Department of Education, 1991), p. 13.

[62] Shirley Downs, *Streamlining and Integrating Human Resource Development Services for Adults* (Washington, DC: National Governors' Association, 1991), p. 19.

[63] U.S. Department of Education, op. cit., footnote 33, p. 16.

[64] Ibid.

responding to public concerns about fraud and abuse, has made a concerted effort to tighten eligibility and related requirements in Federal welfare, job training, and social service programs. The result is an accountability approach that closely tracks individual clients, whereas education programs tend to use aggregate accountability and sampling.

Some local programs resolve the incompatibility of various Federal requirements by establishing self-contained classes of all SLIAG-eligible adults, for example, or all JOBS participants,[65] in order to leave a clear accountability trail (whether or not it is sound educational practice). Others forgo participation in certain programs, feeling that the added paperwork is not worth the burden.[66] Some States, such as Texas, have tried to standardize fiscal and accountability requirements for all adult literacy programs or develop a single eligibility process for needs-based programs, to the extent possible within the parameters of Federal laws.

Several points need to be considered when weighing criticisms of Federal accountability requirements. First, local people are not always clear about which requirements are federally imposed and which are State-imposed. Second, States interpret the same Federal requirements in very different ways and with different amounts of paperwork required. Third, those who complain, with legitimacy, about Federal paperwork and regulations still acknowledge the need for accountability for taxpayers' dollars.

Evaluation Requirements

Evaluation requirements are a particularly important type of accountability mechanism and they, too, differ from program to program, ranging from the very loose (such as a requirement for self-evaluation) to the very prescriptive (such as the JTPA performance standards or the bilingual family literacy technical evaluation standards). Most Federal literacy programs come down somewhere in the middle, with a broad requirement for grantees to conduct an evaluation using objective and quantifiable measures.

In keeping with a national trend toward standard-setting in education and stricter accountability in human resource programs, Congress has strengthened evaluation and program improvement requirements for a number of literacy-related programs.[67] Specific mechanisms differ by program. The JTPA, for example, places relatively few conditions on grantees before they receive funds but is specific about results (performance standards).[68] The JOBS program specifies inputs and outcomes, with individual needs assessments, employability plans, and participation requirements up front and standards of satisfactory progress later.

Performance or outcome standards, as pioneered by the JTPA, are becoming more common in a range of programs. The JTPA itself has become more performance-driven since 1983, with financial incentives and sanctions for failure to meet standards. In the JOBS program, HHS must develop performance standards by 1993. Other new amendments charge the National Institute for Literacy and the State resource centers with advising and providing technical assistance on evaluation and require States to evaluate 20 percent of their AEA-funded programs each year. In addition, the National Literacy Act of 1991 requires that:

> . . . the Secretary, in consultation with appropriate experts, educators and administrators, shall develop indicators of program quality that may be used by State and local programs receiving

---

[65] Hagen and Lurie, op. cit., footnote 30, p. 10.

[66] Mark A. Kutner et al., *Adult Education Programs and Services: A View From Nine Programs* (Washington, DC: Pelavin Associates, 1990), p. 50.

[67] Ibid., p. 15.

[68] Ibid., p. 13.

assistance under this title as models by which to judge the success of such programs, including success in recruitment and retention of students and improvement in the literacy skills of students. Such indicators shall take into account different conditions under which programs operate and shall be modified as better means of assessing program quality are developed.[69]

With all the evaluation data being generated by Federal requirements, there are still some gaps in the area of adult literacy. Much of the information produced by federally mandated evaluations focuses on specific Federal program issues, rather than on the best instructional practices and adult learning models. In addition, good mechanisms do not always exist for managing and analyzing evaluation data and disseminating it to practitioners.

State and local reactions to Federal evaluation requirements raise some important issues that merit consideration as Federal agencies implement new provisions to strengthen evaluation. At the local level, it is not uncommon for a JTPA participant and an AEA participant to sit beside each other in class, work with the same teacher and instructional materials, and yet be judged by different evaluation or performance criteria. From the local perspective, some of these differences may seem unnecessary and at times unfair, especially if some of the funding is tied to outcomes.

While State and local adult literacy professionals would like a higher degree of compatibility, they do not, as a rule, believe that all programs should be measured the same way. Criteria for judging a workplace literacy program, for example, are likely to differ from those used to evaluate a family literacy program.[70] In addition, there

appears to be continued support at the State and local level for accountability systems flexible enough to be "... driven by the individual learner's goals," with measures that evaluate how well those goals are being met.[71]

A second issue is whether evaluation standards are consistent with long-range program goals. For instance, JTPA performance standards are sometimes criticized for overemphasizing job placement, earnings, and corrective action (a criticism addressed in the new reauthorization of the JTPA). Some practitioners say this discourages programs from providing longer term basic skills services to the most educationally disadvantaged, especially if the education services are not likely to lead directly to employment. State and local practitioners also express concern that overambitious standards in a variety of programs can lead to "creaming" of those most likely to succeed or to overenrolling clients in hopes that a sufficient number will meet the standards by the end of the program.

ENCOURAGING TECHNOLOGY USE

The Federal framework sends mixed and sporadic messages about the role of technology in adult literacy programs, and States and local service providers have responded to these signals in different ways.

Federal Provisions for Technology

Several provisions of law and regulation acknowledge, allow, or encourage the use of technologies for delivering literacy services or managing programs (see box 5-D). Some of these are longstanding in Federal law: the JTPA explicitly allows funds to be used for advanced learning

---

[69] Public Law 102-73, Section 301, which amends Section 361 of the Adult Education Act.

[70] In Massachusetts, for example, a workplace literacy program in a manufacturing company judged effectiveness in part by reductions in scrap metal, while an English literacy program in a hospital interviewed patients about the quality of their communications with participating hospital staff. Bob Bozarjian, Massachusetts Department of Education, personal communication, Jan. 27, 1992.

[71] U.S. Department of Education, op. cit., footnote 33, p. 19.

Box 5-D—Key Technology Provisions in Federal Literacy Laws and Regulations

AEA State Resource Centers	Centers may improve and promote diffusion and adoption of technologies. May provide training and technical assistance on effective use of technologies. No more than 10 percent of grant for hardware and software.
National Institute for Literacy	Institute will conduct R&D on best methods, including technology. Will study use of technology to increase literacy knowledge base.
AEA Workplace Literacy	Competitive priority to projects in retooling industries. Projects may update worker basic skills to meet technological demands. Secretary may consider whether applicants have "interactive video curriculum" in making national strategy grants. National strategy grant recipients may use funds to establish "technology-based learning environments," but Secretary may limit expenditures for hardware and software.
AEA English Literacy	Secretary considers use of new instructional technologies in making national demonstration grants.
AEA National Programs	Secretary may evaluate educational technology and software for adults.
Literacy for State and Local Prisoners	Literacy programs must use advanced technologies if possible.
Bilingual Family Literacy	May use funds for technology-based instruction.
DOL Workforce Collaborative	Collaborative will inform businesses and unions about use of technology in workplace literacy and produce video materials.
Job Training Partnership Act (JTPA) Title II-A	Funds may be used for advanced learning technology for education. Funds may be used for commercial technology training packages if bought competitively and include performance criteria.

No special technology provisions	AEA Basic Grants	Commercial Drivers Program
	McKinney Homeless	ED Program for Indian Adults
	Even Start	Library Literacy
	Student Literacy Corps	JTPA Title II
	JTPA Title III	Job Corps
	SLIAG	VISTA Literacy Corps
	JOBS (Welfare Reform)	Refugee Resettlement
	Head Start Family Literacy	

KEY: AEA=Adult Education Act; DOL=Department of Labor; ED=Department of Education; JOBS=Job Opportunities and Basic Skills; SLIAG=State Legalization Impact Assistance Act.

SOURCE: Nancy Kober, "Profiles of Major Federal Literacy Programs," OTA contractor report, July 1992.

technologies, and the Department of Defense is a leading user of adult learning technologies.[72] Other provisions affecting technology are more recent. The National Institute for Literacy and State resource centers are encouraged to conduct research and provide technical assistance on technology. The relatively new workplace literacy partnership program also recognizes the

---

[72] Arnold H. Packer, "Retooling the American Workforce: The Role of Technology in Improving Adult Literacy During the 1990s," background paper for the Project on Adult Literacy, Southport Institute, 1988, p. 39. See also U.S. Congress, Office of Technology Assessment, *Worker Training: Competing in the New Economy*, OTA-ITE-457 (Washington, DC: U.S. Government Printing Office, 1990), pp. 263-267.

This videodisc program incorporates text and pictures to help adult literacy students improve reading skills at Temple University's Center for Learning and Adult Literacy Development.

relationship between basic skills and workplace technology demands.

By and large, however, Federal adult literacy legislation has not kept pace with the reality or promise of technology. The AEA basic grant program contains no provisions explicitly authorizing use of technology, neither do Even Start, SLIAG, refugee resettlement, and homeless education. JOBS regulations mention funding for automated management systems but do not mention use of technology in service delivery. No programs contain capital budgets for equipment purchase or explicit funding for teacher training in technology.

Further, most statutory and regulatory provisions that do recognize technology are options, not mandates. In several programs, Federal administering agencies may consider the use of technology when making competitive grants. In other cases, State and local agencies may use Federal funds for technology. The mandates that do exist—such as those relating to the National Institute for Literacy and the DOL National Workforce Literacy Collaborative—generally affect decisions at the Federal level, not the State and local level. The only quasi-mandate at the grantee level is in the ED functional literacy program for State and local prisoners, which requires the use of advanced technologies "if possible."

Federal intent regarding technology is further obscured by mixed messages. Some laws that explicitly mention technology as an allowable activity also place a cap on the amount that may be spent for hardware or software. (Examples are the State resource centers and the workplace literacy program.)

Moreover, the references to different technologies in laws and regulations are somewhat arbitrary and ill-defined. Various Federal laws mention all the following types of technology without defining them: state-of-the-art technologies, interactive video curriculum, technology-based learning environments, new instructional technologies, technology-based instruction, advanced learning technologies, and commercial technology training packages.

Other Federal requirements not directly related to technology may subtly discourage its use. For example, performance standards may dissuade service providers from making long-term equipment investments or trying out new technology-based instructional approaches, for fear these will not lead to immediate increases in student learning or employment.[73] Eligibility requirements may in effect prohibit federally funded hardware and software from being used by noneligible learners after hours. The absence of multiyear contracts in programs such as JTPA may discourage long-term investment in technology.[74]

Some Federal agencies are undertaking their own efforts to encourage wider and better use of technologies. DOL and ED have supported literacy-related technology demonstrations with discretionary money. States have used AEA section 353

---

[73] Packer, op. cit., footnote 72, p. 55.

[74] Ibid.

experimental funds to promote use of technology.[75]

Why has the Federal Government taken a cautious approach to technology? First, the Federal Government traditionally has tended to be suspicious about capital expenditures in education, especially for expensive equipment that may become obsolete or sit untouched because people are not properly trained. Second, because adult education funding is so limited compared to need, many policymakers see the technology issue as a tradeoff between ''live'' teachers or computers. Third, the pressure for greater Federal leadership is not there, because the adult education field is still in its adolescence regarding technology. Finally, many Federal agencies lack the technical expertise to develop a thoughtful technology policy.[76]

Federal leadership could do a great deal to help the field mature technologically, in terms of research, training, evaluation, dissemination, and adoption. The Office of Educational Research and Improvement National Center for Adult Literacy, the National Institute, and the State centers offer promising starting points, but these efforts are in the early stages.[77]

A final issue for Federal consideration is the use of technology for program management. The growth of Federal literacy-related programs with strict eligibility and documentation requirements has created new data collection and reporting burdens that could be greatly eased through technology-based management systems. Technology also holds promise for better coordination across programs and agencies. A related question is whether Federal policy should encourage broad integration and sharing of instructional and management technology across programs, or whether technology issues should be addressed independently by each program.

State and Local Reaction to Federal Technology Policy

States and local service providers appear to respond in different ways to mixed Federal signals about technology. Some States and local sites are making increasing use of technology in their federally funded adult education programs.[78] In the JTPA program, the majority of service delivery areas use computers for instruction or management.[79] (Often this equipment was purchased with private contributions, Governors' 8-percent money, or national demonstration dollars rather than regular JTPA funds.[80]) Yet despite the existence of successful and sophisticated models, the use of technology is not particularly widespread in federally funded adult literacy programs.

Why is this so? First, many State administrators and local service providers are reluctant to spend limited Federal dollars on equipment and software, believing that they are ''too expensive'' or would drain funds away from direct services.[81] When tight budgets force a choice between buying equipment and paying a salary, an investment in upfront equipment may seem out of the question.

Second, the absence of explicit authorization in many Federal programs for hardware and software or for technology-based instruction seems to have a chilling effect. Although only a few programs actually limit the use of funds for equipment, some State and local program people

---

[75] Seamon, op. cit., footnote 32.

[76] Packer, op. cit., footnote 72, p. 55.

[77] Further along are efforts at the State and local level, such as California's Outreach and Technical Assistance Network (OTAN).

[78] ''Technology in Adult Education: New Opportunities, New Challenges,'' *A.L.L. Points Bulletin*, vol. 3, No. 2, April 1991, p. 1.

[79] Packer, op. cit., footnote 72, p. 17.

[80] Ibid., p. 38.

[81] Ibid., p. 56.

believe such expenditures are discouraged by the Federal Government or interpret Federal silence as lukewarm support. Some State and local program people also seem to perceive, correctly or incorrectly, that Federal administrators are wary of equipment and software purchases, and that if programs make these purchases, they do so at risk of being closely monitored down the road.

Third, the nature of small, highly targeted, or competitive grant programs may present obstacles. In general, expenditures under targeted programs may be used only for services to eligible populations; unless the local target group is large, it may be hard to justify a technology expenditure. Moreover, as noted above, competitive grants are often a short-term and unreliable funding source, and a small one at that. A decision to purchase equipment and software might eat up the entire grant amount, leaving nothing for training, accessories, or instructional services and producing no measurable student outcomes when evaluations come due.

Fourth, some State and local program people feel that there is not yet enough research documenting the effects of technology-based instruction for adult learners, and that technology may not be appropriate for some types of learners. These beliefs seem to be reinforced when State and local people have had prior negative experiences with inappropriately used technology, inferior learning packages, or lack of training. This finding indicates a need for both better research and improved dissemination of existing research, as well as a willingness to experiment, make mistakes, and learn from them.

Fifth, State leadership also seems to be an important influence on the use of technology in federally funded programs. A lack of State encouragement can have a dampening effect at the local level, while a more aggressive State policy can help overcome initial local reluctance. In Texas, for example, where the State has encouraged the use of technology, the majority of the adult education cooperatives reported having access to computers for instructional purposes and administrative purposes; almost one-third had access to integrated learning systems; and some had more than one system, with a wide variety of software being used.[82] Feedback and evaluations from technology-based programs have been quite positive, and Texas officials would like to expand their use. The major obstacle is a lack of funding for capital expenditures.[83]

COORDINATION AMONG ADULT LITERACY PROGRAMS

Recent analyses of the Federal effort in adult literacy have concluded that it is fragmented, poorly coordinated, spread thinly across many agencies, and insufficient in some major ways.[84] Recognizing these problems, Congress has added a range of provisions affecting Federal, State, and local coordination to many literacy-related statutes, most recently the National Literacy Act (see appendix C).

Federal Requirements

The largest programs—AEA, JOBS, and JTPA—have many coordination mandates. Among the most typical are requirements for consultation with other agencies and programs, joint plan review, consultation with broad-based advisory councils, and State plan descriptions of coordination methods. Many programs also include directives to coordinate or collaborate with relevant agencies or service providers at the Federal, State, and local levels. These requirements tend to be specific about the programs with which agencies

[82] Texas Education Agency, "Survey of Computer Usage in Adult Education in Texas," draft report, 1992.

[83] Evelyn Curtis, education specialist, Texas Education Agency, personal communication, Jan. 30, 1992.

[84] See Robert A. Silvanik, *Toward Integrated Adult Learning Systems: The Status of State Literacy Efforts* (Washington, DC: National Governors' Association, 1991); David Harman, *Turning Illiteracy Around: An Agenda for National Action* (New York, NY: Business Council for Effective Literacy, 1985); and Pierce, op. cit., footnote 12.

must coordinate or consult; most frequently mentioned are JTPA, vocational education, elementary and secondary education, vocational rehabilitation, special education, and employment and training programs.

Some statutes give Federal agencies, and to a lesser degree States, joint tasks to carry out. ED, DOL, and HHS are jointly charged with implementing the National Institute for Literacy and providing technical assistance for the JOBS program. Building on this base, the three agencies have undertaken additional shared efforts on their own: sponsoring joint regional planning meetings, initiating relationships at the regional office level, and sitting in on each other's informational meetings.[85] The National Institute for Literacy and the State literacy resource centers have also been given a range of coordination tasks.

The Federal framework also contains some funding incentives for coordination. The Governors' 8-percent education-coordination set-aside under the JTPA is one strong motivator. Other programs, such as workplace literacy, Even Start, and library literacy, attempt to build coordination from the ground up by requiring or urging local programs to be run as partnerships involving more than one agency. In several competitive grant programs, grantees that can demonstrate collaboration or coordination receive priority in selection. Several programs also contain provisions discouraging duplication of services.

Nevertheless, the Federal framework does not go as far as it might to foster coordination. Many of the smaller literacy-related programs do not require or suggest any interagency coordination.[86] In addition, the coordination provisions that exist do not usually specify the nature or degree of coordination expected. As past experience with coordination mandates demonstrates, it is relatively easy to prove that a plan has been reviewed, or an interagency meeting convened. It is harder for the Federal Government to assess whether meaningful coordination is occurring, let alone take enforcement action if it is not. Finally, there is a subtle contradiction in the Federal framework: the same Federal laws that mandate coordination have also created an assortment of programs that, by sheer numbers, make the coordination process more difficult and complicated.

Forging strong collaborative relationships is a time-consuming process and results may not show up immediately. Because of these difficulties, State and local agencies are in effect their own overseers, and the will to achieve results becomes a deciding factor.

State and Local Impact

It is difficult to assess the real effect of Federal coordination requirements on State and local practice. Many successful models of coordination predate or were developed independently of Federal mandates. In addition, grant recipients can comply on paper without really changing their behavior. Nevertheless, coordination requirements in Federal law seem to be having some effect on State and local practice. Coordination requirements in the JTPA, for example— among the earliest mandates—have helped produce a wide range of models and strategies,[87] and many relationships forged under these efforts have carried over into other areas. More recently, the JOBS program coordination requirements have compelled States to make interagency decisions about administration and service delivery.[88]

---

[85] Gerri Fiala, director, Division of Planning, Policy and Legislation, U.S. Department of Labor, personal communication, Jan. 9, 1992; and Seamon, op. cit., footnote 46.

[86] Alamprese and Hughes, op. cit., footnote 14, p. 21.

[87] See U.S. Department of Labor, *An Assessment of the JTPA Role in State and Local Coordination Activities* (Washington, DC: U.S. Government Printing Office, 1991).

[88] Hagen and Lurie, op. cit., footnote 30, pp. 9-10.

Salem Public Library, Salem, Oregon

In many communities the library is an important partner in family, workplace, and adult literacy efforts.

Flexible Federal dollars have also helped grease the wheels of coordination. The JTPA 8-percent education-coordination grants seem particularly important. In 1990, five States had specifically earmarked a portion of this set-aside to support an entity within the Governor's office to coordinate statewide literacy efforts.[89] LSCA Title I funds provide another example: in Kalamazoo, Michigan, for instance, these funds help support a literacy coordinator, maintain a literacy network, and provide a literacy clearinghouse.[90]

There appears to be widespread agreement that Federal mandates alone cannot make coordination happen; individual will and personalities are critical.[91] On the reverse side, no matter how strong the will to coordinate, State and local initiatives can only go so far until they run up against a wall of Federal requirements that cannot be changed without legislative or regulatory action.

What changes do State and local practitioners recommend to eradicate these obstacles? Although some State and local administrators advocate program consolidation or Federal agency reorganization as solutions, these are by no means universal recommendations. A more common recommendation is for Congress and the executive branch to take steps to put the Federal house in order by standardizing requirements, eliminating unnecessary complexity, and charging Fed-

---

89 Silvanik, op. cit., footnote 84, p. 9.

90 Judith A. Alamprese et al., *Patterns of Promise: State and Local Strategies for Improving Coordination in Adult Education Programs* (Washington, DC: Cosmos Corp., 1992), p. 93.

91 U.S. Department of Education, op. cit., footnote 33, p. 14.

eral agencies to undertake joint ventures and forge collaborative relationships. Support for compatible reporting requirements seems particularly strong, with recommendations that Federal agencies decide on standard protocols for evaluations, performance outcomes, eligibility, and reporting timetables. Similarly, the recommendation to move toward compatible application cycles, carryover procedures, and funding cycles (including multiyear grants) is a popular one. Many people also feel that additional, flexible funding specifically for coordination would help.

FEDERAL POLICY ISSUES
Programs and Dollars

Several factors have shaped the Federal role in adult literacy education, but perhaps none more than funding limitations. In essence, the Federal Government has attempted to solve a large, multifaceted problem in a piecemeal fashion. The current array of modest to small programs provides something for almost every type of literacy need and not very much for any, with inefficiencies for all.

Since funding exerts some control over policy, it may make sense for Congress to first face up to the issue of whether adult literacy is a high enough national priority to warrant greatly increased outlays. If the answer is yes, this points toward one set of policy options, which may include a new wide-scale program, with higher visibility in the Federal bureaucracy, that expands, subsumes, or replaces existing efforts. If the answer is no, then policy discussions ought to center on how to use the dollars available more effectively.

One such option is to focus Federal leadership on a few, clear priorities, including any of the following:

- Building capacity and/or improving quality across the whole literacy system;
- Serving a few high-priority target groups, with the aim of reducing costs for other social programs down the road;

- Raising the literacy level, and with it the competitiveness, of the American workforce; and
- Reducing illiteracy in future generations through family literacy.

Any of these choices would suggest a reduction in the number of Federal programs, and perhaps a dramatic refashioning of the Federal role. Some caution might be advisable before a "block grant" approach is taken, however; funding that is too flexible could easily become diffused across the vast pool of literacy needs, and diffusion is already a problem.

In sharpening the focus of the Federal role, Congress might also consider whether the practice of attaching literacy mandates to programs with other goals has expanded funding, participation, and delivery mechanisms for adult literacy, or whether it is has shifted the composition and added to the waiting lists of existing programs.

A final issue is how the Federal Government can make more of its leveraging potential, for example by catalyzing additional private dollars for workplace literacy or providing incentive grants for States to develop cost-effective models of service delivery.

Services, Quality, and Capacity Building

If Congress decides that this is an area where more aggressive Federal leadership could make a difference across the system, then several options seem feasible.

- Building on the missions of the National Institute for Literacy, the National Center for Adult Literacy, and the State resource centers, Congress could expand the funding and scope for research, evaluation, and dissemination of the best instructional practices, curriculum, technology, and training methods. This type of capacity-building agenda could serve as a framework for the entire Federal role.
- Professionalization of the literacy field could begin with a significant Federal staff develop-

ment and preservice training effort for instructors and leaders, as has been done in the mathematics/science education and medical fields. Such approaches as extending grants or loans to talented undergraduates, sponsoring summer institutes, strengthening university programs, and providing high-quality training opportunities could help draw new people to the field and upgrade the skills of existing practitioners, including volunteers. Attention would have to be paid, however, to the substandard pay and working conditions associated with adult education programs.

- In programs as diverse as Chapter 1 and vocational education, the Federal Government has enacted new "program improvement" provisions to identify the weakest local programs and prod them to change their practices. A similar approach could be considered for adult education, although first some consensus would have to be reached about what constitutes success and how to measure it. The forthcoming AEA indicators of program quality could serve as a starting point for a new assessment approach that looks at delivery systems, instructional approaches, and service intensity, in addition to learner outcomes.

- The Federal Government could do more to encourage policies supporting alternative delivery systems for adult literacy services, such as programs in the workplace, the home, or other nontraditional sites. This would require new approaches to crediting student time on task for mandated programs where participation is counted by hours of attendance in a classroom setting, but would offer greater flexibility to the learners.

Target Groups

To date the Federal Government has avoided making hard choices about who should receive highest priority for Federal funds. As States strive to meet mandatory participation levels in the JOBS program, without fully reimbursing local providers for the costs of JOBS services, it is possible that local programs may be forced to make the hard choices themselves, which could lead to polarization among different groups and a backlash against Federal mandates.

Congress could confront the issue directly by deciding on some clear priority groups. A key issue is whether to concentrate on adults who are closest to achieving functional competency and economic self-sufficiency, or on adults who have the most severe disadvantages.

Technology

Federal leadership in adult literacy technology holds promise for improving instruction, coordination, and management. Stronger leadership could be exerted in several ways:

- Stimulating capital investment, through such approaches as a revolving loan fund, incentives for private-sector donations, and technology pools that serve several Federal programs;
- Removing disincentives in Federal law to use of technology;
- Supporting research, development, and dissemination and encouraging private-sector software development;
- Building on the Federal Star Schools program and other distance learning efforts to reach underserved populations of and to expand training and staff development for adult education teachers and volunteers; and
- Piloting use of technology to help manage complex recordkeeping and accountability requirements for multiple Federal programs.

Coordination

Fragmentation at the Federal level undercuts Federal mandates for coordination at the State and local level. Federal leadership is urgently needed. A logical first step would be to develop a common framework to guide Federal accountability, reporting, and eligibility requirements; definitions; and funding cycles. The Federal Government could back up the requirements that already exist in Federal law by providing some incentives, or "glue money," for States and local providers to develop, extend, and improve good models of coordination and effective use of technology.

A stickier issue is whether agency responsibilities should be reorganized to cut down on fragmentation. To some extent the answer would depend on which literacy priorities Congress chooses to emphasize. A Federal role structured around upgrading the workforce, for example, would suggest a different configuration of agency responsibilities, with a stronger role for DOL, than one centered on educational capacity-building and teacher professionalization.

CONCLUSION

In assessing the overall impact of the Federal Government on adult literacy, one must not become so caught up in the criticisms of the Federal role as to forget the positive contributions it has made to the field. The fact that States and local agencies continue to participate in Federal literacy programs year after year, with all the accompanying administrative challenges, suggests that the benefits of participation must outweigh the drawbacks.

The main benefit is not hard to find. Federal dollars continue to be critical to an underfunded field, and States and local service providers continue to do what they must to receive them.

The choice between turning people away and dealing with regulatory complexity is not a difficult one for most literacy providers. In fact, the lengths to which some programs will go to keep their doors open is often remarkable.

Still, it seems fair to ask whether the total Federal literacy effort—given its limited funding, its variable quality and intensity, its scant coverage of the eligible population, and its lack of a cohesive, overarching policy—is really making a dent in the problem of illiteracy. The answer seems to be it is making a real difference in the lives of millions of people, an accomplishment that should not be underestimated. With increased funding, better coordination, greater leadership in the areas of technology and instructional quality, and a richer base of research knowledge, Federal programs could make a difference for millions more.

A final observation: it is beyond the scope of this chapter to analyze the effects of other Federal legislation—such as housing, health, nutrition, tax, and elementary and secondary education policies—on the functional literacy of adult Americans. Suffice it to say, any policy choice that widens or reduces the gap between the haves and have-nots, in this generation or the next, ultimately influences the status of adult literacy in the United States.

Improving the System: Promising Roles for Technology | 6

A dult literacy programs, regardless of funding source or sponsor, share many of the same difficult problems and critical needs. These include issues of recruitment, retention, and mandated attendance; instructional issues regarding curriculum, staff development, and assessment; issues related to the integration of literacy and social services; and administrative issues concerning funding and coordination. Technology offers promise for dealing with many aspects of these common concerns.

FINDINGS

- Recruiting adult learners and retaining them in programs long enough to make significant changes in their literacy levels are persistent concerns for literacy programs of all types. Technology has been used successfully to draw learners into programs, hold their interest, and adapt instruction to their needs and levels.

- Mandated literacy for special populations is affecting literacy programs in a number of ways. The target groups that must be served differ substantially from those who enter programs voluntarily—in terms of education level, motivation, need for support services, and higher incidence of personal problems affecting their literacy quest. Programs must adapt considerably to serve these groups effectively, and these adaptations will likely affect all those served by the programs.

- One of the major challenges for programs is finding curricular materials appropriate for adults, flexible enough for their multiple learning styles and relevant to learners' goals and needs. Survival skills, getting and keeping a job, workplace content, and family needs all provide context for literacy

instruction that is meaningful to adult learners. Technology-based media that use sound, video, graphics, and text and can be adapted easily for the individual learner offer great promise as tools for creating pertinent and engaging curriculum.

- Program evaluation and assessment is stymied by a reliance on school-based models of effectiveness, such as gains in grade-level equivalents on standardized tests. Multiple measures of effectiveness are needed, including performance-based assessments. An effective program must take into account the reality that a learner's personal literacy goals may be different from the outcomes measured for evaluating a program's overall success.

- Maintaining up-to-date student records and program accounting data is costly, time-consuming, and difficult for most programs. Computer-based solutions such as databases containing information on student progress make it possible for programs to streamline operations as well as keep better track of students and their educational needs. Another solution has been the use of personal student data cards; these minimize repeated placement testing and expensive intake procedures, benefiting both programs and learners.

- Professional development of adult educators is unlikely to be achieved without changes in State credentialing requirements, development of master's level programs in adult learning and literacy, and creation of career ladders for those in the field. Better communication is needed between programs and colleges and universities that could provide preservice and inservice training to staff and volunteers. Technology offers a promising resource (via computer networks, distance learning systems, software, and video materials) for training staff and volunteers, sharing information about promising practices, and reducing the isolation of many programs.

- Limited, unstable and short-term funding from multiple sources affects many decisions about staffing, services, and instructional methods, making it difficult to plan, purchase materials, or serve more than a small percentage of those in need. Tight budgets and limited planning capabilities especially affect the ability to make technology a central part of instruction or program management.

- Different and sometimes incompatible Federal funding streams, eligibility restrictions, and accountability requirements are sources of frustration for State and local literacy practitioners and drive these programs in ways that may not always reflect local learner needs or promote efficient management practices. Technology offers resources for improving coordination and consolidating service to improve efficiency, while still allowing local flexibility and control.

RECRUITING, RETAINING, AND SERVING LEARNERS

Bringing learners into literacy programs and keeping them long enough to meet their goals are continuing concerns for programs of all types. Recruitment and retention go hand in hand because the same problems that keep learners from entering programs in the first place resurface as factors contributing to the inability to stay with a literacy program. Indeed, many who enter literacy programs drop out and are then targets for renewed recruitment drives.

Recruitment Issues and Strategies

Many factors make adults reluctant to enter literacy programs. Most common among these are the stigma of admitting one's problems, conflicting demands from family and work that make time commitments difficult, and past negative experiences with schooling.[1] Some adults are overwhelmed by how much time would be required to meet their goals. Remembering that they were unable to succeed as youngsters when attending school all day, every day, they wonder how much progress can be made attending only a few hours a week.[2] For many, the memory of school and their past academic failure makes the idea of returning to school—the scene of so much prior humiliation—a frightening or undesirable prospect.

Public information campaigns have sought to encourage those with literacy needs to come forward. A string of Federal initiatives—from the 1969 "Right to Read Initiative," the 1980 Adult Literacy Initiative, and Barbara Bush's advocacy of literacy for all Americans, as well as the private sector's Project Literacy US (PLUS) and countless State and local efforts—have presented literacy as a problem that can be solved if those in need sign up and others volunteer time and assistance. The message has been delivered through public service announcements on radio and television, on posters, and in newspapers and magazines. However, as discussed in chapter 3, many of those needing help have coped adequately in the past, or cannot be convinced that classes will really help them. Often, as one educator noted: "A person with low literacy skills who has a job which does not demand higher skills will not appreciate the need for instruction until he or she loses that job, the job is eliminated, or the job's demands begin to escalate because of global competition."[3]

With this in mind, some workplace programs have used video as low-pressure but effective recruitment tools to encourage employees to enter their voluntary literacy and training programs. For example, the United Auto Workers and General Motors, with a grant from the U.S. Department of Labor, developed an interactive videodisc to illustrate how quickly the skills needed to succeed in the auto industry are changing.[4] Workers touch the screen to interact with the material and test their knowledge in various skill areas. In one plant, the program was set up in the cafeteria so that employees could work on it for as long as they wanted; many returned over and over, or kept at it for several hours on their own time, trying various self-assessments to see how close they were to having the skills needed for working in the year 2000.[5] In another recruiting approach, the United Auto Workers-Ford video "The Breakfast Club" suggests that there's no stigma attached to improving one's academic skills at all levels.[6] Participation in Ford's Skills Enhancement Program is encouraged by showing a variety of employees including a young engineer working on his master's degree, a worker with many years of seniority pursuing his high school diploma, and a Rumanian immigrant studying English. The message is clear: everyone can pursue higher educational goals with the help of the Skills Enhancement Program.

Literacy programs have discovered that computers can be powerful vehicles for attracting learners and drawing them into programs. For example, the Harlem Community Computing

---

[1] Hal Beder, "Reasons for Nonparticipation in Adult Basic Education," *Adult Education Quarterly*, vol. 40, No. 4, summer 1990, pp. 207-218.

[2] In one study, adults in literacy programs in New York City made the most gain in the first year, and then improved more slowly. By the end of the third year, improvement seems to have leveled off for those with literacy levels below the 7.5-grade level. Thomas Sticht, "How Fast Do Adults Acquire Literacy Skills?" *Mosaic: Research Notes on Literacy*, vol. 2, No. 2, July 1992, p. 2.

[3] Garrett W. Murphy, director, Division of Continuing Education, The State Education Department, New York, personal communication, September 1992.

[4] UAW-GM Human Resource Center and the U.S. Department of Labor, "Skills 2000," brochure, n.d.

[5] OTA site visit, United Auto Workers program, Delco Chassis Plant, Livonia, MI, March 1992.

[6] J.D. Eveland et al., Claremont Graduate School, "Case Studies of Technology in Adult Literacy Programs," OTA contractor report, June 1992.

Center's popular "Playing to Win" program, now in its 10th year, attracts more than 500 people a week. The center's president explained the drawing power of technology:

> Why might a learner respond so willing when a computer is mentioned? Because he or she is no dope, because people who can't read, write, calculate or communicate as well as society could wish are not totally unaware. They know that this is a technologically-based world . . . that acquiring comfort and skill with technology is just as important from their point of view as learning to read, write and calculate more successfully.[7]

Many adult learners associate technology with tomorrow's skills, not yesterday's failures. They find that using computers legitimizes literacy studies; they are proud to be "learning computers" when in fact they are also learning *with* computers. It can be like starting fresh for those who have associated traditional classrooms or textbooks with their past school failures.[8] Others who were frustrated and embarrassed by their slow progress in prior literacy classes or tutorials savor the privacy offered by computers and headphones so that ". . . the guy next to you doesn't have to know what you're working on." They also appreciate the infinite patience of computers. "They will read something over 100 times without (the computer) saying 'You know that word; I just told you that word.' "[9]

Retaining Learners Long Enough to Meet Goals: The Problem of Attrition

Once learners have come forward and secured a place in an adult literacy program, the next big issue is keeping them involved long enough to meet their goals.[10] Student attrition is a central and vexing issue. The statistics are bleak:

- Between 15 and 20 percent of all clients who go through the intake process never actually receive any instruction.[11]
- In the first 5 weeks, from one-quarter to almost one-half of all adult learners stop going to class.[12]
- After 40 weeks, only about 12.5 percent of those who began classes are still active[13]

Overall, attrition rates are in excess of 60 percent in many adult basic education (ABE) and general equivalency diploma (GED) courses and over 70 percent in some State literacy programs.[14] (See figure 6-1.)

Many overlapping factors conspire against completing a program. A longitudinal study of students enrolled in adult literacy programs in New York City in 1988 found that less than 1 in 10 (8.3 percent) said they left because they had

---

[7] Antonia Stone, "Tools for Adult Learners," paper presented at the International Urban Literacy Conference sponsored by the United Nations, August 1992.

[8] See Eveland et al., op. cit., footnote 6.

[9] William M. Bulkeley, "Illiterates Find Computers Are Patient Mentors," *The Wall Street Journal*, Nov. 16, 1992, p. B1.

[10] The high rate of student attrition was placed at the top of the list of program concerns of adult basic education (ABE) and general equivalency diploma (GED) administrators at the 1992 Joint ABE/GED Annual National Administrators Conference and of statewide literacy and ABE administrators in Pennsylvania and Georgia at their 1991 and 1992 professional development conferences. B. Allen Quigley, "The Disappearing Student: The Attrition Problem in Adult Basic Education," *Adult Learning*, vol. 4, No. 1, September/October 1992, p. 25.

[11] Mark Morgan, associate director for Data Processing and Analysis, National Evaluation of Adult Education Programs, Development Associates, Inc., personal communication, February 1993. Data taken from a nationally representative sample of about 21,000 new intakes to Adult Education Act-funded programs. Data based on Development Associates, Inc., "Second Interim Report: Profile of Client Characteristics," draft report, 1993.

[12] Lauren Seiler and Peter Nwakeze, "Attrition in Adult Education: Causes and Recommendations," *Literacy Harvest: The Journal of the Literacy Assistance Center*, vol. 2, No. 1, winter 1993, p. 26.

[13] Morgan, op. cit., footnote 11, p. 2.

[14] Quigley, op. cit., footnote 10.

Figure 6-1—The Pattern of Attrition in Literacy Programs

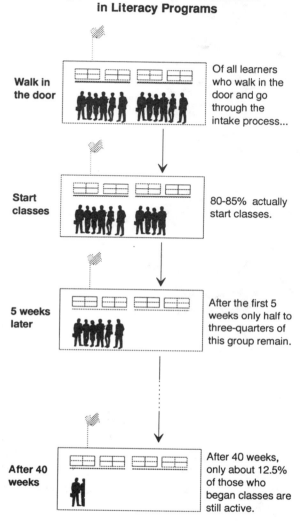

Walk in the door — Of all learners who walk in the door and go through the intake process...

Start classes — 80-85% actually start classes.

5 weeks later — After the first 5 weeks only half to three-quarters of this group remain.

After 40 weeks — After 40 weeks, only about 12.5% of those who began classes are still active.

SOURCE: Office of Technology Assessment, 1993, based on data from Development Associates, Inc., "Second Interim Report: Profile of Client Characteristics," draft report, 1993; and Lauren Seiler and Peter Nwakeze, "Attrition in Adult Education: Causes and Recommendations," *Literacy Harvest: The Journal of the Literacy Assistance Center,* vol. 2, No. 1, winter 1993, p. 26.

learned enough.[15] The vast majority left without completing their educational goals. The reasons for leaving were categorized as follows:

- Situational deterrents (64 percent): work, health, childcare, family, transportation, or other external problems;
- Institutional deterrents (11 percent): uninteresting or inappropriate programs;
- Dispositional deterrents (3.6 percent): tired of school or were not accomplishing goals; and
- Combination of situational, dispositional, and institutional deterrents (7 percent).[16]

It is uncommon to have information on why students drop out, for most who leave literacy programs just stop coming and the factors creating the dissatisfaction leading them to "vote with their feet" are never known or addressed. Furthermore, because many learners leave programs and then return at a later date, there is reluctance to record a learner as "terminated."

Many programs have begun to develop record-keeping systems to help them analyze patterns of attrition. For example, volunteer organizations have developed software packages to help local programs maintain computerized databases on learners and tutors, allowing for more systematic analysis of retention factors.[17] These systems are part of a general effort to improve retention by providing "better matches" between tutors and learners, but there is little data to confirm that this makes learners stay in programs longer.[18]

Even mandatory programs find retention a problem. Education programs for welfare recipients also report that their biggest problem is poor

---

[15] Seiler and Nwakeze, op. cit., footnote 12, p. 27.

[16] Ibid.

[17] The Verse 1.0 data management system, developed by Literacy Volunteers of America (LVA), maintains data for volunteer programs, and helps track mailing information, demographics, tutor-learner matches, hours, and other data on volunteers, tutors, and learners.

[18] An evaluation study of 953 learners at six Literacy Volunteers of America sites throughout the United States showed a slight pattern of correlation between tutor and learner similarity and learner achievement. However, the researchers suggest that the data on which the analysis is made is limited. V.K. Lawson et al., Literacy Volunteers of America, Syracuse, NY, "Evaluation Study of Program Effectiveness," unpublished report, January 1990, p. 24.

Kirkwood Community College

Distance learning projects bring instruction to students in remote locations. This class is being sent from Kirkwood Community College to centers spread across a 4,300-mile service area.

attendance.[19] Only when basic needs are satisfactorily cared for can one concentrate on the difficult task of learning. For those whose financial, emotional, and health situations keep them on the edge, the recurring problems and crises of day-to-day life take precedence over long-term learning goals. Most programs try to deal with the situational, institutional, and dispositional factors that drive students from programs, but it is a huge job.

Community-based organizations are especially sensitive to the need for providing the comprehensive services that remove some situational barriers. Often their literacy activities are part of a broader program that seeks to help clients deal with the myriad issues of housing, employment, childcare, health, and personal relationships. Counseling and social services are as central to their mission as literacy classes. Offering service in

storefronts, libraries, community centers, or housing projects can bring programs to people in places where they feel most comfortable, while alleviating some transportation problems.[20]

In some rural areas, where distance and lack of public transportation are significant problems, distance learning projects have brought programs closer to participants; e.g., adult high school completion programs offered by Kirkwood Community College's telecommunications networks (see box 6-A).

Scheduling programs to accommodate the learners' needs helps boost retention. For example, many programs try to schedule classes in the morning for women whose children are in school; daytime classes also attract women whose safety concerns make them unwilling to attend night classes. However, since many adult literacy teachers work full time in other jobs (most often

---

19 Edward Pauly et al., *Linking Welfare and Education: A Study of New Programs in Five States* (New York, NY: Manpower Demonstration Research Corp., March 1992), p. 14.

20 Some programs provide bus or subway tokens to help learners get to classes.

Box 6-A—Extending Educational Opportunities Through Telecommunications: Kirkwood Community College

For more than a decade, Kirkwood Community College in Cedar Rapids, Iowa, has sought ways to extend its reach to all learners, especially those most cut off from educational services in the past. While the college offers a full range of traditional classroom-based college courses on campus, this is just one method of reaching students. For example, the college is in its 12th year of providing residents of eastern Iowa with live interactive college credit courses over its microwave telecommunications network. Today no resident of Kirkwood's seven-county, 4,300 square-mile service area is more than a 20-minute drive from a distance learning classroom set up in high schools, community centers, and businesses.

Students in these distance learning classes are typically older adults who cannot easily come to the Cedar Rapids campus or are uncomfortable with the idea of attending classes on campus with students much younger than they are. Many build up their confidence once they see that they can compete successfully with "regular" college students. A student can earn an associate's degree exclusively through Kirkwood's distance learning program, without ever coming to the main campus.

At Kirkwood, distance learning has been a success—both in terms of numbers of students served (almost 1,500 students each semester) and by the quality of the instruction. Evaluations of student performance consistently indicate that the distance learning students perform at least as well, if not better, than traditional on-campus students. Some distance learning courses are also offered in conjunction with area high schools, allowing advanced students to earn college credits while still in high school.

Kirkwood also offers alternative programs for students who have dropped out of high school, through secondary-level courses available at learning centers throughout their service area. High school credit courses have been developed using a self-paced format of instruction. These 40 courses complement the traditional courses and individual tutorials. Nearly 400 students took alternative high school classes in the 1992-93 academic year; Kirkwood actually had the largest high school graduating class in the seven-county service area.

Taken together, these experiences have taught Kirkwood administrators important lessons about alternative approaches to delivering instruction. Past assumptions have been proven false, challenging conventional wisdom about who can benefit from alternative educational approaches:

Older students perform as well as younger students; high school level curriculum is as successful as college level curriculum. It is no longer valid to assume that older adults would have an innate fear of technology, or that ABE or GED students would be overly challenged by newer instructional technologies.[1]

Building on what has been learned through these nontraditional self-paced high school credit programs and the telecommunications-based college credit programs, Kirkwood plans to take the next step and offer adults without high school degrees expanded educational opportunities via live interactive telecommunications. In the 1993-94 academic year, the college will work with high school dropouts in off-campus sites, offering distance learning courses that include career development, technical mathematics, and environmental science. The college envisions adding other technologies, including computer-assisted instruction and multimedia courses to augment this program. They also hope to extend similar strategies to adult basic education programs in the near future. The Dean of Telecommunications sums up Kirkwood's attitude and hopes for the future this way: "Telecommunications technology and related instructional technologies certainly hold the promise of extending greater opportunities to those residents who have thus far benefited the least from our educational system."[2]

---

[1] Rich Gross, dean of telecommunications, Kirkwood Community College, Cedar Rapids, Iowa, personal communication, February 1993.

[2] Ibid.

teaching K-12), daytime classes can be difficult to schedule.[21] Workplace programs, held on site between shifts, make it easier for employees to attend. Finally, for some learners, classes can be supplemented with or substituted by study at home, through the use of televised literacy programs such as those offered by Kentucky Educational Television or other public broadcasting stations. These offer the ultimate in convenience, safety, and privacy for learners.

Maintaining regular contact with learners increases likelihood of improving student retention. This may mean serving fewer students in order to do a better job of providing necessary support services such as case management.[22] This involves greater use of counselors or social workers who can provide regular visits to schools or to students' homes to see how students are doing and why they may be missing classes. Teachers or volunteer tutors are often reluctant or unable to take on this role.

Serving Learners: Balancing Supply and Demand

While recruitment and retention are important, the problem goes beyond that. The larger issue is serving all those in need.[23] Although there is variation among local and statewide efforts, on average, most estimates indicate that fewer than 10 percent of those in need are being served.[24] Furthermore, mandated programs are changing the concept of recruitment, often forcing programs to serve one group of learners—those required to attend—at the expense of others who come voluntarily.[25] English as a second language (ESL) programs are often oversubscribed, and many agencies are forced to put a cap on these services so as not to overwhelm and consume their total adult literacy program.[26] A survey taken in New York City in 1988 suggested there were 10,000 people on a waiting list for ESL classes, with indications that the numbers have grown since then.[27]

Technology is extending the range of services. Ironically, as technology makes it possible to reach more people, through hotlines, referral services, and programs brought close to home via distance learning activities, demand is likely to increase. Some communities are finding ways to expand services by involving community resources that can provide technology assistance, often by enlisting the aid of local businesses. Others are tapping into existing public programs like Head Start or public welfare agencies and working with them to offer instruction in these settings (e.g., setting up computer-assisted learning laboratories in daycare centers or in the welfare office—see chapter 4, box 4-E) or through local public broadcasting stations to

---

[21] Providing childcare or offering programs where parents and children attend classes at the same site improves student retention rates, but requires more money, staff, and space—three features many programs lack.

[22] Massachusetts recently took this approach. Murphy, op. cit., footnote 3.

[23] A recent evaluation of adult education programs found waiting lists in 19 percent of local programs. National Evaluation of Adult Education Programs, Bulletin No. 2, January 1991.

[24] The Department of Education estimates that on average 6 percent of those in need are being served. Ron Pugsley, U.S. Department of Education, Division of Adult Education and Literacy, Office of Vocational and Adult Education, unpublished data, October 1992. For example, the Massachusetts Department of Education reports serving about 3 percent of those eligible. OTA site visit, January 1992. See also Robert A. Silvanik, *Toward Integrated Adult Learning Systems: The Status of State Literacy Efforts* (Washington, DC: National Governors' Association, 1991).

[25] For further analysis of this issue, see chapter 5 for a discussion of targeted populations.

[26] Some local programs report long waiting lists among limited-English-proficient adults not eligible for special programs such as State Legalization Impact Assistance Grants (SLIAG). The Community Learning Center in Cambridge, MA, reports an ESL waiting list of 400, and at the Somerville Center for Adult Learning, the average wait for regular ESL is 18 months. OTA site visit, January 1992.

[27] Avi Dogim, "The Workplace in the ESL Class: An Integrated Approach to Job Readiness," *Literacy Harvest: The Journal of the Literacy Assistance Center*, vol. 2, No. 1, winter 1993, p. 6.

provide televised literacy instruction learners can watch at home. These models to "transform the service delivery system via technology" are encouraging, but still limited; most programs facing increasing demand still continue to try to do more of the same, using existing approaches that are already overburdened and limited in their success.

INSTRUCTIONAL ISSUES

At the heart of every adult literacy program are three central issues: what is taught, who teaches it, and how progress is measured. Concerns with each of these are shared across programs of all types.

Curriculum: What Works?

Although the instructional goals for ESL, ABE, GED, and high school completion programs are similar across programs, adult literacy programs use a variety of instructional approaches and materials. Some espouse structured phonetics-based approaches while others prefer whole language materials for beginning readers. Many create materials relevant for their own learners, attempting to "use whatever seems to work," but then find that what works for some students may not work for others.[28] Many programs have the desirable goal of creating individualized instructional plans for each student; however, these must be developed around the philosophy of the program, the time and talents of staff, time available for instruction, and resources (e.g., books, hardware, and software) at hand. Compounding this difficulty is the fact that the student clientele keeps changing. And, while many of the teacher-developed curriculum materials are good and could be shared or replicated, there have not been, until recently, any formal mechanisms to share, evaluate, or disseminate locally developed materials.

Effective instruction is built around a learner's interests. These ESL students celebrate Cinco de Mayo in their Hispanic heritage project.

Furthermore, while there is considerable evidence of what works, the information is not systematically made available to practitioners as a basis for effective practice. Even large curriculum development projects have no system for broad distribution. For example, over a decade ago a California adult literacy curriculum support project led to the development of the Comprehensive Adult Student Assessment System (CASAS). It was designed to provide accurate placement of students in education programs from beginning through advanced levels of ABE, ESL, and preemployment training, and to establish a uniform method for reporting progress, while providing linkages to competency-based instructional materials and instruction. Since 1983, CASAS has been validated by the U.S. Department of Education as an exemplary program for national dissemination through the National Diffusion Network, and agencies implementing CASAS report significant gains in student retention. It has been used effectively in a range of agencies— community colleges, school programs, correctional institutions, and Job Training Partnership

---

[28] Renee S. Lerch, *Effective Adult Literacy Programs: A Practitioner's Guide* (New York, NY: Cambridge Book Co., 1985), p. 101.

Act (JTPA) programs—throughout California and several other States.[29] However, because of the diversity of programs and lack of systematic information-sharing, CASAS and other effective programs are not known by practitioners apart from those directly involved with them.[30]

The problem is repeated as adult literacy programs seek information on effective ways of teaching with technology. The most common software information resource is word-of-mouth, particularly recommendations from other technology-using teachers.[31] While sources for evaluation do exist,[32] more than 60 percent of organizations contacted in a recent survey never consult these sources; most did not even know that these sources were available.[33] If a State or region has an agency that provides information on technology for adult literacy, most computer-using provider organizations in the area will take advantage of its services.[34] However, these State and regional resources are limited.

A promising resource is California's Outreach and Technical Assistance Network (OTAN) (see figure 6-2). OTAN combines a computerized communications system with regional resource libraries that disseminate commercial and teacher-made materials, including training packets with accompanying videotapes, resource documents, and public domain software. OTAN is both an electronic archive and a distribution source for materials, reports, and studies. Several States have signed on to OTAN, hoping to tap into its

base of materials and expertise; however, since much of the material is geared to the California curricula, its use is limited in programs that take a different, less structured approach. Nevertheless, OTAN is seen by some as a model for other State information and dissemination systems, and as a resource for teacher training, the area discussed below.

Helping Teachers, Administrators, and Volunteers Do Their Jobs

It is difficult to define adult education as a profession when most teachers and instructors are part time, certification is rarely required, and no career ladder exists for moving ahead in the field. Furthermore, university programs for specializing in adult literacy are limited, with little agreement or research base specifying what kind of training is needed.

There is a critical need for professional development, both for teachers and for volunteers in adult literacy programs. Teaching adults demands a different set of skills and sensitivities than those required for teaching children. These take time and training to develop, but the transition is often assumed to be automatic. Furthermore, even those with experience teaching adults in community colleges or workplace training programs may not be familiar with the special challenges of teaching adults with low literacy skills. Staff development for ESL instructors appears to be an even greater problem, since many may not be

---

[29] For example, Maryland undertook a review of curricula used in adult literacy programs throughout the State and found content varied enormously, with instruction and materials based on what was available in a center and the background of the instructors. The State director described the situation as a "hodgepodge." Maryland used CASAS as a model for a competency-based curriculum but localized content for Maryland: questions deal with Maryland geography, industries, and other locally relevant topics. Chuck Talbert, director of Adult and Community Education Branch, Maryland Department of Education, personal communication, September 1992.

[30] Paul Delker, consultant, personal communication, April 1992.

[31] Jay Sivin-Kachala and Ellen Bialo, Interactive Educational Systems Design, Inc., "Software for Adult Literacy," OTA contractor report, June 1992, p. 66.

[32] Software guides include: *Guide to Recommended Literacy Software* (Adult Literacy and Technology Project); the *Oregon/Washington Adult Basic Skills Technology Consortium Software Buyers Guide, Educational Software Selector* (EPIE Institute), and manufacturers guides and catalogues, as well as online services. Ibid., p. 68.

[33] Ibid., p. 68.

[34] Ibid., p. 71.

trained in the complexities of second language acquisition and may lack the ability to work with culturally diverse groups and their special needs.[35] Even when programs strive to provide training for their staff and volunteers, they are constrained by a number of factors:

- Minimal State and local policies and certification requirements;
- Limited inservice training requirements;
- The part-time nature of adult education teachers and volunteer instructors;
- The high rate of staff turnover;
- The lack of a unified research base on best practices; and
- Limited financial resources for training.[36]

Most States do not require special certification in adult education for those who teach in literacy programs.[37] Some require an elementary or secondary teaching degree only, some require a few hours of additional coursework or experience, and almost one-half of all States have no certification requirements for adult educators (see figure 6-3). While it is true that some districts and local programs may impose more stringent requirements on teaching staff, it must be said that statewide teaching requirements for adult literacy instructors are less stringent than requirements for K-12 educators. It is ironic that those with the least professional background are asked to help those who need the most help—those for

whom our past education efforts were not successful.

Although inservice training and staff development programs might provide satisfactory alternatives to ABE certification, only 12 States require some type of inservice training.[38] The range of training required is enormous: from 4 hours of preservice and 4 hours of inservice training, to 50 hours of staff development annually.[39] Many local ABE and ESL programs have more stringent staff development requirements than the States, however.

ABE and ESL teachers tend to be part-time employees of adult education programs; 90 percent are paid on an hourly basis and do not receive benefits.[40] Volunteers account for between 25 and 75 percent of total adult education staff members in each State, and these numbers exclude volunteers working in noninstructional activities.[41] This dependence on volunteers and noncertified, part-time instructors keeps program costs down and reduces incentives to increase funding levels. It may also be responsible for the comparatively low salary levels and status of adult educators.

Since so many adult education staff are school teachers during the day and adult education instructors after hours, they have very little time for training, unless weekends or summer vacations are sacrificed. There is little incentive to participate in training, especially since most of the inservice training and staff development activities are undertaken on the instructors' own

---

[35] Pelavin Associates, Inc. et al., ''Study of ABE/ESL Instructor Training Approaches: Phase I Technical Report,'' prepared for the U.S. Department of Education, Office of Vocational and Adult Education, February 1992, p. 12.

[36] Ibid., pp. 11-12.

[37] Pelavin Associates, Inc. et al., ''Study of ABE/ESL Instructor Training Approaches: State Profiles Report,'' prepared for the U.S. Department of Education, Office of Vocational and Adult Education, February 1991.

[38] Pelavin Associates, Inc. et al., ''Study of ABE/ESL Instructor Training Approaches: The Delivery and Content of Training for Adult Education Teachers and Volunteer Instructors,'' prepared for the U.S. Department of Education, Office of Vocational and Adult Education, July 1991, pp. 8-9.

[39] Ibid., p. 8.

[40] For example, in a 1988 report on ABE in North Carolina, 65 percent of programs surveyed reported having no full-time teachers on their staff; Hawaii funded its first full-time ABE staff position in 1989. Ibid., p. 5.

[41] U.S. Department of Education, Office of Vocational and Adult Education, *Exemplary Adult Education Services: Highlights of the Secretary's Award Program Finalists* (Washington, DC: 1988).

Figure 6-2—Outreach and Technical Assistance Network (OTAN)

OTAN provides training, technical assistance, information, and communication links for adult literacy staff. The range of services on the OTAN forum is shown in the menu below. In its first year of operation, the OTAN forum received more than 11,000 queries.

MENU

 About the OTAN Forum has a general explanation of the OTAN project and a detailed description of the electronic communication system.

 The **Master Calendar** will display the latest information on what events are happening in Adult Education.

 Who's Who is a directory containing people information: subscribers, 321 agencies, adult school directors, and U.S. state directors of adult education.

 CDE Info is information from the California Department of Education.

 OTAN Resource Centers are located throughout California and provide inservice activities and have resource libraries.

 Current Articles contain unpublished articles of current interest to Adult Education.

 Course Outlines represent the ten adult education funded areas of adult school instruction. They include: goals, purpose, objectives, instructional strategies, times of instruction, evaluation, and repetition components.

 Curricula Resources list various instructional materials in print, video, or software format. Free instructional materials are also posted.

 Lesson Plans area is under construction. You will find sample lesson plans which you can adapt to fit the needs of your students.

 Public Domain Software is free to be downloaded and used at your agency.

 Demo Software maintains a library of demonstration software from commercial sources. Again, you may download and use at your agency.

 Legislative Information offers up-to-date legislative information as it relates to adult education.

 Reference Materials contains bibliographies of reference information, research reports, lists of library materials to borrow, and actual documents of "hot topics." A full adult education library at your fingertips.

 Educational Grants contains information about funding opportunities available to adult service providers and educators.

 Want Ad users can post/review ads related to job opportunities in education.

 The **Round Table** is the online discussion area. Users can post or respond to others.

 Upload Area is where users can place files that they want to share online.

Using the OTAN Forum: One Example--Here a teacher chooses "lesson plans" from the Forum, then selects a particular example from the file. The teacher can preview and print the entire lesson plan, which contains objectives, materials, preparation time, exercises, and assessment suggestions.

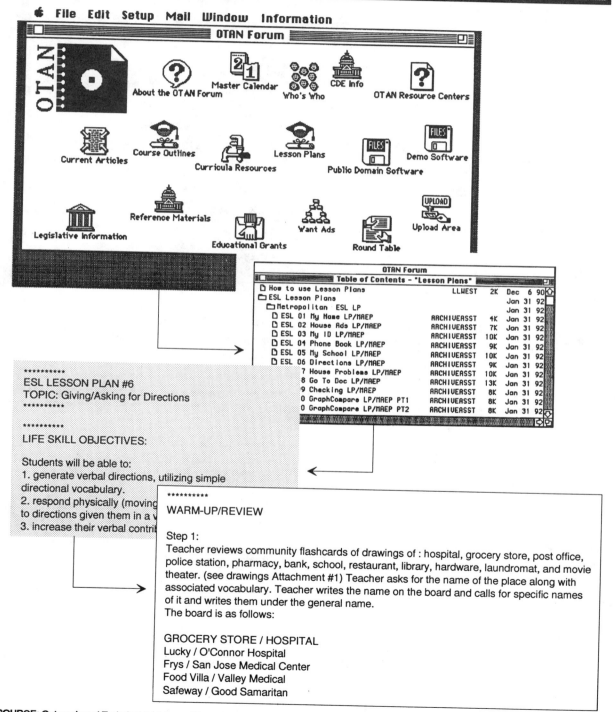

File   Edit   Setup   Mail   Window   Information

OTAN Forum

OTAN

About the OTAN Forum   Master Calendar   Who's Who   CDE Info   OTAN Resource Centers

Current Articles   Course Outlines   Curricula Resources   Lesson Plans   Public Domain Software   Demo Software

Legislative Information   Reference Materials   Educational Grants   Want Ads   Round Table   Upload Area

OTAN Forum

Table of Contents - "Lesson Plans"

How to use Lesson Plans	LLWEST	2K	Dec 6 90
ESL Lesson Plans			Jan 31 92
Metropolitan ESL LP			Jan 31 92
ESL 01 My Name LP/MAEP	ARCHIVEASST	4K	Jan 31 92
ESL 02 House Ads LP/MAEP	ARCHIVEASST	7K	Jan 31 92
ESL 03 My ID LP/MAEP	ARCHIVEASST	10K	Jan 31 92
ESL 04 Phone Book LP/MAEP	ARCHIVEASST	9K	Jan 31 92
ESL 05 My School LP/MAEP	ARCHIVEASST	10K	Jan 31 92
ESL 06 Directions LP/MAEP	ARCHIVEASST	9K	Jan 31 92
7 House Problems LP/MAEP	ARCHIVEASST	10K	Jan 31 92
8 Go To Doc LP/MAEP	ARCHIVEASST	13K	Jan 31 92
9 Checking LP/MAEP	ARCHIVEASST	8K	Jan 31 92
0 GraphCompare LP/MAEP PT1	ARCHIVEASST	8K	Jan 31 92
0 GraphCompare LP/MAEP PT2	ARCHIVEASST	8K	Jan 31 92

****
ESL LESSON PLAN #6
TOPIC: Giving/Asking for Directions
****

****
LIFE SKILL OBJECTIVES:

Students will be able to:
1. generate verbal directions, utilizing simple directional vocabulary.
2. respond physically (moving
to directions given them in a v
3. increase their verbal contri

****
WARM-UP/REVIEW

Step 1:
Teacher reviews community flashcards of drawings of : hospital, grocery store, post office, police station, pharmacy, bank, school, restaurant, library, hardware, laundromat, and movie theater. (see drawings Attachment #1) Teacher asks for the name of the place along with associated vocabulary. Teacher writes the name on the board and calls for specific names of it and writes them under the general name.
The board is as follows:

GROCERY STORE / HOSPITAL
Lucky / O'Connor Hospital
Frys / San Jose Medical Center
Food Villa / Valley Medical
Safeway / Good Samaritan

SOURCE: Outreach and Technical Assistance Network, City of Industry, CA, 1992.

Figure 6-3—State Certification Requirements for Adult Basic Education Teachers

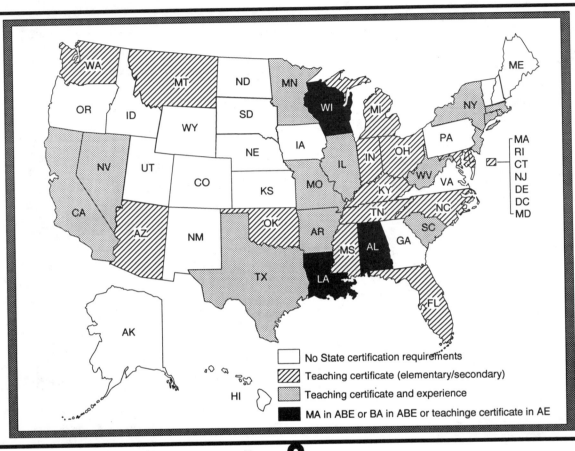

KEY: ABE = adult basic education; AE = adult education; BA = Bachelor of Arts; MA = Master of Arts.

SOURCE: Office of Technology Assessment, 1993, based on Pelavin Associates, Inc. et al., "Study of ABE/ESL Instructors Training Approaches: State Profiles Report," prepared for the U.S. Department of Education, Office of Vocational and Adult Education, February 1991.

time and personal expense.[42] The contrast with K-12 or community college staff development—where teachers are given release time, travel funds, and substitute teachers—is striking.

The high rate of staff turnover also makes training a continuing burden to programs. Nation-wide, comprehensive data on staff turnover is not available, but the experience of one State is indicative of more general problems. The Adult Education Unit of the California Department of Education estimates that it experiences a one-third annual turnover[43] among its adult education

---

[42] Susan E. Foster, "Upgrading the Skills of Literacy Professionals," *Leadership for Literacy: The Agenda for the 1990s*, Forrest P. Chisman and Associates (eds.) (San Francisco, CA: Jossey-Bass, 1990), p. 75.

[43] The scope of training needed is staggering. In 1988-89, approximately 10,000 or more staff needed basic-level inservice training. Cuba Miller, California Department of Education, "Program and Staff Development Support: Working Paper on Strategic Recommendation 9," advisory review draft, Aug. 22, 1990, p. 66.

instructors. When turnover is high, programs are encumbered with the need to provide introductory staff training almost continually.

While there is a clear need for training adult educators in the theory and practice of adult learning, the research base is limited.[44] The intellectual underpinnings for adult learning theory are diverse and multifaceted.[45] Woven within the theoretical base are many strands: theories of cognition, which are themselves far from consistent; understandings derived from developmental and educational psychology; theories of second language learning; and a social science focus that suggests adult learners can only be understood in the socioeconomic and cultural context of their lives and experience. In addition, there are conflicting views as to the appropriate way to teach reading. Finally, there are also diverse views and approaches to instructional management—including conflicting views regarding group instruction versus one-on-one instruction, social interaction versus private time spent alone at a computer terminal, networking across distances via technology versus social contact in a school setting. Perhaps most significant is the concern that, as one practitioner noted:

> Research has shown that some of the most successful teaching has occurred among those who are willing to abandon traditional teaching methods and to adopt methods and materials that are relevant to the learners. Yet we persist in assuming for a major part of our adult literacy system that adequate preparation for adult literacy instructors or facilitators consists of traditional teacher training.[46]

Because there are few State and local policies and guidelines regarding certification, it is difficult for programs to know what adult literacy teachers

KET, The Kentucky Network

Good teaching is both art and science. In a televised lesson, this teacher uses real life applications to make math exciting for his students watching all around the country.

should be expected to know, and to develop appropriate training programs.

Finally, very limited funding is available for training adult education personnel. The major Federal source of support for adult literacy staff development is Section 353 of the Adult Education Act (AEA), which authorizes States to set aside at least 10 percent of their basic grants for training teachers, volunteers, and administrators, or for special projects. In fiscal year 1990, States spent a total of $15.8 million under Section 353. The National Literacy Act increased the set-aside

---

[44] Pelavin Associates, Inc. et al., op. cit., footnote 35, p. 43.

[45] U.S. Department of Education, ''Design Conference for Program Effectiveness Studies in Adult Education,'' unpublished papers, March 1992.

[46] Foster, op. cit., footnote 42, p. 74.

Training adult literacy staff is a major problem. Technology offers a resource for sharing promising practices.

for special projects to 15 percent and specified that at least two-thirds of the set-aside must be devoted to staff development. Even with this increase, the amount spent for adult education training will still be limited; it is estimated that less than $3 million per State will be devoted to training adult literacy personnel.[47]

Technology offers both short- and long-term solutions to the problem of training adult literacy teachers and volunteers. Several media suggest themselves. As video cameras and VCRs become more common, training videos can be taken home for viewing and then discussed in group training sessions. Workshops can be taped for viewing by absentees or new employees. Exemplary teaching models or sample lessons can be demonstrated in videos or live over interactive telecommunications networks. As a part of the selection of new teaching staff, applicants can be taped presenting a demonstration lesson. Current staff can submit videos to demonstrate their competence as a means of improving program evaluation.

Computer networks like OTAN (see above) can be used to help teachers, administrators, and volunteers share information, techniques, and curriculum. Some groups have used telecommunications for live interactive teleconferences on topics of common interest to adult literacy teachers and volunteers across the country. For example, the American Correctional Education Association, Literacy Volunteers of America, and the Public Broadcasting System jointly sponsored a series of teleconferences on the topic of literacy instruction in jails and prisons. Because prisons are often located in isolated settings, personnel who teach in these settings are particularly cut off from traditional professional development opportunities. In another example of distance learning applications, the Los Angeles County Education Department uses its satellite educational telecommunications network (ETN) to reach adult educators on a regular basis.[48] ''The Adult Learners Channel'' on ETN broadcasts programs of interest to adult learners, teachers, and administrators. California plans to use ETN to train all the ESL adult literacy teachers in the State through ESL Teacher Institute training modules. Recent programs and series for the ESL staff development series include the ''ESL Tool Box'' and ''Adult Life Skills ESL Starter Kits'' for teachers, programs for vocational ESL instructors, a series for volunteer ESL tutors, and activities for develop-

---

[47] Pelavin Associates, Inc. et al., op. cit., footnote 35, p. 11. This figure may be optimistic. New York State gets the second highest AEA grant, approximately $17 million, and 10 percent of that would be $1.7 million. Forty-eight States will have lesser amounts. Murphy, op. cit., footnote 3.

[48] ETN is a FCC-licensed satellite broadcasting network owned and operated by the Los Angeles County Office of Education. Courses for teachers, students, administrators, and parents are transmitted to the 95 districts in the 4,083 square-mile area of Los Angeles County, but any site in California or other States capable of receiving the Ku-band satellite system can participate in the live programs. Viewers can telephone studio presenters for immediate discussion and questioning, or telecasts may be interrupted by taping programs for later viewing, allowing participants to discuss ideas and issues among themselves. Los Angeles County Office of Education, Downey, CA, Educational Telecommunications Network brochures, 1992.

ing adult ESL mentor teachers. Other programs for adult education administrators cover topics such as recruitment and retention strategies and new statewide standards and frameworks.[49]

Evaluation and Assessment

State and local literacy practitioners seem far from satisfied with current instruments for both student assessment and program evaluation and are concerned about their being used inappropriately to judge people and programs.[50] Assessments of student progress and evaluations of program success are often used interchangeably, but they are not the same.

Most programs evaluate effectiveness by assessing academic progress (e.g., how many students move to higher levels or the grade-level gains they make on test scores). Effectiveness is also measured by how many acquire a high school diploma or pass the GED. Other indicators of effectiveness vary for specific programs. For example, workplace literacy programs may measure success by reduced employee absenteeism and turnover, by higher productivity and safety records, and by lower product defect and error rates. Prison literacy programs consider long-term improvements in postrelease employment, parole, and recidivism as overall measures of success. Many programs also consider program effectiveness in terms of significant changes in lifestyle, such as the number of students moving off the welfare rolls and into jobs.

Federal program evaluation procedures are changing as programs receiving Federal funds must set up systematic evaluation procedures

showing effectiveness. Counting numbers of those who come and go, or using school-based models of grade-level gains, will no longer suffice. As the goals of programs change, the methods of evaluating success will also need to change. Moving from a 3rd- to a 4th-grade reading level may not be as important to the learner, or the sponsoring agency, as being able to fill out a driver's license application or planning a week's worth of balanced meals on a budget. As one administrator noted: "It's just as legitimate to help people meet short-term goals, such as filling out a job application, as it is to enroll them in a long-term program and measure success by whether they got a high school diploma or advanced so many grade levels."[51]

In compliance with the National Literacy Act, the Department of Education developed model indicators of program quality that will influence adult literacy programs of all types (see table 6-1).

Beyond the question of program evaluation is the issue of individual student assessment. Students are tested when they first enter programs, as a basis for placement; they may or may not be tested when leaving programs. For many, testing is a stressful event, reminding them of past school failures; for others, it is enough to keep them out of programs in the first place. Yet those who enter and exit programs several times often have to repeat the same tests time and again. Some systems have moved to credit-card sized "smart-cards," that store a student's test results and educational program information, enabling the learner to pick up where he or she left off without repeated testing when reentering literacy programs.[52]

---

[49] Los Angeles County Office of Education, "ETN Times," a monthly program directory, October 1992.

[50] U.S. Department of Education, *A Summary Report: National Forums on the Adult Education Delivery System* (Washington, DC: U.S. Government Printing Office, 1991), p. 8.

[51] Terrilyn Turner, quoted in Business Council for Effective Literacy, "Talking Heads: Issues & Challenges in Adult Literacy," newsletter, No. 30, January 1992, p. 1.

[52] The State of California has 2,000 "Educards" for adult learners. Data on student test scores, certification, and other materials are stored on the cards, which cost $4 each, can store approximately two pages worth of typewritten information, and are read by computers using a $100 scanner. John Fleishman and Gerald Kilbert, "Adult Education Technology in the Golden State," *Adult Learning*, vol. 4, No. 3, January/February 1993, p. 15.

Table 6-1—Model Indicators of Program Quality for Adult Education Programs

Topic	Indicators of program quality	Sample measures
Program planning	Program has a planning process that is ongoing and participatory, guided by evaluation, and based on a written plan that considers community demographics, needs, resources, and economic and technological trends, and is implemented to the fullest extent.	• Planning document that specifies program goals and objectives and is regularly reviewed and revised. • Openness to community input via advisory board, staff meetings, student questionnaires, or public hearings; and frequency of consultation with them. • Use of data on community needs (e.g., census data, needs assessments). • Plan matches community needs regarding class location, content, and program services. • Program evaluation component and evidence that evaluation feeds into the planning process. • Congruence between planned and actual activities.
Recruitment	Program successfully recruits the population in the community identified in the Adult Education Act as needing literacy services.	• Types of recruitment activities. • Percent of target population enrolled compared with State demographics. • Percent of students enrolled having specific characteristics compared with the target population having these characteristics in the service area. • Percent of target population enrolled compared with State average.
Retention	Students remain in the program long enough to meet their educational needs.	• Hours in program by type of program and learning gains achieved as measured by student progress. • Percent of students returning to the program within specified time period.
Curriculum and instruction	Program has curriculum and instruction geared to individual student learning styles and levels of student needs.	• Use of student assessment information to inform the instructional progress. • Student goal-setting process linked to decisions on instructional materials, approaches, and strategies. • Instructional content addresses educational needs of individual students. • Instructional strategies used and frequency measured through observation or self-report.
Educational gains	Learners demonstrate progress toward attainment of basic skills and competencies that support their educational needs. Learners advance in the instructional program or complete program educational requirements that allow them to continue their education or training.	• Gains in standardized or competency-based test scores. • Teacher reports of student gains or improvements. • Alternative assessment methods. • Rate of student advancement to a higher level of skill or competency. • Attainment of a competency certificate, GED, or high school diploma. • Percent of students referred to or entering other education or training programs.
Support services	Program identifies students' needs for support services and makes services available to students directly or through referral to other educational and service agencies with which the program coordinates.	• Process for identifying student support service needs. • Agreements or linkages with childcare and transportation providers. • Number and type of support services provided or to which students are referred. • Percent of students obtaining specific needed services through the program or through referral.
Staff development	Program has an ongoing staff development process that considers the specific needs of its staff, offers training in the skills necessary to provide quality instruction, and includes opportunities for practice and systematic followup.	• Presence of preservice and inservice staff development opportunities and average hours of staff development training received by staff. • Process for identifying staff development needs. • Staff development based on promising practices. • Effective staff performance as measured by student ratings or observations of staff. • Percent of staff needs met through training activities.

SOURCE: U.S. Department of Education, Office of Vocational and Adult Education, *Model Indicators of Program Quality for Adult Education Programs* (Washington, DC: July 1992).

Testing has a positive side as well—it is important to learners to know they are making progress, even if the steps forward are small and slow. One of the appeals of computer-based programs is the reinforcement given when learners succeed. For example, in most computer-based instructional programs, when a certain number of correct responses are given, the student is automatically presented more challenging material. In this context, tests are not so much anxiety-provoking events as ongoing checks on one's understanding. Integrated learning systems (ILSs), with their comprehensive instructional and management software packages, are attractive to some literacy programs because of this capability to blend instruction with assessment on a regular basis, and maintain up-to-date records of progress and areas where more help is needed as guides to both instructors and learners. The volume of curricular materials stored in ILS programs can accommodate learners at many levels, allowing students to move ahead in a systematic fashion. Reports on student progress can be accessed immediately and compiled easily for overall program evaluation purposes.[53]

There is some concern among practitioners whether existing assessment tools—multiple-choice paper-and-pencil tests or their computer-based equivalents with their grade-level equivalency mindset—are adequate to meet the demands of new outcome-based assessment systems. Performance measures fit more appropriately with competency-based approaches to instruction, as learners demonstrate learning in the context of such goals as interpreting documents, filling out forms, solving work-related problems, or preparing their own written or video reports.[54] Some programs are using performance assessments, such as portfolio collections of student work illustrating progress over time. As with all performance assessments, concerns are raised about aggregating data and the reliability and validity of these measures. Nonetheless, educators and learners alike are excited about the impact new forms of testing have on teaching and learning.

ADMINISTRATIVE ISSUES

Programs of all types are coping with the central issues of how to provide better service in light of problems with funding, requirements for serving more learners through mandated programs, and issues of coordination.

Funding

Limited funding for literacy programs is in some ways the most critical crosscutting issue, because it constrains everything else that happens in literacy programs—staff training, intensity of services, availability of technology, innovative assessment, and other issues. Further, limited funding severely restricts the vision of all involved—administrators, policymakers, instructors, and students. Why recruit more adults if you cannot serve them? Why enroll in a program that puts you on a long waiting list? Why advance teachers' training if you cannot pay them a competitive salary when they finish? Why learn about technology if your program cannot afford it? Why enact a comprehensive Federal program if appropriations will never be provided?

Public support for adult literacy has been adversely affected by the downturn in the economy, as fiscal belt-tightening continues at every level—Federal, State, and local. Support from the private sector—an important resource for many programs, especially community-based programs—is also soft. Literacy has to fight hard to win its

---

[53] Some of these systems are correlated with the two of the most common tests used for placement: the Test of Adult Basic Education (TABE) and CASAS, sometimes making it unnecessary for a student to take the paper-and-pencil tests.

[54] U.S. Congress, Office of Technology Assessment, *Testing in American Schools: Asking the Right Questions*, OTA-SET-519 (Washington, DC: U.S. Government Printing Office, March 1992). Although this study deals primarily with testing issues in K-12 education, the alternative testing approaches discussed in the report have particular relevance to adult literacy programs.

share of the corporate and philanthropic pie. Although corporations and businesses may support local literacy efforts in the communities where they are located, only a few large foundations provide significant funding for literacy efforts throughout the country.[55] Furthermore, private sector support for adult literacy is uncertain as foundations and businesses change their funding priorities and targets of support from year to year.

Ironically, although technology is expensive, some programs have used it as a magnet for additional funding. In some cases it can be easier to get grants and special donations of technology than support for overall program operation. However, many programs will not spend their own limited resources on technology unless the State or some funding agency makes it a priority.[56] Even those who are informed about technology's potential for adult literacy and eager to use it as a resource for instruction and management are hobbled by the reality of the cost factors associated with technology: the costs of purchasing enough updated hardware and software, the ongoing expense associated with maintenance, and the time and resources necessary to train teachers and volunteers to work with technology as a teaching tool.

Mandated Programs

Recent Federal and State legislation requires certain groups of learners to attend literacy programs—generally welfare recipients and inmates meeting certain educational criteria. These mandated activities affect programs in a number of ways. Since the learners who must attend programs differ from those who enter voluntarily—they tend to have lower average academic achievement on entering, greater need for support services, a higher incidence of personal problems, and, by the nature of their required attendance, a different set of motivational factors—programs must tailor their services to these learners. First, more intense service is required of the provider. Rather than 1 or 2 hours of literacy classes a week, participants attend daily classes of several hours. Services such as childcare and transportation must usually be provided. More intensive programs are more expensive, thus making less funding available to support those who come on a voluntary basis.

Programs often must engage in more comprehensive counseling or case management for students entering from welfare programs. These additional costs are sometimes covered by schools' administrative overhead, sometimes by a share of increased revenues for serving welfare recipients, and sometimes by reimbursement directly from welfare departments.[57] Often the programs are paid based on the number of students and hours spent in a program, which affects recordkeeping and attendance polices. Monitoring attendance on a more rigorous basis means that adult literacy programs are pressed to increase the accuracy and verifiability of attendance data to meet the needs of the welfare programs and to stand up to court challenges.[58] The relationship between teacher and student changes, as does student motivation; rules for attendance and testing for progress are no longer optional.

In Wisconsin, some of the larger school districts have developed computer-matching systems to identify welfare recipients in the districts' data systems and track their attendance. But monitoring has, in general, become a burden for many programs, and teachers especially find it unpleasant to act as "cops" to adult students,

---

[55] For a listing of several foundations supporting adult literacy, see ch. 4, table 4-2.

[56] Nancy Kober, "How States and Local Service Providers Respond to Multiple Federal Literacy Program: Massachusetts and Texas," OTA draft contractor report, Feb. 10, 1992.

[57] Pauly et al., op. cit., footnote 19, p. 15.

[58] Ibid., p. 17.

whose benefit checks may be reduced for poor attendance. Added to this is the difficulty and sensitivity of monitoring some, but not all participants, when some students' attendance is mandated and others' is voluntary.[59] This has been a particular problem in community colleges, night schools and GED programs, and community programs, where students work on individualized programs and detailed attendance and recordkeeping may not be a normal practice. It makes it more likely that welfare recipients will be directed to school-based programs, with their more orderly tradition of attendance and recordkeeping, and less to community-based programs that have a more informal, open approach to attendance.

Other problems in the mandated welfare programs have been created by having to deal with participants who have already initiated education programs on their own—yet now are forced into programs requiring attendance and different arrangements. An important issue for self-initiated participants is their use of proprietary schools. State welfare agencies may be reluctant to accept these programs when they have higher tuition costs and less well-regulated educational offerings.[60] Also at issue is how to measure "satisfactory progress," which in turn affects testing policies that may impact all students in a program.

Lack of Central Focus and Problems of Coordination

The education of America's children has a clearly defined tradition of control by the State education agencies and local school districts, with some assistance from the Federal Government in clearly defined areas. In contrast, adult education has no comparable comprehensive administrative system for organizing thousands of public and private programs in communities across the Nation.

Is diversity an advantage or a problem? On the one hand, the cornucopia of adult literacy programs and providers enriches the field with a multiplicity of resources, approaches, and techniques. On the other hand, this potentially rich resource is squandered without a system that makes it possible to share what works and avoid what does not, that fills in gaps and avoids duplication. A complicated web of service providers makes it difficult for policymakers to see the whole picture, define problems, and identify pressure points where long-term change can be instituted. There are also considerable "turf" battles that can stand in the way of creating effective partnerships.

Furthermore, many literacy program sponsors have other goals and responsibilities that often make literacy service a secondary, rather than primary, goal. Literacy is a means to an end in many of the programs that have the greatest potential for serving learners: in jobs programs, prisons, Head Start programs, workplace programs, and so on. When funding is tight, literacy efforts may be considered expendable. Literacy languishes at the margins.

Federal coordination mandates and incentives for partnerships are producing some positive results, but they are still far from a comprehensive solution. It is too soon to know if the National Institute for Literacy will be able to take on the role of stimulating cooperation and fostering partnerships.[61] Many States and local service providers have gone beyond what is required by law and developed their own approaches for improving coordination of adult literacy pro-

---

[59] Ibid.

[60] "Some JOBS program operators' views of proprietary schools may lead them to disapprove self-initiated participation in those schools' programs. California, Florida, and Oklahoma are beginning to deal with this issue, which promises to be a complex and conflict-filled one." Ibid., p. 24.

[61] The National Institute for Literacy has had an acting director since its creation in 1991. With the appointment of 9 of the 10 board members, the search for a permanent director is now under way.

North Communications, Santa Monica, CA

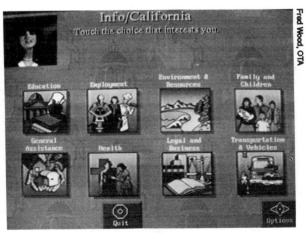

Fred Wood, OTA

The State of California has supported the development of a multimedia kiosk that provides information on public services (see left). Kiosks like the one above have been placed in shopping malls and libraries as part of an experimental project.

grams with each other and with human service agencies and education and training programs.

State Coordination

At the State level, coordination of human service programs has been a front-burner issue for several years, producing a variety of models.[62] In fact, most States have undertaken some sort of initiative to "...bring coherence to the fragmented array of programs and providers that make up the current delivery system for adult literacy and basic skills services." Even so, "...much work remains to be done."[63]

The nature, extent, and success of State literacy coordination efforts vary widely, with some States already into their second generation of

initiatives.[64] Among the most common State coordination mechanisms are:

- New State agencies with broad education and training or human service functions;
- Coordinating bodies and councils;
- Formal and informal interagency agreements or working arrangements among relevant State agencies;
- Jointly funded programs or funding contingent on interagency involvement;
- Incentives, set-asides, or demonstration grants for local coordination, using State funding or discretionary Federal dollars;
- Common program definitions and assessment procedures;

---

[62] See Judith K. Chynoweth, *Enhancing Literacy for Jobs and Productivity* (Washington, DC: The Council of State Policy and Planning Agencies, 1989); U.S. Department of Education, *Making the Connection: Coordinating Education and Training for a Skilled Workforce* (Washington, DC: 1992); Judith A. Alamprese et al., *Patterns of Promise: State and Local Strategies for Improving Coordination in Adult Education Programs* (Washington, DC: Cosmos Corp., 1992); and Silvanik, op. cit., footnote 24.

[63] Silvanik, op. cit., footnote 24, p. viii.

[64] Atelia A. Melaville with Martin J. Blank, *What It Takes: Structuring Interagency Partnerships to Connect Children and Families With Comprehensive Services* (Washington, DC: Education and Human Services Consortium, 1991), p. 19.

- Joint databases to exchange resources and information; and
- Programs that provide technical assistance and training on coordination to State staff and substate entities.

Some of these State mechanisms affect only State agencies, while others seek to foster coordination at the local level.

Perhaps the most prevalent mechanism is the State-level coordinating body. In 1990, 40 States had a coordinating body for adult literacy.[65] These bodies differed significantly in terms of membership, breadth and authority, funding sources, staffing structures, and relationships with local entities. A primary activity of these groups was to raise public awareness about literacy issues. Some groups had broader responsibilities, including directly funding literacy projects, helping States develop policy, providing training and technical assistance, or establishing new initiatives to improve literacy services.[66] Several State umbrella groups have a scope that extends beyond literacy, addressing coordination of workforce development or human service programs.[67]

While having a State-level mechanism is an important first step, it does not guarantee that a coordinated system will naturally evolve.[68] These bodies must also be given the tools to do their job—the power to mandate interagency agreements and collaborative planning, the authority to forge meaningful relationships with local delivery systems, and permission to manage funds from several sources.[69] (See box 6-B.)

Several coordinating groups have begun by identifying all Federal and State resources or programs relevant to the coordination process—a sort of interagency matrix—then developing broad policy statements or strategic planning agendas, and creating interagency agreements to carry out specific components of these agendas.

Some States have given teeth to their agreements and plans by enacting State legislation, providing ''carrots'' such as State incentive grants for certain types of coordination or ''sticks'' such as State mandates for coordination. From 1986 to 1990, 30 States enacted some form of literacy-specific legislation, in most cases providing State funds or authorizing new State agencies for adult literacy.[70]

As several recent experiences demonstrate, State coordination efforts are fragile creatures, sensitive to changes in political climate, funding, and key staff. Governors' initiatives are among the most vulnerable. In at least three States—Massachusetts, Michigan, and Mississippi—a major literacy council or initiative was discontinued or downgraded following a change of Governors.[71] Reductions in Federal or State funding can also negatively affect coordination; staff are cut and forced to try to do more with less money, coordinating bodies lose funding or members, and State agencies guard the dollars they have more carefully. There is concern that coordinating bodies not become yet another State agency or service provider, losing their special neutral character and competing with other State or local entities in an already complex field.

Local Coordination

How do local literacy providers respond to multiple Federal, State, local, and private pro-

---

[65] Silvanik, op. cit., footnote 24, p. 5. (It is likely that the number has decreased since this survey, with some States disbanding their coordinating bodies due to changes in governors or other circumstances.)

[66] Ibid.

[67] Alamprese et al., op. cit., footnote 62, p. 51.

[68] Silvanik, op. cit., footnote 24, p. 5.

[69] For specific examples of State and local literacy program coordination, see Alamprese et al., op. cit., footnote 62.

[70] Silvanik, op. cit., footnote 24, p. 9.

[71] For information on the Michigan experience, see Alamprese et al., op. cit., footnote 62, pp. 71-80.

Box 6-B—Coordinating Literacy Funding: New York State's Approach

One of the most difficult aspects of coordinating social services at the State level is finding ways to merge funding from different sources. The New York State Education Department and the Department of Social Services have jointly developed Adult Centers for Comprehensive Education and Support Services (ACCESS) to deal with this problem. The State's 16 ACCESS centers offer integrated services for adults at each location, including adult basic education and general equivalency diploma (GED) education, English as a second language (ESL), occupational training, life-skills instruction, case management, childcare, assessment and counseling, and other support services. To support the initiative, New York integrates funds from several Federal sources—Adult Education Act basic grants and special experimental grants, Perkins vocational education funding, the Job Training Partnership Act 8-percent set-aside, and Job Opportunities and Basic Skills (JOBS) funding—and from several State programs. The State has overcome the obstacle of different eligibility requirements through a series of interagency agreements transferring funds to the Bureau of Continuing Education Field Services under the Education Department. Based on the types of clients and services addressed by each center or site, the bureau then develops a funding package for each ACCESS grant.

For example, the Board of Cooperative Education Services (BOCES) for Duchess County has been designated as one of the State ACCESS centers. Using a team leadership approach, the program collaborates with 15 State and local agencies, including Social Services, Labor, Vocational and Educational Services for Individuals With Disabilities, and Probation to offer a wide range of comprehensive services. Among the program goals are the creation of a ''one-stop shopping'' concept providing a welfare education program for JOBS clients, an early childhood program for infants, toddlers, and preschoolers, and a program for multihandicapped adults all under one roof. Many other target populations are served through the ACCESS program as well.

Clients are referred by the participating agencies or recruited via direct mailings. (The figure at right illustrates how a client moves through the system.) Students typically attend 6 hours per day, taking a combination of academic courses (basic skills, ESL, GED, and life management), occupational courses (integrated into the high school occupational curriculum), and family literacy courses. They can take advantage of transportation provided to and from the centers, job development and family counseling, and early childhood education onsite. Additional specialized occupational training courses are offered in the evening in areas such as medical secretary, accounting for computers, cabinetmaking, or blueprint reading to add an area of specialization to the skills clients have gained in the daytime programs.

Among the benefits of comprehensive services, the program lists:

- Expanding fragmented services offered at several locations into a more comprehensive program;
- Increasing the cost-effectiveness of programming by coordinating grants and utilizing existing facilities;
- Increasing collaboration and linkages with business, industry, and human resource agencies;
- In the occupational training program, integrating adults and secondary high school students to the benefit of both populations;
- Providing client-centered support services that remove barriers that in the past prevented clients from entering programs (e.g., transportation and onsite childcare); and
- Planning for the future through the initiation of milestones for program operation that are goal-oriented, and provide direction for meeting the needs of the community.

SOURCES: The University of the State of New York, State Education Department, *Adult Literacy: The Key to Lifelong Learning* (Albany, NY: 1992), p. 26; Gary R. Brady, supervisor of Adult and Continuing Education, BOCES, personal communication, March 1993; and Garrett Murphy, director, Division of Continuing Education Planning and Development, New York State Education Department, personal communication, March 1993.

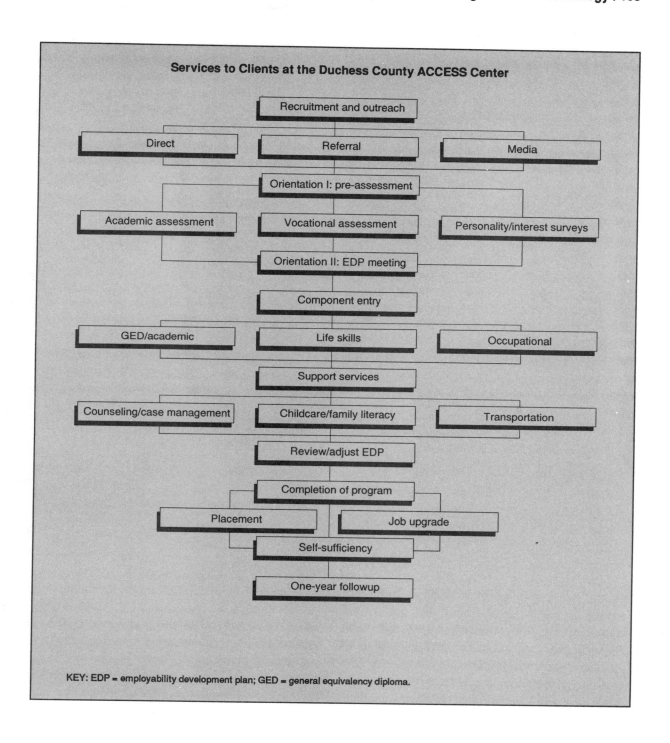

Services to Clients at the Duchess County ACCESS Center

Recruitment and outreach

Direct — Referral — Media

Orientation I: pre-assessment

Academic assessment — Vocational assessment — Personality/interest surveys

Orientation II: EDP meeting

Component entry

GED/academic — Life skills — Occupational

Support services

Counseling/case management — Childcare/family literacy — Transportation

Review/adjust EDP

Completion of program

Placement — Job upgrade

Self-sufficiency

One-year followup

KEY: EDP = employability development plan; GED = general equivalency diploma.

Box 6-C—Cambridge's Community Learning Center: Piecing Together Funding[1]

The Community Learning Center (CLC) is a public agency under the Cambridge, Massachusetts government. For the last 21 years, it has provided literacy instruction to the city's most disadvantaged adults. With 18 full-time staff, 26 part-time staff, and 80 volunteers, the center runs classes from 9 am to 9:30 pm during the week, serving as many as 700 adults at any given time. The center offers regular adult basic education (ABE) classes, intensive 20-hour per week ABE classes, general equivalency diploma (GED) classes, adult diploma programs, seven levels of English as a second language (ESL), family literacy, and workplace education. Sixty-five percent of the students are in ESL classes; 75 to 80 percent are immigrants.

To support these classes, the center receives funding through 12 different grants and contracts, plus local funding from the city of Cambridge and several private sector funding sources. The grants and contracts come through four different State agencies, with funding from eight Federal programs and two State programs (see table at right).

How does CLC coordinate these complex and multiple funding sources? "Primarily by structuring the program around the student's instructional needs and then figuring out how to pay for it," according to the director.[2] A mid-level ESL class, for example, might include 15 students and be funded by State ABE, the Job Training Partnership Act (JTPA), State Legalization Impact Assistance Grants (SLIAG), and the Community Development Block Grant program. The center's 20-hour per-week intensive class is supported with a combination of Job Opportunities and Basic Skills (JOBS) funds, JTPA money, ABE funds, and private funding, as well as rehabilitation funds for one disabled student.

Sometimes it is difficult to maintain separate records and to measure student progress using different performance and evaluation standards. In other cases, the director must shift the funding source for an instructor's salary. And in certain situations, such as workplace literacy classes, which are held at the worksite, or Head Start family literacy programs, which involve children and parents, the Federal requirements necessitate a separate class.

With limited classroom space in its own building, CLC also holds classes in public libraries, in settlement houses and public housing projects, and in homeless shelters. CLC is also looking into the possibility of using a computer room in an elementary school after hours; the problem, however, is finding money for staff. To coordinate ancillary services for its large numbers of limited English proficient students, CLC also works with community-based organizations that serve Hispanic and Haitian families.

[1] Information based on OTA site visit, Jan. 28, 1992.

[2] Mina Reddy, CLC director, personal communication, January 1992.

grams? Some respond by treating each program separately. One study found that local adult education sites did not generally coordinate AEA-funded services with those supported by other adult education and training programs. "For example, a potential student entering . . . as a result of a JTPA recruitment or referral receives JTPA services. . . . No assessment is conducted to determine if the individual might be better suited to receive Adult Education Act-funded services."[72] According to this same study, Federal accountability and reporting requirements were largely responsible for these practices. "Local programs believed that they needed to operate the programs separately in order to ensure that they were complying fully with all Federal require-

---

[72] Mark A. Kutner et al., *Adult Education Programs and Services: A View From Nine Programs* (Washington, DC: Pelavin Associates, Inc., 1990), p. iii.

Cambridge Community Learning Center, Fiscal Year 1992 Funding Sources

Source	Amount	Program	Funding cycle
City of Cambridge local public funds	$277,500	ABE, ASE, ESL, adult diploma	Annual allotment
Mass Dept of Ed ABE instruction State funds	274,500	ABE, ASE, ESL, volunteer coordination	3-year grant
Mass Dept of Ed SLIAG Federal funds	25,000	ABE, ASE, ESL for immigrants in amnesty program	3-year grant
Mass Dept of Ed ABE for homeless Federal funds	44,000	ABE, ASE, ESL for homeless adults	Two 6-month grants
Mass Dept of Ed Workplace education Federal funds	60,000	ABE, ESL classes with workplace specific curriculum	18-month grant
Employment Resources, Inc. (Metro North SDA) Mass Dept of Ed State funds	18,060	ESL for residents of Metro North area	3-year grant
Employment Resources, Inc. Mass Dept of Public Welfare JTPA and JOBS Federal program funds	58,225	Intensive ABE for AFDC recipients and other low-income adults residing in Metro North	1-year contract
Economic Development Industry Corp. (Boston SDA) Mass Dept of Public Welfare JOBS Federal program funds	37,494	Intensive ABE for welfare recipients in Boston	1-year contract
City of Cambridge Community Development Block Grant Federal funds	15,000	ESL for Cambridge residents	1-year grant
Massachusetts Rehabilitation Commission State vocational rehabilitation funds	2,100	Intensive ABE for one learning disabled student	Two 6-month contracts
Cambridge Head Start Federal funds	9,391	ESL, ABE, and GED for Head Start parents	1-year grant
The Cambridge Hospital local funds	15,563	Adult diploma program for employees	15-month grant
Neville Manor Nursing Home local funds	12,407	Adult diploma program for employees	8-month grant

KEY: ABE=adult basic education; AFDC=Aid for Families With Dependent Children; ASE=adult secondary education; ESL=English as a second language; GED=general equivalency diploma; JOBS=Job Opportunities and Basic Skills; JTPA=Job Training Partnership Act; Mass Dept of ED= Massachusetts Department of Education; SDA=service delivery area; SLIAG=State Legalization Impact Assistance Grants.

Coordination of literacy services requires leadership at all levels. Houston's Mayor Bob Lanier brought city leaders together and told his Commission on Literacy: ''I will do whatever I can to help.''

ments''[73]—even when this degree of separation was not mandated by Federal law.

Other local providers use more creative approaches, such as channeling funds through a single fiscal agent who contracts with other community agencies, or combining funding from different programs to support a single class of learners (see box 6-C). However, coordinating funding from different sources does not necessarily reduce, and may actually increase, recordkeeping, management, and reporting burdens as local programs struggle to leave a clear accountability and audit trail. Technology can reduce some of this burden if agreement can be reached on developing common data elements, definitions, data collection procedures, and reporting formats.

Some Federal programs make local coordination difficult because of their requirements concerning location of classes, student eligibility, or intensity of service. Examples include workplace literacy programs that must be conducted at the job site, family literacy programs with strict eligibility as to the kinds of children and families that can be served, or Job Opportunities and Basic Skills programs requiring 20 hours of instruction per week, an almost impossible schedule for adults working full time.

A FINAL NOTE

As the above issues illustrate, all policies—whether at the Federal, State, or local level—have two interrelated goals: serving more learners with high-quality programs that meet their educational goals, and operating programs more efficiently and effectively. The efforts of thousands of dedicated adult literacy volunteers and staff are especially impressive for their persistence in the face of severe constraints. But it is difficult to look at a system that, at best, *may serve* less than 10 percent of those in need and say it has come far enough. It is impossible to look at a system that has, at best, *met the full literacy* needs of fewer than one in 10 of these learners and say it is successful. The system as it stands cannot be expected to meet the current problems, much less ever increasing demands as the horizons of literacy continue to push forward. New approaches and solutions are required. Technology is increasingly being considered an engine for changing the ways adult learners can be served. This is discussed in greater detail in the next chapters.

---

[73] Ibid.

Technology Today: Practice vs. Promise | 7

A dvances in technology have "upped the ante" for adult literacy by redefining the skills people need to function successfully at work and in everyday life. At the same time, technology offers new tools with enormous potential for improving adult literacy—provided that learners and education programs can obtain and use them effectively.

Computer and video technologies, telecommunications, and consumer electronics all have features well-suited to adult education. Within each type of technology, an array of hardware, software, and learning materials is available. Hardware for literacy ranges from interstate satellite networks to pocket-sized language translators; from dazzling multimedia systems integrating words, pictures, sound, and touch, to the familiar telephone. Software ranges from basic drill programs that permit learners to practice a skill repeatedly, to sophisticated simulations that allow adults to interact with realistic reproductions of work or social situations.

As earlier chapters have suggested, technology has the potential to attract and motivate adults with limited literacy skills, give them greater privacy and control over their learning, adjust instruction to different paces and learning styles, transport education to new locations, reach more students at lower cost, train teachers, and improve program management and coordination. But is this potential being met? To answer that question, this chapter explores several questions:

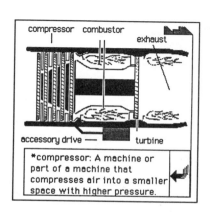

- How much real access do literacy programs and learners currently have to hardware and software?
- How do literacy programs use technology now, and how could they use it more effectively?
- What are the barriers to broader access and more effective use of technology?

189

FINDINGS

- Computers are the most widely used technology in literacy programs, but even the use of this technology is limited. It is estimated that not more than 15 percent of literacy providers use computers regularly for instruction. Still rarer in literacy programs is the use of newer, computer-related technologies—digitized speech, videodisc players, and CD-ROM (compact disc-read only memory)—that offer promising multimedia applications.

- As literacy educators gain more experience, the uses of computers move far beyond traditional drill and practice. However, even experienced programs generally use technology as a supplement to traditional classroom-based instruction, rather than as a fundamental tool for learning.

- Video technology is surprisingly underused given its familiarity and availability. Lower end, inexpensive technologies—such as audio recorders, closed-caption decoders, and hand-held electronic devices—are largely ignored.

- Available computer software does not adequately meet the demands of literacy programs. Courseware for video and other technologies is even more limited.

- A significant amount of hardware and software in businesses, homes, schools, colleges, and libraries is underutilized for literacy education.

- The promise of technologies to enable adults to learn anywhere, any time, is still largely unexplored. Technology is rarely used to reach learners outside of classrooms or to provide flexibility for learners.

- Significant barriers that inhibit widespread access and effective use of technologies include the cost and funding of technology, a highly fragmented marketplace, the lack of information about technology applications, and the institutional challenges faced by a diverse literacy field.

ACCESS TO TECHNOLOGIES FOR LITERACY

Recent advances have made technology more adaptable than ever before for adults with limited literacy skills. Computers with speech synthesizers can transform written text into spoken words, which is especially helpful to limited English proficient (LEP) adults and those with minimal reading skills. Touch screens, pointing devices, and icons have made computers less intimidating and easier to operate. Hand-held electronic devices make it possible for adults to learn on the bus, at home, on a coffee break, or in a waiting room. Distance learning technologies can extend opportunities for education and peer interaction to adults in remote locations. And the diversity of technologies means that something is available for almost every type of learning style or program need (see box 7-A).

In order to take advantage of these features, however, adult learners and literacy programs must have access to hardware and equipment and to software and other learning materials. Determining the extent to which literacy programs have access to technology is difficult because data are so limited, especially for some of the newer technologies. To supplement the limited existing research, the Office of Technology Assessment (OTA) initiated several studies and made staff visits to technology-using literacy sites.[1]

Access to Computer Hardware

Having access to hardware is the first, most obvious gateway to using technology. Literacy

---

[1] J.D. Eveland et al., Claremont Graduate School, "Case Studies of Technology Use in Adult Literacy Programs," OTA contractor report, June 1992; Jay P. Sivin-Kachala and Ellen R. Bialo, Interactive Educational Systems Design, Inc., "Software for Adult Literacy: Scope, Suitability, Available Sources of Information, and Implications for Federal Policy," OTA contractor report, June 1992; Christine Holland, SL Productions, "Observations: Technologies for Literacy in Mississippi and New York City," OTA contractor report and video footage, April 1992; and Education TURNKEY Systems, Inc. and Wujcik and Associates, "The Educational Software Marketplace and Adult Literacy Niches," OTA contractor report, April 1992. See appendix H for information on obtaining these reports.

Box 7-A—Technologies for Literacy

Computer-Based Technologies

- Computer and peripheral hardware (monitors, keyboards, printers, drives, mice, modems).
- Computer input devices (scanners, touch screens, pens, microphones).
- Local- or wide-area networks (computers and terminals linked over short or long distances), electronic mail, electronic bulletin boards.
- Multimedia systems that combine text, graphics, sound, animation, and video (computers connected with devices such as video monitors, laserdisc or videodisc players, CD-ROM players, speech synthesizers, speech boards, audio speakers).

Some applications: Computer laboratories for instruction and self-tutoring; audio for help with pronunciation and vocabulary (especially useful with beginning readers and English as a second language students); presentation of information through multiple media (e.g., text, graphics, moving pictures, sound) to reach learners with different learning styles; information networks for teachers and administrators.

Telecommunications Technologies

- Broadcast, radio, cable, and satellite networks.
- Television sets, VCRs, videodisc players, camcorders, closed-caption decoders, and videocassettes.
- Telephone networks, telephones, touch tone, voice mail (see also local- or wide-area networks above).
- Facsimile (fax) machines.

Some applications: Two-way interactive distance learning; videoconferencing for learners and teachers; television, videocassette, and radio courses to facilitate learning at home; informing public about literacy programs; sharing of courseware and effective practices; large installed base in order to reach many prospective learners who cannot or will not come to programs.

Consumer Electronic Devices

- Portable electronic devices (calculator, language translator, hand-held dictionary and encyclopedia, digital books).
- Home videogame machines.
- Audio equipment (stereo, compact disc player, tape player, cassettes, books on tape).

Some applications: Learning "on the go" or at home, renting courseware for VCRs or game machines, translating between English and another language, hearing correct pronunciation of unfamiliar words, reading books on tape or electronic books.

SOURCE: Office of Technology Assessment, 1993.

---

programs with computers are most often found in public schools, community colleges, and large corporations—institutions that have funds for hardware purchases, a prior commitment to learning technologies, and opportunities for buying in quantity at reduced prices. Although literacy programs benefit from being located in such institutions, it is rarely the literacy program alone that drives hardware acquisition.

Correctional facilities are another group of literacy providers likely to have access to computers. Federal prisons, for example, were early users of computer-based training in basic and vocational skills. Although comprehensive statistics are not available regarding technology access in correctional institutions, 35 of 65 Federal prisons use computers in their educational programs, as do the correctional systems in such States as

Texas, New York, Michigan, and Minnesota and such large cities as Los Angeles.[2]

Reliable estimates of access to computers among community-based organizations (CBOs) are particularly difficult to obtain, because these providers are so diverse. An OTA survey of 33 technology-using programs found that community-based literacy programs had fewer computers than programs in public schools, businesses, and community colleges.[3] Even so, many community-based and volunteer literacy programs do acquire hardware. A 1991 survey conducted by Literacy Volunteers of America (LVA) reported that 72 percent of LVA programs were using computers in some capacity (though not necessarily for instruction).[4] In addition, the Job Training Partnership Act (JTPA), which funds many CBOs, encourages computer-based instruction and allows Federal funds to be used for hardware and software (see chapter 5). Similarly, the Federal Job Corps program for severely disadvantaged youth has promoted the use of computers for education and training in its centers.[5]

Furthermore, most literacy programs with computers do not appear to have access to newer more powerful, computer-related technologies—such as scanners, speech boards, CD-ROM, videodisc players, modems, and touch screens—that make the technology more accessible and open up promising multimedia applications for adult learners. Typically, the 33 technology-using programs surveyed by OTA had stand-alone computers with color monitors and mouses. About one-half of the programs surveyed had some hardware with speech capabilities. Scanners, which allow teachers and students to customize software by copying photos, drawings, and text into their computer applications, appeared in only one-third of the sites. Videodisc players, CD-ROM, modems, and touch screens were even less available.[6] Access to newer technologies seems to depend on whether a "critical mass" of technology resources exists in a literacy education setting. Programs with relatively fewer computers (less than 15) also tend to have fewer of the more advanced technologies.[7]

Little is known about which factors create demand for instructional computers or how much technology planning precedes acquisition. Anecdotal evidence suggests that the motivation to purchase hardware comes from any of four sources: word-of-mouth success stories, the desire to attract students, the initiative of a technology crusader on staff, or an attempt to serve more learners when space, time, or personnel are limited.[8] Very few literacy providers, especially those outside of community colleges or large school districts, appear to develop a comprehensive, long-range technology plan. Even workplace literacy programs operated by businesses sometimes fail to tap in-house technology expertise from other departments.[9]

Access to Other Hardware

Estimating the number of literacy programs with access to video and telecommunications

---

2 Education TURNKEY, Inc. and Wujcik and Associates, op. cit., footnote 1, pp. 34-35.

3 Sivin-Kachala and Bialo, op. cit., footnote 1, p. 26.

4 Literacy Volunteers of America, Inc., New York, NY, "Computer Use Survey, 1984-1991," 1991. Forty percent of the LVA programs with computers reported using them for program management only.

5 Jo Ann Intili et al., *An Evaluation Feasibility Study of the Use of Various Technologies to Assist in the Instruction of JTPA Participants*, vol. 1 (Berkeley, CA: Micro Methods, June 30, 1989).

6 Sivin-Kachala and Bialo, op. cit., footnote 1, pp. 28-29.

7 Ibid., p. 29.

8 Ibid., p. 66; Eveland et al., op. cit., footnote 1; Holland, op. cit., footnote 1; and Arnold H. Packer, *Retooling the American Workforce: The Role of Technology in Improving Adult Literacy During the 1990s* (Washington, DC: Southport Institute for Policy Analysis, 1988).

9 Eveland et al., op. cit., footnote 1, pp. 133-159.

Despite a growing base of distance learning systems, few are being used to serve adults in literacy programs. Some schools, like Kirkwood Community College, are exploring the possibilities of reaching adult learners.

hardware is even more difficult than determining computer availability. While statistics exist about the presence of these technologies in different institutional settings, it is unclear to what extent video and telecommunications technologies are actually being used for adult literacy education. OTA studies indicate that very few literacy providers use video and telecommunications technologies, even when a parent institution, such as a public school, has access to hardware.

Community colleges, for instance, frequently use broadcast and cable television to offer college-level telecourses. Over one-half of the community colleges responding to a recent survey reported having a distance learning program,[10] but few use these for adult literacy education.

The private sector also appears to have access to video technologies that are used for general training activities. *Training* magazine reports that 92 percent of U.S. businesses with 100 or more employees use videotape materials for training purposes, 20 percent use interactive videodiscs, and 10 percent use videoconferencing, with higher percentages among larger businesses. This survey did not distinguish between training for basic skills/literacy and other types of corporate training, although 19 percent of the businesses reported providing some kind of remedial courses in reading, writing, basic mathematics, or English as a second language (ESL).[11]

A potential source of telecommunications hardware for literacy programs is the Federal Star Schools Program. The 10 telecommunications partnerships created by this program have provided over 3,000 elementary and secondary schools with satellite dishes and 1 project is

---

[10] Ron Brey, *U.S. Postsecondary Distance Learning Programs in the 1990s: A Decade of Growth* (Washington, DC: American Association of Community and Junior Colleges, 1991), pp. 6-11.

[11] ''Industry Report 1992: 11th Annual Survey of Employer-Sponsored Training in America,'' *Training*, vol. 29, No. 10, October 1992, pp. 31-59. When businesses were allowed to set the criterion for which courses qualify as ''remedial education,'' 40 percent reported offering such a course.

helping build a statewide fiber optic network in Iowa. Although the program is primarily a K-12 venture, several of the Star Schools projects are serving adults with limited literacy skills or adults who want to learn English.[12]

Personal electronic devices, such as language translators, hand-held dictionaries, and encyclopedias, are available in a limited number of literacy programs, although almost one-half million of these products are now in public schools and providers such as correctional institutions are beginning to acquire them. Several million individuals also own hand-held language devices.[13] To date these devices have had limited learning applications. Most were developed for a limited purpose, with preprogrammed contents on a microchip. Now that vendors are placing content on cartridges (e.g., whole books) sold separately with features like a built-in dictionary, these products are likely to become more serviceable for literacy in the future.

Availability of Computer Courseware[14]

A second prerequisite to using technology is access to appropriate computer or video courseware or other technology-based learning materials. Although it is estimated that as many as 2,000 computer software products are marketed to the literacy community, relatively few are specifi-

cally designed for use in literacy programs.[15] Most of the marketed software products are "stand-alone," designed to run on an individual computer. Stand-alone products are generally quite affordable—most cost less than $100 per program—although a few exceed $1,000.[16]

Reading/language arts was the most commonly addressed subject among the 1,451 stand-alone software products identified by OTA, accounting for more than one-half of the products (see table 7-1). Mathematics was the next most popular subject, with about 22 percent of the products. Also common were so-called productivity tools, such as keyboarding, word processing, and spreadsheet software. Other subjects, such as social studies, science, job preparation, life skills, and problem solving, accounted for less than 10 percent each of the products. Most stand-alone software was targeted at adult basic education (ABE) programs, followed by ESL, and general equivalency diploma (GED) preparation.[17]

These stand-alone programs are only one type of courseware for literacy. Larger, more expensive integrated learning systems (ILSs) are also aimed at the adult literacy community. An ILS is a special type of computer network that typically includes a centralized "server," linked to less-powerful terminals. It also includes instructional software covering one or more subject areas and

---

[12] Presentations by Brian Talbot, Pacific Northwest Star Schools Partnership, and Mabel Phifer, United States Educational Network, at the Federal Star Schools Project Directors Meeting, Washington, DC, Nov. 24, 1992.

[13] Arthur Sisk, president, Franklin Learning Resources, The Educational Division of Franklin Electronic Publishers, Inc., personal communication, Nov. 19, 1992.

[14] Courseware is educational software or video programming packaged with supporting materials such as student manuals, teacher guides, and operating manuals.

[15] The database of existing software marketed to adult literacy was assembled by Sivin-Kachala and Bialo (op. cit., footnote 1, pp. 2-4) from the following sources: Marjorie DeWert and Beverly U. Student (eds.), *Apple Access: Adult Basic Skills Curriculum Software Guide* (Cupertino, CA: Apple Computer, Inc., 1991); Jeffrey H. Orloff (ed.), *Apple Access: Macintosh Educational Software Guide* (Cupertino, CA: Apple Computer, Inc., 1991); Tina Ruppelt (ed.), *Apple Adult Basic Education Resource Guide* (Cupertino, CA: Apple Computer, Inc., 1988); Barbara A.W. Wright (ed.), *Oregon/Washington Adult Basic Skills Technology Consortium Software Buyers Guide* (Seattle, WA: Oregon/Washington Adult Basic Skills Technology Consortium, 1991); Deborah Healey and Norman Johnson (eds.), *TESOL CALL Interest Section Software List 1991* (Alexandria, VA: Teachers of English to Speakers of Other Languages, 1991); and Education TURNKEY Systems, Inc. (compiler), "IBM Educational Systems Educational Software and Courseware," unpublished document, September 1991. Additional titles were provided by the sites responding to OTA's survey.

[16] Sivin-Kachala and Bialo, op. cit., footnote 1, p. 10.

[17] Ibid., pp. I-3 to I-11.

Table 7-1—Distribution of Available Literacy Software Products by Subject

Major subjects	Number	Percent	Major subjects	Number	Percent
Language arts	769	53.0%	**Language arts topics**		
Mathematics	313	21.6	Grammar and punctuation	234	30.5
General purpose	126	8.6	Spelling and vocabulary	231	30.2
Life skills	122	8.4	Reading comprehension	218	28.5
Social studies	111	7.6	Basic reading	206	26.9
Problem solving	65	4.5	Writing	107	14.0
Science	58	4.0	*Distribution of language arts products (total=769)*		
ESL/LEP specific	49	3.4			
Career guidance	39	2.7	**Mathematics topics**		
Computers and keyboard	31	2.1	Basic skills	225	71.9
Health	19	1.3	Applications	95	30.4
GED specific	17	1.2	Advanced	31	9.9
Employment	11	0.8	*Distribution of mathematics products (total=313)*		

KEY: ESL=English as a second language; GED=general equivalency diploma; LEP=limited English proficient.

NOTE: A total of 1,451 stand-alone computer software products used in literacy programs were identified for this analysis. As some products covered more than one subject, the totals do not add up to 100 percent.

SOFTWARE TYPES:
General purpose: Open-ended software that is not subject-specific.
Career guidance: Helps students learn about different careers and match their interests to various fields of work.
Computers and keyboard: Includes learning how to use a computer (e.g., booting up, inserting disks, standard keys) and learning how people use computer-based technology.
Employment: Combines both preemployment/work maturity skills (e.g., good work habits and on-the-job etiquette) and vocation-specific skills.
Life skills: Includes skills necessary for success at everyday living (e.g., coping with stress, balancing a checkbook, reading a bus schedule).
Problem solving: Addresses general problem-solving skills with application across domains rather than subject-specific skills.

SOURCE: Jay P. Sivin-Kachala and Ellen Bialo, Interactive Educational Systems Design, Inc., "Software for Adult Literacy: Scope, Suitability, Available Sources of Information, and Implications for Federal Policy," OTA contractor report, June 1992.

a range of grade levels; computer-based activities and a curriculum framework correlated to a widely used test instrument; and a management system that sequences student activities, records student performance, and generates summary reports. The OTA survey identified nine ILS products that are marketed to adult literacy programs.[18]

Despite this volume and variety, OTA finds that available computer software is not adequately meeting the demands of literacy programs. Literacy providers canvassed in site visits, surveys, workshops, and personal interviews agree that more appropriate applications are

desired—applications that cater to adult interests and tie directly to the context of learners' lives.[19] Many of the existing software products were designed for children and young adults and may be inappropriate for adult learners. As one adult educator noted:

> Most of the software that is on the market has been written for "larger markets" and then sold to "submarkets" as being appropriate for their populations. This is an immediate turn off to teachers of adult literacy who are very concerned with the dignity of adult learners and want to use technology as a motivator. Sitting at a computer is an "adult activity" and should not be under-

---

[18] Of the nine ILS products currently sold to adult literacy programs, six are correlated to the Test of Adult Basic Education (TABE) and five are correlated to the Comprehensive Adult Student Assessment System (CASAS). See ibid., pp. 12-14.

[19] Stephen Reder, Northwest Regional Educational Laboratory, "On-Line Literacy Development: A Context for Technology in Adult Literacy Education," OTA contractor report, April 1992; Center for Literacy Studies, University of Tennessee, Knoxville, "Life at the Margins: Profiles of Adults With Low Literacy Skills," OTA contractor report, March 1992; and Joyce Hakansson, "The Developer's Dilemma," OTA contractor report, October 1991.

mined by programs that are written for kindergarten to grade three.[20]

Many subjects and applications are not well-covered. Among them are writing; problem solving and critical thinking; adult-oriented courseware for GED preparation and ESL; career planning, preemployment skills, and workplace readiness; life skills; parenting skills; and reading and language arts for nonreaders and low-level readers, especially products that take advantage of human speech.[21]

Availability of Other Courseware and Programming

Video courseware and programming for adult literacy are extremely limited in quantity and scope. Other types of learning materials, such as courseware for consumer electronics, are rare.

Video courseware can include content on videotape, videodisc, or CD-ROM; live interactive distance learning courses; and television programming for broadcast, cable, and satellite transmission. They range in sophistication from the basic and inexpensive, such as ''teacher and blackboard'' public access television courses; to the slick and expensive, such as professional videotape productions involving location filming, professional actors, scriptwriters, teachers, and editors. The formats for video courseware vary from interviews, lectures, and discussions, to dramatizations, demonstrations, and storytelling.

A recent report surveying the current availability and use of broadcast-quality video programming identified five literacy series created for broadcast and cablecast. Kentucky Educational Television (KET) accounts for four of the five series and 99 percent of the use.[22] The fifth series, called *On Your Own*, is produced by WPSX-TV, a public television station in Pennsylvania in partnership with Prentice Hall. It consists of 33 5- to 15-minute segments designed for use by a teacher. Although the series is carried into 800,000 homes and learning centers throughout one-third of the State, it is not designed for free-standing home viewing.

The most widely used video courseware for adult literacy is KET's *GED on TV* (see box 7-B). This series is distributed to literacy programs in all 50 States, many of which use it to supplement classroom instruction. The three other KET products include *Another Page*, which is designed to teach reading skills at the 5th- through 7th-grade level; *Learn to Read*, a 30-segment series aimed at beginning readers; and *Math Basics*, a new series of 11 half-hour segments.

Over 750 training and education courseware titles exist for videodisc; however, only about 50 target basic skills.[23] Several other video titles relevant to adult literacy address issues such as parenting skills, health, consumer issues, job-readiness, and staff development.

An Untapped Base of Technology

OTA finds that a significant amount of technology in businesses, homes, schools, colleges, and libraries could be tapped for literacy and learning. Many companies have an impressive base of technology that is used for training. Large corporations also own videoconferencing and other telecommunications equipment, but it is used primarily for executive business meetings,

---

[20] Inaam Mansoor, director, Arlington Education and Employment Program (Project REEP), Arlington, VA, personal communication, Apr. 22, 1992.

[21] Sivin-Kachala and Bialo, op. cit., footnote 1, pp. 61-62.

[22] Marian L. Schwarz, ''Television and Adult Literacy: Potential for Access to Learning for an Unserved Population,'' report prepared for the Ford Foundation, June 1992, p. 25.

[23] Richard Pollak, ''Titles Available for Adult Training and Adult Literacy,'' unpublished data compiled from *Videodisc Compendium, 1993* (St. Paul, MN: Emerging Technology Consultants Inc., 1992).

Box 7-B—Broadcast Programming: The *GED on TV* Example

On Tuesday and Thursday evenings, while his children are doing homework, a 35-year-old father watches GED on TV. *Several months ago, while channel browsing, he stumbled upon a 2-minute video pretest on the local public television station. His self-score was high enough to qualify for the* GED on TV *program. Now, more than half-way through the series, he is stuck for the first time. He picks up the phone to call a tutor at the public television station's GED help line.*

In 1962, the Federal Appalachian Regional Commission (ARC) helped establish Kentucky Educational Television (KET) to produce and carry instructional programming to schools. With $100,000 from ARC, KET created a prototype for the first version of *GED on TV*, a series of programs to help viewers prepare for the general equivalency diploma (GED) examination. An additional $400,000 in State funds enabled KET to begin broadcasting *GED on TV* to Kentucky homes in 1975; since then the series has enrolled an average of 1,400 Kentuckians per year.[1] In 1986, KET revised *GED on TV* at a cost of $2 million, producing 43 half-hour segments and 3 workbooks. Today the series is also available in Spanish and is delivered in a variety of ways—broadcast, satellite downlink, videotape, and interactive videodisc.

Community outreach for *GED on TV* takes many forms—from print campaigns to involvement of social service agencies. In Kentucky, the process, contracted by KET to Morehead State University, works as follows: before the series begins, KET conducts a promotion on television and in newspapers, giving out an 800 number. Callers are screened over the phone and mailed pretests and enrollment forms when appropriate. Those who pass the pretest are sent schedules and workbooks. They watch the programs at home and can use the 800 line for tutorial help. At the end of the course, KET sends a practice test to enrollees, scores it with feedback, and returns it to the student with a certificate that pays the $10 GED test fee. In 1990, 54 percent of Kentucky's enrollees took the GED examination and 74 percent of those passed it—comparing favorably with national pass rates overall that are reported to be about 70 percent.

GED on TV has been distributed nationally since 1982. It is currently licensed to Public Broadcasting Service stations in 36 States and learning centers in all 50 States, including over 600 military bases and all Federal and many State prisons. Schools, businesses, and libraries can license the programs to provide videotapes to their learners for $132 per half-hour.[2] Several educational cable services also carry the series. At present, over 150,000 persons are either formally enrolled in the home study course or have sent for the study guides. Since the beginning of the broadcasts in 1975, more that 2 million adults have been involved in the course in one of these two ways.

There is compelling evidence that *GED on TV* brings in students who do not respond to other literacy programs. For example, in a survey of Indiana's 2,763 enrolled students, 82 percent said they would not have attempted to get a GED if they could not study at home. Furthermore, "... of all the enrollees who responded from the six-county pilot area, 58.9 percent said that they were making their first contact with any adult education program when they called about studying at home."[3]

---

[1] KET-Kentucky Educational Television, "KET/GED on TV Use and Benefits, 1975-1989," unpublished data, May 1990.

[2] Tape prices do not include broadcast or tape duplication rights. KET-Kentucky Educational Television, *The KET Instructional Video Catalogue* (Lexington, KY: 1992.)

[3] Summary of the Indiana Learn-at-Home Project, cited in Marion L. Schwarz, *Television and Adult Literacy: Potential for Access to Learning for an Unserved Population*, a report for the Ford Foundation, June 1992, p. 30.

Continued on next page

---

file exchange, or electronic mail and less often for training.[24]

Colleges and universities also have a base of technology, plus wide experience using it for teaching and learning. According to a 1991 survey, 2-year public colleges have a total of 356,000 desktop computers, or a ratio of 1 for every 24 students. These computers are not

---

[24] James Posko, "AT&T Video Conferencing," *Procomm Enterprises Magazine*, April 1991; Jeff Charles, "There Is a Video in Your Future," *1992 Ten-Year Forecast* (Menlo Park, CA: Institute for the Future, 1992), pp. 159-164; and "Industry Report 1992," op. cit., footnote 11, p. 46.

Box 7-B—Broadcast Programming: The *GED on TV* Example—Continued

Directors of programs in Kentucky, Indiana, Arkansas, and West Virginia suggest that several elements are important to success of the GED program. All the State directors agree that television advertising, particularly on commercial television, is critical. ''There is general agreement that the greater the promotional effort, the greater the response.''[4] Another important lesson is that both enrollment procedures and viewing opportunities need to be made as accessible and easy as possible. Videocassette recorders have become an important tool for increasing accessibility as learners can control the pace and schedule of their viewing—one outreach coordinator reports that everyone who has passed the test in her program had one.[5] The State directors also felt that support services (e.g., the 800 line) can make a difference, but are less crucial than advertising or accessibility.

New outreach activities are under way. The Public Television Outreach Alliance will promote the *GED on TV* series in a national effort. Targeted for fall of 1993, these efforts include: production of a 60-minute special to improve public awareness and motivation, a newspaper supplement that will reach 25 million readers, and an offer of 16 months of free use of the series by any public television station.

Cost Analysis

What does it cost to produce and deliver broadcast-quality instructional television and support services to adult learners? In the KET example, three elements are involved.

Production. The 1986 revision cost $2 million. If the programming has a life of 10 years, then Kentucky, which will serve an estimated 14,000 enrollees during those 10 years, will have spent $142.86 per student. However, if these costs are averaged out nationally—150,000 enrollees per year over 10 years—the cost drops to $1.33 per student. Furthermore, through licensing arrangements, KET expects to recoup its production costs.

Advertising and promotion. This is widely considered to be one of the most important investments in ensuring program success with an at-home audience. In 1990, this part of KET's budget was $60,000. Averaged out over the 1,100 Kentucky students who enrolled during that year, the cost was about $55 per student. However, there is some evidence that small increases in this budget can increase enrollment substantially, thereby driving down the other per capita costs. In 1987, when the Governor of Kentucky made *GED on TV* a special initiative, the advertising budget was $80,000 and the enrollment almost tripled to 3,000 (bringing advertising costs down to $27 per student).

Student support services. This budget was $166,000, paying for an administrator, a data manager, and 2 $1/2$ full-time telephone instructors. Per capita costs for enrollees in 1990 was $151. If, however, the additional advertising dollars had been spent as they were in 1987 and 3,000 learners were brought in, the per capita costs for student support services would be reduced to $55 (assuming a constant level of student support services—an assumption that may not be realistic).

---

4 Schwarz, op. cit., footnote 3, p. 31

5 Nellie Lawrence, outreach coordinator, KRMA-TV, Denver, CO, personal communication, Nov. 6, 1992.

evenly distributed within institutions, however, nor are they used exclusively for student instruction,[25] let alone for adult literacy. In addition, the majority of community colleges use distance learning and video technologies for instruction.[26]

Public schools have more than 2.5 million computers. Because many elementary and secondary schools are not open in the evening and because some school computers are restricted to use by special programs (e.g., the Federal Chapter 1 program), adult education programs often do not have access to these resources. In addition, virtually all elementary and secondary schools have televisions, 98 percent have videocassette

---

25 Kenneth C. Green and Skip Eastman, *Campus Computing 1991: The EDUCOM-USC Survey of Desktop Computing in Higher Education* (Los Angeles, CA: Center for Scholarly Technology, University of Southern California, 1992), p. 12.

26 Brey, op. cit., footnote 10, pp. 10-13, 67.

recorders (VCRs),[27] and 61 percent have access to cable, although schools in the poorest communities are often the least likely to have cable.[28] A growing number of public schools have videodisc players, satellite dishes, and interactive distance learning systems.[29] Despite the fact that many adult learning programs are held in public schools, use of these school-based technologies for adult literacy instruction is rare.

Perhaps the greatest untapped resources for literacy are home technologies (see figure 7-1). Telephones and televisions are the most widely available. Ninety-three percent of households have telephones,[30] but over one-third of these are rotary or pulse phones, which limits their access to hotlines, voice mail, and audio text.[31] In 1990, 98 percent of households had at least one television, over 72 percent of households owned VCRs, and 55 percent subscribed to cable. Only 3 percent of households had a home satellite dish system, mostly in rural areas or small towns.[32]

Home computers are far from pervasive, especially among low-income and minority households, but the number is growing. In 1989, 17.3 percent of adults had a computer in their home, up from 9.1 percent in 1984. However only about 58 percent of adults who have access to a home computer report actually using it. Home computers were used most frequently by adults for word processing (62 percent of users), video games (44 percent) and household records (36 percent).[33]

Figure 7-1—Technologies in the Home, 1990

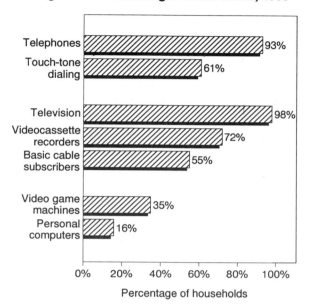

Percentage of households

NOTE: Total number of households is approximately 93 million.

SOURCES: Personal computer data from Robert Kominski, *Computer Use in the United States: 1989*, Special Studies Series, No. 171 (Washington, DC: U.S. Department of Commerce, Bureau of the Census, February 1991), p. 23; extrapolations to 1990 based on rates of change between 1984 and 1989. Video game data from Julia Marsh and Lawrence K. Vanston, *Interactive Multimedia and Telecommunications: Forecasts of Markets and Technologies* (Austin, TX: Technology Futures, Inc., 1992), p. 67. Telephone data from the U.S. Department of Commerce, *The NTIA Infrastructure Report*, NTIA Special Publication 91-26 (Washington, DC: October 1991). Touch-tone data from an AT&T survey cited in Bob Bentz, "Reaching Rotary Dialers With Voice Recognition," *Infotext*, July 1991, pp. 64-65. All television data from Henry T. Ingle, "A Nation of Learners: The Demographics of Access to Video and Telecommunications Technology," *New Visions for Video: Use of Cable, Satellite, Broadcast, and Interactive Systems for Literacy and Learning*, Annenberg Washington Program (ed.) (Washington, DC: 1992).

---

[27] Quality Education Data, Inc., *1992-1992 Catalog & Education Market Reference Guide* (Denver, CO: 1992).

[28] Steven L. Schongar, *Education and Technology, 1991: A Survey of the K-12 Market* (Shelton, CT: Market Data Retrieval, and New York, NY: LINK Resources, 1991), p. 61.

[29] Ibid., p. 54.

[30] Alexander Belinfante, *Telephone Subscribership in the U.S.* (Washington, DC: Federal Communications Commission, September 1991) cited in U.S. Department of Commerce, *The NTIA Infrastructure Report*, NTIA Special Publication 91-26 (Washington, DC: October 1991), app. F.

[31] 1991 AT&T survey cited in Bob Bentz, "Reaching Rotary Dialers With Voice Recognition," *Infotext*, July 1991, pp. 64-65.

[32] Henry T. Ingle, "A Nation of Learners: The Demographics of Access to Video and Telecommunications Technology," *New Visions for Video: Use of Cable, Satellite, Broadcast, and Interactive Systems for Literacy and Learning*, Annenberg Washington Program (ed.) (Washington, DC: 1992), p. 14.

[33] Robert Kominski, *Computer Use in the United States: 1989*, Special Studies Series P-23, No. 171 (Washington, DC: U.S. Department of Commerce, Bureau of the Census, February 1991).

Game machines such as Nintendo or Sega are one of the fastest growing consumer technologies. As of 1990, at least 35 percent of households were estimated to have acquired home video game machines.[34] In the past, software for these machines has been strictly entertainment. Recently the attachment of compact discs to these technologies and the advent of more powerful microprocessors have facilitated the introduction of new kinds of video game machines. As new devices, e.g., compact disc-interactive (CD-I), are brought to market, the manufacturers are negotiating with educational developers to create products for their platforms. In some cases, educational titles are included with the purchase of hardware. This trend is expected to continue.[35]

USES OF TECHNOLOGY

Most literacy programs do not have access to technology. But what about those that do? How are they using it? Are the technologies bringing the expected advantages? Are they realizing their promise? Because systematic data are not available to answer these questions, OTA has taken some "snapshots" of technology use in literacy programs through a survey of software use in 33 programs,[36] 6 intensive case studies,[37] and many site visits.[38] (For a list of all the sites, see appendix G). Taken together these sources suggest some patterns and lessons regarding technology use.

General Findings About Technology Use

Preceding chapters of this report have already mentioned several potential advantages of technology. These are summarized in boxes 7-C and 7-D as a way of framing the discussion that follows about how programs are *actually* using technology, what they are learning about its strengths and drawbacks, and whether technology is fulfilling its potential.[39]

In its site visits and surveys, OTA found that for most programs "technology" means computers; other technologies are used only sporadically. In addition, the proportion of programs that use computers regularly for instruction is surprisingly small—probably not more than 15 percent of all literacy providers.[40] Research shows that when computers are first introduced into educational settings, they are used in ways that often mirror current instructional practices,[41] and literacy is no exception. Educators who are least experienced with technology tend to use computers more for drill, practice, and automated tutorials than for other types of activities,[42] reflecting the overall prevalence of drill and practice in literacy instruction.

As programs become more experienced with technologies, they are more likely to use them as tools to assist all learning, and in ways that go well beyond drill and practice. Literacy providers with more technology experience use computers with word processors, spreadsheets, desktop pub-

---

[34] Julia A. Marsh and Lawrence K. Vanston, *Interactive Multimedia and Telecommunications: Forecasts of Markets and Technologies* (Austin, TX: Technology Futures, Inc., 1992), pp. 66-67.

[35] John Lowry, chairman and CEO, Discis Knowledge Research, Inc., personal communication, Dec. 2, 1992.

[36] Sivin-Kachala and Bialo, op. cit., footnote 1.

[37] J.D. Eveland et al., op. cit., footnote 1.

[38] For example, see Holland, op. cit., footnote 1.

[39] For further discussion of the issues in box 7-D, see ch. 3, and of those in box 7-E, see ch. 6.

[40] Development Associates, Inc., *National Evaluation of Adult Education Programs: Profiles of Service Providers* (Washington, DC: U.S. Department of Education, 1992), p. 72; Education TURNKEY Systems, Inc. and Wujcik and Associates, op. cit., footnote 1; and Holland, op. cit., footnote 1.

[41] Karen Sheingold and Martha Hadley, *Accomplished Teachers: Integrating Computers Into Classroom Practice* (New York, NY: Bank Street College of Education, September 1990).

[42] Sivin-Kachala and Bialo, op. cit., footnote 1, p. 53.

Many adults use computers in the LA Times Learning Center.

lishing, and databases—the same ways they are used in the "real world."[43] Students learn to use computers for practical things like writing letters or resumes, planning a budget, creating a business card or publishing a community newsletter. Educational games and simulations are also more common in sites with more computer experience.[44]

All of the technology-using programs surveyed by OTA also reported using computers for administrative purposes, such as general correspondence, registration and scheduling, recordkeeping, budgeting and payroll, student tracking, evaluation and planning, and mandated reports.[45]

The clearest finding from the case studies is that most programs are using computers principally as a supplement to a traditional program of classroom-based instruction. Two programs

drawn from OTA's case studies illustrate this point.

The Metro Campus Adult Learning Center is located on the fourth floor of the Cuyahoga County Community College in Cleveland, Ohio. Students, who must have at least a 4th-grade reading level to enroll, attend either a basic skills course or GED classes. Primary funding for the program is from JTPA: many of the students are single mothers who receive Aid to Families with Dependent Children (AFDC). The center has a computer laboratory with 31 Tandy computers, 26 of which have no hard drives. All are linked to one of two file servers that contain PLATO courseware.[46] The computer laboratory is open to students between 8:30 am and 4 pm. Classes are from 9 am to 1 pm every day. For 2 hours, students work in the computer laboratory, the

---

[43] Holland, op. cit., footnote 1.

[44] Sivin-Kachala and Bialo, op. cit., footnote 1, p. 53.

[45] Ibid., p. 31.

[46] PLATO—Programmed Logic for Automatic Teaching Operations—is an integrated learning system designed for adults reading at grade levels 4 through 12.

Box 7-C—Advantages of Technology for Adult Learners

Reaching Learners Outside of Classrooms

- With portable technology, adults can learn almost anywhere, any time, and can use small parcels of time more efficiently.
- Technology can carry instruction to nonschool settings—workplaces, homes, prisons, or the community.
- Adults can be served who would otherwise be left out, because of barriers such as inconvenient class scheduling, lack of childcare, or transportation.
- Learning at home can be more convenient and private for those who would feel stigmatized by attending a literacy program.

Using Learning Time Efficiently

- Learners can move at their own pace, have greater control over their own learning, and make better use of their learning time.
- Learners can handle some routine tasks more quickly through such processes as computer spell checking.
- Some learners advance more quickly with computers or interactive videodiscs than with conventional teaching methods.

Sustaining Motivation

- Novelty factor can be a "drawing card."
- Technology can be more engaging, can add interest to repetitive learning tasks.
- Importance of computers in society can enhance the status of literacy instruction.
- Privacy and confidentiality are added to the learning environment, reducing embarrassment adults often experience.
- Technology-based learning environments do not resemble those of past school failures.
- Intense, nonjudgmental drill and practice is available for those who need it.
- Instantaneous feedback and assessment are provided.

Individualizing Instruction

- Computers can serve as "personal tutors"—instruction and scheduling can be individualized without one-on-one staffing; suitable for open-entry, open-exit programs.
- Materials and presentation formats can be customized to suit different learning styles, interests, or workplace needs.
- Images and sound can help some adults learn better, especially those who cannot read text well.
- Computers with digitized and synthesized speech can help with pronunciation and vocabulary.
- Adults with learning disabilities and certain physical disabilities can be accommodated.

Providing Access to Information Tools

- Adults need to learn to use today's electronic tools for accessing information.
- Adults believe familiarity with computers will make them more employable.

SOURCE: Office of Technology Assessment, 1993.

other 2 hours they spend in a classroom that primarily uses traditional paper-and-pencil instructional methods. Student progress is tracked by the PLATO system and can be accessed readily by the teacher.

The Ripken Center is the first learning center established by the Baltimore City Literacy Corporation. Classes here are set up in 6-month

segments, because most of its students generate enough funding from JTPA to cover that period. Current capacity is 85 students. Courses include ABE, pre-GED, life skills, counseling, and career orientation. Each student attends class for 3 hours a day, 5 days a week. Each day a student spends half of the time (1 1/2 hours) doing classroom work; the other 1 1/2 hours are spent either in the

Box 7-D—Advantages of Technology for Literacy Programs

Recruiting and Retaining Learners

- Technology can be a magnet, attracting learners.
- More learners can be served and teachers used more productively.
- Programs can broaden their reach, serving those in remote locations.
- Teachers and counselors can maintain regular contact with learners.

Improving Curriculum

- Teachers can create individualized, engaging instructional materials related to the learner's needs and interests.
- Programs can share "what works" in terms of instructional materials and techniques.

Meeting Staff Development Challenges

- Teachers, volunteers, and administrators can be trained via video, distance learning, and self-study computer modules.
- Career ladders can be developed and information about vacancies can be posted nationwide.
- Staff can collaborate with their peers across town or cross country about problems, solutions, resources, and opportunities.

Enhancing Assessment and Evaluation

- Technology can track student progress continually, minimizing the need for "high anxiety" testing.
- Technology can provide diagnostic assistance for the teacher.
- Video and audiotape records, portfolio collections of writings, and other performance assessment measures can give more complete evidence of student progress.
- Program evaluation can be simplified by more systematic evaluation procedures and common data elements.

Streamlining Administration and Management

- Technology can more efficiently handle routine administrative tasks, freeing staff for instruction and providing comprehensive services to clients.
- Computer-based systems provide more efficient, accessible records on attendance, scheduling, personnel, budgeting, evaluation, and client tracking.

Augmenting Funding and Coordination

- Technology can serve as a magnet for fundraising and business contributions.
- Programs can pool resources and coordinate services, including social services, to serve learners better and avoid duplication of effort.
- Programs can share and access experts, databases, curriculum, public access software, government information, and national pools of literacy expertise.

SOURCE: Office of Technology Assessment, 1993.

computer laboratory (3 days a week for a total of 4 1/2 hours per week), a life skills class (1 day), or a career preparation class (1 day). The Ripken Center has a laboratory with 14 IBM-compatible personal computers, one of which operates as a file server. These computers are set up to use the WICAT system;[47] teachers select appropriate components from WICAT to supplement classroom activities. Considerable diversity of lessons characterizes activities in the laboratory; in 1 site visit at least 10 different applications were being used among the 15 students in the room. Word processing software is also available and many students use it regularly.

---

[47] The WICAT system is an integrated learning system.

Making computers a more fundamental part of the education experience requires accumulated skill and sustained effort. However, even programs with well-versed staff do not always have enough hardware to center instruction around technology.

Benefits and Limitations of Technologies for Literacy

OTA found that some of the anticipated benefits of technology are indeed being realized in the field—the good news. Case studies suggest caution, however, about overstating the advantages; technology has its limitations and can create new problems and challenges—the bad news.

The Good News

Learners like the tools. The overwhelming majority of people interviewed were highly enthusiastic about the benefits of computers in adult literacy. Almost everyone agreed that technology helps attract adult learners to the programs and keep them there. Mastering technology enhances self-esteem and increases motivation to learn. In addition, adults often view computers as a pathway to a vocational skill. Computer literacy programs designed to familiarize users with word processing, keyboarding, operating systems, and other applications are often more popular than classroom-oriented basic skills courses.

Information tools help teachers but do not replace them. There is no substitute for the dedicated and effective teacher. Contrary to the fears of some, there is no evidence from case studies that technology will usurp the critical relationship between teacher and learner. Rather, the tools can sharpen and focus the teacher-student interaction, and can spell the teacher during the more repetitive parts of the learning process; they can also ease some administrative tasks for the teacher. But ultimately it is the teacher who must guide the use of technology and shape its contribution to the overall learning context.

Information tools do meet some of the special learning needs of adults with low literacy skills. Creative use of information technology can support the open-entry, open-exit programs that many believe are essential for adult literacy instruction. The programs currently using computers describe many advantages: technology supports self-paced instruction, is nonjudgmental, adjusts to different skill levels, provides a "private" environment, and offers immediate feedback. Technology seems to help create a different type of educational experience, one that does not repeat the conditions of past failures.

The Bad News

Technology can be intimidating to some learners. Not everyone is equally enchanted by information technology. Any program that hopes to reach the full range of clients needs to provide learning opportunities that include a variety of methods. Those for whom technology does not work deserve as much consideration and alternative learning opportunities as those who are more comfortable with state-of-the-art tools. While technology draws many learners into programs, it may scare others away.

Tools require learner investment. Even the most "user friendly" software takes some time to learn. Most adults in literacy programs must invest time orienting themselves to the technology and learning how to use the tools before the tools can improve their learning. Additionally, since most learners have little or no access to information tools in their everyday lives, they may be unable to practice and gain familiarity during relatively brief computer laboratory times in programs.

Technical problems with hardware and software are common; special expertise is often needed to get technology working optimally. As programs come to depend more on systems made up of widely differing combinations of machines and software, they are more likely to need specialized personnel to evaluate hardware and software, perform systems integration, troubleshoot, and switch equipment over to different applications. In most of the sites visited, there were one or more ''gurus'' who, by virtue of interest and capability (seldom formal training), had acquired the expertise and knowledge needed to keep the technology working for their less mechanically minded colleagues. These gurus are critical to the functioning of the programs—it is they who patch together the systems with baling wire and cellophane tape—not to mention with recycled disc drives and self-taught midnight programming.

Decisions about technology implementation— what to buy, how to use it, what works with different kinds of learners—often must be made by trial and error. In OTA's survey of technology users, word-of-mouth—especially from adult education colleagues and educational technology experts—was cited as the most important source of information on software. If a State or region has an agency that provides information on technology for adult literacy, most computer-using programs in the region will take advantage of its services. But technology users did not typically consult available resources such as reviews from online services or software guides, mostly because they did not know about these sources. In addition, most technology applications have not been formally evaluated. As a result almost no data on effectiveness is available to help guide technology implementation decisions (see the section on ''Barriers'' below).

Information technology requires new skills of teachers. Traditional methods of training teachers and volunteers for adult literacy are not generally oriented toward technology use. Many adult educators lack computing experience and, even when they can operate the equipment, cannot keep it running smoothly. Those uncomfortable with technology are unlikely to recommend it to their students; some fear it will replace them, or come between them and their students. Furthermore, effective teaching with technology requires new approaches that integrate technology with classroom work and make the most of technology's capabilities.

Integrated learning systems can be a mixed blessing. ILSs are designed to be all-inclusive, simplified arrangements for handling the complete teaching task. They are often especially valuable to smaller programs because they can reduce the need for specialized support personnel. The broad content coverage offered can provide materials for practicing what was covered in class as well as materials that can ''fill in the gaps'' in a program's curriculum. The automated management system takes care of placement, assessment, and diagnosis, and allows for self-paced, individualized instruction and testing.

However ILSs also have some disadvantages. Often they are difficult to customize for specific learner needs; some have materials designed for children that appear condescending to adults; some lack opportunities for learner control which can undermine motivation; and others are limited in their ''save and resume'' capabilities which creates problems for students who only have a short amount of time to work on lessons. Most newer systems now targeting adult literacy are tackling these concerns in their design and software.

The Promise Unfulfilled

OTA finds that in many critical respects the technologies that are accessible to adult literacy programs are vastly underutilized and the potential of technology remains largely unfulfilled. Yet there are enough promising, effective, and exciting models of technology use to suggest that the potential is more than visionary and to encourage continued implementation.

Technology is rarely used to reach learners outside of classrooms or to provide flexibility for learners. Information technology for adult learning seems to have made little headway in delivering services to learners whenever and wherever they need it. Typically there is little use of ''distance learning'' in the programs visited;

Motorola employees enrolled in Project SALSA learned at home on loaned computers and modems.

most programs still require students to come to program sites within specified hours. Often there are good reasons for this—e.g., to provide social reinforcement or to develop employability skills such as punctuality. However, in most programs, learners experienced major difficulties in going to program facilities. Program administrators talked about difficulties in providing access to the technology whenever and wherever it was needed —they described situations in which equipment sat idle at some times and could not meet demand at others. There was little evidence of "portable" technologies that learners could take home or to other learning sites.

Yet the potential remains. Individual experiments are being tried by a few; innovative ideas bloom where nourished.

- In a workplace literacy program at several of Motorola's plants in Arizona, students enrolled in a reading course were given computers and modems to take home. Throughout the 6-month course, they had access to a networked reading curriculum; families of the workers were encouraged to use the computers as well (see box 7-E).

- "Playing to Win" is a neighborhood technology center in the basement of a housing project in East Harlem, New York. The center, which serves about 500 people and has about 40 computers, is designed to give neighborhood residents access to computers and computer-based learning. The schedule at the center is filled with a mixture of classes from neighboring public schools, adult literacy programs, vocational groups, Head Start, and plenty of open laboratory time where any East Harlem resident can use the computers for a nominal sum. Trained counselors are on hand to help novices; learners can work on their own, or sign up for workshops and classes.[48]

- The Mississippi Mobile Learning Lab, equipped with 12 computer workstations, travels to towns in northeast Mississippi and provides computer-assisted basic skills instruction. The laboratory offers basic computer literacy and word processing, job skill development, ABE, GED, and commercial motor vehicle drivers license review. The laboratory serves six counties and stays for about 8 weeks in each location. Each learner who comes has an individualized course designed for him or her.[49]

- At the Euclid Adult Learning Center, students can watch KET tapes during classroom times. They then complete related exercises in an accompanying workbook. To help students work at home, an 800 number is available that can be accessed from any touch-tone phone. A student can direct the phone system to a particular lesson and can review the lesson as many times as necessary by pressing "0."[50]

Networking—of both people and machines— is also limited. There is a striking absence of networking among sites and even within sites. At

---

[48] See Steven Levy, "Access for All," *MacWorld*, August 1989, pp. 43-44.

[49] Holland, op. cit., footnote 1.

[50] Eveland et al., op. cit., footnote 1.

Box 7-E—Project SALSA: Sending Computers Home With Learners

Many Motorola employees participate in basic skills classes (reading, writing, and mathematics) at the worksite. What if computers were also available at home? Would there be an increase in learning gains? Would employees' families benefit too? These questions formed the basis for Motorola's Project SALSA, a research project involving U.S. West Communications, Apple Computer, University Communications, Businessland, the University of Illinois, and Rio Salado Community College.

Fifty-three employees enrolled in a traditional reading course at Motorola's semiconductor facilities in Mesa and Tempe, Arizona, also received a computer and modem that connected them to the University of Illinois' NovaNET system. These workers, mostly female, single parents, had access to over 10,000 hours of educational software and received 14 hours of training in its use. A control group of 30 Motorola employees was enrolled in the same reading course, but not given computers. Teachers did not know who had the computers.

A formal evaluation at the end of 6 months compared the learning gains of those with computers at home to those in the control group. Although on average computer users made larger gains on a standardized reading test, the results were not statistically significant. However, some interesting lessons emerged.

First, the amount of time learners used the computers at home was quite low—users averaged only about 30 to 45 minutes a week. Learners varied widely in how much they used the equipment—some logged on only once or twice after the initial training, others used it quite a bit. Several factors seemed to affect use, the first being scheduling. The NovaNET hours were not optimal for most learners as the network was down from 7 to 9 pm and on weekends. In addition, many employees described having little time to use the computer and, even when they did, being too tired. This suggests that at-home systems will work best if they can be available whenever the learner has free time to use them. Individuals are likely to vary considerably in the extent to which they are able to study at home, feel comfortable using computers, or prefer face-to-face instruction.

A second problem was separation of the at-home coursework and classroom content. Because of the constraints of this experiment, teachers were not aware that some students had access to a computer and a software curriculum and, therefore, could not design classroom work to complement these educational resources. Students were pretty much "on their own" with regard to integrating computer materials into their coursework. As one student noted: "The reading class on NovaNET was not anything like the reading class at the plant." These results suggest that at-home work should be reinforced and integrated into what is being taught in class. Furthermore, teachers need to be trained in how to implement computers and software into their teaching.

Third, the need for technical support related to using the computers emerged as a central issue. If participants were confused during the training sessions, they became more frustrated when they took the computer home. Some eventually stopped trying to use the computer or NovaNET altogether. The evaluation suggested the importance of creating a team of instructors/trainers with responsibility for visiting employees, troubleshooting hardware, software, and communications problems, and creating user groups to share experiences over the system.

Despite the difficulties, anecdotal evidence suggested that family members benefited from the experiment. Of the 150 family members, 120 signed in and logged a total of 2,600 hours, sampling many software options. Some participants described family members working together with the computer—grandparents with parents and parents with children. Employees were excited and proud to participate in the project. The computer and NovaNET introduced learners to new subjects, technological capabilities, skills, and experiences. Participants appreciated the patient and private environment provided by the computer. Most participants liked having a computer in the home and appreciated the extra support. Many were reluctant to give up the computers at the end of the project and expressed an interest in purchasing a computer if Motorola offered to split the cost.

SOURCES: Linda Thor et al., *SALSA (Southwest Advanced Learning System for Adults) Pilot Project Research Report* (Phoenix, AZ: Rio Salado Community College, April 1991); Jim Frasier, manager of education research, Motorola University, personal communication, 1992; and Karen Mills, associate dean of instruction, Rio Salado Community College, personal communication, 1992.

the most basic level, there is far less use of computer networks than is possible or desirable. Although there are numerous examples of networked systems that combine electronic mail, bulletin boards, and other capabilities to create exciting learning environments for children,[51] these methods are not being employed in adult literacy programs. This is paralleled by a general isolation of personnel in one facility from those at other facilities even when programs fall under one central administrative system. Programs often seem to be functioning in an intellectual and operational vacuum.

Coordination of services with other agencies is frequently desired, but seldom achieved. Few programs use their technology to identify or access other social services available to adult learners, except for some welfare reform initiatives where such coordination is mandated. In short, the potential for information exchange is singularly untapped in agencies visited, despite their desire for it.

Several projects and States are experimenting with networking and data coordination:

- In Philadelphia "Power Learning," a pilot project, implemented by the Mayor's Commission on Literacy, is linking together learners and teachers from eight community-based adult education projects. One-hundred learners, each enrolled in a program at one of the eight sites, have been loaned a computer and a modem to take home. The system allows electronic conferencing among teachers and learners, access to PLATO courseware, and word processing. Learners are using the computers in many ways, but writing is the predominant activity. Students are writing about themselves, talking

to each other online, and sending messages to their teachers.[52]
- The Outreach and Technical Assistance Network (OTAN) Online Communication System has been set up as part of California's strategic plan for adult education. This system provides electronic mail through which people working in adult education can contact others in California and throughout the Nation (see chapter 6, figure 6-2). In addition, it provides an electronic database full of resources and information for teachers and administrators.[53]

Video technology is surprisingly underused given its familiarity and availability. The virtual explosion of easily accessible and relatively inexpensive video technologies, in particular VCRs and videotapes, offers exciting new possibilities for using video as a learning and teaching tool. Yet video use in literacy programs is limited. Videos are used largely to provide information or stimulate group discussions in class. A few programs have videocameras or other video production equipment, which they use to tape special events or mock job interviews, but producing video or using video as a classroom resource is a rare activity.

Examples of innovations include:

- To help employees who want to improve their reading skills at home, one company is distributing a 5 1/2-hour beginning reader video series called *I Want to Read*.[54] As part of the service, this company conducts a promotional campaign with an 800 number, mails videos and support materials to interested employees, offers telephone counseling, and helps employees to find a community literacy program.
- Arlington Community Television has produced a video series called *Communicating Survival*

---

[51] See Reder, op. cit., footnote 19.

[52] Donna Cooper, executive director, Mayor's Commission on Literacy, Philadelphia, PA, personal communication, Mar. 26, 1993.

[53] John Fleischman and Gerald H. Kilbert, "Adult Education Technology in the Golden State," *Adult Learning*, January/February 1993, pp. 15-16.

[54] The series was produced by Anabel Newman of the University of Indiana.

that provides information critical to new immigrants, such as the use of 911, emergency health care, the supermarket, and so forth. The tapes are produced in several languages and are being distributed for use by individuals, ESL classes, and refugee assistance groups.

- A collaboration between El Paso Community College and Levi Strauss is the first major project attempting to design and implement a video-based workplace literacy curriculum. A series of 60 ESL videos that focus on textile production and manufacturing techniques used in Strauss' 7 El Paso plants have been completed; the project is about to begin production of another 60 episodes to teach reading, writing, and mathematics skills within the workplace context. Using employee input and formative research, the video series is being designed for initial use with the predominantly Spanish-speaking workers in these plants.[55]

- The Children's Television Workshop has recently produced a children's literacy program called *Ghostwriter*. The series is targeted toward 2nd to 4th graders, particularly those who are "... becoming reluctant readers and writers—who do not see the personal relevance of the printed word or are experiencing difficulty understanding and creating text."[56] The program, which is being broadcast on many Public Broadcasting Service (PBS) stations during the 1992-93 television season, focuses on a multiethnic group of three boys and three girls who solve mysteries in their neighborhood by reading and writing. Viewers are encouraged to write and read through a host of print-based activities like letter writing and contests.[57] While not aimed at adults, the engaging format

has attracted a number of parents seeking to enhance their literacy skills.

- The Annenberg/Corporation for Public Broadcasting (CPB) project is soliciting proposals for funding to develop an adult television course that teaches ESL. The course will include a series of at least 20 broadcast-quality television programs (30 minutes in length) with integrated print and audio materials. The first phase (year 1) will fund one planning and formative research effort ($100,000). Annenberg/CPB expects to provide $1.5 million for production and distribution (to be matched by an additional $1.5 million in outside funds). The programs will have wide distribution through broadcast and cable, in community-based ESL programs, in community college ESL programs, and through public libraries, corporations, and other community organizations.[58]

- Vermont Interactive Television is a statewide telecommunications system that allows people all over the State ready access to education and training resources. Currently nine sites are connected via two-way interactive television. Learners go to the site nearest their home and attend classes that may be taught by teachers in another part of the State. Learners can use the system to work on their GED. All classes are preserved on videotape for learners who may miss a class or want to review material.[59]

Simpler, inexpensive technologies—such as audio recorders, closed-caption decoders, and hand-held electronic devices—are largely ignored. Although many literacy educators described the virtues of audio for learners who lack reading skills, audiotape recorders were seldom being used. Few literacy programs seemed aware

---

[55] All three of the above examples are drawn from Schwarz, op. cit., footnote 22.

[56] Children's Television Workshop, "Literacy Project Snapshot," unpublished manuscript, Nov. 19, 1990, p. 2.

[57] Children's Television Workshop, *Ghostwriter Activity Guide* (New York, NY: 1992).

[58] Annenberg/CPB Project, "English as a Second Language Solicitation Guidelines," unpublished document, 1993.

[59] "Adult Basic Education: Expanding Horizons Over VIT," *Online: The Newsletter of Vermont Interactive Television*, vol. 2, No. 1, August 1991.

of other, less well-known devices such as closed-caption decoders or hand-held dictionaries and translators (see box 7-F).

There are some experiments that indicate these technologies have much to offer:

- The Mott Haven Library Center for Reading and Writing in New York City (see chapter 4), which serves mostly adults who read below grade-4 level, has an extensive collection of books on tape that are very popular with these learners. The collection is large because a pool of volunteers reads and records books; the collection can easily and inexpensively be updated to keep up with the interests and requests of the learners.

- The Institute for Communication Disorders offers a special literacy program for learning disabled adults with 0 to 3rd-grade reading ability at the International Center for the Disabled in New York City. The teacher, a learning disabilities specialist, reports that calculators and the Franklin Speaking Spelling Ace are extremely helpful to her students. Cassette tape recorders, which students use to listen to books on tape and to make audio notes, are at the top of the teacher's list as useful technology.

- The Arlington Education and Employment Program (REEP) in Arlington, Virginia, and the National Captioning Institute (NCI) have proposed a project to use closed captioning in ESL classes. After REEP has identified videos relevant to their ESL curriculum, NCI will provide captions (available at two different paces) and will provide training to teachers using the captioned videos. Anecdotal reports suggest that many non-native speakers of English find captioning helpful; NCI reports that 50 percent of individuals who purchased

decoders in 1990 did so in order to learn English.[60]

The availability of relevant and versatile software is limited. Providers repeatedly mentioned the need for software that addresses the specific needs of adults with low literacy skills. They ask for content that is meaningful to adults, not just a refashioning of something originally made for children. There is a great need for high-quality programming that can be easily customized by instructors to meet the special needs of local client populations.

Interesting possibilities are being explored as programs acquire technology and software that enable them to create their own products.

- Design tools, such as software shells, make it increasingly easy to create courseware that reinforces basic skills through materials specific to the workplace (see box 7-G).

- The Correctional Educational Division (CED) of the Los Angeles County jail system (see chapter 4, box 4-F) has supported the onsite development of computer software and video programming that more closely meets the needs of their inmate population. For example, they have developed computer reading materials for the 3rd- and 4th-grade reading levels that make use of idioms frequently heard by inmates in the jails. CED also has impressive video production facilities; one of their main purposes is to produce short videos, requested by teachers, to illustrate concepts or skills that teachers find themselves demonstrating repeatedly (e.g., the safe use of hand tools).

- Chemeketa Community College in Salem, Oregon, has recently created software for teachers called *Textbook Toolbox*. This software allows teachers with no programming experience to create electronic textbooks using

---

[60] These data come from decoder warranty registrations. C. Eric Kirkland, National Captioning Institute, Inc., personal communication, August 1992.

Box 7-F—Closed Captioning

Captioning is a way of displaying a "script" on the television screen, much like subtitles in foreign language films. Originally developed for the hearing impaired, applications of captioning technology may prove to be an important resource for literacy. The first captioning system was pioneered in 1971. By the late 1970s, it was possible to embed the text into the Vertical Blanking Interval of the video signal. The development of "closed" captions made the text visible only on those sets equipped with a special decoder. Until recently, viewers were required to buy and install this decoder (about $160 to $200), if they wanted to view captions. However, as a result of Federal legislation, all television sets with screen sizes 13 inches or larger, whether manufactured or imported for use in the United States after June 30, 1993, will have captioning capability built directly into the television receiver.[1]

This legislation accelerated the development of hardware circuitry and put captioned programming within reach of large numbers of people who can benefit, including an estimated 24 million Americans who are hearing impaired, 38 percent of older adults with some hearing loss, children and adults learning to read, and those who are not proficient in English. The cost of captioning technology was lowered by aggregating demand. High-volume production of the chip and installation during manufacturing will reduce the unit cost of decoders to under $5. Since about 20 percent of households purchase a new television each year, well over 40 million households are expected to have a caption-capable television by 1996.

By enlarging the audience with access to captioning, the legislation sought to provide marketplace incentives to pay for more captioned programming. The production of captions for programming, which is quite expensive, started with Federal dollars but, in recent years, has been supported by a mix of government, television network, and advertiser funding.[2] All prime-time network broadcasts are captioned, as are many sporting events, newscasts, and public affairs programs. The library of captioned movies on videotape is expanding as well, with over 3,000 titles available in 1992. However, basic cable networks, such as CNN, and pay cable networks, such as HBO, offer limited access to captioned programming.

Greater access to closed captioning has spurred a renewed interest in its potential educational uses. Studies of the effects of closed captioning on adult learners, adults and children with learning disabilities, and limited English proficient adults and children indicate that captioning may benefit these populations.[3] For example, there is limited evidence that closed captioning motivates these learners to read and helps improve their reading skills. Further research and experimentation are needed to exploit the potential of captioning as an educational tool. Some of the major questions are: 1) Can captioning, particularly as a part of incidental television viewing, improve reading and writing skills? Under what circumstances? For what kinds of learners (i.e., limited English proficient or nonreaders)? 2) How should captions be designed? 3) What are cost-effective ways to produce and distribute captions widely? A few studies on these questions and pilot projects are under way.[4]

---

[1] Public Law 101-431, The Television Decoder Circuitry Act of 1990.

[2] According to the National Captioning Institute (NCI), the Federal Government covers about 25 percent of the production costs for captioning. NCI estimates the cost of an hour of captioning at about $500 to $1,800 and up to 20 person-hours, depending on the application. Morgan Bramlet, manager of public relations, National Captioning Institute, personal communication, Feb. 12, 1993.

[3] See Rita M. Bean and Robert M. Wilson, "Using Closed Captioned Television to Teach Reading to Adults," *Reading Research and Instruction*, vol. 28, No. 4, 1989, pp. 27-37; E. Askov et al., Pennsylvania State University, Institute for the Study of Adult Literacy, "Adult Literacy, Computer Technology and the Hearing Impaired," unpublished manuscript, 1989; Susan B. Neuman and Patricia Koskinen, "Captioned Television as 'Comprehensible Input': Effects of Incidental Word Learning From Context for Language Minority Students," *Reading Research Quarterly*, vol. 27, No. 1, 1992, pp. 94-106; and Robert M. Wilson et al., "Using Closed Captioned Television to Enhance Reading Skills of Learning Disabled Students," *Yearbook of the National Reading Conference*, vol. 35, 1986, pp. 61-65.

[4] The Media Access Research and Development Office at the WGBH Caption Center, funded by the Corporation for Public Broadcasting and the U.S. Department of Education, conducts research on human factors and design issues related to captions for adults and children and delivery of simultaneous Spanish translation. Larry Goldberg, Executive Director, WGBH Caption Center, "Closed Captioned Programming: Changing Development in the Television Landscape," presentation at the Annenberg Washington Program, Oct. 17, 1991.

Box 7-G—Basic Skills Instruction Embedded in Job Training Materials

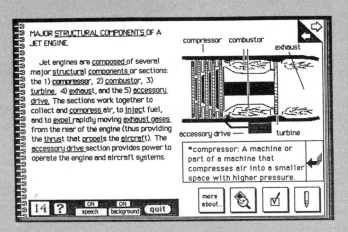

One of the difficulties experienced by some companies in upgrading the skills of their employees is the complexity of job-related technical documents and training manuals required for learning new systems. The technical vocabulary and complex concepts require high-level reading skills that may be beyond the capabilities of many employees.

The General Electric (GE) aircraft engine factory in Rutland, Vermont, faced this problem when GE sought to upgrade the production system. GE wanted to change operating procedures from line work, with its single repetitive tasks, to a team approach, in which groups of employees would be responsible for a cluster of tasks. When a training program was instituted, many employees were unable to understand the training materials. Rather than "dummy down" the manuals, GE took a different approach. Under a Federal workplace literacy grant with the Vermont Department of Education, GE converted the written manuals to software and used them as basic texts for their workplace literacy efforts.

The complex manuals are made more understandable to workers through the addition of speech and graphics using a hypertext/hypermedia system that offers links to supplemental information that help the user read and understand the text (see figure above). The user can "click" on a word or concept that is not understood and hear it read aloud and may request its definition in written format. A feature called "more about" gives more detail on complex concepts; e.g., if the employee wants to find out more about a "compressor," he or she clicks on the more about button, which brings up a graphic representation of a compressor and a description of how it works (see figure below). This "closeup" feature provides the context known by a good reader, but necessary for more

limited readers to comprehend the material. In choosing the closeup option, alternative wording of a passage can be provided, removing some of the nonessential information that can be confusing; other techniques include explicit numbering of sequential steps, highlighting causal relationships in the text, and graphic representations or animations of descriptive passages. Checkup questions help students monitor their comprehension as they go along.

Adult education teachers like using the software in their classes because it teaches basic skills in a meaningful

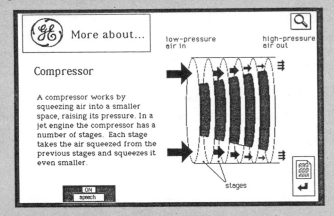

context, using the manuals the employees must understand for success on the job. Employers see it as a way to "sneak" basic skills training into job training, making it more palatable for both management and workers. Because the materials are so tied to the workplace changes, all employees benefit: some are "brushing up" on rusty skills, while those whose literacy skills may be very limited are not stigmatized by their participation.

SOURCE: Based on Michael Hillinger, Lexicon Systems, Sharon, VT, personal communication, August 1992. See also Michael L. Hillinger, "Computer Speech and Responsive Text," *Reading and Writing: An Interdisciplinary Journal*, vol. 4, No. 2, 1992, pp. 219-229.

notes, sounds, graphics, movies, and dictionary features.[61]

BARRIERS TO USE OF TECHNOLOGY

Why are literacy programs not taking greater advantage of technology? OTA identified several barriers that inhibit widespread access and effective use of technologies. They include funding, market, informational, and institutional problems. Many of these barriers are interrelated: e.g., funding barriers contribute to market barriers and vice versa.

Funding Barriers

Hardware and software cost money. Even technology that is reasonably priced by the standards of public schools, small businesses, or middle-income consumers may be out of range for literacy programs, since most cannot buy in quantity and thus take advantage of reduced prices. As discussed in chapters 4 and 6, most literacy programs operate on very tight budgets (average spending of $217 per student[62]), using funding from multiple and sometimes unreliable sources. Most literacy providers, especially small community-based organizations, cannot afford technology.

The median annual technology budget of the technology-using programs in OTA's survey (those with less than 15 computers) was $500.[63] Compare this with the average cost of $1,000 to $1,500 for a computer with color monitor, keyboard, and mouse. The startup price of an ILS generally ranges from $18,000 to $65,000, including equipment, the management and instruc-tional software, setup, and initial training. Annual support and software updates for ILSs cost from $1,500 to $6,000.

Newer technologies such as computer-based multimedia systems and interactive videodisc systems are even less affordable (see box 7-H). Among the most expensive technologies are two-way interactive telecommunications systems. Initial capital costs are high, and continuing outlays, such as subscriber fees, can also be expensive, making distance learning prohibitive for most programs.

The cost of technology is also an obstacle for the millions of adults who could benefit from literacy-related technology in the home or at work. As noted above, televisions, VCRs, telephones, computers, and game machines are commonplace features in many homes and work-places. But adults with limited literacy skills are among the least affluent consumer groups. Many cannot afford technological devices, even at mass market prices. They are also less likely to come in contact with technologies on the job.[64]

Although telephone service is often thought of as universal, only 93 percent of households actually have telephones (fewer than have televi-sions). Furthermore there are disparities related to ethnicity—while 95 percent of white house-holds have phones, only 84 percent of African-American and 83 percent of Latino households do so.[65] Those households with annual incomes of less than $15,000 also have lower rates of phone service.[66] A 1991 survey of cable and VCR penetration also shows a strong relationship to

---

[61] Lucy Tribble MacDonald, Chemeketa Community College, Salem, OR, presentation at Literacy Volunteers of America National Conference, Denver, CO, November 1992.

[62] This amount is for fiscal year 1990 programs funded by the Adult Education Act and includes Federal and State/local contribution. See ch. 4, table 4-1.

[63] Sivin-Kachala and Bialo, op. cit., footnote 1, p. 24.

[64] Center for Literacy Studies, op. cit., footnote 19.

[65] Belinfante, op. cit., footnote 30.

[66] Ibid.

Box 7-H—Multimedia, Hypermedia, and Adult Learning

Multimedia is the integrated use of sound, text, graphics, animation, still images, and motion video. Multimedia applications use a variety of hardware configurations, typically a computer linked to an interactive videodisc, CD-ROM player, television, and/or videocassette recorder. More recent technology configurations bundle the hardware together so that all images—text, graphics, animation, and full-motion video—can be displayed simultaneously on multiple windows on a single, desktop monitor.

Multimedia and hypermedia are often used interchangeably, but they are not identical. Multimedia refers to hardware that makes it possible to present multiple types of media, or to the applications (software) running on multimedia hardware platforms. One of the more powerful of these applications is hypermedia, a process that links software images in an associative, rather than linear fashion. Like hypertext software, used for many years to allow a user to link text by following an associative line of inquiry, hypermedia software makes it possible to take this concept further, creating associative links across media forms (e.g., text to video, or sound to graphics and animation). Hypermedia authoring tools are becoming easier to use, allowing teachers and learners to create their own lessons. Three illustrations follow:

1. Books on CD-ROM can be used with a computer. As the "pages" appear on the computer screen, the user can hear the book read aloud in English or in a different language. The user can interrupt to request a definition or clarify a concept. Supplementary material can feature video, graphics, or animation as well as sound and text.[1]

2. An interactive videodisc application simulates a jury trial. The learner joins the jury and views short video segments. The vignettes dramatize the courtroom procedure and show other members of the jury discussing the trial and making inferences. After each segment, multiple-choice questions are displayed on the monitor.

3. A CD-ROM presents the history of Native American tribes who lived in Mendocino County, California. The tribes are presented through photographs from the turn of the century, pictures of artifacts, sound recordings, and oral histories. Students can use segments from the CD and integrate them with their own videos and interviews with members of the tribes today to create a multimedia report.

Multimedia and hypermedia can incorporate a mix of learning techniques in one piece of courseware. Many adult learners, unable to use text for information, have developed alternative skills for understanding, organizing, and remembering information that draw on imagery, sound, and spatial memory.[2] Multimedia materials can incorporate these skills as a basis for learning, rather than relying on text alone. Hypermedia is also a powerful tool, because it puts adults in control of the learning path, allowing them to make information links based on personal choice and logic. Hypermedia makes it easy to "browse" through information, encouraging learners' intellectual curiosity.[3]

Each generation of computers includes more multimedia capability; new courseware releases increasingly use video, sound, and graphics. Though highly promising, there are also challenges. Multimedia courseware applications are more expensive and complex; it may be difficult for literacy programs to select appropriate courseware. Teachers will need training in order to take the fullest advantage of the power of multimedia. Most vexing is that little or no compatibility exists from vendor to vendor and from one generation of equipment to the next. With the proliferation of formats now vying for commercial acceptance (e.g., CD-ROM, CDI, DVI), many educational users will wait to make large-scale commitments to multimedia.

---

[1] Recent examples include *The Tell-Tale Heart*, by Discis Books, and *Who Built America?* a multimedia social studies textbook developed by the Voyager Co. in cooperation with the American Social History Project in New York City. Voyager also created the *Expanded Book Tool Kit*, a tool for converting existing texts to multimedia electronic books.

[2] See J. Gretes and T. Songer, "Validation of the Learning Style Survey: An Interactive Videodisc Instrument," *Educational and Psychological Measurement*, vol. 49, No. 1, spring 1989, pp. 235-241.

[3] Wayne Nelson and David Palumbo, "Learning, Instruction, and Hypermedia," *Journal of Educational Multimedia and Hypermedia*, vol. 1, No. 3, 1992; Antonietta Lanza and Teresa Roselli, "Effects of the Hypertextual Approach Versus the Stuctured Approach on Students' Achievement," *Journal of Computer-Based Instruction*, vol. 18, No. 2, spring 1991, pp. 48-50.

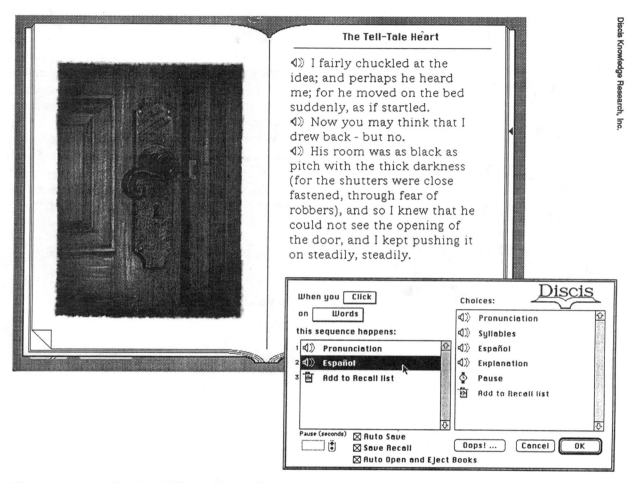

This software version of the Tell-Tale Heart *allows the reader to choose either a Spanish or English reading of the text, the tempo of the reading, and words to be defined.*

income (see figure 7-2); 41 percent of households in the lowest income bracket (under $15,000) have cable and 39 percent have VCRs, compared with 69 and 93 percent respectively for those in the highest income bracket ($60,000 or more).[67]

Computer ownership is related to income, education, and ethnicity. While 15 percent of all households had a computer in 1989, only 6 percent of households with incomes under $20,000 had them compared with 39 percent of house-

holds with incomes of $50,000 or more. Computers are found in the homes of 18 percent of white adults, but only in 8 percent of African-American and 8 percent of Latino adults.[68] Both access to and use of home computers are related to the educational level of adults. For example, only 4.6 percent of those with less than a high school degree have a home computer, compared with 33.7 percent of those with a college degree. Furthermore, 25.6 percent of those without a high

---

[67] A.C. Nielsen Co., National (50-State) Sample of 4,000 Households (Nielsen Peoplemeter Service), as reported in Boston Consulting Group, ''Public Television: Developing a Ready-to-Learn Service,'' report prepared for the Public Broadcasting Service, January 1993. Data collected by Nielsen in 1991.

[68] Kominski, op. cit., footnote 33.

Figure 7-2—Households With Videocassette Recorders and Cable Subscriptions, by Income, 1991

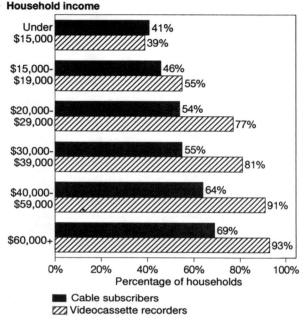

Household income

NOTE: The average for all households in 1991 is 57 percent cable subscribers and 73 percent with VCRs.

SOURCE: A.C. Nielsen Co., National (50-State) Sample of 4,000 Households (Nielsen Peoplemeter Service), as reported in Boston Consulting Group, "Public Television: Developing a Ready-to-Learn Service," report prepared for the Public Broadcasting Service, January 1993. Data collected by Nielsen in 1991.

ment process have become cheaper in recent years, consumers have also come to expect better presentation quality (i.e., the use of graphics and sound) and educational value (i.e., the incorporation of critical thinking skills and contexts relevant to the learners). These features increase the cost of development.

Without some reasonable hope of a return, companies are unlikely to invest the startup costs for specialized technology aimed at limited, fragile submarkets. Such is the case with the literacy market—by any measure small, fragmented, underfinanced, and underdeveloped.[69]

Figure 7-3—Adults With Home Computers, by Level of Schooling

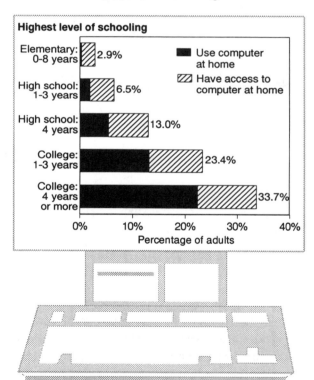

NOTE: Figure includes persons 18 years and older in 1989.

SOURCE: Robert Kominski, *Computer Use in the United States: 1989*, Current Population Reports, Special Series P-23, No. 171 (Washington, DC: U.S. Department of Commerce, Bureau of the Census, February 1991).

school degree report using their computers, compared with 71.2 percent of those with college degrees (see figure 7-3).

Market Barriers

The costs to research, develop, market, distribute, and support technology aimed at the specialized needs of adult learners can be very high. To develop a courseware package, the needs of learners must be researched, educational experts must be consulted, and courseware must be tested in the field. In some cases, focus groups are convened and formal assessments conducted. Although some technical aspects of the develop-

---

[69] Education TURNKEY Systems, Inc. and Wujcik and Associates, op. cit., footnote 1.

The universe of literacy programs—or potential "customers"—is small compared with other educational or corporate markets. In addition, as explained above, funding limitations prevent many literacy programs from purchasing hardware, which further shrinks the potential customer base. Although individual learners theoretically comprise a much larger market, they are least likely to be able to afford technology.[70]

Definitive data are not available on total sales of literacy-related technologies, but statistics on sales of computer software corroborate the notion that in the large pond of the technology market, the adult literacy market is a small fish indeed. The entire personal software industry had annual sales of about $4.6 billion in 1990. In that same year, elementary and secondary schools spent about $230 million for educational courseware.[71] By comparison, OTA estimates that the adult literacy market had annual software sales in 1990 of roughly $10 to $15 million (see figure 7-4).[72]

Without a large and visible base of potential customers or a healthy record of past sales to attract them, even software companies with considerable expertise in "crossover marketing" may shy away from the literacy market. Developers outside the education field seem particularly uninterested. Consequently, most of the active competitors in the literacy market are those with a stake in larger education and training markets, such as K-12 schools or corporate training. Some of these vendors simply sell their existing educational products to literacy clients. Others successfully revise products originally designed for the K-12 education market. Only a few companies market high-quality products designed especially for adult literacy (see box 7-I).

Figure 7-4—The Personal Computer Software Market, 1990

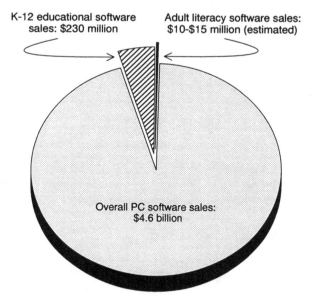

K-12 educational software sales: $230 million

Adult literacy software sales: $10-$15 million (estimated)

Overall PC software sales: $4.6 billion

NOTE: Does not include software purchased or licensed as part of an integrated learning system.

SOURCE: Office of Technology Assessment, 1993, based on data from Education TURNKEY Systems, Inc. and Wujcik Associates, "The Educational Software Marketplace and Adult Literacy Niches," OTA contractor report, June 1992.

The literacy software market is in an early stage of development. There are currently few people with both expertise in adult literacy and know-how in technology to develop applications for the literacy market. In addition, slow economic growth and a lack of other factors make it unlikely that technology "seeding" will occur for adult literacy.[73] However, some firms have been able to locate funding to cover the high costs of developing literacy software, including multimedia with

---

[70] OTA/Annenberg Workshop, "New Visions for Video Use of Cable, Satellite, Broadcast, and Interactive Systems for Literacy and Learning," Jan. 27, 1992.

[71] Figures for educational courseware are for the 1989-90 school year and do not include software purchased or licensed as part of an integrated learning system. Education TURNKEY Systems, Inc. and Wujcik and Associates, op. cit., footnote 1, pp. 12-13.

[72] Estimates based on OTA conversations with vendors and programs.

[73] Seeding is grants of computers by hardware companies to stimulate future sales. It also stimulates the development of courseware and peripherals. Seeding has occurred in the K-12 and higher education markets.

Box 7-I—Franklin Electronic Learning Resources

It takes a worker three bus changes and 2 hours to go from her city apartment to her suburban house cleaning job every day. Her husband, an unemployed construction worker, takes their disabled teenager to the local public health clinic every 2 weeks for physical therapy. On each visit the pair waits at least 1 hour before seeing the therapist. This family spends much of their commute and wait time in bored frustration.

Portable, electronic learning aids could provide an interesting resource for thousands of individuals with similar stories. With hand-held electronic units, waiting time at bus stops, in clinics, and many other places could be spent practicing vocabulary, mathematics, English, or grammar skills. For those trying to learn to read or to speak English, these devices can serve as personal "tutors," translating and pronouncing unfamiliar words encountered in everyday life.

One vendor of portable electronic devices, Franklin Electronic Learning Resources, is creating a niche in the literacy market. Its products include English and bilingual dictionaries, a thesaurus, a spelling tutor, and an encyclopedia. On average these units weigh about 4 ounces, display up to six lines of text, and often include a speaker. The Spanish Master, for example, enables a user to type in an unfamiliar English word, hear it pronounced, and see a written Spanish translation. It also provides spelling and grammar assistance and word games. For someone with limited English proficiency, the tool could be an invaluable resource in everyday life—used, for example, to translate labels on products in the grocery store, to help ask a salesperson a question, or to understand signs and directions.

Although most of its sales to date have been in the consumer electronics market (6 million devices), the company anticipates future sales of these devices in community colleges, prisons, libraries, and community-based literacy sites. Anecdotal evidence from the literacy field has been very encouraging. Users like portable devices because they are easy to use, affordable, and flexible. Franklin staff believe that adults with limited literacy skills are not ashamed to be seen in public using hand-held devices because they feel part of the high-tech age. Once learners in literacy programs are exposed to hand-held learning devices, the company feels, an increased market will develop among personal users.

Why does this company see a market for personal literacy tools, while other vendors with similar products have not? The company views adult education as a logical extension of its long involvement with the K-12 education market and the leadership at Franklin has taken a personal interest in adult literacy. Reference materials and language translation have broad appeal without the need for much customization. In addition, the company has redefined itself from hardware vendor to electronic publisher. As a publisher, Franklin believes that it can effectively serve several niches cost-effectively. For example, the company's latest product, *The Digital Book System* (see photograph), includes a library of digital books that range from health to Spanish/English translation to religion.

As the technology becomes more powerful, cheaper, and smaller, Franklin's president envisions new ways it can serve adult literacy. For example, an adult learner newly enrolled in a literacy program could use a personal learning tool in the following ways:

After orientation to a Franklin portable electronic unit, the student takes a pretest. . . . [A] plan of activities is downloaded into the unit, and the student is asked to work through the activities [at the literacy site]. . . . Now comes the neat part! Instead of going away to come back for 3 hours tomorrow night, the student once again has a set of activities downloaded into the portable unit. . . . He can work through the set of activities as needed at home, on the bus, at work during lunch breaks and even during television commercials! . . . At long last, the instructional package travels with the student instead of demanding that the student come to the instruction.[1]

---

[1] Arthur J. Sisk, president, Franklin Learning Resources, The Educational Division of Franklin Electronic Publishers, Inc., personal communication, Oct. 28, 1992.

opportunities for customization (see box 7-J). Virtually all of the technology firms included in OTA industry case studies raised the necessary funding internally or through partnerships with other groups.

Information Barriers

OTA finds that there is inadequate information available to both consumers and producers of adult literacy technologies. From the consumer end, most literacy educators, even those with some technology expertise, are not aware of the range of technology options available. The problem exists at all levels but is most obvious among novice technology users, who do not fully understand the capabilities of technology and who rarely or never consult software reviews.[74] Literacy program administrators often have little training in or experience with technology, hence do not know what to look for or how it could benefit programs.

From the vendor end, there is a shortage of specific market information on potential or existing literacy customers and their needs. Particularly lacking is more comprehensive data on the current uses of educational technology by literacy programs and home consumers; their current and anticipated expenditures for hardware, courseware, and other instructional materials; and effective product design features for hard-to-reach literacy populations.[75]

Technology vendors in OTA's case studies adopted various strategies to cope with this lack of information, including hiring consultants and market research firms to conduct limited studies or develop "best estimate" projections; conducting their own design research during prototype testing, rather than relying on existing research; hiring experienced developers and marketers who had their own information sources in the literacy

Digital books on many different topics can be plugged into this small hand-held device, making it possible to read and learn anywhere, anytime.

field; and refining existing products based on feedback from their customer base.[76]

Both literacy programs and technology developers could benefit from more information on the effectiveness of different types of technologies in improving literacy skills. This is especially true for specific subgroups of learners such as adults with the very lowest reading skills, with limited English proficiency, or with learning disabilities. Similarly, there is little hard data available on the effectiveness of some newer technologies for adult literacy, such as interactive distance learning. Some literacy providers are reluctant to adopt technology-based approaches because they have doubts about their effectiveness, especially when weighed against their cost. More evidence of effectiveness might help persuade adult educators to buy hardware and convince technology vendors to invest in developing better software.

Institutional Barriers

Some of the common institutional challenges faced by literacy programs constrain their use of technology and work against the development of

---

[74] Sivin-Kachala and Bialo, op. cit., footnote 1, p. 68.

[75] Education TURNKEY, Inc. and Wujcik Associates, op. cit., footnote 1.

[76] Ibid.

Box 7-J—Developing Innovative Software: The Example of Interactive Knowledge, Inc.[1]

In the last decade, startup companies have contributed to the development of computer software for K-12 education and corporate training. For some companies, public funding played a significant role. There are signs that software development in the adult literacy submarket could follow a similar pattern.

Interactive Knowledge, Inc. (IK), a firm that designs, develops, and distributes multimedia courseware for adult education, is one example. The company evolved from a 6-year research effort that began in 1985 at Central Piedmont Community College (CPCC) in Charlotte, North Carolina. At that time, CPCC hired Tim Songer and Chuck Barger, two media and instructional designers with experience in adult education, to create adult reading comprehension courseware. With grants from the U.S. Department of Education and the North Carolina Department of Community Colleges, CPCC staff developed two programs: *The READY Course*, 50 hours of reading comprehension instruction on topics of interest to adults (e.g., using credit cards and medical concerns) for those reading between the 5th- and 9th-grade levels and *The New Reader Bookstore*, a CD-ROM-based curriculum with over 120 hours of audio-based instruction to help adult nonreaders develop decoding skills. In conducting product-development research, the designers learned that effective courseware: 1) incorporates high-quality digital audio, 2) gives the learner control and choice throughout each lesson, and 3) integrates instructional content into real-life contexts.

In 1991, Songer and Barger, along with a third *Ready* employee, Sam Hess, left CPCC and founded Interactive Knowledge. They negotiated the exclusive rights to package and market the two reading programs and pay royalties to CPCC on the sales. Since that time, the company has prepared several other multimedia products aimed at adult, family, and workplace needs. The company markets its courseware to a variety of adult education providers including public schools, community colleges, community-based organizations, correctional facilities, libraries, and businesses.

In the process of creating these "off-the-shelf" products, IK has also developed software shells that can be easily customized for a particular industrial or educational client. The shell makes it possible to combine reading, mathematics, and critical thinking instruction with content from any business or subject area. Producing IK's custom products cost about $3,000 to $4,000 per hour of instruction compared with typical costs for custom courseware of $15,000 to $18,000 per hour.

The firm's use of multimedia to develop an innovative product line would not have been possible without the $800,000 in Federal, State, and private grants. Notes Songer: "This business would not exist without the research and development funds available to us at the college . . . We were able to start the business with many important contacts in place and an established reputation for developing effective adult literacy solutions."

IK is unusual because its founders began to design multimedia for adult literacy at a time when there was almost no installed base of videodisc players and CD-ROM drives among providers. The future of IK is still uncertain. The lack of funding and technology know-how among adult educators and learners creates serious market impediments, and small technology firms often have limited resources and business experience. In the little-explored literacy submarket, companies like IK have many questions to answer: Does the company have the products that educators and learners want? Are the prices realistic? How can a small company identify and inform potential customers about products? How can they identify customers who have multimedia capacity? How will State economies affect the funds available to literacy programs for hardware upgrades? For small innovative firms like IK, designing for an emerging technology that is not yet installed in literacy programs, viability rests on many players in an unpredictable marketplace.

---

[1] Based on Tim Songer, president, Interactive Knowledge, Inc., Charlotte, NC, personal communication, Oct. 28, 1992. See also Tim Songer, "Why Multimedia Works: Perspective on Literacy Courseware," *Literacy Practitioner*, a Publication of Literacy Volunteers of America—New York State, Inc., vol. 1, No. 1, December 1992.

a viable literacy market. The diverse and sometimes fragmented nature of the literacy field is one such barrier. Different types of literacy programs, such as ABE, GED preparation, ESL, correctional education, workplace skills enhancement, and family literacy, require different kinds of instructional content. The apparent need for customized products for each submarket, however small or seemingly unprofitable, increases development and customer support costs and may dissuade developers from entering the market. In addition, the diversity of service providers means that there is no identifiable, formal market relationship, no clear purchasing pattern, and no single organizational structure; this makes it difficult for companies to obtain market-relevant information and complicates marketing and distribution.[77] The fragmentation of funding sources presents still another barrier, especially when some Federal grant-in-aid programs limit expenditures for hardware and equipment (see chapter 5).

Another institutional barrier cited by technology developers is the lack of common performance objectives for literacy programs. Industry respondents believed that commonly accepted standards and objectives could reduce customization costs and over time bring down prices.

The shortage of experienced professional staff for adult literacy, who could help develop software and programming, is also perceived as a barrier, particularly among firms that have decided not to enter the adult literacy market. Virtually all of the case study firms in the literacy marketplace had a core team with directly related experience, which the firm could supplement through consultants and reassignment of staff from other divisions within the company.

CONCLUSIONS

The use of technology to address the problem of adult literacy is limited but growing. Technology has the potential both to improve the existing system of literacy education and to reach people in new ways. Although some literacy providers are experienced users of technology, the potential of technology for programs has barely been exploited. Of equal import but even less explored is the potential of technology to help individual learners and give them access to information and learning tools. The promise of technology needs to be realized. There are encouraging signs that investment and interest in technologies for literacy are increasing. Rapid technology development is occurring simultaneously with a growing recognition of the importance of lifelong learning. These factors have created an opportune time to stimulate the private sector, aggregate the market, and encourage innovative uses of technology.

---

[77] Ibid., pp. 34-35.

Looking Ahead to a Future With Technology | 8

Today's literacy programs are unable to meet the current demand, much less projected future requirements, for literacy services. Many learners cannot or will not participate in the literacy programs now in place. It may be impossible to provide enough teachers, classes, and programs no matter how much money is pumped into the current system. Ways must be found to extend the range and increase the impact of existing teachers, programs, and expertise.

This chapter looks ahead to tomorrow, with three scenarios offering a vision of adult literacy for the next 5 to 10 years. The scenarios combine several themes raised throughout this report. First, they reflect a desire to go beyond reliance on school-based programs and classroom-oriented instruction; instead, they assume more flexible ways of providing service. Second, the scenarios present literacy instruction integrated into and reflective of the daily activities of a learner's life. Because adults spend most of their time and energy either at home or at work, family and workplace are both setting and context for much of the literacy instruction in the scenarios. The goals of workplace and family literacy—economic security, professional advancement, and improving the opportunities of one's children—are naturally motivating to learners. Because these goals complement goals held by our society—international competitiveness and personal economic self-sufficiency—workplace and family literacy activities may be able to elicit broad-based support and financial commitment. Finally, the scenarios assume a primary role for technology—increasingly powerful, portable, flexible, and affordable tools that can empower the learner any time, any place, and in a range of applications.

223

A LOOK INTO THE FUTURE: THREE SCENARIOS

What futures are possible if technology, flexibility, and comprehensive services could be provided to learners in contexts relevant to their daily living and long-term goals? The scenarios provide one way of envisioning these possibilities, using three fictional learners typical of many who need literacy assistance. The technology depicted in them is suggestive of possible applications, based on current trends and developments.[1] They exemplify the kind of changes that *could* occur by the year 2000 and are meant to illustrate ideas, not to make specific predictions.

Carla King: Moving Ahead With a Changing Industry

Carla King, a vivacious 32-year-old, lives with her mother and 10-year-old daughter Latanya in a garden apartment on the outskirts of a small midwestern city. Since graduating from high school, Carla has worked in jobs as a cashier, mail room clerk, receptionist, and school bus driver, with her mother providing babysitting. Although they have few extras, Carla has been able to support the family adequately on her income, supplemented by her mother's social security check. Carla hopes her 4-year relationship with her boyfriend, a truck driver, will lead to marriage and greater financial stability.

Carla has worked for the Cobra Alarm Company for 3 years. Cobra sells, installs, services, and monitors alarms for residences and businesses. Working the 3 pm to 11 pm shift, Carla monitors incoming signals that indicate a triggered alarm and responds by contacting the police, fire, or emergency medical departments, and home or business owners or their designees. She also takes requests for repairs, writes work orders, and directs the incoming calls not handled by voice mail.

The company was founded by Scott Webster, a 43-year-old entrepreneur. In the last 6 years the company has grown from Scott, his brother, and two sisters to 35 employees. Scott was able to get his business off the ground with assistance from the Coalition—a collaborative of local businesses and city and State government that helps develop and support small businesses and create jobs for community residents. The Coalition helped Scott obtain low-interest financing, develop a business plan, and recruit employees from the local area. The Coalition provides continuing support and management expertise. The Coalition has been particularly supportive in helping companies develop workplace education programs.

Cobra's 5-year business plan calls for a substantial increase in the number of large commercial customers. This change will accompany the move to a new "smart alarm" system. The company plans to acquire new telecommunications and computer equipment with sophisticated voice-recognition capability that automates telephone operations and monitors alarms automatically. Once smart alarms replace older models, human telephone operators will no longer be needed. Customers will give oral instructions, such as changing the party to be notified in an emergency, directly to their smart alarm. The alarm's computer will recognize, execute, and

---

[1] The ways in which technology is conceptualized in these scenarios comes from the OTA Workshop on Emerging Communications and Information Technologies: Implications for Literacy and Learning, Sept. 26-27, 1991; and OTA/Annenberg Workshop, "New Visions for Video: Use of Cable, Satellite, Broadcast, and Interactive Systems for Literacy and Learning," Jan. 27, 1992. See also Robert Olsen et al., *21st Century Learning and Health Care in the Home: Creating a National Telecommunications Network* (Washington, DC: Institute for Alternative Futures/Consumer Interest Research Institute, 1992); Julia A. Marsh and Lawrence K. Vanston, *Interactive Multimedia and Telecommunications: Forecasts of Markets and Technologies* (Austin, TX: Technology Futures Inc., 1992); "Newton's World," *MacUser*, August 1992, pp. 45-48. Finally, these scenarios build on previous OTA work including *Linking for Learning: A New Course for Education*, OTA-SET-430 (Washington, DC: U.S. Government Printing Office, November 1989); *Worker Training: Competing in the New International Economy*, OTA-ITE-457 (Washington, DC: U.S. Government Printing Office, September 1990); and *Rural America at the Crossroads: Networking for the Future*, OTA-TCT-471 (Washington, DC: U.S. Government Printing Office, April 1991).

verify the owner's request, relaying it directly to Cobra's central computer.

With this change to a more competitive high-tech product, Scott plans to reorganize the company around the principles of total quality management. Each employee will be expected to know several jobs well and understand the entire operation.

Carla's current job will phase out with the changeover. She wants to stay on at Cobra, but she realizes that she has little opportunity for advancement without additional education. As a general track student in high school, she bypassed both challenging academic courses, such as algebra and geometry, and practical vocational courses. Although her oral communication skills are adequate, her written skills are limited. She is concerned about the new responsibilities she will have as a team member. Carla will be expected to read and comprehend technical material and diagrams, troubleshoot problems for customers, make well-reasoned judgments using technical information, write reports, and make suggestions for change.

As a part of preparing for the reorganization, Scott meets with the State government workplace training coordinator, the community college adult education director, and Cobra's employee committee to design the education and training that will be needed to move the company into its new role. An assessment reveals that one-half of Cobra's employees need to improve their writing and reading skills. One-third need to learn (or brush up on) mathematics for technical work and statistical process control.

With help from education advisers at the community college, the company develops a customized skills enhancement program. All employees are given 2 to 5 work-hours per week, company time, to participate in skills enhancement and training, providing they contribute at least 2 additional hours a week of their own time. Profit-sharing credits are offered to employees who spend 4 hours per week or more of their own time at learning activities for their individualized

learning plan. Scott admits it is unlikely he would be able to provide these incentives without the recently passed Federal tax credits for companies offering workplace literacy programs like Cobra's.

In part because there is no room onsite to conduct classes, Scott has purchased from the Coalition, at a reduced rate, several lightweight, battery-operated, notebook-sized personal learning devices (PLDs) for his employees to check out. The PLD functions like a combination computer, television, and telephone; it unfolds to show a screen for the display of both video and graphic information. Screen text is as clear and easy to read as a book. With a touch of the network button on the screen, the PLD opens a telephone line to transmit or receive data over a distance. The PLD has a built-in pen-based data entry system and touch screen, microphone and speaker, a detachable keyboard, and an external hard disk drive for extra data storage.

Carla likes the PLD because it is powerful and easy to use. When she first went to her Coalition education counselor, Carla was given a personal interest inventory and skills assessment software package to complete at home on the PLD. Results were downloaded into the Coalition's office, and the next afternoon Carla and her counselor met online and discussed her academic strengths and areas for improvement in relation to the needs of the new job. Carla's learning style preferences were matched to available program resources. Carla's profile indicated she likes to study independently and works well in small groups, but is intimidated by structured classroom settings. Consequently, her counselor suggested self-study modules and distance learning options for her personal learning plan.

The distance learning capabilities of the PLD enable Carla to enroll in a mathematics class, identified through a national database of distance learning classes, that matches her learning needs and time schedule. In this class she has two study partners in two different cities. Using PLDs, all three study together as if they were in the same room. On her PLD, Carla prepares mathematics assignments by entering data, plotting graphs, and graphically rendering mathematical concepts. This whole process helps demystify the subject matter, and real-world problems show her the practicality of having good mathematics skills. The PLD's calculator helps her avoid arithmetic errors and permits her to concentrate on mathematical concepts.

Carla also signs onto a current events reading club. Based on her interest profile, Carla is matched with seven other young women around the city. They meet for 2 hours on Saturday mornings in the local library, but most of the discussion goes on over the electronic-mail connection of the PLD. While at the library, Carla downloads articles from *The Washington Post*, *The New York Times*, and weekly news magazines onto her PLD. She shares these with her daughter and mother, and together they compare the different emphases of these news accounts with what they see on the evening television news. The PLD software helps Carla generate, outline, and organize ideas for her written pieces for the club, and the word processor with voice, pen, and keyboard input makes writing easier. Carla reorganizes, revises, and edits with the help of software language aids—spelling, grammar, punctuation and style checkers, and a thesaurus—before sending her reports to other members of the club.

Ten months later, Carla has overcome her school anxieties and now enjoys her education. She has checked out the PLD so often that she has considered purchasing one on her own. She likes the fact that, when she practices skills on her own time, the software records her study time and she receives "educredits" that can be applied to a certificate program at the community college and for reduced-cost purchase of her own PLD through the Coalition's lease/purchase plan for member businesses. After completing the mathematics course, Carla feels ready to tackle a module on basic principles of electricity and electronics. This course uses multimedia software and scientific probes that can be added to the

PLD. Course materials have been customized by a team from the Coalition's technology advisers and Cobra technicians. The software simulates the actions of redesigning wiring diagrams, replacing computer chips, and reprogramming a smart alarm.

Carla uses the PLD in many more ways: pursuing her hobby of home gardening by accessing a horticultural database, locating a Spanish tutor for Latanya through a database of local educational resources, and using the multimedia encyclopedia software and other references to assist with her school projects. Carla's mother communicates electronically with new friends on "seniornet," a national network she subscribes to at a reduced rate through her church's senior citizens center.

Carla is making steady progress and plans to enroll at the community college for an associate degree in electronics next year. She will already have several credits under her belt through her self-study modules. Her new confidence is showing up at work, where she is participating more actively in team meetings and suggesting new approaches to tasks. In training sessions that require the use of technical manuals, Carla keeps pace with other workers. Best of all, she has been given a promotion and pay raise to reflect her increased responsibilities.

Dave Decker: Changing a Life, Starting a Future

Nineteen-year-old Dave Decker officially left school when he turned 16, but he dropped out intellectually years before. He always had trouble reading and repeated both the 4th and 7th grades. By the time he was in the 8th grade, when he was a foot taller and several years older than the other kids, he knew he did not fit in. Instead, he found a new circle of friends—the older guys that hung out at the pool hall, drank beer, and stole cars for kicks. Dave and his friends were arrested several times for car theft and vandalism. After his fourth arrest, this time with a drunk and disorderly charge, Dave's mother refused to bail him out. The judge ordered him to enroll in a substance abuse program and assigned him to a detention center for juvenile offenders.

His first week in detention, Dave's literacy skills were assessed using a procedure developed by a four-State consortium of correctional educational programs. Dave took a battery of multimedia diagnostic assessments that included a series of science experiments, writing assignments, and social studies miniprojects. The tests required him to read documents; write reports, memoranda, and essays; collect and interpret scientific data to formulate and test hypotheses; draw conclusions from multiple historical source documents and maps; apply mathematics to solve real-life problems; and create charts and graphs in several subject areas. Other assessment software helped Dave learn more about his aptitudes and interests in areas such as music, art, mathematics, mechanics, physical strength and dexterity, leadership, and interpersonal relations. Multimedia materials were also used to help Dave identify possible career directions. When Dave expressed interest in the job of a physical therapist, he called up a database of health career simulations that let him "shadow" a therapist for a day, ask questions about the job, and practice providing therapy to patients.

Dave's assessment results—test scores and interpretive analyses—were sent to the State detention education offices for processing and returned to the local staff within 24 hours. An individualized educational plan was developed for Dave by the second week in the program and he signed an education contract, spelling out his goals and the requirements for meeting them. He was given a personal "educard" containing data on his testing results and plan. As he progressed through his plan, each step was credited on the card, and time was deducted from his open-ended sentence.

Dave worked especially hard on language arts skills. During class he used a small personal multimedia computer connected with the State's online database of courseware and reading material. After class, he downloaded materials he needed extra work onto a notebook-sized PLD he checked out to use in his room and repeat lessons as many times as he wanted. The PLD held Dave's attention, did not make fun of his mistakes, and rewarded him with bonus points for center privileges when he completed a unit. It held no preconceptions about his ability and turned his lefthanded "chicken scratch" handwriting into fine-looking typed words and sentences, especially when he remembered to use the spell, punctuation, and grammar guides.

Several months after entering the center, Dave received a card with no letter inside, only a picture of a smiling red-headed baby with the word "Georgette" written in his mother's handwriting. His girlfriend Kathy had given birth to his child. Dave stared at the photograph with a mixture of shock, denial, pride, shame, and tenderness. Until then, Dave had drifted aimlessly through life, his low self-esteem leading him to doubt his ability to succeed at anything. For the first time he felt he had a goal to work toward. Dave resolved to stay sober and assume the responsibility of fatherhood.

After his release from detention, Dave returned home. Because he had received so many educredits while in the center, his high school diploma was finally within reach. But he swore he would never again set foot in the local high school, and he had to work to help support his little girl while Kathy lived with her parents and finished high school. Dave enrolled in a general equivalency diploma (GED) course offered on the local Public Broadcasting Service (PBS) channel, watching at home in the evenings and taping lessons he had to miss when caring for Georgette. He spent his days working in his uncle's feed store, and his uncle let him use the computer to hook up with an electronic mail support group for teen alcoholics. Dave found it reassuring to know that he could use the 24-hour "chat" line whenever he needed support. Each day he also dialed into the computer's video connect to check in with his probation officer.

One night, when Dave was feeling particularly low, he was thrown out of a local bar for drunk and disorderly behavior. His probation officer realized Dave was at a crisis point and sent Rick Carter over to the house. Rick, also a recovering alcoholic, described the We Are Family (WAF) Program he had created to help other adolescent parents avoid the mistakes he made as an angry young man. While most teen parents entered the program voluntarily, for a few like Dave, participation was a condition of his parole.

Dave was reluctant, but did not want to lose his parole or the delicate relationship he was trying to reestablish with Kathy and Georgette. Rick explained that the goal of the program is to improve self-esteem through increasing literacy skills, working around three themes: parenting, health and safety, and job preparation. Reading, mathematics, science, and writing skills are introduced and reinforced within the three themes by professional teachers, both onsite and through distance networks. Because the community is a rural one, spread across hundreds of miles, they meet electronically through satellite downlinks and telephone/computer connections. Study groups form around multimedia lessons, supported by a library of interactive CDs, which students can order up through touch screens on the television. Those who do not have the necessary hardware are given loaners through the library.

Dave's work on the family skills activities supports his evening GED studies. He recently worked on reading comprehension by trying to infer meaning from context clues, using a CD on child immunization downloaded from the system. While watching the CD, he tries out various options that test his understanding, resulting in scenarios created by his choices. Shocked by the negative effect his response has had on the characters in the story, Dave realizes he has not understood the material sufficiently, and decides to watch a more detailed explanation of the concept. He can repeat portions of the CD, asking

for definitions of concepts or terms, pursuing his own interests indepth or just following along with the written student guide. Kathy and Dave work on some modules separately, since he is still living at his parents house. When they get together at Kathy's, they share what they have learned with each other.

Dave spends a great deal of time with his daughter and fully shares child-rearing responsibilities, working from 2 to 9 pm so he can care for the baby while Kathy is at school. Dave is also learning ways to interact with Georgette that will help stimulate the baby's communication skills. He borrows paper and electronic books from the library to read to her. His favorites are interactive books that contain music, animation, voice narration, and video. Georgette's favorites are any books where her father supplies the sound effects.

His affectionate and increasingly skilled parenting of Georgette has won over Kathy's parents, and they see that his commitment to his family is helping him to stay sober. They have given their blessing to their marriage when Kathy finishes high school.

Fifteen months out of the detention center, Dave passes the GED on his second try. He plans to enroll in a laboratory technician certification program through the community college's distance learning network. Later, after he gets his confidence up, he may take some classes on campus, but, right now, without a car and so little free time, the class at the community center is all he can handle. With a certificate, he hopes to work in a new biogenetics laboratory that is located in the area.

Although Dave has finished his parole and no longer has to participate in WAF's teen dad program, he will continue to participate as a volunteer. It has helped him get his life on track.

Tina Lopez: Family Support Through a Multipurpose Literacy Center

Tina Lopez, age 24, lives in a small town in south Texas. She left school in her native

Guatemala to marry Eduardo when she was 15, and followed him to the United States when she was 18. When Eduardo lost his job and became abusive they separated, leaving her to raise her two young children alone on a small welfare check.

Through her Spanish-speaking counselor at the welfare office, Tina learned about the River Family Literacy Program. With 5-year-old Jimmy and 2-year-old Maria old enough for school and daycare, Tina has been told that, by participating in the literacy and job preparation activities offered through the center, her check will be increased for each of the educredits she earns toward her high school degree. The program guarantees her a job paying, at a minimum, 10 percent more than her welfare check when she graduates from the program. Her health insurance benefits will be transferred from State support to employer support automatically under the national health assurance program.

Tina did not like being told what she had to do, and was initially reluctant to participate because of unpleasant memories of school. She recognized, however, it was her only choice for a better future. When her girlfriend Dolores showed her the PLDs and other learning tools that participants can check out of the center's library and bragged about how much English she learned in her 6 months at the center, Tina signed up.

River School, the location of the family program, is a center for community life. It houses an elementary school, an after-school program, an infant care and early learning center for children from 6 months, and English as a second language (ESL) literacy classes based around parenting support and job preparation. The building also contains a medical clinic, a mental health center, a buying cooperative, and a Food Stamp outlet. Videoconferencing booths at the school give local residents access to case workers at the county office for other social services not available onsite.

Tina's reception at the River Family Literacy Program is warm and respectful. The director of the program, Elena Martinez, shows great sensitivity in serving this multicultural community. Computer-scheduled minibuses are on call to take participants to and from the River School at all hours.

Tina participates in the program 5 days a week. After getting Maria settled in the early childhood center and Jimmy in kindergarten, Maria goes down the hall to her ESL parenting support group. After the children and Tina have lunch together, she goes to the job training center, where ESL instruction is integrated with all the materials.

Tina and other family literacy participants spend several hours each morning working alone or in small groups, using the multimedia library of parenting materials. Tina is working with simulations helping her understand and handle common childhood conditions, such as tantrums and bed-wetting. Although the material is presented in English, at any point the user can click to an audio assist in Spanish, Creole, Cantonese, or Vietnamese. Materials are presented in stages of reading difficulty geared to the user's responses to questions that routinely check on comprehension. If the user answers these correctly in a certain amount of time, the material gradually increases the vocabulary and difficulty of material. These embedded tests are so low key that Tina moves through them without any of the anxiety she used to associate with testing in school. Since the tutorials are private, each participant is moving at her own pace, but progress is automatically recorded on the system. Tina enjoys this activity, particularly since she can choose the content she wants to study from a huge topic menu. When she asks Elena about how to deal with Maria's tendency to bite her brother when he pushes her around, Elena added a segment on dealing with aggressiveness in children at that age. Tina particularly enjoys the small group discussion sessions held after each of these private tutorials; this is when she can discuss her approach to these issues with the other women and clarify points she found difficult. A trained literacy tutor acts as a facilitator in these group learning sessions.

"Aggressive," "discipline," "appropriate," and "sense of humor": Tina adds these words to the electronic pocket translator she checks out of the library each week. Her friend Dolores has bought her own, but Tina has been unable to put aside the money to buy one, and cannot unless she collects enough attendance and improvement credits to qualify for the "top students' discount." The device has a vocabulary of 25,000 commonly used words. With this device, Tina can speak a word (in English or Spanish) into the built-in microphone, see the word in English or Spanish translation on a small screen, and hear the translated word spoken, defined, and used in a sentence. Since it can be customized by adding vocabulary, Tina, Jimmy, and even Maria add words they are learning together, and play word games with it on the bus to and from the center. Tina now knows the secret of Dolores' English success.

Tina goes to the after-school center to work with the children two afternoons each week. One of her favorite activities is creating slide shows and videos with the children. The center has a full supply of minicameras that the children use for videowriting, and plug-in units for editing and adding sound effects and graphics. Tina works with the children to help them appreciate how carefully they must plan and edit their materials to create the best stories. In one project, Tina works with Jimmy, several of his friends, and some 6th graders from the school and their teacher to create a history of Central American children's games. They record interviews with community residents of all ages and videotape them demonstrating the games they know. Students also graphically illustrate the games step-by-step. The 6th-grade students research the African, European, and Indian origins of the games. The grateful teacher lends Tina her own notebook multimedia sketchpad so she can work on the games project at home. The project becomes a rich family learning experience as Tina and her children talk about it and work together on it after school. After her children go to bed, Tina spends time writing storyboards, sketching graphics, and trying out various animations. She previews supplemental video segments downloaded from the cable station. The county librarian is so impressed with the final product that he requests permission to make copies to place in the library. It is the first real school-related success Tina has ever experienced.

Tina soon has enough English skills to move into the next phase of the program: job search. Although job opportunities in town are limited, the River Family Literacy Program has a "service information kiosk" that Tina has used for information about finalizing her divorce, changing her name back, and other legal concerns. The kiosk also maintains a database of job openings, salary levels, and requirements for positions offered by public and private employers in specified geographic areas in the region. Although Tina first thought she would like to work at the River Family Center, openings there are scarce, so she has been checking the kiosk database on a regular basis. The relatively high pay and opportunity to work outdoors attract Tina to highway construction. Her job counselor sets up a videoconference with women who are already working in this male-dominated vocation so Tina can learn first-hand about working conditions.

Tina learns that to advance in the field, she will need to read technical manuals, operate computers that control the latest road construction equipment, and make decisions that require an understanding of geometry and geology. She signs up for job training to prepare her for highway construction. Several of the courses she needs are not available at the center, but Tina enrolls in a geometry class at the community college. She takes the course via satellite at River School, because she cannot rely on her car to make the 100-mile round-trip to the college twice a week. She downloads mathematics software onto her loaner PLD to help her prepare for the examination.

Through her ESL, parenting, job preparation, and mathematics courses, Tina eventually gains enough credits to earn a high school degree after 2 years. She could have taken the GED sooner to shorten the process, but the concept of a formal examination scared her off. She begins to work for a highway construction contractor. With support from the family literacy program staff, she and her children have tried to prepare for the extended absences her job requires. Her friend Dolores cares for Maria and Jimmy while Tina is away from home, with support from the center should any crises arise. While she is on the road, Tina visits with her children through the videophone at the center and a videophone at her construction office.

After 5 years, Tina has made steady progress on her job and is the first woman in her company to supervise a road construction crew. She has bought her own electronic pocket translator, to which she has added her specialized construction-related vocabulary. She keeps up with the center's parenting classes through a videophone linkup to the computer at work. Tina continues to monitor the children's homework when she is at home and by electronic means when she is on the road. She has also been browsing through several online college catalogs; she and the children have a bet going on who will be the first one to get a degree in engineering.

QUESTIONS RAISED BY THE SCENARIOS: HOW TO CREATE A FUTURE FOR LITERACY

These scenarios show how people, institutions, programs, and technology could come together to increase adult learners' options for learning. They look ahead to the year 2000, and offer an optimistic vision. The challenge lies in turning these visions of the future into a reality for the millions of Americans with limited literacy skills. This view of the future includes several key elements:

- Providing new options for those who wish to participate in literacy programs but are overwhelmed by barriers such as transportation, childcare, and competing demands on their time;
- Motivating people to enter programs, and providing successful learning experiences to help them persevere until they have reached their literacy goals; and
- Offering affordable, flexible technology tools to help people pursue learning in classes or on their own.

The scenarios assume continuing advances in hardware, software, and networking capabilities, along with public commitment and financial support to guarantee access to these resources for those who need them most.

Hardware Advances

The scenarios assume that current trends in telecommunications and hardware development will produce an array of important capabilities. They include:

- more and cheaper computing power;
- integrated video, sound, text, and graphics on the same display;
- smaller, portable hardware;
- higher resolution screens;
- variety in input devices;
- embedded intelligence;
- greater channel capacity for television; and
- interactivity between computers, telephones, and other hardware.

As computing power continues to expand, new capabilities will become increasingly affordable. These hardware advances will take many forms and offer capabilities beyond today's realities. For example, the ability to deliver, process, or display video, text, graphics, and audio from a single box is reducing the number of components needed for multimedia. Additionally, the ability to use natural speech for input and control of

Box 8-A—Computers That Speak, Computers That Listen: Speech Production and Speech Recognition Technologies

There are two forms of speech-related activity on computers: speech production and speech recognition. Speech production has been available for a number of years, and uses either speech synthesis or digitized speech. Speech synthesis is computer-created speech based on a set of algorithms that provide rules for translating letters to sounds, using the 44 basic sounds (phonemes) on which most English words are built, along with rules for considering grammar and context when words are not phonetic. An alternative form of speech output is digitized speech, produced by translating the analog sound waves of human speech into digitized bits of information. Digitized speech is more memory-intensive but more natural sounding than synthesized speech.

As computer chips increase in power and decline in cost, the number of applications using speech is growing and speech output has become a valuable learning aid in educational software. If the learner does not understand a word or phrase, the option of actually hearing it spoken may make it possible to understand the material; the addition of headphones makes this assistance entirely private. The combination of spoken and written cues is particularly important to adults with limited reading skills. It is also valuable for English as a second language or foreign language instruction by reinforcing written and oral language skills at the same time.

Speech recognition, the ability of a computer to respond to spoken language, is a much more complicated process. Speech recognition is categorized by whether it can accommodate a range of speakers and how precisely words must be spoken. A computer that can understand many voices is called speaker independent; these systems are designed to understand certain phrases or numbers as spoken by a range of users. For example, a system is being designed in which policemen will be able to read a car's registration number into a radio, which connects to a computer that listens to the number and checks a database to see whether or not the car has been stolen.[1] If a computer responds only to particular voices, it is known as speaker dependent. Speaker-dependent systems must be "trained" to understand the pronunciation, inflection, and rhythms of a user's voice. These systems provide some measure of security, as the computer, like a trained dog, responds only to its master's voice. Currently, a computer requires about 30 minutes or more of training to be able to respond to a user.

Discrete-word speech recognition systems require clearly enunciated words with a distinct pause between each word. Continuous recognition systems enable the user to string words together naturally. Most speech recognition systems in use today are discrete-word, speaker-independent systems with limited vocabularies. Currently, there is no true continuous speech system commercially available; when users leave less than a 0.10-second pause between utterances, some words are skipped.

In the first step of the speech recognition process, words spoken into a computer microphone are digitized. The computer analyzes the pattern of the data in millisecond chunks, by comparing it to stored patterns of words represented phonetically and by applying a set of grammatical rules and contextual clues. The computer makes the best match possible, guessing where the sounds should be divided into words and choosing specific words. For example, the spoken sounds, "aieewahntoduhpahszeht" (phonetically) could be matched to several word

---

1 "Answer Me," *The Economist*, July 25, 1992, p. 7.

---

computers is a particularly promising development[2] (see box 8-A). Computers, regardless of manufacturer, will be able to share data more easily in the future. Improvements in digital transmission and advances in compression technology will increase channel capacity. The number of captioned television programs will be much greater, because of the standard for closed captioning on all televisions manufactured after 1993. Displays with high resolution will increase text readability and reduce eye fatigue, making applications such as computer-based books more attractive. New switching techniques will make television more like telephones and both of them

---

2 Robert E. Calem, "Coming Soon: The PC With Ears," *The New York Times*, Aug. 30, 1992, sec. 3, p. 9; and "Answer Me," *The Economist*, July 25, 1992, pp. 79-80.

combinations including "eye went toad a posse it" or "Aye one toe dub a set," but considering grammar and context are displayed as, "I want to deposit."[2] Accuracy depends largely on the quality of the comparison database for matching input sounds and the effectiveness of the comparison rules.

Irregularities in the English language, regional accents, colloquial expressions, background noises, and other problems are challenges to the development of speech recognition. Furthermore, developers must take into account the amount of time users are willing to devote to pretraining and the error rate users are willing to tolerate. Many speech recognition developers do not think this technology will gain mass acceptance until it is continuous, speaker independent, self-training, at least 90 percent accurate, has real-time speed (about 135 words per minute), the ability connect to a variety of communications devices, and is priced for the consumer as well as business market. Nevertheless, speech recognition technologies are advancing rapidly, due to research efforts conducted by major hardware, software, and telecommunications companies. Ameritech recently unveiled a "Voice Controlled Work Station" that has a 30,000-word dictionary and enables a user to dictate correspondence at 45 to 55 words per minute, read electronic mail, access library databases, and even dial and answer the telephone.[3] The system represents the integrating of a series of technologies developed by a number of companies, including Dragon Dictate. Dragon's system, compatible with most off-the-shelf MS-Dos PC-based applications, is bridging the gap between speaker-dependent and independent systems.[4] Apple Computer plans to release its "Casper" advanced speech recognition command and control technology as an option for Macintosh computers by the end of 1993.

The ability to give spoken commands to a computer, or to enter the first draft of a document orally, could be very useful in a multitude of contexts. Speech recognition applications in the workplace today include postal workers sorting mail, brokers on Wall Street barking rapid trading commands into computers, doctors entering patient information, and radiologists scanning x-rays as they read the results into computers. Schools and employers will be able to accommodate the computing needs of physically challenged adults and children and comply with the requirements of the Americans with Disabilities Act. Systems are now being tested with dyslexic children who "talk their ideas down" as a way of overcoming their inability to express thoughts in written form.[5] Adults with limited keyboarding and reading skills may find speaking into a computer makes the prospect of writing significantly less daunting and more rewarding. Furthermore, with a keyboard no longer a necessity, computers can be much smaller, making portability a viable feature, with all the benefits of "go anywhere, use anytime" computing.

---

[2] Robert E. Calem, "Coming Soon: The PC With Ears," *The New York Times*, Aug. 30, 1992, sec. 3, p. 9.

[3] The basic system requires a 386 MS-Dos computer, 8 meg of RAM, voice platform, a microphone, and a standard modem. The upgraded 12-meg version, packaged with a mouse and Lotus and WordPerfect software, currently sells for approximately $5,000, with distribution rights given to the Central Indiana Easter Seals Society. Dorsey Ruley, Ameritech Information Services, Chicago, IL, personal communication, April 1993.

[4] Keith Wetzel, "Speaking to Read and Write: A Report on the Status of Speech Recognition," *The Computing Teacher*, vol. 19, No. 1, August/September 1991, p. 9.

[5] Ruley, op. cit., footnote 3.

---

more like computers, making vast amounts of video, text, and data available instantly to homes and businesses.

All of these trends *could* promote greater opportunities for adult learning. It is reasonable to expect that, in the next 5 years, machines with the power of today's high-end personal computers could be sold for prices similar to today's televisions, making them more affordable to literacy providers.[3] Miniaturization of hardware

---

[3] The horizon of computing power continues to move forward, however, and today's high-end computing power is unlikely to meet tomorrow's expectations. Nonetheless, the computer industry's product evolution and marketing strategies have kept the price of personal computers fairly level from year to year. For example, computers that sold in 1987 for about $1,000 (e.g., IBM PCjr. and Apple IIC) to $2,500 (IBM MS-Dos 286 and Apple Macintosh) have been replaced by a new generation of vastly more powerful computers—still in the $1,000 to $2,500 price range.

Advancements in speech recognition technologies allow users to operate a computer and input data by speaking into a microphone. In addition to the importance of this resource for persons with disabilities, speech recognition will make computers easier to use for a range of applications.

components will permit powerful uses of learning technologies in sizes that vary from desktop to notebook to pocket or pocketbook sized. High-resolution screen displays will be flatter. Storage devices will be more compact. As the range of possible sizes increases, the technology will become more flexible and small, portable equipment will expand opportunities for literacy education anytime or anyplace (on the bus, during work breaks, or waiting in a doctor's office) and in places where space is limited, such as in crowded working and living quarters. A researcher notes:

> Ubiquitous computers will also come in different sizes, each suited to a particular task. My colleagues and I have built what we call tabs, pads and boards: Inch-scale machines that approximate active Post-it notes, foot-scale ones that behave something like a sheet of paper (or a book

or a magazine) and yard-scale displays that are the equivalent of a blackboard or bulletin board.[4]

Speech recognition technology could help people express complex ideas more capably than they can read or write. When commands or information can be entered by speaking into a computer, the learner can focus on content and not be distracted or intimidated by the technicalities of operating a computer. Speech recognition technology could also help boost English proficiency in daily tasks. Speaking into a pocket translator for assistance with unknown or difficult words could facilitate communication in real-life situations when learners might find themselves at a loss for words.

It will be important to assure interconnectivity between various kinds of hardware. Literacy practitioners will need to participate in standard-setting, in order to guarantee that features appropriate for education and adult literacy are assured (see box 8-B).

Small but powerful and easy to use, portable computers like this could make it possible for learners to study anywhere, anytime.

---

[4] Mark Weiser, "The Computer for the 21st Century," *Scientific American*, September 1991, p. 98. The author is head of the Computer Science Laboratory at the Xerox Palo Alto Research Center.

Box 8-B—Understanding How Standards Are Set

Three types of standards affect the development of computer, video, and communications technologies.[1] *Product standards* establish product quality, reliability, and compatibility. *Process standards* determine how technologies operate when they are interconnected and set procedures for acceptable, smooth, and consistent operation. *Control standards* relate to how a technology affects health and safety, rights of privacy and free speech, and similar issues of public interest. Standards are important because they can: 1) drive product costs up or down, 2) facilitate or hinder technological advances, and 3) contribute to or obstruct ease of use for teachers and learners.

There is considerable variation in the way technology standards are set. They can be established, *de facto*, by market forces; i.e., developers sell products with different standards and wait for one dominant standard to emerge. In videocassette recorder development, for example, Sony developed the Beta standard and Panasonic developed the VHS standard. The market eventually settled on VHS, the standard that currently prevails industrywide. Some standards are set by governmental action. For example, in 1991, new legislation required closed-captioning circuitry on all new televisions produced in the United States after 1993. This law created a new standard for television. Finally, standards can be established through a voluntary consensus-building process where key technology manufacturers come together and negotiate standards. For example, Sony and Phillips, the two largest and original developers of compact disc technology, negotiated one standard, called the "High Sierra Standards," after the place where they hammered out the details of the agreement.

When market forces work well, a standard emerges at an "optimal" time in the development of a new technology. The standard evolves from the give and take between producer-driven supply factors such as production costs, market share, and profitability, and consumer-driven demand factors such as quality, utility, and affordability.

When the market does not work well, standards can be set too early or late. If standards are set prematurely, the pace of technological advancement can be slowed and improvements in product capabilities, ease of use, and product quality can be retarded. The "qwerty" typewriter key layout is an example of premature standard setting.[2] Conversely, when standards are set too late, consumers suffer from lack of connectivity or correspondence between similar products. For example, a community college with a mix of faculty-selected desktop computers of various types will experience greater costs and technical difficulties when attempting to install a collegewide computing network than if it had set a common computing standard early in the hardware selection process.

Setting optimal standards can be hindered by a number of factors. The size of the installed base of an early standard can restrain market forces from developing a better standard. Lack of consumer information can also prevent market forces from setting a good standard. The government can set standards that are not optimal if heavily influenced by a particular special interest.

Adult learners and educators could benefit from participating in standard-setting processes. By keeping abreast of emerging technical standards, they may be able to influence the content of those standards. Opportunities for adult learners and educators to participate in *de facto* standard setting are likely to remain limited, however. For, example, markets for computer-based technologies have operated efficiently and profitably while ignoring the lowest end consumers. By the time adult learners and educators enter the market, standards are unlikely to be malleable. However, better and more complete information about the options and features of new technologies and discussion of their advantages and disadvantages would enable early adopting users to contribute to the standard-setting process by purchasing products wisely. Additionally, standards for technologies that require startup with a relatively large installed base, for example, computer networks and telecommunications, often involve voluntary standard setting and offer greater opportunity for participation by adult learners and educators.

---

[1] U.S. Congress, Office of Technology Assessment, *Global Standards: Building Blocks for the Future*, OTA-TCT-512 (Washington, DC: U.S. Government Printing Office, March 1992), pp. 5-6.

[2] The "qwerty" layout of the keyboard was established to prevent jamming on Charles Latham Sholes' early typewriter. If a standard for key placement had not been adopted until the keys could be placed in any arrangement without jamming, today's keyboard could be easier to learn and faster to use. Donald A. Norman, *The Design of Everyday Things* (New York, NY: Doubleday, 1990), pp. 145-151.

Networking Advances

Telecommunications networks play an important role in all of the scenarios: learners, teachers, and other classmates were able to converse or send text, graphics, or video to each other, and access online databases. Location was no longer a barrier. Books without pages could be sent from libraries without walls;[5] curriculum was distributed from classrooms without doors.

As telecommunications networking grows, it will expand opportunities to reach workers and families by providing:

- greater convenience to learners;
- new ways for teachers to serve larger numbers of learners;
- a broader range of courses and learning modules;
- expanded access to information, expertise, and learning resources;
- more resources for informal, interactive learning; and
- informational resources to meet social, health, and housing needs.

The scenarios assume the availability of some mix of coaxial cable, Integrated Service Digital Network (ISDN), fiber, and satellite transmissions to homes, businesses, schools, and community centers. High-speed, two-way communications for text, graphics, video, and voice in the home could provide the most complete range of instructional options and accommodate a wide range of learning styles, but will require greater broadband capacity than available in most homes today. Fiber optic cable, with its bandwidth capacity far in excess of copper wire or cable, has always been considered the key to more rapid two-way transmission of voice, data, and video.[6] While the expansion of high-bandwidth fiber optic cable has been dramatic, the majority of the new fiber deployment has been for long-distance carriers.

It has been thought until recently that a full range of interactive multimedia networking capabilities would not be available until fiber optic cable could be brought the "last mile" from the local provider (cable or telephone company) to the home, a task anticipated to cost from $200 to $400 billion and possibly taking as long as 20 years.[7] However, recent research breakthroughs by both cable and telephone companies have created alternative solutions to carry information beyond the bottlenecks of existing systems. With cable, the breakthrough came with appreciation that, for short distances, coaxial cable has almost as much bandwidth as fiber. Using a combination of fiber for the main lines, and no more than one-quarter mile of coaxial wire for the delivery to the home, two-way interactivity over existing cable systems may indeed be practical and affordable. Similarly, research conducted by the telephone companies, using Asymmetric Digital Subscriber Line (ADSL) technology, stretches copper wire to its outer limit, also extending the capabilities of existing networks.

Also important to the fulfillment of this vision of a networked information system are continuing advances in switching or routing. It is switching that "makes the connection" between the user and the information service, data, or product.[8] Efficient high-speed switching is required to move digitized information (a phone call, movie, newscast, teleconference, book, catalog order, financial transaction, video game, software program, medical report, travel order, or any other information product or service) from any one of millions of points on a network to another.

Continuing research is necessary to enhance and expand these and other promising telecom-

---

5 See John Browning, "Libraries Without Walls for Books Without Pages," *Wired*, premiere issue, January 1993, pp. 62-65, 110.

6 Olson et al., op. cit., footnote 1, pp. 19-25.

7 Philip Elmer-Dewitt, "Electronic Superhighway," *Time Magazine*, Apr. 12, 1993, p. 54.

8 Olson et al., op. cit., footnote 1, p. 25.

munications capabilities. Ultimately, the availability of these technologies will be determined by the high capital outlays required to upgrade and expand the overall national communications infrastructure.[9]

Software Advances

No matter how fast, how small, how interconnected the technology, without high-quality courseware—computer software, video, and printed materials—technology will not be used effectively for learning. The scenarios suggest courseware applications that personalize content, heighten the appeal of learning, and help learners monitor their own progress to increase the rate and quality of learning.

Anecdotal evidence suggests that some learners will approach new technologies timidly (see chapter 3). As computer-based technologies become more "user-friendly," like televisions, radios, and telephones, they will be less intimidating. The easier the technologies are to use, the more likely it is that adult learners will accept them. The design of software and person-computer interfaces plays an important role in making computers user-friendly. Such features as consistency across applications, the use of "windows" to display more than one piece of information at a time, and icons (e.g., a picture of a trash can to represent the concept of deleting material the user has been working on but does not want to save; a picture of a magnifying glass to represent the concept "find out more about") have already made technology easier to use. High-resolution graphics, sound, and video also make information more engaging and understandable. Multiple ways of interacting with the computer (e.g.,

Residents in Cerritos, California, can pay bills, get stock quotes, make airline reservations, take SAT preparation courses, or find out about municipal services on Main Street, *an interactive information video service that uses a combination of the telephone network and a local cable channel.*

handwriting and voice input, in addition to today's touch screens, keyboards, and mouse) will improve user-friendliness. Collaborative work spaces are being designed to make it easier for groups of people to create a document, implement a project, or solve a problem in shared computer spaces.[10] Programming and editing tools are making it easier and less expensive for adult educators and learners to create or customize their own multimedia courseware, enhancing the connection between meaningful context and learning.[11]

Finally, new knowledge about cognitive processes in general, and adult learning in particular, can lead to better educational applications. As instructional theory and design evolve over the

---

[9] See U.S. Congress, Office of Technology Assessment, "Advanced Networking Technologies," background paper, draft, April 1993.

[10] See Denis Newman, "Technology as Support for School Structure and School Restructuring," *Phi Delta Kappan,* vol. 74, No. 4, December 1992, pp. 308-315; Olsen et al., op. cit., footnote 1; and Bernajean Porter, "Aspects: Creative Word Processing in the Classroom," *The Writing Notebook,* vol. 9, No. 4, April/May 1992, pp. 14-15; and Marlene Scardamalia et al., "Educational Applications of a Networked Communal Database," *Interactive Learning Environments,* vol. 2, No. 1, 1992, pp. 45-71.

[11] David L. Wilson, "Computer Programs Without Programmers," *The Chronicle of Higher Education,* vol. 38, No. 37, May 20, 1992, pp. A15-16.

Good software is crucial for effective learning with computers. Material must be engaging and related to learners' needs and interests.

next decade, instruction in basic skills and applications that require higher order thinking skills will become more fully integrated into functional contexts. Flexible applications and learner-designed materials can empower adults and reward them for independent study, while better diagnostic tools, improved tutorials, and automated ''checkups'' and recordkeeping can help learners manage their own instruction and know when to seek extra assistance.

The expansion of broadcast and cable television programming also provides greater resources for adult literacy. Within the next 5 to 10 years, compressed digital video technology will make it possible to carry at least eight broadcast-quality signals on a channel that today carries just one. Given these improvements in technology, cable channel capacity is expected to increase to at least 500 channels; PBS plans to increase its capacity correspondingly. What will people watch on all these channels? One possible future suggests high-quality literacy programming targeted for various groups of adults (e.g., senior citizens, rural farmers, or parents of teenagers), similar to the programming for young children now offered many hours a day.

One area of special concern to the development and use of literacy courseware is clarification of copyright issues (see box 8-C).

Issues of Access and Equity

These technology advances can provide resources that go beyond what is available today. However, unless those who need them most—people like Carla, Dave, Tina, and their families—have convenient, timely, and affordable access to them, the futures projected in the scenarios will not occur. In fact, these learners and millions like them may become further disadvantaged if they do not have access to these resources.

People learn best when they have frequent and regular opportunities to practice new knowledge.[12] As the scenarios illustrate, it is more convenient and easier to practice when technology is available at home. Yet those who most need literacy assistance are those with the most limited incomes, and thus least likely to have access to these empowering technologies.

To analyze the access barriers to future technology, it is useful to look at current patterns of access to the backbones of future learning technologies: the personal computer, telephone, and television. Access is affected by income, race, and ethnicity.[13] Many more adults have access to telephones in their homes than to home computers, but television is currently the most widely distributed technology (see chapter 7, figure 7-1). Despite high purchase prices, the widespread availability of television and, more recently, telephones provide models for greater computer access. Unlike computers, televisions and telephones are sold in a variety of stores, in urban areas and small rural towns. Televisions can be rented, mail-ordered, or purchased new or used. Future learning technologies could become as available as today's television and telephone if

Adults learn best when they can practice new skills repeatedly. It is critical that those most in need of adult literacy services have easy access to technologies for learning.

they, too, were sold, rented, and leased to learners at reasonable cost, on installment plans or through other financing schemes, through workplaces, community-based organizations, schools, and post-secondary institutions.

In the scenarios, the pocket translator is an example of limited purpose, specialized equipment that could be developed at prices most learners could afford or that businesses could make available to their workers. Similarly, PLDs could be priced at a cost affordable to most workers and families, or provided by the workplace and family literacy programs. According to current projections, equipment with capabilities similar to those described for the PLD will cost about $500 in 1997, if purchased in bulk.[14] Even at that cost, some learners like Tina may be unable to afford these tools unless some subsidy is provided.

---

[12] See, for example, David Twitchell (ed.), "Robert Gagne and M. David Merrill in Conversation: The Cognitive Psychological Basis for Instructional Design," *Educational Technology*, vol. 30, No. 12, December 1990, pp. 35–46; and Robert Gagne et al., *Principles of Instructional Design*, 3rd ed. (New York, NY: Holt Rinehart and Winston, 1988).

[13] For example, among African-American and Hispanic households with incomes at minimum wage level, about 20 and 25 percent, respectively, do not have home telephones, compared with an overall rate of 93 percent. Federal Communications Commission, "Telephone Subscribership in the U.S.," unpublished document, February 1992.

[14] Gary Simons, Summer Institute of Linguistics, "Hardware Projections for Project '95 Target Machine," unpublished paper, 1992; and Marsh and Vanston, op. cit., footnote 1, pp. 63–77.

Box 8-C—Copyright Issues: How They Affect the Development and Use of Literacy Courseware

Copyright law grants authors and other copyright holders the right to control the reproduction, distribution, performance, display, and derivative use of their creations. Copyright law applies to specific types of intellectual property, including literary, dramatic, musical, and artistic works.[1] Emerging technologies are producing new forms of intellectual property, such as electronic databases and multimedia courseware, as well as new means of reproducing them or making derivative works by "downloading" or "sampling." New technologies also create new means of potentially infringing copyright, thus exacerbating tensions between the interests of the producers and users of intellectual property.

Copyright questions have traditionally been resolved through a combination of legislation, negotiation, licensing, and litigation. There is often uncertainty about the scope of copyright in software and multimedia applications, and how permission and licensing will be handled for multimedia works. Litigation to resolve these questions could take years, and legislation even longer. Licenses usually specify what types of users and uses (including any modifications) are permitted. License negotiations can be time-consuming, especially when several sets of copyright holders are involved. These lengthy, often costly, processes could limit access to adult literacy courseware by making startup development too risky for small companies, by increasing product prices and licensing fees, and by limiting creative use of courseware by teachers and learners.

Experiences with multimedia provide examples of how copyright issues can complicate the development of educational courseware. Systematic procedures for granting permission to use copyrighted material for multimedia have yet to be established by most institutions and individuals and there are few established "standard" terms and fees for licensing materials for use in multimedia works.[2] In order to include copyrighted film or music, courseware developers must negotiate fees and the conditions under which the material can be used. Film rights generally must be negotiated with individual copyright holders. Music performance rights are

---

[1] For further information about copyright and technological change see U.S. Congress, Office of Technology Assessment, *Finding a Balance: Computer Software, Intellectual Property, and the Challenge of Technological Change*, OTA-TCT-527 (Washington DC: U.S. Government Printing Office, May, 1992). See also 17 USC 101 *et seq.* (1988). U.S. copyright law treats computer software as a literary work.

[2] For example, fee structures for music rights are geared to use of the entire song or composition, not use of small pieces of dozens or hundreds of songs. See Office of Technology Assessment, op. cit., footnote 1, pp. 172-73. Early in the development of multimedia, demands for exclusivity or rights in perpetuity strained relations between intellectual property rights holders and software developers. See "Turning Up the Heat on Titles," *Digital Media*, vol. 2, No. 5, Oct. 12, 1992, pp. 5-6.

The rapid pace of development in computer, video, and telecommunications hardware and software typically has been stimulated by profitable markets in business, entertainment, or consumer products. Most hardware is created with these other markets in mind and later adapted for educational applications; eventually, education (K-12 as well as adult literacy) has been able to benefit from these advances in technological power and flexibility. However, some analysts suggest that, to assure that important social goals are not ignored, it is necessary to stimulate the market to assure innovations focused specifically on improving learning.

Although some computer companies that began with education as their primary activity are thriving, as are some educational software companies, serving adult learners in particular requires extra efforts in development and marketing.[15] There is no zip code promoters can target, and developers do not consider those most in need of literacy assistance an appealing market. Yet,

---

[15] Education TURNKEY Systems, Inc. and Wujcik and Associates, "The Educational Software Marketplace and Adult Literacy Niches," OTA contractor report, April 1992.

generally negotiated with organizations such as the American Society of Composers, Authors, and Publishers (ASCAP), Broadcast Music, Inc. (BMI), and other rights holders such as individual record companies. Thus, development of one courseware package can require a large number of separate negotiations. A lower cost alternative is a ''stock house'' that collects film and music from public-domain sources or independent artists and packages them to sell to users for a flat fee. However, stock houses usually do not have access to identifiable work by well-known stars that have instant popular appeal.

Many small courseware development companies are finding the complex, costly copyright permissions and licensing processes a barrier to entering the multimedia market. Obtaining permission to use copyrighted material is difficult for even the largest developers. For example, for Microsoft's *Encarta*, a multimedia encyclopedia costing several million dollars to develop, five people were hired solely to handle rights acquisitions.[3] Funds spent in copyright acquisition leave less money for developing creative, new approaches to learning. Also, when vendors spend hundreds of thousands of dollars or more to develop a product, they may be tempted to recoup their investment by marketing the courseware aggressively, regardless of its educational effectiveness.

Copyright issues cause difficulties for users as well as developers. Literacy programs and learners are often confused about how ''fair use''[4] principles, in particular, and copyright law, in general, apply to emerging technologies. For example, when is it proper to reproduce multimedia material? How much can be reproduced and how long can it be kept? Under what circumstances can teachers share materials with other classes or other centers? Under what conditions can adults borrow materials to take home? How does copyright protection apply to student-created materials that incorporate commercial media clips or electronic database material?

These confusions will only be exacerbated if copyright provisions and informal (negotiated) guidelines change frequently, or, as at present, different provisions continue to apply within and between text, video, and music sources.[5] Adult literacy programs typically do not have access to detailed, timely information about copyright provisions and what practices constitute infringement. Consequently, if vendors believe that adult literacy teachers and volunteers are likely to infringe copyrights, whether intentionally or inadvertently, they may raise their prices to compensate for what they believe to be lost sales. In the worst case, they could discontinue their participation in the adult literacy courseware market together.

---

[3] ''Setting a New Precedent, Microsoft Spends $5 Million to Make New Encyclopedia Designed 'For the Computer,' '' *Digital Media*, vol. 2, No. 5, Oct. 12, 1992, p. 10.

[4] ''Fair use'' refers to a set of statutory and nonstatutory guidelines that govern ways in which copyrighted material can be used for education or in other not-for-profit circumstances. See 17 USC 107 (1988).

[5] See ch. 5 in Office of Technology Assessment, op. cit., footnote 1, for further discussion and ch. 1, pp. 35-36, for potential ways of ameliorating these difficulties.

---

the number of potential consumers of adult literacy products is large and growing, whether diffused as individual learners or aggregated as members of preexisting groups such as job training or welfare programs.

Similarly, information and telecommunications applications are also driven by the needs of their markets. Where the information is of value to the society as a whole—e.g., access to timely information regarding education, training, health, political participation, and efficient access to government services—user payments alone may not be enough to support information dissemination. Thus, some have suggested that ''universal service'' should include not just the technology of communication but also a body of information, access to which should be guaranteed for everyone, providing an ''information safety net'' to all.[16]

The power of networked telecommunications, and the policy of universal access, are significant:

---

[16] Francis D. Fisher, ''What the Coming Telecommunications Infrastructure Could Mean to Our Family,'' *The Aspen Institute Quarterly*, vol. 5, No. 1, winter 1993, pp. 135, 138.

For meeting the widely disparate information needs of a large and heterogeneous population, the switching capability of a network is its single most important characteristic. . . . Once we are switched and connected to an information source, interactivity provides the means to further refine our choice of information. . . . Universal access implies overcoming not only the boundaries of poverty but geographical boundaries as well. . . . But offering services to rural users may be worthwhile for society as a whole where alternatives involving travel, ignorance, and economic underdevelopment are expensive.[17]

CONCLUSIONS

Technologies that expand literacy options in the directions suggested in the scenarios will require substantial investment by all segments of society. Businesses will need to commit resources for continuing education and training of personnel as jobs and skills change. Adult learners will be required to contribute the money, time, and effort necessary to learn. The technology industry will have to create hardware, courseware, and networks that serve a wide spectrum of learners. The public sector will need to underwrite the early development of technologies and materials, and test their use in literacy applications.

Motivated adults with appropriate materials learn faster, persevere longer, and retain more of what they learn. Many who are reluctant to enter formal programs could benefit from new models of customized personal instruction, guided by teachers and mentors but facilitated by portable learning technologies. Technologies could improve motivation by providing immediate feedback and more opportunities to practice learning privately. Technology-based diagnostic aids and instructional management systems could ensure that learning tasks are well matched to learning needs. Finally, adults could learn new skills not even offered when they were in school.

However, access and use of new information technologies are likely to be limited if current trends continue. Although there will be notable exceptions, the quality of most adult literacy courseware is likely to improve slowly. Moreover, many useful learning technologies, such as computers and online databases, are likely to remain too expensive for economically disadvantaged families. This forecast could be altered through Federal policies that encourage the development, access, and use of technologies to expand the quantity and quality of adult literacy options.

---

[17] Ibid., pp. 132, 138.

Appendix A: List of Boxes, Figures, and Tables

Boxes

Figures

Tables

Appendix B: Major Federal Adult Literacy and Basic Skills Programs

Federal agency	Program	Purpose	Fiscal year 1992 funding (in millions of dollars)
Department of Education	Adult Education Act (AEA) Basic Grants	Primary Federal program for adults with inadequate basic skills. Formula grants to State education agencies (SEAs) for adult basic education, secondary education, and English literacy. State set-asides for incarcerated and institutionalized adults, and teacher training and innovation.	$235.8
	AEA State Literacy Resource Centers	Centers chosen by Governor perform coordinating, research, training, and technical assistance functions.	5.0
	AEA Workplace Literacy Partnerships	Secretary makes competitive grants to partnerships of education providers and private sector partners. Literacy programs for workers with less than high school education. (If appropriations exceed $50 million, program administered by States.)	19.3
	AEA English Literacy Grants	SEAs receive competitive grants for English literacy programs for limited English proficient (LEP) adults. Secretary also may fund demonstrations of innovative approaches for English literacy instruction.	1.0
	AEA National Programs	Secretary carries out range of national research and evaluations in adult literacy; provides technical assistance; supports demonstration projects; and, with Department of Health and Human Services (HHS) and Department of Labor (DOL), funds National Institute for Literacy.	9.0
	Literacy for State and Local Prisoners	Grants to State or local correctional agencies. Literacy training for inmates.	5.0
	Commercial Drivers Program	Competitive grants to business, labor, apprenticeship programs, and education agencies. Literacy programs help commercial drivers pass mandated test.	2.5
	Adult Education for the Homeless	Discretionary grants to SEAs provide basic skills and literacy training for the homeless.	9.8
	Special Programs for Indian Adults	Competitive grants to Indian tribes and organizations improve education below the college level for Indian adults.	4.3

Federal agency	Program	Purpose	Fiscal year 1992 funding (In millions of dollars)
	Even Start Family Literacy	SEAs receive formula grants for family literacy projects run by local education agencies, community-based organizations, and others. Participants are educationally disadvantaged parents and their children ages 0 to 7 who live in areas eligible for Chapter 1 and Elementary and Secondary Education Act (ESEA) grants. Parents taught literacy and parenting skills; children receive education and school readiness.	$70.0[a]
	Bilingual Family English Literacy	Competitive grants to educational institutions to help LEP adults and out-of-school youth achieve competence in English, support their children in school, and gain citizenship knowledge. Preference to families with children in Title VII, ESEA.	6.1
	Library Services and Construction Act (LSCA) Title VI Library Literacy Program	Secretary makes discretionary grants to State and local public libraries to support literacy programs in public libraries.	8.2
	LSCA Title I Public Library Services	Formula grants to State library agencies. Primary purpose: to expand public library services in underserved areas. States may also use funds to help public libraries provide adult literacy programs and to support model library literacy centers.	83.9[a]
	Student Literacy Corps	Competitive grants to higher education institutions. Projects encourage undergraduates to volunteer as literacy tutors for adults and children.	5.4
	Migrant Education High School Equivalency Program (HEP)	Competitive grants help migrant farmworkers or their children ages 17 or older obtain general equivalency diploma (GED) and proceed to job or higher education.	8.3
Department of Health and Human Services	Job Opportunities and Basic Skills (JOBS)	Provides Aid for Families With Dependent Children (AFDC) recipients with education and training in order to avoid welfare dependence. State welfare agencies receive entitlements. Services must include basic education, GED education, English as a second language (ESL), and job training. Participation mandated for some parents.	1,000.0[a]
	State Legalization Impact Assistance Grants (SLIAG)	Reimburses States for costs of public assistance, public health, and adult education for newly legalized aliens. Services include basic education, GED education, English literacy instruction, and citizenship instruction.	0 ($1,122.9[a] deferred until fiscal year 1993)
	Refugee Resettlement Program	States receive formula grants for social services for eligible refugees. Funds may be used for English language instruction.	83.0[a]
	Head Start Family Literacy Initiative	Head Start provides education, social services, and school readiness activities for low-income preschool children and their families. As of 1992, HHS requires every Head Start project to integrate family literacy activities into regular practices.	9.0 (Minimum for family literacy. Total fiscal year 1992 funding for Head Start was $2,202.0.)

Federal agency	Program	Purpose	Fiscal year 1992 funding (in millions of dollars)
Department of Labor	Job Training Partnership Act (JTPA) Title II-A Training for Disadvantaged Youth and Adults	Aims to increase employability of economically disadvantaged adults and youth ages 16 to 21. States receive formula grants. Governors keep 8 percent for education and training coordination, literacy services, and other activities. Seventy-eight percent of grant distributed to regional service delivery areas (SDAs). Services are primarily job training, but also include remedial, basic skills, literacy, and bilingual education.	$1,773.5[a]
	JTPA Title II-B Summer Youth Employment and Training	Summer education and training programs for economically disadvantaged youth ages 14 to 21. States receive formula grants; funds channeled to local SDAs. Private industry councils determine local service providers. Programs must include basic skills and remedial education; other allowable activities are work experience, job training, and employability skills.	495.2[a]
	JTPA Title III Dislocated Worker Assistance	Grants to States for retraining, education, and readjustment services for workers displaced from jobs. Basic and remedial education, literacy training, and English literacy, as well as job retraining. Secretary also funds special and emergency projects.	577.0[a]
	JTPA Title IV-B Job Corps	Federal Government directly administers residential Job Corps centers. Program aims to help severely disadvantaged youth ages 14 to 22 become more responsible, employable, and productive. Highly intensive program provides basic education and GED education, along with training, work experience, and support services.	846.5[a]
	National Workforce Literacy Collaborative	Helps small and medium-sized businesses and labor organizations develop literacy programs tailored to workforce needs. DOL plans to expand to include broader technical assistance.	0 (DOL requests $1.2 for fiscal year 1993 for this and National Literacy Act duties.)
Department of Defense	Army Basic Skills Education Programs (BSEP) I and II	BSEP I and BSEP II provide basic education to soldiers who need to improve their skills to complete initial entry training, as well as job-related basic skills competencies.	6.5 (estimate)
	Navy Skills Enhancement Program	Provides basic skills training to help sailors achieve competency and perform jobs.	3.1 (estimate)
Department of the Interior	Bureau of Indian Affairs Adult Education Program	Bureau of Indian Affairs contracts with Indian tribes to operate basic literacy and GED programs for Indian adults.	3.4
Department of Justice	Bureau of Prisons Literacy Program	Inmates in Federal prisons who perform below high school diploma literacy level must participate in literacy program until they meet GED level, or for a minimum of 120 days. LEP inmates must attend ESL program until they function at 8th-grade competency level.	16.1 (estimate)
ACTION	Volunteers in Service to America (VISTA) Literacy Corps	Volunteer tutors assigned to adult literacy projects in needy communities. Projects are competitively selected.	4.8

[a] Amounts are for entire program; specific expenditures for adult literacy and basic skills education are not available.

SOURCE: Information for this appendix is from Nancy Kober, "Profiles of Major Federal Programs," OTA contractor report, July 1992.

Appendix C: Key Coordination Provisions in Literacy Laws and Regulations

R = required; E = encouraged; O = optional		
Adult Education Act (AEA) Basic Grants	Joint review of State plan by other State boards.	R
	State plans and coordinates programs with job training, vocational education, immigration, rehabilitation, special education, Indian education, higher education, and Volunteers in Service to America (VISTA).	R
	State plan describes how delivery system will be expanded through coordination and how volunteers will be used.	R
	State considers degree of coordination in selecting local providers.	R
	Local coordination with Job Training Partnership Act (JTPA), vocational education, and other programs cited in law.	R
	Local cooperative arrangements with business, industry, volunteer groups, and others.	R
	Limited English proficient (LEP) programs coordinate with Federal bilingual education and vocational education programs.	R
	Public housing Gateway grantees consult with other adult education service providers.	R
	Set-aside of 10 percent for incarcerated should be coordinated with services for ex-offenders and may support cooperative projects with education agencies, community-based organizations (CBOs), and businesses.	E
	Set-aside of 15 percent for teacher training and innovation may be used for promising coordination programs.	O
	State advisory council includes broad representation and advises on coordination.	O
AEA State Resource Centers	Centers develop innovative approaches to Federal-State, interstate, and intrastate coordination; assist public and private agencies in coordinating service delivery; and encourage government and industry partnerships.	E
Workplace Literacy	Department of Education (ED) consults with Department of Labor (DOL) and the Small Business Administration in making grants.	R
	Programs run by partnerships of public/private sector groups.	R
	Programs that collaborate with other providers receive priority for national strategies grants.	E

R = required; E = encouraged; O = optional

English Literacy	Funds may be combined with other LEP literacy funds.	O
Commercial Drivers	Grantees refer adults with serious literacy problems to other providers.	R
National Institute for Literacy	Joint administration by ED, DOL, and Department of Health and Human Services (HHS).	R
	Institute helps government agencies develop model coordinating systems and advises on uniform requirements.	R
	Institute research coordinated with other relevant Federal research activities.	R
McKinney Homeless Literacy	State programs coordinate with existing resources.	R
	Secretary considers cooperative arrangements in selecting grantees.	E
Even Start Family Literacy	Local programs coordinate with AEA, JTPA, Chapter 1 and Chapter 2 of Elementary and Secondary Education Act, Head Start, special education, volunteer literacy, and other programs.	R
	Local projects should build on community resources.	E
Bilingual Family Literacy	ED coordinates with all relevant programs.	R
	Nonlocal education agency applicants coordinate with local education agencies (LEAs).	E
Library Services and Construction Act (LSCA) Title I	Model library literacy centers coordinate with other State agencies and nonprofit organizations.	R
	Local projects cooperate with other agencies if appropriate.	E
Library Literacy (LSCA Title VI)	ED coordinates with other LSCA programs.	R
	ED gives priority to projects that coordinate with literacy organizations and CBOs.	R
	State plans describe how projects will be coordinated with education and library services.	R
	Projects coordinate with volunteer literacy.	E
Student Literacy Corps	Institutes of higher education collaborate with community agencies to run projects.	R
DOL Workforce Collaborative	Promotes cooperation among State and local agencies and private sector; cooperates with National Institute for Literacy and other Federal centers.	R
JTPA Title II-A	Governor establishes criteria for service delivery areas (SDAs) to coordinate with other key programs.	R
	Governor reserves 8 percent to support coordination between education agencies and JTPA entities.	R
	Governor develops coordination plan.	R
	Mandated State Job Training Coordinating Committee (SJTCC) reviews plans of relevant State agencies and advises on statewide coordination.	R
	SDA plan reviewed by LEA and other public agencies.	R
	Private industry councils (PICs) include representatives of educational agencies in SDA.	R
	Funds may not duplicate existing services.	R

R = required; E = encouraged; O = optional

JTPA Title II-B	Same as JTPA II-A above.	
	Local program goals may include demonstrated coordination with other community organizations.	O
JTPA Title III	States coordinate with other State programs, consult with labor organizations, and coordinate services with 1974 Trade Act.	R
	Labor organizations involved in substate planning and implementation.	R
	Substate grantees coordinate services with other programs.	R
	Funds may be used for joint services with vocational education.	O
	SJTCC reviews State plan.	R
Job Corps	DOL cooperates with ED and Department of Defense.	E
	Centers develop relationships with communities.	E
Job Opportunities and Basic Skills (JOBS)	HHS consults with ED and DOL to ensure service coordination.	R
	HHS, ED, and DOL support joint technical assistance.	R
	State welfare agencies coordinate with JTPA, AEA, vocational education, preschool and early childhood, and other State agencies.	R
	Governor ensures coordination with JTPA and employment, training, and education.	R
	State welfare agency consults with State education agency (SEA), State employment service, and State agencies for JTPA, vocational and adult education, employment service, childcare, and public housing.	R
	SJTCC and SEA review State plan.	R
	Local welfare agencies consult with PICs.	R
	Local programs coordinate with PICs and LEAs.	E
	State ensures that JOBS funds are not used for services already available.	R
Refugee Resettlement	States ensure coordination of public and private resources.	E
	Local volunteer agencies cooperate with State and local government.	E
Head Start Family Literacy	Grantees collaborate with community literacy programs.	E
VISTA Literacy Corps	ACTION coordinates with community action programs and other Federal, State, and local programs.	R
	ACTION consults with other Federal agencies to encourage use of volunteers in agency programs.	R
	Projects encouraging intrastate coordination receive preference.	E

SOURCE: Information for this appendix is from Nancy Kober, "Profiles of Major Federal Programs," OTA contractor report, July 1992.

Appendix D: Glossary

Analog communication: A communication format in which information is transmitted by modulating a continuous signal, such as a radio wave. Voice and video messages originate in analog form since sound and light are wave-like functions; thus, they must be converted into digital messages in order to communicate along digital communications formats or media.

Animation: Animation is apparent movement produced by recording step-by-step a series of still drawings, three-dimensional objects, or computer-generated graphics. Movement over time is shown by replacing each image (frame) by the next one in the series at a uniform speed—frames per second (fps). The human eye perceives fluid movement at 30 fps—the approximate rate of film, television, and VCR-quality video.

Application tools: Computer software that enables the user to manipulate information to create documents or reports.

Artificial intelligence: The use of computer processing to simulate intelligent behavior. Current research includes natural language recognition and use, problem solving, selection from alternatives, pattern recognition, generalization based on experience, and analysis of novel situations.

Asynchronous communication: Two-way communication in which there is a time delay between when a message is sent and when it is received. Examples include electronic-mail and voice-mail systems. In contrast, synchronous communication is simultaneous two-way exchange of information—e.g., a telephone conversation.

Audioconferencing: An electronic meeting in which participants in different locations use telephones and audio bridges (devices that connect and control multiple telephone lines) to communicate simultaneously with each other.

Audiotext: An automated telephone information service with branching capability accessed through a touch-tone telephone. Audiotext services are often used by businesses or public agencies to provide commonly requested information, such as instructions for obtaining a drivers license.

Authoring: The process of building or modifying computer software using a computer program designed for that purpose. Generally, authoring software applications require less technical expertise compared to use of programming languages.

Bit (BInary digiT): The smallest unit of information a computer can use. A bit is represented as a "0" or a "1" (also "on" or "off"). A group of 8 bits is called a byte. Bits are used to measure the speed of digital transmission systems. Speeds are commonly expressed in kilobits (Kbps), i.e., thousand per second; megabits (Mbps), i.e., million per second; and gigabits (Gbps), i.e., billion per second.

Bulletin board service (BBS): A computer service that is modeled after a community bulletin board. Using a computer, modem, and phone line, individuals connect to a central "host" computer to post or read messages or to upload and download software. Communication is usually asynchronous.

CD-ROM (compact disc-read only memory): An optical storage system for computers that permits data to be randomly accessed from a disc. With read only discs, new data cannot be stored nor can the disc be erased for reuse. Other optical storage systems allow users to record or write and rewrite information.

Coaxial cable: Shielded wire cable that connects communications components. Coaxial cable is commonly used in cable television systems because of its ability to carry multiple video (or other broadband) signals.

Codec: An electronic device that converts analog video signals into a digital format for transmission, and vice versa. The name is an abbreviated form of ''coder-decoder'' or ''compressor-decompressor'' when compression is also involved.

Compression: Squeezing information so that it requires less space to store or transmit. When speech is compressed, for example, pauses are eliminated. Compression is generally expressed as a ratio. For example, an 8-to-1 ratio means that the information requires one-eighth of its original space. In compressed video, digital technology is used to encode and compress the signal. Picture quality is generally not as good as full motion; quick movements often appear blurred. The greater the compression ratio, the higher the chance for loss of quality in image, sound, or motion.

Computer graphics: Drawings and figures that can be digitized, altered, created, stored, and produced with a computer. Application tools allow users to draw or ''paint'' original images with a mouse or graphics tablet.

Consumer electronics: A class of electronic products that are typically designed, marketed, and sold to the consumer mass market. Televisions, videocassette recorders, video game systems, walk-about radios, pocket calculators, and portable compact disc players are examples.

Courseware: A package used for teaching and learning, which includes computer or video software and related print materials such as a teacher's guide and student activity books.

Digital communications: A communications format used with both electronic and light-based systems that transmits audio, video, and data as bits of information.

Digital video: A format used to store, manipulate, and transmit moving images as bits of information. Codecs are used to convert traditional analog

signals into a digital format and back again. Digital video can be compressed for more efficient storage and transmission.

Digitize: To change analog information to a digital format. Once information has been converted to this form, it can be conveniently stored, manipulated, and compressed. It can also be transmitted over a distance with little or no loss in quality. Sound (such as speech or music), stills (such as transparencies), and motion video are commonly converted into digitized form.

Downlink: An antenna shaped like a dish that receives signals from a satellite. Often referred to as a satellite dish, terminal, Earth station, or TVRO (television receive only).

Electronic mail (e-mail): A computer application for exchanging information over a distance. Communication is asynchronous. E-mail typically consists of text, but multimedia formats are under development.

Facsimile machine (fax): A device that converts hard-copy images and text into an electronic form for transmission over telephone lines to similar devices at another location.

Fiber optic cable: Hair thin, flexible glass rods that use light signals to transmit information in either analog or digital formats. Fiber optic cable has much higher capacity than copper or coaxial cable, and is not as subject to interference or noise. Fiber optic cable has the bandwidth to accommodate high-speed, multimedia networking.

Flat-panel display: A video or computer screen that is relatively thin, lightweight, and typically used in portable computers.

Gbps: See bit.

Groupware: A computer software program that allows the same information to be shared among several computer users simultaneously. With some applications, users can see each other and from their own computers, add to or edit text and graphics in a single document.

Icon: A symbol displayed on the computer screen that represents a command or program (e.g., a trash can symbolizing the command to delete a document). Icons help make computer operating systems and applications easier to use.

Interface: A general term used in the computer world to designate the hardware and associated software needed to enable one device to communicate with another or to enable a person to communicate with computers and related devices. A user interface can be a keyboard, a mouse, commands, icons, or menus that facilitate communication between the user and computer.

ISDN (Integrated Services Digital Network): A protocol for high-speed digital transmission. ISDN provides simultaneous voice and high-speed data transmission along a single conduit to users' premises. Two ISDN protocols have been standardized: narrowband ISDN—two 64 Kbps channels carry voice or data messages and one 16 Kbps data channel is used for signaling; and broadband ISDN—twenty-three 64 Kbps channels carry voice or data messages and one 64 Kbps channel is used for signaling.

Kbps: See **bit.**

Laserdisc: See **videodisc.**

LEOS (low-Earth orbiting satellites): Small satellites with a lower orbit (hundreds of miles) than geosynchronous satellites (22,300 miles). In the future, LEOS could be used to provide data and voice communications to portable computers, telephones, and other devices without the use of wires.

Local area networks (LANs): Data communication networks that are relatively limited in their reach. They generally cover the premises of a building or a school. Like all networking technologies, LANs facilitate communication and sharing of information and computer resources by the members of a group.

Mbps: See **bit.**

Microwave: High-frequency radio waves used for point-to-point and omnidirectional communication of data, video, and voice.

Modem: A device that allows two computers to communicate over telephone lines. It converts digital computer signals into analog format for transmission. A similar device at the other end converts the analog signal back into a digital format that the computer can understand. The name is an abbreviated form of "modulator-demodulator."

Mouse: A pointing device that connects to a computer. With a mouse, users can control pointer movements on a computer screen by rolling the mouse over a flat surface and clicking a button on the device. The mouse is also commonly used to define and move blocks of text; open or close windows, documents, or applications; and draw or paint graphics.

Optical storage: High-density disc storage that uses a laser to "write" information on the surface. Erasable or rewritable optical storage enables written information to be erased and new information written.

Pen: See **stylus.**

PSTN (Public Switched Telephone Network): The public telephone network that allows point-to-point connections anywhere in the system.

RAM (random access memory): Computer memory where any location can be read from, or written to, in a random access fashion. Information in RAM is destroyed when the computer is turned off.

ROM (read only memory): Once information has been entered into this memory, it can be read as often as required, but cannot normally be changed.

Satellite dish: See **downlink.**

Scanner: An input device that attaches to a computer that makes a digital image of a hard-copy document such as a photograph. Scanned pictures, graphs, maps, and other graphical data are often used in desktop publishing.

Simulation: Software that enables the user to experience a realistic reproduction of an actual situation. Computer-based simulations often involve situations that are very costly or high risk (e.g., flight simulation training for pilots).

Smart Card: A small plastic card containing information that can be read by a computer reader. For example, a smart card can be used to keep track of Food Stamp eligibility and qualify the holder for other social services that use the same criteria.

Software: Programming that controls computer, video, or electronic hardware. Software takes many forms including application tools, operating systems, instructional drills, and games.

Storyboard: A board or panel containing small drawings or pictures that show the sequence of action for a script of a video or computer software.

Stylus: A tool similar to a pen with no ink used for marking or drawing on a touch-sensitive surface. In pen-based computing, a stylus, rather than a keyboard, is used as the primary input device.

Synchronous communication: See **asynchronous communication.**

Tablet or graphics tablet: A computer input device resembling a normal pad of paper on which images are drawn with a pointing instrument such as a stylus. The tablet converts hand-drawn images into digital information that can be processed and displayed on a computer monitor.

Teleconferencing: A general term for any conferencing system using telecommunications links to connect remote sites. There are many types of teleconferencing including: videoconferencing, computer conferencing, and audioconferencing.

Touch window: A computer screen that allows data to be entered by using a specialized stylus to write on the screen, or by making direct physical contact between the finger and the screen.

Uplink: A satellite dish that transmits signals up to a satellite.

Videoconference: A form of teleconferencing where participants see, as well as hear, other participants in remote locations. Video cameras, monitors, codecs, and networks allow synchronous communication between sites.

Videodisc: An optical disc that contains recorded still images, motion video, and sounds that can be played back through a television monitor. Videodiscs can be used alone or as a part of a computer-based application.

Voice mail: An electronic system for transmitting and storing voice messages, which can be accessed later by the person to whom they are addressed. Voice mail operates like an electronic-mail system.

Voice recognition: Computer hardware and software systems that recognize spoken words and convert them to digital signals that can be used for input.

Wide area networks (WANs): Data communication networks that provide long-haul connectivity among separate networks located in different geographic areas. WANs make use of a variety of transmission media, which can be provided on a leased or dial-up basis.

Window: A part of the computer screen that is given over to a different display from the rest of the screen (e.g., a text window in a graphics screen). It can also be a portion of a file or image currently on the screen, when multiple windows are displayed simultaneously.

Wireless: Voice, data, or video communications without the use of connecting wires. In wireless communications, radio signals make use of microwave towers or satellites. Cellular telephones and pagers are examples of wireless communications.

Workstation: A computer that is intended for individual use, but is generally more powerful than a personal computer. A workstation may also act as a terminal for a central mainframe.

Appendix E:
List of
Acronyms

ABE	adult basic education	ESEA	Elementary and Secondary Education Act
ACCESS	Adult Centers for Comprehensive Education and Support Services	ESL	English as a second language
ADSL	Asymmetric Digital Subscriber Line	GED	general equivalency diploma
AEA	Adult Education Act		
AFDC	Aid for Families with Dependent Children	HHS	Department of Health and Human Services
APL	Adult Performance Level		
ARC	Appalachian Regional Commission	ILS	integrated learning system
ASE	adult secondary education		
		JOBS	Job Opportunities and Basic Skills
BCLC	Baltimore City Literacy Corp.	JTPA	Job Training Partnership Act
BIA	Bureau of Indian Affairs		
BOCES	Board of Cooperative Education Services	KET	Kentucky Educational Television
BRI	Baltimore Reads, Inc.		
BSEP	Basic Skills Education Programs	LEA	local education agency
		LEP	limited English proficient
CASAS	Comprehensive Adult Student Assessment System	LLA	Laubach Literacy Action
		LSCA	Library Services and Construction Act
CBE	computer-based education	LVA	Literacy Volunteers of America
CBO	community-based organization		
CD	compact disc	NAEP	National Assessment of Educational Progress
CD-I	compact disc-interactive		
CD-ROM	compact disc-read only memory	NCAL	National Center for Adult Literacy
CED	Correctional Education Division	NCI	National Captioning Institute
CLC	Community Learning Center	NIL	National Institute for Literacy
CPB	Corporation for Public Broadcasting	NLA	National Literacy Act
CPCC	Central Piedmont Community College	NSF	National Science Foundation
DOD	Department of Defense	OEO	Office of Economic Opportunity
DOL	Department of Labor	OTAN	Outreach and Technical Assistance Network
ED	Department of Education		
ES	Employment System	PACE	Parent and Childhood Education

PBS	Public Broadcasting Service
PIC	private industry council
PLUS	Project Literacy US
R&D	research and development
REEP	Arlington Education and Employment Program
SBIR	Small Business Innovation Research
SCANS	Secretary's Commission on Achieving Necessary Skills
SDA	service delivery area
SEA	State education agency
SEP	Skills Enhancement Program
SJTCC	State Job Training Coordinating Committee

SLIAG	State Legalization Impact Assistance Grants
TABE	Test of Adult Basic Education
TOEFL	Test of English for Foreign Learners
UI	Unemployment Insurance
UTC	United Technologies Center
VISTA	Volunteers in Service to America
VIT	Vermont Interactive Television
WIC	Women, Infants, and Children

Appendix F:
Workshop Participants, and Reviewers and Contributors

Workshop on Emerging Communication and Information Technologies: Implications for Literacy and Learning, September 26 and 27, 1991

Vivian Horner, *Chairperson*
Bell Atlantic

Burt Arnowitz
Arnowitz Productions

Peter Bradford
Cement Boat Company, Inc.

Doug Carlston
Broderbund Software

Susan Goldman
Vanderbilt University

Charles House
Informix Software, Inc.

Alan Kay
Apple Computer, Inc.

Ray Kurzweil
Kurzweil Applied Intelligence

Martin Lamb
University of Toronto

Michael North
North Communications

George Peterson
National Geographic Society

Stephen Reder
Northwest Regional Educational Laboratory

Antonia Stone
Playing to Win

Richard Venezky
University of Delaware

Bud Wonsiewicz
US WEST Communications

OTA/Annenberg Workshop New Visions for Video: Use of Cable, Satellite, Broadcast, and Interactive Systems for Literacy and Learning, January 27, 1992

Milda K. Hedblom, *Chairperson*
Augsburg College

Walter Baer
Rand Corp.

Patricia Cabrera
Educational Telecommunications Network

R.L. Capell III
Bell South

J. Ronald Castell
Blockbuster Entertainment Corp.

Nathan I. Felde
NYNEX Science and Technology Center

David Forman
National Education Training Group

Rich Gross
Kirkwood Community College

Henry Ingle
Claremont Graduate School

Newton N. Minow
The Annenberg Washington Program

Barbara Popovic
Chicago Access Corp.

Marian L. Schwarz
Consultant

Don Sutton
Jones Intercable, Inc.

Sandra Welch
Public Broadcasting Service

William Wilson
The Kentucky Network

Kristina Hooper Woolsey
Apple Computer, Inc.

Reviewers and Contributors

Emily Vargas Adams
Ceden Family Resource Center

Judith A. Alamprese
COSMOS Corp.

Eunice Askov
Institute for the Study of Adult Literacy

Elsa Auerbach
University of Massachusetts

John Avolio
Redford Union School

Lynn Barnett
American Association of Community and Junior
   Colleges

Hal Beder
Rutgers University

Brenda Bell
National Alliance of Business

Robert Bickerton
Massachusetts Department of Education

Karen Billings
CLARIS

Jan Biros
Drexel University

Brian Black
Black Light Design

Janet Bolen
Education is Essential Foundation, Inc.

Bob Bozarjian
Massachusetts Department of Education

Gary Brady
Dutchess County BOCES, NY

Morgan Bramlet
National Captioning Institute

Frances Buchanan
Watts Adult Learning Center

David Buzard
Outreach and Technical Assistance Network

Marge Cappo
WINGS for Learning/Sunburst

Chip Carlin
Literacy Volunteers of America, Inc.

Nguyen Minh Chau
Opportunity Systems, Inc.

Forrest Chisman
Southport Institute for Policy Analysis

Daryl Chubin
Office of Technology Assessment

Robert Clausen
Clausen Associates

Donna Cooper
Mayor's Commision on Literacy, Philadelphia

John Cradler
Far West Laboratories

Jodi Crandall
Center for Applied Linguistics

Barbara Crosby
Texas State Library

Jinx Crouch
Literacy Volunteers of America, Inc.

Evelyn Curtis
Texas Education Agency

Jan Davidson
Davidson and Associates

Catherine Carroll Day
Massachusetts Department of Employment
and Training

Chris Dede
George Mason University

Paul Delker
Consultant

Bryna Diamond
New York Public Library
Centers for Reading and Writing

Mark Dillon
GTE Imagitrek

Margaret Douherty
Houston Read Commission

Roger Dovner
Literacy Assistance Center

Richard Erdmann
Wasatch Education Systems

Gerard Fiala
U.S. Department of Labor

Hanna Arlene Fingeret
Literacy South

John Fleischman
Outreach and Technical Assistance Network

Ronald Fortune
Computer Curriculum Corp.

Rob Foshay
TRO Learning, Inc.

Michael Fox
Consultant

Jim Frasier
Motorola, Inc.

Maggi Gaines
Baltimore City Literacy Corp.

Linda Garcia
Office of Technology Assessment

Carol Goertzel
Lutheran Settlement House Women's Program

Marshall Goldberg
The Alliance

Sheryl Gowen
Georgia State University

Bill Grimes
San Diego Community College

Michael Grubbs
Tandy Corp.

Bob Guy
Jostens Learning Corp.

Pat Hartgrove
Texas Literacy Council

Ted Hasselbring
Vanderbilt University

Jan Hawkins
Bank Street College of Education

Jeanne Hayes
Quality Education Data, Inc.

Mike Hillinger
Lexicon Systems

Harold L. Hodgkinson
Center for Demographic Policy

Yvonne Howard
U.S. Department of Health and Human Services

Kathy Hurley
IBM Corp.

Paul Irwin
Congressional Research Service

Linda Jacobus
Lexington Technology Center

Paul Jurmo
Consultant

S. James Katz
Bellcore

Peter Kelman
Scholastic, Inc.

Brenda Kempster
Knowledge Network
Pacific Bell

Becky King
National Center for Family Literacy

C. Eric Kirkland
National Captioning Institute, Inc.

Peter Kleinbard
Young Adult Learning Academy

Judy Koloski
National Adult Education
    Professional Development Consortium

Andrew Kolstad
National Center for Education Statistics
U.S. Department of Education

Robert A. Kominski
Bureau of the Census
U.S. Department of Commerce

Mark Kutner
Pelavin Associates, Inc.

Jane Nissen Laidley
People's Computer Co.

Donna Lane
Oregon Office of Community College Services

Mary Leonard
Council on Foundations

Judith Loucks
Jostens Learning

Mary Lovell
U.S. Department of Education

Jeanne Lowe
GED Testing Service

John Lowery
Discis Knowledge Research, Inc.

Lucy Trible MacDonald
Chemeketa Community College

Shirley Malcom
American Association for the Advancement of Science

Ray Manak
Center for Training and Economic Development

Inaam Mansoor
Arlington (VA) Education and Employment Program

Laura Martin
Children's Television Workshop

Bodie Marx
Scott, Foresman and Co.

Sylvia McCollen
Federal Bureau of Prisons

Garry McDaniels
Skills Bank Corp.

Harry R. Miller
U.S. Distance Learning Association

Ken Miller
IBM Corp.

Preston Miller
Literacy Volunteers of Franklin County, NY

Karen Mills
Rio Salado Community College

Mark Morgan
Development Associates, Inc.

Garrett Murphy
New York State Office of Adult Education

Monroe C. Neff
Houston Community College System

Sara Newcomb
U.S. Department of Education

David Newman
The Roach Organization

James Olsen
WICAT Systems

Edward Pauly
Manpower Demonstration Research Corp.

Karen Pearl
New York City Literacy Assistance Center, Inc.

Pamela Pease
Jones Intercable, Inc.

Pedro Pedraza
Hunter College

Aqueda Pena
Creative Academic Achievement Pro-Success
    Learning Center

Robert Pepper
Federal Communications Commission

Dennis Poe
U.S. Department of Health and Human Services

Curtis Priest
Center for Information Technology and Society

Ronald S. Pugsley
U.S. Department of Education

Diane Rapley
Broderbund Software

Mina Reddy
Cambridge Community Learning Center

Craig Riecke
Literacy Volunteers of America

Andrew Rock
U.S. Department of Health and Human Services

Pavlos Roussos
Texas Education Agency

C. Dorsey Ruley
Illinois Bell

Tony Sarmiento
AFL/CIO

Rose Saylin
Huntington Beach Library

Ernestine Schnulle
Correctional Educational Division
Los Angeles County Jail System

Gail Schwartz
U.S. Department of Education

Sylvia Scribner
City University of New York

Joan Seamon
U.S. Department of Education

John Sener
U.S. BASICS

Ruth Shaw
Central Piedmont Community College

Paul Siegel
Bureau of the Census
U.S. Department of Commerce

Robert Silvanic
National Governors' Association

Arthur Sisk
Franklin Electronic Publications

Ellen Skinner
Texas Department of Human Services

Margaret Smith
Texas Department of Criminal Justice

Tim Songer
Interactive Knowledge, Inc.

Gail Spangenberg
Business Council for Effective Literacy

Richard K. Sparks
Idaho State University

Brian Stecher
Rand Corp.

Sondra Stein
Consultant

Thomas G. Sticht
Applied Behavioral and Cognitive Sciences, Inc.

Betty Stone
Sommerville Center for Adult Learning Experiences

Nancy Stover
The Discovery Channel

Beverly Student
LIST Services, Inc.

Andrew Sum
Northeastern University

Charles Talbert
Adult and Community Education Branch
Maryland Department of Education

Sue Talley
Foundation for Educational Software

James Tollefson
University of Washington

Gaye Tolman
Literacy Volunteers of Maricopa County, AZ

Jay Tucker
United Auto Workers/Ford Program

Terilyn C. Turner
St. Paul Lifelong Literacy Center

Daniel Wagner
National Center for Adult Literacy

Peter Waite
Laubach Literacy Action

Sharlene Walker
Oregon Office of Community Colleges

Dave Weaver
LIST Services, Inc.

William Weder
U.S. Department of Health and Human Services

Michael Weiner
Selectronics Corp.

Joan Winston
Office of Technology Assessment

Barbara Wright
Oregon/Washington Adult Basic Skills Technology
    Consortium

David Wye
Office of Technology Assessment

Malcom Young
Development Associates, Inc.

Chris Zachariadis
Association for Community Board Education

Appendix G: Contributing Sites

Throughout the course of this assessment, OTA received invaluable information and assistance from many literacy programs located across the United States. The following is a listing of the sites that participated in OTA's case studies and the survey of software, as well as programs that were visited by OTA staff.

ACCESS Center
Duchess County Board of Cooperative Services
Poughkeepsie, NY

Adult Learning Center
White Plains, NY

Adult Success Center
Idaho State University
Pocatello, ID

Allenwood Federal Prison Camp
Montgomery, PA

Baltimore Reads, Inc.
Baltimore, MD
  Ripken Learning Center
  Words for Life

Baltimore Urban League Job Training Center
Baltimore, MD

Bronx Educational Services
Bronx, NY

Center for Reading and Writing
Mott Haven Public Library
Bronx, NY

Center for Training and Economic Development
Cuyahoga Community College
Cleveland, OH
  Metro Campus Adult Learning Center, Cleveland, OH
  Euclid Adult Learning Center, Cleveland, OH
  Multi-Media Community Literacy Program,
    Garfield Heights, OH
  Job Readiness Program, Cleveland, OH

Chinese-American Civic Association
Boston, MA

Columbia Basin College
Learning Opportunity Center
Pasco, WA

Community Learning Center
Cambridge, MA

Continuing Education Learning Center
Jackson, MS

Correctional Educational Division
Los Angeles County Jail System
Hacienda La Puente Unified School District
Los Angeles, CA

Creative Academic Achievement Pro-Success
(CAAP) Learning Center
McAllen, TX

Eastern Idaho Technical College
Idaho Falls, ID

Eastern Michigan University Academy
United Auto Workers/Ford Motor Co.
Ypsilanti, MI

El Barrio Popular Education Program
Harlem, NY

El Centro del Cardenal
Boston, MA

Estill County Parent and Child Education Program
Ravenna Elementary School
Ravenna, KY

Eva Bowlby Library
Workplace and Adult Literacy Projects
Waynesburg, PA

Garrett Heyns Education Center
Shelton, WA

Greater Columbus Learning Center
Columbus, MS

Hattiesburg Education Literacy Project
Hattiesburg, MS

Institute for Communication Disorders
International Center for the Disabled
New York, NY

Job Skills Enhancement Program
Meridian Community College
Meridian, MS

Lane Community College Adult Basic
and Secondary Education
Eugene, OR

Laramie County Community College
Laramie, WY

Lewisburg Federal Penitentiary
Lewisburg, PA

Lexington Technology Center
Lexington, SC

Literacy Action Center
Seattle, WA

Literacy Assistance Center
New York, NY

Longfellow Adult Learning Center
Owensboro, KY

Lutheran Settlement House
Women's Project
Philadelphia, PA

Metropolitan Education Program
San Jose, CA

Mid-Manhattan Learning Center
Harlem, NY

Mississippi Gulf Coast Community College
Perkinston, MS

Mississippi Mobile Learning Lab
Northeast Region
Booneville, MS

Mobile Automated Learning Laboratory
Mississippi Delta Community College
Delta Region, Moorhead, MS

National Education, Development and Training Center
United Auto Workers/Ford Motor Co.
Dearborn, MI
  Walton Hills Stamping Plant, Walton Hills, OH
  Wixom Assembly Plant, Wixom, MI

New York City Public Schools
Office of Adult and Continuing Education
  Queens Adult Learning Center, Queens, NY
  Brooklyn Adult Learning Center, Brooklyn, NY

Northwest Tri-County Intermediate Unit Center
Erie, PA

Odessa Community College
Adult Education Co-op
Odessa, TX

Playing to Win
Harlem, NY

REEP Program
Arlington, VA

Rouge Academy
Ford Motor Co. Dearborn Engine Plant
Dearborn, MI

St. Bernadine's Head Start Center
Baltimore, MD

South Dade Skills Center
Leisure City, FL

STAR Adult Education Center
(Formerly Literacy Volunteers of America of Biloxi)
Biloxi, MS

Sunflower County Library Adult Learners Program
Sunflower, MS
    Henry M. Seymour Library, Indianola, MS
    East Sunflower Elementary School, Sunflower, MS
    Ruleville Library, Ruleville, MS

Support for Training and Educational Services, Inc.
New York, NY

Technology for Literacy Center
St. Paul, MN

Tillamook Bay Community College
Tillamook, OR

United South End Settlement
Boston, MA

Ventura Adult/Continuing Education
Ventura, CA

Watsonville/Aptos Adult School
Watsonville, CA

Watts Adult Learning Center
Los Angeles, CA

York College Community Learning Center
City University of New York
Queens, NY

York College Learning Center
Literacy Initiative
Jamaica, NY

Young Adult Learning Academy
New York, NY

Appendix H:
Contractor
Reports
Prepared for
This Assessment

Copies of contractor reports done for this study are available through the National Technical Information Service (NTIS), either by mail (U.S. Department of Commerce, National Technical Information Service, Springfield, VA 22161) or by calling NTIS directly at (703) 487-4650.

Center for Literacy Studies, The University of Tennessee, Knoxville, "Life at the Margins: Profiles of Adults With Low Literacy Skills," PB 93-163871.

Education TURNKEY Systems, Inc. and Wujcik and Associates, "The Educational Software Marketplace and Adult Literacy Niches," PB 93-163897.

J.D. Eveland et al., Claremont Graduate School, "Case Studies of Technology Use in Adult Literacy Programs," PB 93-163905.

Nancy Kober, "Profiles of Major Federal Literacy Programs," PB 93-163863.

Stephen Reder, Northwest Regional Educational Laboratory, "On-Line Literacy Development: A Context for Technology in Adult Literacy Education," PB 93-163889.

Jay P. Sivin-Kachala and Ellen R. Bialo, Interactive Educational Systems Design (IESD), Inc., "Software for Adult Literacy: Scope, Suitability, Available Sources of Information, and Implications for Federal Policy," PB 93-163913.

Index

U.S. GOVERNMENT PRINTING OFFICE : 1993 O - 331-048 QL 3

Superintendent of Documents **Publications** Order Form

P3

Order Processing Code:
*7079

Telephone orders (202) 783-3238
To fax your orders (202) 512-2250
Charge your order.
It's Easy!

☐ **YES**, please send me the following:

_____ copies of *Adult Literacy and New Technologies: Tools for a Lifetime (288 pages)*,
S/N 052-003-01330-4 at $16.00 each.

The total cost of my order is $_____. International customers please add 25%. Prices include regular domestic postage and handling and are subject to change.

Please Choose Method of Payment:

_____
(Company or Personal Name)   (Please type or print)

☐ Check Payable to the Superintendent of Documents

_____
(Additional address/attention line)

☐ GPO Deposit Account ☐☐☐☐☐☐☐ — ☐

_____
(Street address)

☐ VISA or MasterCard Account

☐☐☐☐☐☐☐☐☐☐☐☐☐☐☐☐☐☐☐☐☐☐

_____
(City, State, ZIP Code)

☐☐☐☐ (Credit card expiration date)

Thank you for your order!

_____
(Daytime phone including area code)

_____
(Authorizing Signature)   (7/93)

_____
(Purchase Order No.)

YES NO
May we make your name/address available to other mailers? ☐ ☐

Mail To: New Orders, Superintendent of Documents, P.O. Box 371954, Pittsburgh, PA 15250-7954

THIS FORM MAY BE PHOTOCOPIED

- -

Superintendent of Documents **Publications** Order Form

P3

Order Processing Code:
*7079

Telephone orders (202) 783-3238
To fax your orders (202) 512-2250
Charge your order.
It's Easy!

☐ **YES**, please send me the following:

_____ copies of *Adult Literacy and New Technologies: Tools for a Lifetime (288 pages)*,
S/N 052-003-01330-4 at $16.00 each.

The total cost of my order is $_____. International customers please add 25%. Prices include regular domestic postage and handling and are subject to change.

Please Choose Method of Payment:

_____
(Company or Personal Name)   (Please type or print)

☐ Check Payable to the Superintendent of Documents

_____
(Additional address/attention line)

☐ GPO Deposit Account ☐☐☐☐☐☐☐ — ☐

_____
(Street address)

☐ VISA or MasterCard Account

☐☐☐☐☐☐☐☐☐☐☐☐☐☐☐☐☐☐☐☐☐☐

_____
(City, State, ZIP Code)

☐☐☐☐ (Credit card expiration date)

Thank you for your order!

_____
(Daytime phone including area code)

_____
(Authorizing Signature)   (7/93)

_____
(Purchase Order No.)

YES NO
May we make your name/address available to other mailers? ☐ ☐

Mail To: New Orders, Superintendent of Documents, P.O. Box 371954, Pittsburgh, PA 15250-7954

THIS FORM MAY BE PHOTOCOPIED